A GRAVE TOO FAR AWAY

KATHRYN SPURLING

A GRAVE
TOO FAR AWAY

A TRIBUTE TO AUSTRALIANS
IN BOMBER COMMAND
EUROPE

NEW
HOLLAND

DEDICATION

To the truly amazing Australian aircrew who served with RAF Bomber Command, Europe, 1939–45, and their families.

To my parents, Flying Officer Maxwell Alton Norris, RAAF and Hilda Norris (née Ludlow)

Published in 2022 by New Holland Publishers
First published in Australia in 2008 by New Holland Publishers
Sydney • Auckland

Level 1, 178 Fox Valley Road, Wahroonga, NSW 2076, Australia
5/39 Woodside Ave, Northcote, Auckland 0627, New Zealand

newhollandpublishers.com

A record of this book is held at the National Library of Australia.

ISBN 9781760794798

Group Managing Director: Fiona Schultz
Project Editor: Simona Hill
Designer: Andrew Davies
Production Director: Arlene Gippert
Printed in Australia by SOS Print + Media Group

10 9 8 7 6 5 4 3 2 1

Keep up with New Holland Publishers:

 NewHollandPublishers
 @newhollandpublishers

Picture previous page: Bedankt (Thank you) RAAF Heroes of Bomber Command, courtesy of Margaret Hadfield (Zorgdrager).

ACKNOWLEDGEMENTS

This book took much longer than anticipated, too many RAAF personnel files "not yet examined", more indicative of families disappearing, with the death of an only son, than lack of interest on the part of those left behind. It is sad that no one had before examined forms written in the neat or untidy handwriting of eager, youthful men, wishing to enlist and go to war: or looked at photographs of bright faces with RAAF numbers either held or hung around necks. Clearly they had been told to keep a sombre expression, clearly some could not. I applied for more files than I needed just because it seemed the right thing to do – but alas there are thousands more. The National Archives of Australia is to be congratulated for their comprehensive listings and ongoing programme to digitise military personnel files – and I give thanks to the patient, helpful research staff there. Thanks to Elizabeth Van Der Hor for untwisting language and to Air Commodore Geoff Michael, AO, (RAAF rtd) for that also, and technical advice. Credit too, to the Australian government's *World War Two Nominal Roll* www.ww2roll.gov.au, and *the Commonwealth War Graves Commission* www.cwgc.org which lists 1,700,000 men and women of the Commonwealth forces who died in World War I and World War II. Each name, each person, each family, represents a legacy of war and each has their own story, most are simply amazing. I have endeavoured to ensure names and dates and the maze of facts are correct but if I have failed, I apologise.

I greatly appreciate the individuals and families who shared their stories; the response was overwhelming and there were too many stories to do justice to in one volume. Nonetheless I hope this book will convey the story of Australian aircrew attached to RAF Bomber Command Europe, 1939–45, through the lives and deaths of those who participated and those they left behind.

CONTENTS

Foreword		10
Abbreviations		11
Introduction		13

One	"I knew that the young men…in their shining machines were the chivalrous warriors of the 20th century."	20
Two	"God alone knows when I will see you again."	49
Three	"When it was dark I made my way to this lone aircraft."	76
Four	"I had a little difficulty crossing the canal"	106
Five	"They were your boys, now they are ours and we shall take care of them."	137
Six	Although my son is believed killed…I still hope that he is coming back.	169
Seven	"All being well! We may be all home for next Xmas – Wishful thinking!!! I really can't see this mess being cleared up in one year."	199
Eight	"Our planes become our shrouds."	234
Nine	"Where was the justice of it all, and where was God in this mad slaughter?"	271
Ten	"Rest peacefully, youngster, rest peacefully."	309
Eleven	"Five aircraft were a heavier loss we were reminded, than the five crews."	343
Twelve	"No one has asked me before how much I have missed my brother all these years"	379
Thirteen	"You know our mother never recovered from losing Michael. Michael was the very best of us."	415

Endnotes		436
Bibliography		447

FOREWORD

The families of members of Royal Air Force Bomber Command who were killed during the five-year campaign in World War II are rarely given a mention in such detail as has been written in this book. Kathryn Spurling has conducted considerable research into the lives of those who were lost in operations or during training, and has met with numerous families to enable the sadness endured by them to be expressed with obvious feeling. Memories of sons, brothers and close friends makes one realise that those who are left at home to worry about their loved ones are those who suffer the most in times of war.

The author has emphasised the role contributed by crews of Bomber Command during the 1942/1943 period and recorded in graphic detail the many losses mainly involving aircrews of the listed Australian Squadrons and the involvement of the Pathfinder Force (PFF).

Kathryn Spurling brings out the thoughts of prime minister Winston Churchill and the controversial Commander-in-Chief of Bomber Command, Air Chief Marshal Sir Arthur Harris, both of whom expressed vehemently that the war against Germany could only be won by Bomber Command, and that this could only be achieved by breaking the morale of the German people through continuous heavy bombing of the major German cities and communication centres.

This book is very informative and is recommended reading. The horrors of war in the air in bombers, for the aircrews involved, are presented in detail. Much can be learned about Bomber Command operations and the affect on participating crews and the families left at home. I was a pilot in Bomber Command flying Lancaster aircraft in 1944/1945.

Geoff Michael AO, OBE, AFC
Air Commodore RAAF (Ret)

ABBREVIATIONS

AFC	Australian Flying Corps
AIF	Australian Imperial Force
ANZAC	Australian New Zealand Army Corps
Anzacs	Members of ANZAC but popularly referred to serving army
AWAS	Australian Women's Army Service
CMF	Civilian Military Force
EATS	Empire Air Training Scheme
EFTS	Elementary Flying Training Scheme
ITS	Initial Training Scheme
RAAF	Royal Australian Air Force
RAF	Royal Air Force
RAFVR	Royal Air Force Volunteer Reserve
RAN	Royal Australian Navy
RCAF	Royal Canadian Air Force
RFC	Royal Flying Corps
RN	Royal Navy
SFTS	Service Flying Training School
WAAAF	Women's Australian Auxiliary Air Force
WAAF	Women's Auxiliary Air Force
WRANS	Women's Royal Australian Naval Service
DFC	Distinguished Flying Cross
DFM	Distinguished Flying Medal
DSO	Distinguished Service Order
AWOL	Absence without leave
GPS	Greater Public School

OTU	Operating Training Unit
PFF	Pathfinders Force
POW	Prisoner of War
PTSD	Post Dramatic Stress Disorder
Sqn	Squadron
TI	Target Indicators
WWI	World War One
WWII	World War Two
AC	Aircraftsman
BA	Bomb Aimer; Air Bomber; Bombadier
C-in-C	Commander in Chief
CO	Commanding Officer
Cpl	Corporal
F/L	Flight Lieutenant
F/S	Flight Sergeant
FO	Flying Officer
G/C	Group Captain
LAC	Leading Aircraftsman
M/U/G	Middle Upper Gunner
Nav	Navigator; Observer
NCO	Non-commissioned Officer (not an officer)
P	Pilot
PO	Pilot Officer
R/G	Rear Gunner
S/L	Squadron Leader
Sgt	Sergeant
W/C	Wing Commander
WO	Warrant Officer
WOP/AG	Wireless Operator/Air Gunner
ACT	Australian Capital Territory
NSW	New South Wales
Q	Queensland

SA	South Australia	USA	United States of America
Tas	Tasmania	Vic	Victoria
UK	United Kingdom	WA	Western Australia

INTRODUCTION

The wind rustles the leaves gently. Foliage fallen during an earlier season remains sprinkled across the small cemetery, the brilliant reds and yellows now reduced to brittle brown – perhaps fittingly dead on dead. An elderly Dutch man rests his hand respectfully on the top of a gravestone. The inscription etched on white stone reads:

Pilot Officer W. W. Bell-Towers
Royal Australian Air Force
15th August 1941 Age 32

There is a sense of tranquility in this tiny cemetery, which is tucked away on the Dutch island of Terschelling, and a strange beauty in the gravestones that mark the 67 graves of Allied aircrew. Islanders respectfully tend the graves, honouring those who lie within.

Local islander Unna (Anne) Maas never met Wadja Wellesley Bell-Towers named on the grave's inscription. Being just seven when the war began, he says, "we did not know what war meant...for us the war lasted only five days and then we surrendered". Soon there were 1,500 German soldiers living among the Dutch island population of 3,600. He recalls that the island was turned into a German fortress with bunkers, radar stations and gun emplacements, essentially directed at Allied aircraft. Life was difficult. Behaviour by occupying military force could be harsh. Anything could be confiscated, and treatment of individuals could be, and invariably was, merciless. Hendrik Maas struggled to support his wife Sieke and two sons, "he did all kinds of jobs and started selling coals and other firing", says son Unna, but this was not enough so he "accepted the job of grave-digger".

Under German guard Hendrik and Unna (Anne) travelled the broad Terschelling beaches to collect the remains of men whose world had exploded into flames, falling with their shattered bombers into the North Sea. Invariably, says Unna, "the bodies were damaged very badly". It was a grim task for the boy and his father. On 17 August 1941 they were ordered to retrieve the bodies of Pilot Officer Wadja Wellesley Bell-Towers, Royal Australian Air Force, and three other crew of aircraft Whitley Z6829 from where it had crashed on the windswept beach. That day would have been Wadja Bell-Towers' 33rd birthday. Unna Maas wondered where these men who fought the occupying Germans had come from. He and his countrymen knew nothing of this country Australia, which was to be etched onto gravestones. When they looked at a map of the world they shook their heads – these aircrew came from the end of the earth.

In a home overlooking a New South Wales beach, another elderly man considers a photo of Wadja Bell-Towers' gravestone and speaks tenderly of a brother he has missed for 70 years, and of growing up in the shadow of Wadja Bell-Towers. Wadja and Arthur were born into privilege, sons of a high society Melbourne family. Their East Malvern mansion was large, with five servants and a private zoo. "Wadja was named after a Syrian friend of my father." The family had a history in academia, music and business, but: "Wadja was athletic, a fitness fanatic with an outgoing personality. He had huge arms and was very powerful, with the strength of a lion. He was very handsome and had a tremendous personality."

Arthur smiles when he remembers how his much older brother took him to the Tivoli Theatre and to vaudeville, saying "Wadja was very much a ladies' man". In 1940 Wadja's marriage to Merla featured on the social pages of Melbourne's print media.

Wadja had been a Cadet Lieutenant at Scotch College, Melbourne, and entered the militia as soon as war was declared, becoming a 6th Battalion Lieutenant. He had already trained as a pilot, flying Tiger Moths, and transferred to the RAAF at the first opportunity. By May 1941 he was in England, attached to 102 Squadron Royal Air Force (RAF) as a crew member of a Whitley twin-engine medium bomber. The RAF was reluctant to accept Australians of Wadja's age as pilots – he was 32 and 30 was considered old – so instead he trained as an observer (navigator). Though disappointed he hoped the RAF would soon accept his credentials and allow him to pilot a bomber and be captain of a crew. Wadja was a Pilot Officer, his RAF Pilot and skipper was a 21-year-old Sergeant from London. The RAF Wireless Operators/Air Gunners were a 20 year old from the Irish Republic and a 21 year old from Northern Ireland, which ensured lively discussion. There was one other Australian in the six-man crew: Sergeant Frank Walace Penn (400233) was from Melbourne and held the position of second pilot, he was not yet 20. The nickname "grey beard" was a title Wadja would just have to accept with grace.

On the night of 14 August 1941 the crew was tasked to bomb Hanover, Germany. The Whitley took off from RAF Topcliffe (North Yorkshire) at 2218 none too graciously, "gracious" and "Whitley" could never fit comfortably together, but the aircrew had confidence in the machine that carried them with their deadly cargo into the English sky. With their bomb load dropped on target they breathed more easily as their aircraft settled on a course for the home base. The burst of cannon fire from a German Messerschmitt Bf 110 came without warning and shell fragments penetrated the left boot of Frank Penn causing him pain. The Messerschmitt night fighter piloted by Oberfeldwebel (Platoon Leader) Paul Gildner attacked again and fire broke out on the Whitley near the escape hatch. It was extinguished, but again the German fighter attacked and strafing fire destroyed the bomber's controls. The command to bale out was given and the RAF Rear Gunner Sergeant T A Vermiglio exited immediately. The Whitley was on fire, out of control and diving towards the island of Terschelling. Another crew member hesitated at the escape hatch and accidentally inflated his life jacket. His body now jammed the hatch preventing others from escape. Wadja Bell-Towers realised he was trapped. He grabbed the small Frank Penn and pushed him out of the aircraft between the other crewman's legs. Penn and Vermiglio were captured and spent the remainder of the war incarcerated as German prisoners of war.

Arthur Bell-Towers was a student at Melbourne's Scotch College when his brother was killed. He remembers well the stunning news that his hero was dead. "My parents said little but clearly my father was very upset. My mother had a breakdown and struggled with her health for

Anne Maas.   *Burying Australian aircrew on Terschelling.*

the rest of her life." Pilot Officer Wadja Bell-Towers never met his baby son Ian. Following the war Arthur suggested to his sister-in-law that she should consider remarrying. Merla replied: "When I meet someone as fine as your brother, I'll marry him". She never did.

Over the ensuing war years more bodies were cast ashore and collected by Hendrik and Unna Mass and reverently buried on Terschelling. The cemetery became the resting place of aircrew from the United Kingdom, Canada, New Zealand, and other unknown countries. These men included aircrew from all over Australia: Sergeant Douglas Howie McIntosh (407603), a 31-year old from Berri, South Australia; Sergeant Robert George Ashby Braithwaite (403312), a 27-year-old barrister from Sydney who died on 26 June 1942; Pilot Officers Arthur Leonard Gibbons (415245) 21, from Perth, Western Australia; Kevin Herbert Hoffman (414798) 22, from Mount Morgan, Queensland; and James Thomas Buchanan (405998) 31, from Brisbane, came ashore in July 1943; Flight Sergeant George Herbert Williamson (414741) 29, a former fireman and assistant engine driver from Lismore, New South Wales, was buried on 28 April 1944; Sergeant William Bird (417330) 28, from Hilton, South Australia, was buried two months later.

During World War II, 488 bombers are thought to have crashed in The Netherlands. Of the 2,972 aircrew (with an average age of 24) 46 evaded capture and 614 were taken prisoner of war; the greater number died and were buried in The Netherlands or had no known grave. In total, 374 of those buried in 99 Dutch cemeteries were Australian. Though these Australian aircrew were latterly known and defined by their military rank, it is their life stories preceding and through the war and the influence that their lives had on others that is their legacy to the world. These men were sons, brothers, husbands, fathers and friends, and their stories are interwoven with those of others whose lives they touched.

Pilot Officer Wadja Bell-Towers (courtesy of Arthur Bell-Towers).

Arthur Bell-Towers enlisted because his brother was killed. He survived combat in the war in the Pacific and received a visit from a grateful Warrant Officer Penn who spoke of his brother's bravery and how Wadja had saved his life. The visit forged a bond between the families. In time, another generation of Bell-Towers would visit the small island off the Dutch coast. In 2010, an Australian Ambassador to The Netherlands, Lydia Morton, would commemorate the Australian aircrew buried in the sandy loam of Terschelling; with dignitaries from several nations and the people of Terschelling, including the elderly Unna Maas.

Years later, Margaret Hadfield, an Australian-born artist, would commit to canvas the face of Wadja Bell-Towers to honour the fallen in her painting *Standing Room Only for Heroes*.

Margaret Hadfield is the daughter of Pieter Zorgdrager. Pieter spent the war years working as a house painter when allowed, driving a truck for the Germans when ordered, and working in the shadows with the Terschelling resistance movement. He watched as young Australians fell with their bombers and were buried on his island. At war's end Pieter emigrated from Terschelling with his family, to the New South Wales country town of Coonabarabran.

Standing Room Only For Heroes
(courtesy Margaret Hadfield, née Zorgdrager).

While strategy and tactics of Bomber Command Europe monopolised the attention of those in RAF High Command, Australian aircrew were simply intent on doing the best they could and staying alive. They came from all over their country, from all social echelons and occupations – chosen because of their ability to understand and operate complex technical equipment. They were the best of the best. Their stories were as different as they were similar. They enlisted to rid the world of what they believed was evil; to protect the values they held sacred, to protect their families and their nation. They also joined for the adventure and for many the ensuing two, three or four years were the most important and exciting of their lives. Many would never have the luxury of retrospection. They were brothers – like Flight Sergeants Ron and Ed Osborne from Benalla Victoria, and the Borrett boys from Western Australia. They became Bomber Command brothers

Terschelling Resistance, Pieter Zorgdrager fourth from right top row.

in arms – like Queenslanders Max Norris and Peter (Stuart) Wade; Jim Chigwidden and William (Lionel) Gibbs from New South Wales; Victorians Harold Boal, and Ron Waldon; Merv Whittenbury from South Australia; Ted Deveson and Bob Emrose from Western Australia; and a bloke from King Island, Tasmania, with the hard-to-believe name of Bill Cheese. These recruits of the war in the air joined others in close-knit crews, bonded in squadrons, and struggled together as prisoners of war (POWs). After World War II these Australian aircrew of Bomber Command faced derision and fought their own demons, but their service and sacrifice continue to reverberate for generations around the globe.

ONE

"I knew that the young men...in their shining machines were the chivalrous warriors of the 20th century."

Flying Officer Arthur Hoyle

It was the first day of September 1939 and German tanks rumbled into Poland. The assault was brisk and ruthless. Great Britain declared war two days later. In a Brisbane, Australia, home Hilda Ludlow bent over the large wireless which dominated the lounge of her family home listening intently to the sombre words, "we are now at war", of British prime minister Neville Chamberlain relayed by BBC news. The words seemed ominous but this war Britain had embarked upon seemed a very long way away; surely it would not have too much effect on Australia? Even though her generation had been raised in the long dark shadow of World War I (1914–18), and so many of her beliefs and values had been shaped by it and by the Great Depression, there was no way Hilda could gauge how a global conflict was to change the course of her life and of those around her. On the evening of 3 September 1939 families listened to the words of prime minister, Robert Gordon Menzies: "fellow Australians, it is my melancholy duty to inform you officially that...Australia is also at war". His words continued, "neither is there any doubt that where Great Britain stands there stand the people of the entire British world".[1]

Since Federation in 1901 the nation's history had been dominated by war in defence of the interests of the British Empire. Men from Australian colonies fought in the Sudan and the Boxer Rebellion in China. More joined British forces in South Africa from 1899. During 1901 and 1902 the new Australian Commonwealth continued this tradition. Around 16,000 men who called Australia home fought in the Boer War – some 282 died in action or from wounds sustained in battle, 286 died from illness and another 38 died in accidents or unknown causes. Six Australians received the Victoria Cross. The Great War of 1914–18 came at a terrible cost with 331,781 Australians sent overseas to fight for British integrity. The innocence of the new nation was extinguished with the horrors of modern warfare and the death of 61,720 of their own, notably at Gallipoli, Turkey, and on the Western Front. A further 153,865 were wounded.[2] The casualty rate of 64.98 per cent was the worst of the Allied nations bar New Zealand. For a nation of just seven million the repercussions of this lost generation were immeasurable.[3] And now, again, Australians were called upon to don military uniforms, take up weapons and be transported around the world to face warring European nations. In 1914 Australia's prime minister Andrew Fisher had immortalised the words that Australia would support Britain "to the last man and the last shilling". Now another prime minister echoed similar patriotic sentiment as he announced that Australians "were a British people" and they would "face the crisis with cheerful fortitude and confidence".[4] Prime minister Menzies realised the emotive nature of his broadcast to the Australian radio audience: "It is no wonder that at this hour of suspense, or real peril, and of supreme effort, Great Britain should have turned to her children, the dominions, and to us perhaps not least of all."[5]

There was little dissent in the country. In the Australian Parliament the debate to commit Australia to war was short and the vote unanimous: Australians believed their destiny was inextricably tied to Britain.

In this regard Hilda Ludlow and her family were typical. They were of Scottish and English ancestry. They regarded Britain as the "motherland" and believed that should the "motherland" be threatened it was the duty of Australians to go to Britain's aid. The lessons of the earlier war, which was supposed to end all wars, were lost in jingoism. Returned soldiers, sailors and aircrew may have paused for reflection and offered cautionary comment but their children, like all children, believed parents' fears were exaggerated. It was unconscionable that they themselves would not participate and scant thought was given to their own mortality. Hilda's male friends and relatives decided it was their sworn duty to enlist in what they also saw as a great adventure. Hilda was "keen on" John MacKay whose parents ran the corner store in her Brisbane suburb of Toowong. There was also Max Norris who spent more time than usual visiting his grandmother who lived across the road from the Ludlows, most of which seemed to be spent at the fence talking to Hilda. Max Norris worked for the Commonwealth Bank and was likeable enough, though Hilda's brothers mocked him because he was a part-time soldier with the Militia, a member of the 61st Battalion, (Queensland Cameron Highlanders) – and part of the uniform was a kilt.[6] Brothers Tom and Ray Ludlow took every opportunity to point out that real men didn't wear kilts. In retaliation Max pointed out that they played soccer, whereas real Australian gentlemen played rugby, and he was already playing rugby for Brisbane. Hilda was an amused onlooker until John MacKay introduced her to his friend Tom Freeman. Tom liked Hilda a lot. Within a couple of years Tom, John and Max were in the RAAF and only one would be alive at war's end.

World War II recruitment posters.

While the first recruiting posters were quickly hammered to walls, Australia was not ready for war. The Great Depression had caused government financial stringency measures during the late 1920s and 1930s which had greatly reduced the size and effectiveness of the nation's defence forces. Faith in Britain and Britain's policy of appeasement towards Nazi Germany also induced a careless indifference to the outbreak of war and an almost universal belief in imperial defence. Australia's defence budget was largely spent on fortifying the British Singapore naval base. In return Australians were promised that the Royal Navy would protect British dominions in the south. Those who cautioned against such policy, and pointed to the goose-stepping German military boots which had begun to crush democracy in the name of fascism, and to Japanese military expansion in the east, were met with disbelief, even ridicule.

At the time of committing to war the Royal Australian Navy was small and equipped with two heavy cruisers, four light cruisers, two "sloop-of-war" sloops, five obsolete destroyers and a number of small and auxiliary warships. RAN personnel numbered 6,340.[7] It was a navy controlled by the Admiralty in London. The Australian Army comprised a small permanent cadre of 3,000 men, and an 80,000-strong "Australian Army Reserve" Citizen Military Force, which was legally restricted to service in Australia and its external territories. The "Royal Australian Air Force" RAAF was the weakest of the services. The Australian Flying Corps had been in action within weeks of the ANZAC landing at Gallipoli in 1915.[8] Though small in number their war of 1914–18 was "heroic, bloody, and ultimately tragic".[9] Regardless of the daring feats of these magnificent men in their flying machines, the Australian Flying Corps was disbanded at that war's end.

In the decades following World War I Australian defence dogma was controlled by the Australian Army. Two of its most influential generals Sir John Monash and Sir Brudenall (Cyril) White believed there should not be a separate air force.[10] They could not contemplate that the next world conflict may be a war largely fought in the air. After spirited resistance, the Australian Air Force was formed on 31 March 1921 and, following the approval of King George V, the prefix 'Royal' became effective from August of that year. At formation the RAAF boasted a force of 151 men, and 164 mainly obsolescent aircraft. Over the next decades there was little improvement and "the RAAF's greatest achievement in its first 18 years was...simply to survive as an independent service".[11] Political inertia, defence jealousies, and a steadfast belief in imperial defence, meant Australia was ill prepared for war.

Within a fortnight of war being declared prime minister Robert Menzies announced the formation of the second Australian Imperial Force. This was an expeditionary force, initially to consist of 20,000 men organised into an infantry division (the 6th Division) and auxiliary units. It was intended that the division would join the British expeditionary force in France, but the speed with which German forces invaded their neighbours meant this did not eventuate. It was 29 November 1939 before the Australian prime minister could announce that the 6th Division Australian Imperial Force would be sent overseas. He did this with typical imperial rhetoric: "if Britain is lost, Australia is lost with her".[12] In early 1940 the 6th Division embarked for the Middle East. The *Sydney Morning Herald* headline was nationalistic and called on ANZAC legends of the past to herald this first contingent of the second AIF who marched through the city's streets. The newspaper believed they were "the proud bearers of the standard bequeathed to them by the original Anzacs".[13]

Just a few weeks before, on 5 November 1939, Menzies had announced the reintroduction of conscription for home defence service to be effective from 1 January 1940. Recruitment for military service, however, progressed slowly. Only after the fall of France in June 1940, when Britain seemed under direct threat, did the number of Australian men wishing to sign up increase. While the media continued to headline "unstinted help and sacrifice to the Empire and Allied cause"[14] and regale men in khaki as the "sons of those Gallipoli heroes", it was not the army that caught the imagination of young men in 1940 but the RAAF.

Arthur Hoyle remembered that in the early 1930s: "Like many another boy, I was fascinated by the feats of the young aircrew who had fought and usually died in the skies over France, and by the deeds of the aerial pioneers such as Kingsford Smith, Ulm, Cobham, Hinkler and Amy Johnson."[15] Hoyle followed the 1935 Great Air Race from London to Melbourne and sitting at his school desk would daydream: "My pencil became a Zeppelin flying in the dark skies…and I was a daring young pilot intent on destroying the great raider". His generation was raised on the very popular adventures of *Biggles*. Biggles was the nickname for James Bigglesworth, an adventurer, pilot and hero, in the series of youth-oriented adventure books written by William Earl Johns. *Biggles* was a teenage World War I fighter pilot in the Royal Flying Corps who flew daring, heroic missions fighting the Germans commonly referred to as 'Huns'. The first *Biggles* book, *The Camels Are Coming*, was published in 1932. In total, 17 *Biggles* books filled the imaginations of teenagers who lined up now in front of air force recruiters, wanting their own adventures fighting the "Huns" in flying machines. They were also of a generation who, unlike those who controlled military dogma, "realised that, if this was to be a technological, aerial war, then the air force would be the centre of attention".[16] In 1935, 15-year-old Arthur Hoyle watched the crews of Avro-Ansons walk from their aircraft: "I could not articulate it but I knew that the young men in their ugly flying suits, in their shining machines, were the chivalrous warriors of the 20th century. Far more than the marching infantry in their khaki uniforms or the jingling light horse with emu feathers in their hats, they were the future."[17]

At the end of 1939 there were 3,179 airmen and 310 officers in the RAAF. The 246 aircraft were mostly obsolescent. Around 450 members of the RAAF, mostly pilots, had been sent to Britain on short service commissions in the RAF. While it was decided the RAAF needed fewer than 170 volunteers in the initial intake, recruiting offices were swamped. In Melbourne alone 2,000 came to sign up.[18] Harassed recruiters accepted the first 1,000 and sent the others away to apply in writing. By March, applications for aircrew had grown to 11,500 and another 56,777 sought ground crew places.[19] Authorities indoctrinated with the minimalist training regimes of foot soldiers now struggled to catch up with the training regimes required to prepare civilians to crew aircraft for modern warfare.

In World War I as much as 50 per cent of the flying personnel in British squadrons came from the dominions.[20] In World War II the

Australian government initially approved a plan to raise a six squadron expeditionary air force but Britain asked the dominions to contribute instead to an empire air force under RAF control.

Menzies, without first consulting the Australian Air Board, agreed. James V Fairbairn, the Minister for Civil Aviation, who would become Minister for Air in November, conferred with representatives from other Commonwealth nations in Ottawa, Canada. The Canadians were less acquiescent in accepting the British ideal, but New Zealand promised to provide the United Kingdom with 1,000 pilots a year.[21] Australia came under pressure to do likewise but even before this could be properly considered the British Air Member for Personnel, Sir Charles Portal, believed a figure of roughly 20,000 pilots alone were needed and, even in 1939, it was foreseen that Britain could produce no more than half of the 50,000 aircrew required – the expectation was that dominions would need to provide the bulk of the manpower.[22] Furthermore the dominions would pay for the training. For the estimated expenditure of Can $888,500,000 Canada would donate $359,280,000, Australia $299,400,000 and New Zealand $89,00/0,000. The UK would, it was proposed, restrict itself to making "an important free capital contribution" in equipment and aircraft of $140,000.[23] Finally, the Empire Air Training Scheme (EATS) was initiated, whereby Australia would provide and partially train around 10,000 aircrew a year for the RAF. Australians would provide aircrew to fight battles but not the policy advisers on how the battles would be fought. The scheme perpetuated the mistakes and lack of control over Australian volunteers of the Hughes' government in World War I, because while the scheme would undoubtedly benefit the British war effort it would do little to defend the Australian mainland. "Australia largely lost control of its trained airmen who went into the Royal Air Force."[24] From the standpoint of Australian national defence as distinct from imperial defence, the scheme was defective policy.

Basic training was to be undertaken in Australia before most would receive advanced training in Canada and a smaller group in Rhodesia. The RAAF would establish two air navigation schools, three bombing and gunnery schools, three air observers schools, 12 elementary flying training schools, six initial flying training schools and eight service flying training schools. The organisational task ahead was huge and there was already a shortage of instructors. From the word "go" the RAAF was running to catch up. Ultimately it was an amazing achievement and instead of training 10,000 airmen, by 1943 when the scheme ended, 37,730 aircrew had been trained under EATS. By March 1940, only 184 RAAF aircrew were in training and the waiting lists were very long. Within a month the first EATS trainees were inducted. It was 15 months before the first EATS graduates arrived in Britain.

Ron Waldon was a school teacher with the Victorian Education Department. He applied for the RAAF in April 1940. He waited and waited, for seven months. "I was certainly impatient. In November 1940 I was called up. What Joy!"[25] For him and the thousands who followed, the politics were unknown and of no concern – they just wanted to join the RAAF and fight another generation of "Hun". Also unknown was the shocking fatality rate they would face.

Immediate assistance in the air war in Europe was restricted to those 450 Australian pilots on RAF short service commissions and members of RAAF 10 Squadron who were in England to fly nine Sunderland flying boats back to Australia. For them, combat was immediate. Attached to Coastal Command this squadron was tasked to protect shipping from submarine attack and surface raiders. By the end of the war the squadron had sustained 150 casualties and lost 19 aircraft.[26]

The first Australian to take part in a World War II bombing operation was West Australian James Frederick Powell Brough (257416). In January 1936, Brough, aged 19, joined RAAF Point Cook to become a Pilot. As was common, he departed for Britain and was transferred to the RAF. On 4 September 1939, as captain of a Wellington bomber, he was sent to attack German warships based at Wilhelmshaven, Germany. The inexperience of those who commanded the operation and the aircrews detailed to carry it out was blatantly obvious. Of the 15 Blenheim bombers and 14 Wellingtons dispatched, five from each force failed to find the targets in the low-cloud conditions. Additionally bombs failed to explode. The greatest damage caused to the German warship Emden was when a Blenheim crashed on to it. Owing to a navigational error one Wellington dropped bombs on the Danish town of Esbjerg killing two civilians. Seven aircraft were lost and the RAF had its first bomber casualties of the war. The Australian pilot Brough returned his aircraft and crew safely and prepared himself for the next operation. For Flight Lieutenant Brough, his war was long and dangerous but he, at least, defied the odds and returned to Australia. After a posting as an Instructor at No 6 Service Flying Training School (FTS) during the last days of a war in the Pacific he retired from on 1 July 1947. Many Australians followed Brough's path and it was in Bomber Command that Australians left their most enduring impression and made the greatest sacrifice.

The evacuation of the British Expeditionary Force from Dunkirk in May and June 1940 astounded Australians who traditionally assumed British superiority. Indignation followed as the Battle of Britain, the air campaign being waged by the German Air Force Luftwaffe against Britain, raged. It commenced in the European summer with the German objective being to achieve air superiority, the first major campaign to be fought entirely by air forces. From July 1940, British shipping, then RAF airfields and infrastructure, were targeted in an attempt to destroy Britain's ability to wage war. Of the 37 Australian aircrew who participated in the Battle of France, ending in the Dunkirk evacuations, 13 died and one was shot down and taken prisoner of war (POW).[27]

There was no respite; those who survived became immersed in the following Battle of Britain. The very survival of Britain now depended on the battle in the air. Britain's prime minister, Winston Churchill, immortalised the airmen with the words, "never in the field of human conflict was so much owed by so many to so few". He also called them, "these splendid men, this brilliant youth, who will have the glory of saving their native land, their island home, and all they love, from the most deadly of all attacks". Churchill failed to mention that the native land of 574 of the estimated 2,353 aircrew who took on the German fury was not Britain. These flyers were Polish, Czechoslovakian, Canadian, New Zealander, French, South African, American, Belgian, Irish, Rhodesian, and even one born in Palestine and another in Jamaica. It was part of the war propaganda to strengthen citizen belief in a beleaguered Britain, but it took for granted the service and sacrifice of many thousands of non-British residents. Twenty-one Australian names were eventually added to the official honour roll of those who fought in the Battle of Britain.[28]

The Battle of Britain galvanised Australian support. Sergeant Ronald Gustave Damman (400051), a 27 year old from Warburton, Victoria, felt he had something to prove, given his ancestry was German. He was one of the first EATS recruits accepted, as a trainee pilot, on 29 April 1940. He watched developments in Europe and wished his training could progress faster. Initially he was at RAAF Somers on Victoria's Mornington Peninsula for two months, then No 5 Elementary Flying Training Scheme (EFTS) at RAAF Narromine, New South Wales, until 19 August 1940. At Narromine he flew Tiger Moths and gained confidence. There were accidents, even deaths, and many aspiring pilots washed out. One trainee pilot said, "I just felt that they were in too much of a hurry...to get people to be able to fly an aeroplane".[29] In September 1940, Damman went to train in Canada where his flying progress was further honed, until he arrived in Britain to join Bomber Command on Christmas Day. As soon as his operational and conversion training was over Damman was attached to RAF 9 Squadron on, 28 March 1941, with an all RAF crew.

At 2044 on 26 April 1941, Damman eased Wellington R1281 from the Suffolk RAF Honington airfield to bomb Emden, the "seaport of the Ruhr area". The navigator had difficulties and soon the aircraft was well off course and not far from Berlin. A hurried course change was made and at 0223 the bomber was south of Emden. Within an hour Damman felt, as well as heard, a change in depth of the sound of the engines. The aircraft dropped height rapidly and they were too low to bale out. The intercom chatter came to an abrupt halt as Damman announced he was putting the Wellington down. The rest happened quickly, the landing was not one of his best but everyone escaped. Unfortunately they were 15 miles (24 kilometres) northwest of Almelo, Holland. At this time German forces were advancing on several fronts,[30] and on 10 May The Netherlands were invaded. Five days later the Dutch military capitulated.

The letter with the Australian Red Cross emblem dated 5 June 1941 arrived at Damman's parents' home in Victoria. The initial relief was wonderful, "Ron was alive", but it was soon tempered with the realisation that their son was a POW. They had no understanding of what this meant and how long his imprisonment would last. For Sergeant Ron Damman the future was unknown and scary. He realised quickly the importance of staying busy and concentrating on the future and not the present. Over the next four years he studied and sat qualification exams. When finally liberated, Damman had passed Institute of Bookkeepers examinations in bookkeeping; business methods and organisation; and economics; the Incorporated Sales Managers' Association qualifications; and, through the Faculty of Social Studies of Oxford University, courses in economics, banking, industrial organisation and statistics.

The earliest EATS recruits were able to choose their own mustering but as numbers increased and the demands from Britain for particular aircrew musterings dictated, this option ceased. Of course the early pilot trainees fancied their chances of flying fighters rather than bombers. They wanted to be real pilots rather than "bus drivers", it just seemed more glamorous, more exciting. Once in England, RAF OTUs tested humour as well as ability. Australians struggled with the contrasting weather conditions and, being used to a wide brown land, they struggled with the size of Britain:

We were at a place called Unsworth near Newcastle-upon-Tyne, right in the north of England, a dreadful part of the world really in the sense that the weather was so bad...anywhere in Australia I flew, the visibility was unlimited. Over there at Unsworth, if you could see the other side of the airfield it was good flying weather. ...A proportion of pilots that flew out of that place never came back because you were so near the sea.[31]

Marcel France Dekyvere had enlisted on 27 May 1940 and found the RAF 550 OTU very different from his flight training in Wagga Wagga. A confidential report cited this Australian airman as "adaptable and quick and resourceful". Yet so much of the early training regime was simply hit and miss. Dekyvere was instructed to do a height test in training. He had never heard of a height test. It was explained to him that he should keep climbing until his aircraft wouldn't climb any further. The aircraft would then fall out of the sky and he would learn a valuable lesson. This seemed to come with the assumption that he would save himself and the aircraft. The cloud cover was incredibly thick and he climbed until he could climb no further. Levelling out he could see nothing below except cloud so he turned north. There was no radio contact. Finally there was a crackle in his headphones and he answered his call sign. "Are you over the sea?" The Australian answered he was in thick cloud and had no idea where he was. The answer included a couple of "Australianisms". He took the aircraft down in a spiral and came out of cloud at around 200 feet (60 metres). Yep, he was over the sea and the compass was "going round and round". His mind was spinning too. "If I'm on the right-hand side of England and I fly east I'm going to hit France and the French are going to shoot me on sight. If I fly west I should hit England. If I'm on the left-hand side and I fly west I'll hit Ireland."

So he turned his aircraft onto what he thought was a south-west course. There was momentary relief when the familiar landscape of England appeared, momentary because anti-aircraft batteries assumed he was the enemy and "all the ack-ack opened up on me. Fortunately they were pretty poor shots and I wasn't hit".[32] Dekyvere believed it was "pure luck" that he made his way back to his home airfield. He believed it was more pure luck that saw him survive service with Fighter Command. After being awarded the Distinguished Flying Cross he joined air-sea rescue. Flying Walrus aircraft, Flight Lieutenant Dekyvere, Distinguished Flying Cross, found it rewarding to patrol, land and pick up downed aircrew from the sea he once got lost over.

Albert Bingley (Bing) and Peter Goldie grew up in the Western Australian mining centre of Kalgoorlie, their lives "very happy as we shared in the simple pleasures of growing up during the Great Depression years".[33] Bing had the audacity to question this and was simply told non-acceptance meant he would be "returned to civilian life".[34] With so many men besieging recruiting offices, the RAAF was not starved for choice: "Some of us suffered the frailties of the system by being re-mustered from pilots to air gunners, simply because we happened to be standing in the wrong part of the squad on that particular Parade."[35]

They had visions of blazing guns and sending enemy fighters afire and plummeting to the ground, but it was a little disappointing to find that all aircrew were not equal. As training progressed "school and family connections did appear to have influence". Peter and Bing tried to tell themselves that "it was natural for pilots and observers to consider themselves the elite...with wireless air gunners and air gunners being at the bottom of the scale".[36] Just the same, it was hard when the RAAF introduced pay scales which formalised this difference in status. In war Bing believed "each crew member was dependent upon the other". As stories began to filter through on the vulnerability on air gunners, particularly rear gunners – that "an air gunner's body, or what remained of it, often had to be washed from the aircraft"[37,] for reason only comprehensible to young aircrew recruits, the status of air gunners also rose a little.

The next months were exciting for the men who stood to attention on RAAF Pearce parade ground in November 1940. Young men like Peter and Bing, two boys from Kalgoorlie who marvelled at the city of Perth, and whose travel dreams "extended as far as our pushbikes might transport us", would now traverse the world. The huge adventure commenced when they set sail from Sydney on the converted troopship *Johan Van Oldenbarnevelt*. They were eager and confident, their arms resplendent with sergeant stripes and their caps slightly more tilted. Peter decided to write a diary, he was excited, he had never been on a ship before. Within the first day he wished he could get off. Feeling the effects of sea sickness he wondered if they would ever make New Zealand because the RAN escort ship was the ancient HMAS *Adelaide* and the troopship was slowing down so the RAN could keep up. He was very impressed with Auckland "exceedingly pretty city, harbour a beautiful sight". The long trip across the Pacific Ocean was tedious and his diary came to life when he saw the coastline of the Republic of Panama and the "rugged mountains rising to many hundreds of feet, to be lost in the clouds"[38] His fountain pen flew across the pages as he delighted in everything he saw, "scenery most picturesque, dense tropical growth, beautiful birds, waterfalls, gaudily coloured butterflies, towering hills of rock". Bing was not as impressed, he had the flu. Halifax, Canada, was so old and so sophisticated and had "pictures (movies) all through the night". It was 19 August 1941 and Peter enjoyed shopping in Halifax, wandering "through the big stores talking to the girls" as well as purchasing a copy of "Byron's poetical works". Bing had recovered enough to help his childhood friend celebrate his 19th birthday on 20 August: "Went to the pictures in the evening with a beautiful little girl... went for a walk...I went dancing. The end of...18 years...and a happy beginning for the 19th."[39]

Peter Goldie celebrated a little too hard and returned to the ship late. His Commanding Officer failed to be impressed that turning 19 was a suitable excuse and Peter received extra duty. For the remainder of his time in Halifax Peter spent every second he could ashore with Lila. He was in love. When he couldn't get ashore he wrote her notes, and when he could, he bought her gifts, including a ring. The troopship sailed on 25 August and Sergeant Peter Goldie was heartbroken. He scribbled in his diary, "another two days and Lila and I would have been engaged. Now at least I know what it is to be in love". It was Monday 1 September when the ship sailed into Liverpool. "Our first sight of England was not very encouraging, heavy cloud and dense smoke and fumes from the large industries."

War for the first time became reality, sunken superstructures of ships scarred the harbour, the streets were pockmarked with bombed buildings, and the city "was cloaked by hundreds of barrage balloons". As they left the city, the boys from Kalgoorlie were more impressed with the "marvellous" English countryside and surprised by how "happy" the people were. They were soon billeted in coastal Bournemouth. This city was gentler on the eye than industrial Liverpool but the Aussie boys were not enamoured with the beach; "there was no surf and the beach itself had a lot of stone". The RAF wasn't ready for them so their time was their own. There was the occasional annoying "encounter with some RAF officers for not saluting...not the custom in our country to run around saluting everyone". Within a few days Peter was on report for being intoxicated. He also believed he was in love again and her name was Janet.

There was supposed to be a war on yet no one appeared to want responsibility for the contingent of Australian EATS graduates who arrived in England on 1 September 1941. They were sharp and enthusiastic when they paraded for the last time in Australia and now a month in England they idled away their time spending their money, drinking too much and chatting up any pretty girl. The local police were beginning to lose patience. Finally the RAF acted and postings were issued. On 6 October Peter Goldie was one of a group posted to 25 OTU. On arriving at Doncaster: "As we fully expected no one knew who we were or what we were doing there. There were no beds in the sergeants' quarters, so we bedded down with the airmen."

Bomber Command's first RAAF squadron – 455 Squadron – was formed at RAF Swinderby, Lincolnshire, on 6 June 1941. Under the EATS agreement the dominions were to retain their own nationality. Facilities and equipment would be supplied by the RAF. Australian squadrons would be numbered 450–467, seven of which would be part of Bomber Command. Although the first EATS graduates had finished their Australian training in November 1940, when RAAF 455 Squadron was founded in England it had no Australian personnel. Due to misunderstanding and lack of liaison ground crew were not available. RAAF 455 Squadron ground crew had been trained and assembled at Williamtown, New South Wales, but were stuck in Australia due to lack of overseas transport. The promised Handley Page Hampden aircraft had not eventuated; they didn't arrive until 10 July.

The first RAAF 455 Squadron Commanding Officer was Squadron Leader Dereck Jack French, RAAF (257540). The son of Australia's Chief Commonwealth Auditor, Dereck French had joined RAAF Point Cook in Victoria to become a pilot in January 1937. On the night of 29 August 1941 French spearheaded RAAF 455 Squadron's first bombing raid, against Frankfurt. French and his crew were the only representatives of RAAF 455 Squadron in the 100 aircraft force as there was only one serviceable 455 Squadron Hampden.[40] Nevertheless they became "the first Australian squadron to bomb Germany".

The Australian Minister for Air, James Valentine Fairbairn, was well respected by members of the nascent RAAF because he had journeyed to the UK during World War I and joined the Royal Flying Corp. While flying over enemy lines he had been shot down and became a POW. Having returned to Australia he entered politics. His position within the Menzies Cabinet was a popular one with those who wished to fly or were already dressed in air force blue. Fairbairn issued a glowing press release on 20 April 1940 announcing the award of Commanding Officer French's Distinguished Flying Cross for "gallantry in flying operations against the enemy". Fairbairn was "delighted to learn that an Australian trained pilot, had earned this highly coveted decoration so early in the war".[41]

For domestic morale Fairbairn again accentuated that the "policy of the RAAF training pilots for direct entry in the RAF had been of material assistance to that service". Prominent British officers "had frequently commented on the fine type of Australians who had joined the Force, and on their initiative and ability". He declared that the system was limited but the "big difference" now was "that air crews proceeding abroad under the EATS would preserve their identity as members of the RAAF". He believed "thousands of Australians would soon have an opportunity of doing battle for the Mother country and the Empire generally" while "adding further prestige to a young nation already famed for its air heroes and pioneers". Fairbairn was killed in August 1940 when his commuter aircraft crashed close to Canberra airport. From this point the RAAF as an entity struggled to preserve its identity in the European war. It is debatable whether Fairbairn's strong belief in the "Mother country and the Empire" was responsible; or it was the lack of his governance; but the RAAF lost control over their own personnel. Theoretically RAAF 455 Squadron was supposed to be Australian but it became a "League of Nations" squadron with Australians never making up more than 70 per cent. Then in April 1942 RAF hierarchy transferred RAAF 455 Squadron to Coastal Command.

Few of the Australian aircrew, like Bing Bingley and Peter Goldie, trying to "preserve their identity as members of the RAAF", could fathom the delays and poor organization, particularly given the Australian recruiting drives and propaganda. They felt forgotten and certainly not appreciated. Having just arrived in Doncaster in October 1941 Sergeant Peter Goldie wrote in his diary: "We were told we would probably be sent back to Bournemouth. So we just had to sit tight till they [made] up their minds what to do with us."

On 10 October he wrote "still waiting around". His frustration had become acute so perhaps unwisely he approached his superior officer and, "told him we were fed up with it all...I am now a marked man". A course was organised for the Australians, "a complete mess up, we are on a conversion course, and have never been on operations". The men had too much time on their hands, they spent the next days and weeks "playing dice", "went to pictures", "slept in late", "loafed around all day", "we messed around again today", and were involved with way too many "pub crawls". Some had by the end of October been "admitted to hospital with the DTs (delirium tremens) as a result of the beer". Another unchallenging course commenced on 27 October which was to take three weeks meaning Peter Goldie and others "loafed all day... fed up". The deteriorating winter weather was not helping to humour the Australians and they were, according to Goldie, "fed up with the RAF". His diary entries had been effusive and enthusiastic, now they were short and indifferent: "Sunday 2nd November. Messed around. Wrote to Janet". Goldie and his companions could make no sense of why they were not being utilised, why the RAF had chosen to return them to elementary training. On Monday 17 November he wrote, "sadly learnt that two RAAF boys had been killed". It is difficult to know which RAAF boys Goldie referred to – there had been many deaths in the first half of 1941 and more in the second half.

In August 1940 the first heavyweight four-engine bombers arrived. The first Stirling was given to RAF 7 Squadron. Three months later RAF 35 Squadron received the first Halifax bombers. Nearly a year later in July 1941 Flying Officer John Kinnane (407077) was skipper of an RAF 7 Squadron Stirling which took off at midday to bomb Borkum, the westernmost and largest of the seven East Frisian Islands in the southern North Sea. Kinnane joined from Yorktown, South Australia, in May 1940 and received his wings in Australia. Kinnane's Stirling was seen being attacked by two Messerschmitt Me109s over the sea off the Dutch island of Texel. The British air gunners were desperately trying to fend off the German fighters and a dinghy had been dropped suggesting the crew realised their situation was dire. The Stirling was not seen again. The bodies of Kinnane and two of his crew were washed ashore on the west coast of Jutland and buried in a cemetery at Esbjerg, Denmark.

Almost a year after Germany forced the French to accept an armistice, Germany attacked the Soviet Union nullifying their two-nation Non-Aggression Pact signed in 1939. World War II entered a dramatic new stage, with Germany now committed on two fronts. On 8 July 1940 an RAF 214 (Federated Malay States) Squadron Wellington, in which RAAF Pilot Officer Donald Noel Robert Armstrong (400009) 27, of Melbourne was the Navigator, crashed in Belgium, at Limburg. That night two RAF 78 Squadron Whitleys took off three minutes apart, to attack Hamm, Germany. Both aircraft skippers were RAAF. Sergeant Oliver Wiley McLean (404112) 24, from scenic Maleny in the hinterland of the Queensland's Sunshine Coast, and his crew never returned. The second aircraft met a similar fate. Tasmanian Sergeant William (Bill) Morrison McQuitty (408014) held the Wellington at 12,000 feet (3,660 metres). The target was clearly identified and within seconds the observer called "steady, steady, steady". The Wellington was caught in searchlights and subjected to heavy anti-aircraft fire. Only when the bombs were released could McQuitty attempt evasive action. The Wellington was silhouetted in a large cone of searchlights and hit repeatedly by shells. One struck the starboard engine and a fire started. It burnt itself out but the starboard engine was dead. McQuitty headed for home on one engine and with the air speed indicator also useless.

As the Wellington limped across the Dutch coast the rear gunner shouted into the intercom that a Messerschmitt 110 had commenced its attack and started firing. For whatever reason, the fighter broke off and the crew again sighed with relief. But McQuitty was struggling to keep the aircraft on course and they were losing more and more height. He ordered the second pilot to go aft, to the back of the bomber, and get the dinghy ready, but the port engine overheated and cut out. The Wellington crashed nose first into the North Sea. The fuselage began to fill with water quickly and the crew struggled aft through breast high water and pulled themselves clear through the tail turret. They struck out for the dinghy only to find it punctured by shell fragments and unable to take their weight. It was still dark and they realised it would be hours before they could hope to be seen. The Observer Sergeant J Hafferden (RAF) was a strong swimmer and he told them he intended to strike out for the light on the horizon. After covering some distance, through the dim light of dawn he saw a light ship but realised the current would prevent him from reaching it. He hesitated and decided to return to his crew. He could find no sign of them. Nearing exhaustion he turned again and headed for the English coast. He swam about nine miles (15 kilometres) when he finally tumbled ashore. Hafferden then walked more than two miles (three kilometres) before he came across a cottage from which he immediately telephoned for assistance. Rescue services could find no trace of his crew. Bill McQuitty was only 20.

The letter sent to Sergeant Bill McQuitty's father, James, by RAAF officialdom concluded with, "your pride in your gallant son will be a consolation to you in your great loss". In January 1944, James McQuitty acknowledged the final official Casualty Section correspondence. He apologised for the delay but he had been hospitalised. James McQuitty's wife Kathleen was dead and their youngest daughter was very ill; he was not coping well. The loss of his "good son" had been "a grievous blow". James had served as a private in the Australian Imperial Force in World War I and named his eldest son William in honour of his own brother who was killed in that war. His acute anguish was not yet over. His second son, 18-year-old Robert (Bob) McQuitty enlisted in the RAAF in November of the same year in which his brother Bill was killed. Flight Sergeant Bob McQuitty (408338) was killed on 24 June 1944 when his RAF 149 Squadron Stirling was shot down. He was buried in St. Charles de Percy War Cemetery, France. Their brother David Henry McQuitty (428144) enlisted in the RAAF in January 1943 at 18 and his father James must have had great misgivings. David survived the war as a Flying Officer. James, his health already debilitated from service in

38

World War I, now undermined by anxiety and grief from another war, did not.

The "seeds" for the round-the-clock bombing strategy "were sown in the spring and high summer of 1941".[42] For crews there would be no respite and more Australians died. On 15 July an RAF 75 Squadron Wellington took off from RAF Feltwell in Norfolk. The squadron was RAF but there was no member of the RAF onboard. The bombing operation was on Duisburg in the western Ruhr. The engineer Sergeant Joseph Roberts was Royal Canadian Air Force (RCAF), from Notre Dame de Grace, Quebec, Canada. The second pilot was RAAF Sergeant Eric Vincent Keiran Higgins (400277) 27, from Windsor, Victoria. The skipper of the aircraft and the other three members of the crew were from New Zealand.[43] Wellington R31771 crashed off the Dutch coast and the bodies of the crew were never found.

At 1854 on 29 September 1941, Sergeant John Ernest Turner (406018) took off with his RAF 58 Squadron Whitley crew from their Yorkshire base, RAF Linton-on-Ouse. Turner, from Perth, had been lucky to gain entry into the RAAF in the very early days of recruitment – he was 35 on entry and had been employed for 18 years. His age would be seen as far too old in future. His Observer training commenced on the 19 December 1940, he embarked from Fremantle on 3 March 1941, arrived in the UK on 15 May 1941, and finished his training with 19 OTU on 13 August 1941 when he joined RAF 58. Hunter was the only Australian onboard a Whitley which dropped its bomb load on port facilities at Stettin, Poland. The worst was over and the airfield was a welcome sight. It was 0420 on 30 September and still dark. There seemed no reason why it was not a straightforward landing but it wasn't. The pilot missed the airfield and came down in a wood beside the strip. The Whitley burst into flames. Although the tail gunner was uninjured, the two in the cockpit died, John Turner was dragged out of the flames and died of his burns four days later.

The same night RAAF Navigator Sergeant Duncan John McKenzie (400283) 24, from the Murray River hub Echuca, was onboard RAF 115 Wellington, X9673. Sergeant James Henry Goodey (402656) 23, was onboard another RAF 115 Wellington, X9910. The bombers took off ten minutes apart from RAF Marham, Norfolk, to attack the German city of Hamburg. The city was ringed by anti-aircraft installations and the bombers were lit up by powerful searchlights. Goodey had been born in Ottawa, Canada, and enlisted in the RAAF in Sydney, just over a year earlier. His Wellington was shot down by a German night fighter piloted by Oberleutnant Ludwig Becker and crashed into the spire of the Blijham Dutch Reform Church at 2252. Goodey and four other crew were buried in Wedde (Blijham) Protestant Churchyard. McKenzie's Wellington was shot down by a night fighter flown by Feldwebel Kalinowski at 0026; the crew were buried in Becklingen War Cemetery, Soltau, Germany.

The British War Cabinet believed the bombing campaign was not achieving expectation. A detailed analysis had been ordered in mid 1941. The August report suggested "bombing results were judged to be poor with only a small percentage of bombs falling anywhere near their intended target".[44] "Bomber wastage" was of concern. Bomber Command was struggling with the growing sophistication of German defences and the "inadequate technical advances within Bomber Command to overcome the inherent weaknesses within the bomber fleet."[45] There was a serious lack of suitable radio and navigational capabilities. Trials on the "Gee" navigational device were promising. By the end of August 1941 an estimated 1,170 bombers had been lost since the beginning of the war. This was seen as taxing the aircraft industry to keep up with replacing the vehicles of the air war, but worse still was an estimate of 5,500 airmen missing or dead.

Pilot Officer Keith John Miller (404348), a 22 year old from Moree, New South Wales, was the pilot and skipper of RAF 57 Wellington X9978 tasked to bomb Cologne on 15 October. It was a night fighter piloted by Feldwebel Wilheim Mayer that sent the bomber plummeting into Holland. The bodies of the six-man crew lie in Jonkerbos War Cemetery, The Netherlands. On the same bombing operation Sergeant Harold Dawson Grimes (404532) 25, who had been born in Bala Sore, India, but enlisted in Brisbane, died when his RAF Squadron 75 Wellington, W5663, crashed in Germany. Grimes was the 20-year-old son of a Baptist missionary. Prior to enlisting he worked as a plants' inspector with the Agriculture and Stock Department at Nambour, Queensland. RAAF 458 Squadron was designated an Australian squadron but Sergeant Philip George Crittenden (400410), the second pilot, was the only Australian in an otherwise all RAF crew designated to undertake the squadron's first bombing operation, to bomb Antwerp, Belgium. His body was distinguished from those of his crew by the word "Australia" stitched on his upper sleeves.

October 1941 saw more Australians attached to RAF Bomber Command die. On 22 October two more were killed. Sergeant James Roberts (400310) was a Scot, from Hawick, whose family had migrated to Melbourne and who couldn't wait to defend what he still saw as home. He was 18 when the RAAF accepted his enlistment and 20 when he died. His RAF 75 Squadron Wellington, X9914, set off to bomb Mannheim, Germany, and crashed near Werken, Belgium. He was the only Australian in his crew. At 1830 the same night, RAAF 458 Wellington, R1765, took off from RAF Holme-on-Spalding Moor, Yorkshire, to bomb the French port of le Havre. The aircraft was hit by flak. Once more over English territory the crew were ordered to bale out. Five did so, landing in the vicinity of Aldershot, Hampshire. Twenty-four-year-old Sergeant Morris William Shapir (400357) RAAF from Melbourne suffered internal injuries and fractured a leg. He was admitted to Cambridge Military Hospital at Aldershot but died later.

The Allied bombing of Hamburg was deemed important for numerous strategic reasons. The city was an industrial hub with oil refineries. Its shipyards and U-boat pens would be the focus of many bomber command sorties. On the night of 31 October, Australians were among the 123 aircrew sent to bomb Hamburg. Unusually RAF 51 Squadron Whitley Z9220, was piloted by RAAF Sergeant Charles Guan (402349) 25, with an RAAF Navigator Sergeant Bill Bourke (402645) 29. Both were from Sydney's North Shore. Charles Guan's written application was impressive. He had attended Sydney High School but never felt comfortable in that city, yearning instead for wide open spaces. Charles was a good student so was sent to Hawkesbury Agriculture College between 1933 and 1935. He then left the city and became a jackaroo on sheep and cattle properties in western New South

Wales where he felt far more at home. Charles Guan was working on a station near Coonamble, New South Wales, when he decided to apply to be a pilot. The medical officer noted that everything about this candidate was dark. His complexion, eyes and hair were dark or dark brown. He was healthy and the doctor had no grounds for preventing Guan from entering the air force. It was hard to avoid the possibility that Guan was indigenous. It was something not discussed openly in North Shore society, and the RAAF being a young service had no entrenched racism – the expression "The Stolen Generation" was more than half a century from being explored. Aircraftsman Charles Guan commenced his RAAF training in September 1940 and travelled to Narromine for his flying course. In December 1940 his training continued in Canada before he was posted to Britain in May 1941. On 31st October 1941 Guan and his crew took off at 1738 to bomb Hamburg. A radio broadcast was received just off the English coast at 0035, calling for help. Nothing more was heard.

The Royal Navy still did not control the North Sea and the Battle of the Atlantic continued. The dangers to convoys were enormously high. In March 1941 Winston Churchill had issued a "directive ordering Bomber Command to devote its energy towards countering the growing threat posed by U-Boats".[46] Operations concentrated over the next four months on German submarine construction as well as their bases along the Brittany coast. Sergeant Ronald James Brownee Rost (402170) was the pilot of a Blenheim Bomber that was sent to attack shipping at Rotterdam on 16 July 1941. His aircraft was brought down by flak. He lived for several hours following the crash and died in Delft hospital. The 20 year old had been born in the Sydney beach suburb of Coogee and died on the coastline of Holland.

Pilot Officer Bruce Bertram Barber (400456) was the pilot of an RAF 82 Squadron Blenheim (V6146) seeking German ships when his aircraft was shot down by Feldwebel Josef Ederer off Katwijk aan Zee, Holland. Ederer had just shot down another Blenheim, V5634, from RAF 82 Squadron. The bodies of Barber – who had been born in Cairo, Egypt, and had enlisted in the RAAF in Melbourne in September 1940 – and his crew were never found. On 20 September 1941 an RAF 226

Squadron Blenheim bomber (V6422) took off from RAF Wattisham, Suffolk, to attack enemy shipping. RAAF Sergeant Gordon Kenneth Bartlett (407190) from Sydney was part of the Blenheim crew. Bartlett had celebrated his 21st birthday in July. Growing up he never envisaged that he would celebrate his coming of age in England, in a war. Now he was the only Aussie in a three-man crew searching the vast sea off the Dutch coast. There was a blast of adrenalin when they spotted a German convoy off Hoek van Holland. The pilot dropped altitude, too much altitude. The Blenheim blew up, the crew caught up in the blast of their own bombs. Gordon Bartlett's remains lie in the New Eastern Cemetery, Amsterdam.

More anti-shipping operations were conducted by 2 Group Blenheim bombers over 16 days during October 1941. These required a high degree of skill and courage because aircraft needed to attack enemy shipping at an extremely low level thus subjecting them to a withering barrage of anti-aircraft fire. They also had to be quick to react to German fighters. The Blenheims were ill equipped for these operations which were finally curtailed in early November, but not before 205 Blenheims and their crews joined the casualty statistics of 1941.[47] Sergeant Christian Samuel Balzer (404229) 22, from Lismore, New South Wales, was one of the few Australians to be pilot and captain of RAF 114 Squadron Blenheim. His orders on 15 October 1941 were to find and attack enemy shipping. It didn't matter how good a pilot he was; Balzer's Blenheim was no match for the night fighters. V5875 crashed into the sea 81 miles (130 kilometres) west northwest of Den Helder, Holland. The body of Sergeant Balzer was eventually washed ashore and buried in Harlingen General Cemetery.

Peter Goldie heard of the fatalities but it made him even keener to play his part. When he was finally posted to RAF 21 OTU he was pleased and excited. His diary entries returned to their descriptive nature of months earlier but the content was different – no longer "beautiful scenery" but "a Spitfire crashed into a formation of Manchesters. ...Eight chaps were killed and burnt to cinders". The next day: "an Australian was killed in the crash yesterday". Goldie was sent on another five-day course and finally this one was "interesting". He still managed to visit 21 pubs with his 23-year-old mate Sergeant Rex Seymour (407808) from Port Pirie, South Australia. They were fog bound and unable to fly for days on training operations. The weather was appalling. On 5 December 1941 he took off in a Wellington and nearly came to grief when the pilot put down on the airfield which had become a sea of mud. Thoughts went home as he wrote an entry on 7 December: "Japan enters war". Finally he believed his chance had come to fight in this European war when he was posted to RAF 207 Squadron and on 11 December 1941: "have been picked as rear gunner for a crack veteran crew. Am feeling rather happy". The pilot and skipper of the Manchester six-man crew was RAF Flying Officer George Bayley. The Wireless Operator/Air Gunner was Flight Sergeant J E Jones (RAF), who had a DFM[48], and to top it off his mate and fellow gunner Sergeant Rex Seymour was also picked up for the crew. Rex was "a fine friend". Goldie's excitement was diminished by a letter from Bing to say that he had been in a nasty crash.

Like his childhood mate Peter Goldie, Sergeant Bing Bingley had been pleased to be posted out of 21 OTU to RAF 148 Squadron. The crew's task was to ferry aircraft to Malta and then on to Egypt where they were likely to become part of RAF 149. He found himself in a crew with a New Zealander, an Argentine and three British airmen. It was their first flight onboard an almost new Wellington bomber. The Commanding Officer decided that although the weather was cold and inclement they would go on a test flight. "We were elated and thinking only of the adventure ahead." The Wellingtons hit a violent electrical storm. The electrical system on Bingley's aircraft failed. Through a break in the clouds the Australian saw one of the Wellingtons burning on the ground and shock gripped his body as it blew up. Within minutes his own aircraft crashed. "From 9,000 feet [2740 metres] we suddenly went into a steep dive straight into the earth." The Wellington broke into two, caught fire and exploded. When Bing recovered consciousness he was in a hospital in Oxford, England. His family had received a telegram notifying them that he was "seriously injured and was not expected to live". Bing was transferred to the Princess Mary's RAF Hospital, Buckinghamshire, with a fractured skull and a severely damaged leg. The leg was saved but it was the start of four years in hospitals and rehabilitation units.

Bing had plenty of time to think: "It is somewhat of a paradox that life is considered such a disposable commodity in the cause of conflict, yet when one is injured it becomes so precious and worthy and a challenge to preserve."[49]

On 15 December Peter Goldie and Rex Seymour were pleased to discover that another Australian had joined their crew as second pilot. Sergeant Noel Messines Toohill (404786) was more than 6 feet (1.8 metres) tall and weighed more than 13 stone (80 kilos). He was born in the difficult-to-pronounce town of Toogoolawah, in Queensland, enlisting at age 18, during the same month as Peter and Bing. Toohill was educated at "Churchie", Brisbane's illustrious Church of England Grammar School. He successfully passed flying training at RAAF Amberley, Queensland. Now here he was, 19 and second pilot – pretty exciting stuff. Training runs and gunnery examinations kept Peter busy. His crew was told to prepare for daylight operations.

On 17 December the weather was so cold that as the Manchester gained height Goldie suffered slight frost bite. Two days later, Peter heard daylight operation losses were estimated to be 20 per cent. Disgruntled he wrote: "the Commanding personnel of this station are not capable of running a sewerage system let alone a defence force". On 20 December another airman was surprised to see him because he had heard Goldie had been killed. Peter addressed himself in his diary as "the living dead". His crew was given eight days leave. Peter returned to Bournemouth and Janet. Leave was "glorious". On 2 January 1942 his crew was briefed on a raid against U-boats stationed at the harbour in the French coastal town of St Nazaire. There was cloud over the target and the Manchester was hit by flak, but the crew jettisoned the bomb load and returned to base. On 4 January the operation was scrubbed due to adverse weather.

The following day the weather cleared sufficiently for the crew to take off at 0352 for Brest, France, with the brief to hit German warships and submarines. Brest was a major centre with a large German U-boat base and dockyards. The French peninsula of île Longue was a strategic location for German anti-aircraft batteries from which to protect Brest. With its cliffs and local water resources the peninsula could only be accessed at low tide, making it easy to defend. Sergeant Alexander Hollingworth (404246) 22, of Brisbane from RAF 102 Squadron was the skipper of a Whitley that turned back when the starboard engine failed. The Whitley made the English coast but the failed engine burst into flames. Hollingworth ordered his crew to bale out. He attempted to crash land, but died and was buried in Doncaster Cemetery.

An RAF 12 Squadron Wellington piloted by 23-year-old Sergeant Peter Collin Voller (404270) from Brisbane was hit by flak and, on fire, crashed into the sea. Voller and Hollingworth had joined together in Brisbane on 19 July 1940 and they died on the same night on the same operation. Also on the operation was an RAAF 458 Squadron Wellington which took off at 0437 from Holme-on-Spalding Moor. Ice and snow on the main planes resulted in the bomber crashing shortly after. Second pilot, Pilot Officer David Norris Carmichael RAAF (403040) from Sydney, was killed along with Pilot Officer Edward John Norman MacDonald (404346) from Brisbane. They were buried in the All Saints Churchyard near their airfield. The Wellington skipper, Australian Flying Officer Harold Maxwell Moran (400596) was injured, as were British and New Zealand crew members. Moran recovered from his injuries and continued to fight in the war. He left the RAAF as a Squadron Leader in 1946. Some members of the World War II RAAF would be left to wonder why they had survived when the men sitting next to them in the cockpit had died. Sergeant Peter Goldie's crew had survived despite flak and "many fighters". He was already tired and sick and wrote in his diary "Thank God" when an operation was cancelled. Peter wanted to be brave but he was only 19 and the adventure had already turned into a nightmare. He confided in his diary: "Two consecutive trips would give a man a nervous breakdown. Operations are very hard on me. You are keyed up the whole time, especially when you see fighters. If oxygen supply is weak you tire and begin to see things." On 8 January 1942 it was Brest again.

The telegram arrived at the Kalgoorlie home on 17 January 1942. There was nowhere for Lillian Goldie to hide. She knew that this might happen, but was not prepared for it when it did. The shock of those words: "regret to inform you that your son Sergeant Peter Charles

Herbert Goldie is reported missing". You pretended you were ready for such a message but you never were. The next of kin form listed Lillian only as she had separated from her husband. Alexander Goldie was a Bombadier on an anti-aircraft battery on Buckland Hill overlooking Fremantle Harbour. Opening the newspaper on 5 February 1942 Alexander found his son listed as "missing". RAAF Headquarters Western Australia signalled the Air Board in Melbourne that the father should have been informed. Air Board was blunt in reply; the father was not down as first next of kin and advising other persons "duplicates work". "This headquarters would appreciate your co-operation in discouraging enquiries likely to increase heavy burden of work for casualty section."

The signal was not well received in Perth. An official letter was dispatched to Air Board by RAAF Headquarters, Western Australia. They were "endeavouring to co-operate" and had avoided raising enquiries unless shown to be "genuine". HQ Western Australia believed a father's concern was genuine enough. When it came to Western Australian RAAF enlistees and their families it was believed casualty notification should also be received by RAAF Headquarters in that state. Casualties were increasing and thus their own workload, it was time for more RAAF staff dealing with this; "it is now considered desirable that a sub-section of your Casualty Section should be established in this area".[50] Air Board had no inkling of how many Australians would die in Bomber Command. In January 1942 RAAF Headquarters was already struggling to keep up and the situation would become dramatically worse.

By July 1946 the war was over but there was still no closure for Lillian Goldie. She wrote to the Air Board that she had received no information for "four and a half years" and she pleaded to know more about her son's "end of life". The same appeal came from William and Eliza Seymour of Port Pirie, South Australia. They too had received the same brief upsetting telegrams, they too needed to know more of the fate of the crew of Manchester L7322 and their son Bill (known as Rex): "The news we have received from the Air Board has been very brief. We feel we would like to hear more information as to his whereabouts at the time of his 'presumed death'."

The same entreaty came from Queensland. Miriam Toohill asked if there was any further news on "our son? We feel this blow more than words can express, such a promising young man, a good son".

The RAF Missing Research & Enquiry Unit finally sent a report to the Australian Air Board. The situation after the war was as chaotic as the war itself. Disintegration of villages, of regions, meant that piecing together the puzzle of missing airmen and their machines was difficult at best. Brest was totally destroyed in 1944 with the Allied invasion of Normandy. French citizens who had survived were homeless and scattered, yet witnesses needed to be interviewed and often statements and leads were confused and false. Graves with no markings were exhumed. There had been little German regard given the crew of the Manchester L7322 which was brought down by the anti-aircraft batteries on île Longue. The bodies that came ashore were given to villagers to bury without proper identification and no ceremony. RAF pilot Flying Officer George Bayley lay in one grave. Sergeant Noel Toohill had no known grave. Exhumation revealed one grave contained two bodies, and dental charts showed them to be Sergeant Rex Seymour and Sergeant Peter Goldie. Lillian Goldie was spared the more upsetting details of the report. She was simply told on 2 July 1947 that 19-year-old Peter was buried in Crozon Communal Cemetery, France, not far from his "fine friend" Rex Seymour. She had hoped for closure but there was none and his grave was too far away.

TWO

"God alone knows when I will see you again."

Sergeant Bill (Buff) Cheese

The trench warfare of World War I in which so many Australians died and where the nation's male youth had been used as cannon fodder, had left a lasting impression on the psyche of their countrymen. Fathers who survived the carnage of World War I did not wish their sons to be subjected to the same. In the early years of World War II the romance of swashbuckling men in fur-lined leather flying jackets or tailor-made blue uniforms offered a very different and more palatable option of serving your country and defending the principles this generation held to be true. The RAAF was largely unknown, few had direct contact with anyone who had flown in the Australian Flying Corps and commonly airmen were portrayed by the media as gentlemen, almost friendly with the enemy as they passed each other in the air and saluted. The romantic ideal for aircrew would not survive – the bombing campaign would prove it an apparition – as aircrew became the expendable commodity in much the same way as men in khaki were in World War I. For those caught up in the initial flush of patriotic fervour, but were under 21, the unknown worked in their favour. Being under 21, Arthur Hoyle approached his father about joining the army and was firmly rebuffed. Arthur was on a university scholarship to become a teacher so all he could do was join the Sydney University Regiment, a part-time militia battalion consisting mainly of students. Here he would mark time until his father agreed. Like many 18 year olds, Arthur "expected to become a glamour boy", but the thick woollen khaki uniform "which fitted rather poorly on my slight frame", a pair of heavy boots and a slouch hat that came almost over his ears, was not what he had in mind. Neither was the khaki initiation. "We were given nothing to eat but just lined up in the hot sun, given a vaccination and an injection in each arm and then set to work. The needles were blunt and several of the would-be soldiers fainted."[1]

Arthur persisted with his hopes of enlistment into the "real" military but his father continued to refuse. When one day Arthur spoke of becoming an aircrew trainee he "was amazed" that his father agreed with him. He was surprised too, by the "ridiculously strict medical examination" he endured to enter the RAAF. Having passed, he counted down the days until that morning of 6 December 1941 when he reported to the RAAF reception centre at Woolloomooloo. "I felt some trepidation but it was overwhelmed by the excitement of the day." Arthur, who as a 15-year-old boy had watched enthralled as aircrew alighted from their Ansons, was now embarking on "the greatest adventure of my life", living the "dreams of heroism as I swept in on the tails of a Messerschmitt or ploughed through the sky at the controls of my Wellington bomber".[2]

Pre-war career opportunities were limited for Australian middle class men. There were primarily three choices – teacher, clerk or accountant. Arthur Hoyle was studying to become a teacher, Victorian Ron Waldon was a student teacher at schools in his home town of Beechworth and in Tallangatta, before entering the Melbourne Teachers College in 1939. On graduation Waldon was sent to the small one-teacher towns of Mount Alfred and Barwidgee Creek. The RAAF seemed rather more exciting, war or no war, so he enlisted in April 1940 but "had to wait about seven months" before being called up.[3] Ron was sent to RAAF Bradfield Park Station, Lindfield, Sydney. He made friends quickly with those in his course. He had heard of the camaraderie of the military and quickly realised this to be true. It was still early days in this wartime

RAAF and volunteers were kept marking time "because there were no schools available". Finally with Australian training over they were ready to embark for overseas. He wrote in his diary "farewells were sad and will always be remembered".[4]

As his troopship slipped its moorings, "there were about 200 of us...I shall always remember sailing down the beautiful Sydney Harbour". The next days were grim as Ron Waldon struggled with sea sickness. "I was sick. The ship just swayed and rolled – up and down". The next day he was "still sick". The following day, 25 February 1941, was such relief, calmer waters and mooring in Auckland harbour. Ron decided New Zealanders were "very nice people". He was impressed with the scenery and even delighted in "the smell of sulphur, boiling geysers". He would have preferred to stay given that as soon as the ship was in open ocean "that rolling again" was cause for concern until he realised that he was no longer sea sick. Some New Zealander airmen had swelled their numbers and he considered them "great chaps". This was developing into an amazing trip, the sort of round the world trip he could never have contemplated even a year ago. The next stop was Suva, Fiji, and here he had time for some souvenir shopping.

Doug Butterworth and his brothers were "fanatics about the exciting advancements in aviation".[5] Although they were bush kids and grew up in North Queensland they were still "definitely subjected to the 'British Empire Syndrome'...we were intensely patriotic towards the British Empire". Les Butterworth already had a commercial pilot's licence so was immediately accepted by the RAAF as an instructor. Doug was a sugar chemist at Kalmia Sugar Mill in Ayr and enlisted with mates Ian Whitson, a fellow employee of the Kalmia Sugar Mill, Frank Bower, a former student of Ayr state and high schools, now a clerk with Ayr Shire Council, and Bernie Whyte from Townsville. They were taken into the reserve and then told to wait because the RAAF was not yet ready for them; "we were sure the war would be over before we got there (how naive can you be?)".[6] The report notices finally came and together they boarded a train in north Queensland for the trip south. These were heady exciting days. They marched with other Queensland recruits down the broad streets of their state capital not yet in uniform, but off to war as far as the cheering Brisbane crowds were concerned. It was a proud day with flags and bunting; perhaps just a trifle embarrassing because in their minds they had not as yet become true heroes.

The train trip down to Sydney improved when beer was brought onboard at South Grafton railway station and quite a party atmosphere ensued. On arrival in Bradfield Park the Queenslanders were a little bothered – since their entire intake was mustered as Wireless Operators/Air Gunners. They were in no position to ask why. Strangely it seemed that the majority of Victorians and New South Welshmen were mustered Pilots, whereas the majority of aircrew trainees from other states were mustered otherwise. At least it meant they were likely to remain together throughout their training.

In the short term, the Queensland boys were more intent on finding uniforms that actually fitted; "uniforms, boots and all the accoutrements of war were flung at us willy nilly, regardless of size" recalled Doug Butterworth. If you had the audacity to complain "you received snarls from the back of the counter as well as your own sadistic Non-commissioned Officer screaming at you".[7] A barrage of injections for diseases they had never heard of was given followed by a great deal of marching accompanied by the standard high RAAF arm swing. For Doug Butterworth the pain from his swollen arms was offset by the blisters on his feet caused by wearing boots that were at least two sizes too small. The passage "from civilian to service life was fairly traumatic for some of us". On the few short leave periods Doug Butterworth was led astray by his mate Bernie Whyte "a mischievous extrovert".

As they prepared to board the ship to Canada at the end of October 1940 there was one last medical inspection, nicknamed the "Short Arm Inspection". Aircrew recruits were ordered to line up and approach a medical officer who was armed with a 12 in (30 cm) ruler. Upon command the recruit would drop his pants and the doctor would use the ruler "to stir up your credentials to have a good peek to see if venereal disease is prevalent". Needless to say there were many wisecracks about having to measure up for this man's RAAF and if there was a prize for the man who measured up the longest. Undoubtedly for those assembled who as yet had not even experienced the briefest interaction with a member of the opposite sex, the examination was a little confronting, but this they kept to themselves.

For RAAF aircrew trainees their first overseas deployment was a dream. They found themselves in Auckland, New Zealand, and Fiji. They would have loved to explore Honolulu but because the United States was not at war these Australian British Empire war recruits were not allowed ashore. The sea journey was just becoming boring when they finally arrived in Vancouver, Canada, on 20 November 1940. "The view coming into Vancouver was spectacular – majestic snow-capped mountains", wrote Doug Butterworth. The journey was far from over as they immediately caught the train for Calgary, Alberta, journeying through the Rocky Mountains. For the boys from Queensland's sugar cane tropics snow was a new phenomenon. It was the middle of the Canadian winter, which meant there was a great deal of snow to come. In the beginning there were plenty of snowball fights but after months of winter their enthusiasm waned. They were issued with warmer caps with ear flaps but Royal Canadian Air Force (RCAF) parade tradition was to tie the flaps above the top of head. There was friction when the Australians decided that in no way were their cap flaps budging from over their ears in −29°C (20°F).

The Queensland intake was sent to the bombing and gunnery school at Mossbank, Saskatchewan. Canada, like Australia, was not ready for war and it was almost comical to see guards patrolling the base fence line with sticks over their shoulders because rifles were unavailable. The ensuing weeks at school were spent firing Vickers gas-operated machine guns at a drogue towed by another aircraft from the open cockpit of Fairey Battles. Both guns and aircraft were antiquated. "The state of unpreparedness was unreal" wrote Doug Butterworth. Nonetheless those visions of World War I air aces were rekindled as the trainees stood in the open cockpit firing machine guns; all that was missing was the white scarf streaming behind in the slip stream. In June their training was over. With Wireless Operator insignias proudly fastened to their uniforms Butterworth and his classmates were sent on another ship bound for Britain and the war. The Atlantic was fogbound.

Newly promoted Sergeant Doug Butterworth wrote in his 1941 diary: "Friday 27 June – Cold as Christ. Tuesday 1 July – Colder than Christ".

For reasons unexplained their ship left the convoy and took the airmen to Iceland and "the most primitive, disorganised military camp imaginable" where they slept on concrete floors. Furthermore the Icelanders were not friendly given that their loyalties were towards Germany. The Australians were left to their own devices and found this confusing; Wasn't there a war on? What on earth were Australian aircrew doing in Iceland? When it seemed they had been completely forgotten they departed Iceland for England "amongst disorganised chaos – the Poms seemed to have a flair for it" wrote a slightly disgruntled Doug Butterworth.

The recruits were keen to start their operational life, but tragically on the day they arrived at 20 Operating Training Unit at Lossiemouth, northern Scotland, two Wellington bombers crashed and burst into flames. Doug Butterworth wrote "very impressive military funerals – made one realise a war was on". In Lossiemouth there were Marconi radio sets to familiarise themselves with, and a great deal of cross-country flights and gunnery practice. There were "circuits and bumps" – flights with inexperienced pilots, which were always nerve wracking. The element of urgency had finally arrived, as rising casualties increased in line with Bomber Command intensity. The weather, nonetheless, intervened and trainees spent more time "playing pontoon than in training".[8] By late December 1941 and January 1942 dispersal of the trainees from 20 Operating Training Unit commenced. The vagaries of the RAF posting system meant that most of the Queensland boys who entered and trained together would not remain together. This was also true for others. During World War II the Royal Australian Navy (RAN) endeavoured to draft wartime sailors in state groups and if at all possible to ships which bore the name of the sailor's state capital. For these RAAF men it may well have encouraged a closer-knit group and eased the burden of what they were to face so far from home. Those in RAF command who controlled the movements of RAAF personnel never considered this. There was no attempt to understand the distances involved or the state loyalties imbued in a nation 27 times the size of

Britain. They were simply intent on rapid resolution of RAF crewing for the war against Germany and Italy.

Doug Butterworth's Queensland intake departed in numerous directions. Doug and Frank Bower spent a fun Christmas 1941 together before joining RAF 109 Squadron. Sergeant Frank Bower (404478) the son of a Blacksmith in Ayr, North Queensland, was part of a crew whose Wellington was shot down on 28/29 March 1942. No trace of aircraft or crew was found. Warrant Officer Jack Bernard Whyte (404473), known as Bernie Whyte, was posted to RAF 215 Squadron on 22 March 1942. The squadron was transferred to RAF India Command via the Middle East and arrived in the sub-continent on April Fools' Day 1942. He was killed when his Wellington bomber was shot down in the region of Meiktila, Burma (modern-day Myanmar), on 17 May 1943. Also onboard was classmate Warrant Officer Arthur Barnes (404541), a Brisbane clerk storeman educated at Yeronga State High School and Brisbane's Commercial High School. No trace of aircraft or crew was ever found.

Flying Officer Ian Whitson (404593), who worked with Doug Butterworth at Ayr's Kalmia Sugar Mill, was posted to RAAF 455 Squadron and teamed up with 23-year-old Sydney-born Pilot Flight Sergeant John Samuel Freeth (411768). Freeth had enlisted in May 1941 and embarked for overseas service five months later. He had 303 hours of flying service and his quiet confidence belied his 23 years. By October 1941 he was in England and by January 1943 was flying with RAAF 455 Squadron. His crew was a mix of airmen with the Navigator RAF Sergeant Bert Wheatcroft (1330814) and Canadian Sergeant Horace Downing (R/74871) as the other gunner. On 24 May 1943 they were undertaking an "attack liaison" training exercise out of RAF Leuchars, Fifeshire, Scotland. These training runs came with a degree of fear mixed with excitement when dodging and weaving fighters, even if they were your own. Freeth's Hampden was at a level height until his gunners sighted a Spitfire. He took evasive action and levelled out. A Beaufighter on the same exercise also took evasive action but failed to properly observe the position of the Hampden. The Beaufighter tore through the Hampden, severing its tail, and the Hampden plunged into the sea off Scotland's

Fraser Borough. The bodies of Wheatcroft and Downing were retrieved but the two Australians were never found. The Commanding Officer of RAF Leuchars advised the British Air Board that the fault for the accident clearly lay with the pilot of the Beaufighter and a board of enquiry was unwarranted. That their deaths were deemed "non-operational" and caused by friendly fire somehow seemed even more tragic.

By coincidence Pilot John Freeth had attended the prestigious Sydney Grammar School between 1932 and 1935; Flying Officer John Walter Keene (402742), pilot of Doug Butterworth's crew, also attended Sydney Grammar School at the same time. Doug was posted to the nascent RAAF 460 Squadron where the worlds and destinies of hundreds of Australians merged from 6 January when 460 Squadron was formed initially at RAF Molesworth, Cambridgeshire, and then on 4 January 1942 moved to Breighton, Yorkshire. RAAF 460 ended the war with a proud history. Of all British Bomber Command squadrons this one flew the most operations, carried the highest bomb tonnages and its aircrew were awarded the most decorations. It also suffered the heaviest casualties with 60 per cent of squadron airmen killed, another 3 per cent seriously injured in crashes, and a further 12 per cent became prisoners of war.

Shocking weather delayed the first RAAF 460 Squadron operational flights but offered instead the opportunity for the men to settle in as best they could and for crews to form and bond. Doug Butterworth's Aussie crew had followed different EATS routes. Doug was made Front Gunner. The Rear Gunner, Flight Sergeant Reg Biglands (407282) from Adelaide, had enlisted in August 1940, a month earlier than Doug. Reg was seen as pretty "old". Not only was he turning 28 in May but he was married to Olive and had a six year old son, Peter. Reg had finished his apprenticeship and was working as a letterpress machinist prior to entering the RAAF. The Wireless Operator was 24-year-old Flight Sergeant Graham Berry (407281) a former driver with Great Boulder Goldmine Co. He and Reg Biglands trained together. Their South Australian intake completed RAAF training at Ballarat and Evans Head, not leaving Australia until May 1941 to travel to Britain. Unlike EATS trainees like Doug Butterworth, their training had not been interrupted and shortened due to the winter weather of Canada and Britain. Still, joining 20 OTU in a cold 1941 Scots autumn and then winter was rather a rude shock.

The Navigator was Ron Waldon, the Victorian teacher whose episodes with sea sickness cleared in time to buy souvenirs in Suva. Ron Waldon discovered how difficult his training was as soon as he entered the navigation school in Edmonton, and how he had to "work like blazes. We do a two-year university course in three months". Now it made sense why it was "necessary to have a fairly high education to get admittance with the air force" and to be mustered Observer/Navigator.

His Canadian sojourn was amusing, and he particularly liked the Canadian manner of speaking which he likened to the accents of the first American "talkies" (movies). Like Doug Butterworth, Ron was amazed by the beauty of the Rocky Mountains which he thought "impossible" to do justice to in words. "High rugged peaks covered with white snow, lakes covered with ice, green pine trees, winding creeks and rivers". They would impress forever the aircrew from the driest continent. "You can imagine how enjoyable that day was to me" Ron Waldon wrote in his letter home, it was "impossible for me to describe the splendour and grandeur of the scenes I saw that day". He looked forward to when he returned home so he could tell his family "much, much more". By August Ron was in Ottawa attached to a Canadian flight: "They are a grand bunch of fellows". On the first day of August 1941 he wrote, "I have my wings and Sergeant stripes – Boy oh Boy...Next step, I hope will be a commission after actual warfare". At this time he was in Ottawa and the only Aussie attached to a Canadian flight: "They are a grand bunch of fellows". From here he travelled to the UK to join an Operating Training Unit: "By the time you receive this I hope I shall have dropped a few eggs in Jerry land". Like other Australians he was struggling with the weather in this "Damned cold country. At present I have a hell of a lot of chilblains – wow". The white Christmas was a novelty but it didn't really feel like Christmas and Ron missed his family "it is really grand to receive Aussie mail". "The weather is just b••••• awful".[9] By the time the crew of Keene, Waldon, Berry, Biglands and Butterworth had teamed up, Australia was at war with Japan. Doug Butterworth wrote in his diary: "Heard the bad news of Jap lands and atrocities, so Ron [Waldon] and I went to the local pub and drowned our sorrows – All boys very worried and discontented."[10]

Australians serving with RAAF 460 Squadron were grateful to see the end of snow and ice. Though English spring weather was unpredictable at least it gave hope of warmer weather to come and that the Nissen huts in which they stayed may become a fraction less cold and draughty. The closest village to RAF Breighton was Bubwith and the quiet rustic countryside was turned upside down by a wartime airfield and its accompanying noise and urgency. The village folk were still getting accustomed to the rowdy, raucous airmen and their strange Australian accents and likewise, the RAAF 460 airmen were still getting accustomed to the locals and their strange Yorkshire brogue. The two village pubs did a roaring trade although the elegant name of one, the "Black Swan", was now popularly referred to by Australian aircrew as the "Dirty Duck" and the other, the "Seven Sisters Hotel", was even less graciously nicknamed the "Fourteen Titties".[11]

The RAAF 460 Squadron Commanding Officer was the highly respected Wing Commander Arthur Leonard George Hubbard (267508). He was born in Echuca, a town which hugged a bend of the Murray River, and watched as steamboats plied a trade of wool and supplies when the muddy brown river ran. But the imagination of 19-year-old Hubbard was engaged by faster, more futuristic transportation and the mechanic's assistant was accepted as a cadet at RAAF Point Cook in July 1936. As was the way in the 1930s junior RAAF officers went to Britain for further training and Arthur Hubbard arrived in August 1937. He commenced service with RAF 38 Squadron and in the first year of the war was flying war planes in the Middle East. He returned to Britain to observe RAAF EATS trainees undergoing heavy bomber conversion training. Hubbard was a solidly built man of medium height whose natural presence was obvious without being daunting. He was admired by the Australians he commanded because he led from the front, joining his men on dangerous operations. He commanded 460 until posted back to Australia in March 1943. The following month he was awarded the Distinguished Service Order. He had already been awarded the Distinguished Flying Cross. The citation read "this officer had displayed exceptional qualities of leadership". Before the end of World War II he saw service in New Guinea, before retiring from the RAAF in July 1947.

The RAAF 460 Squadron Flight Commanders were South Australian Squadron Leader Colin Leslie Gilbert and RAF Squadron Leader Frank (DFC). Both were airmen of great experience and Gilbert in particular was tremendously respected because of his "great love" for "operational flying" and his "enthusiasm for life" which "quickly inspired the new fledglings coming on to the squadron and made him a most popular figure".[12] Squadron Leader Frank was replaced by Australian Squadron Leader John William Edward Leighton, DFC, early in 1942 and quickly impressed younger flyers because he was "similarly disposed to the joys of life as Gilbert".[13] They watched as the training of RAAF 460 personnel progressed and was fine tuned.

On 12 March 1942 RAAF 460 Squadron took off at 2030 hours and struck the German city of Emden. The bombing height was 15,000 feet (4,500 metres), and each bomb load consisted of six 500 lb (225 kg) bombs. The weather was expected to be mostly clear with light cumulus cloud. At the same time five other crews took off to bomb harbour installations at Dunkirk. In keeping with Bomber Command operations generally, this first 460 operation was haphazard due to a lack of navigational aids. By the small hours of the morning RAAF 460 Squadron had lost its first crew on the attack on Dunkirk. That aircrew was made up of New Zealander Flight Sergeant Patrick Cooney, (403951) RNZAF, who piloted a crew of two Australians, Sergeants John Sivyer Turnock (404688) a 28 year old from the Tweed River in NSW, and 23-year-old Ian Eric Hart (400413) from Melbourne; and three RAF Sergeants George Winter (989226), Jack Woodward (135986) and William Pascoe (1380051). Their Wellington Z1251 crashed at St Joris les Nieuwpoort (West Flanders), Belgium.

Sergeant Bill (Buff) Cheese (408046) was one of the young aircrew watched carefully by Leighton. Like so many inexperienced youthful EATS trainees, Buff was just busting to cease the training and begin real operations. He was 19 when he gained RAAF entry in August

1940. He had been a good student in Hobart, passing English, French, arithmetic, algebra, Latin and chemistry at intermediate level. He was studying technical subjects through the Australian Insurance Institute, Melbourne, and achieved honours in the subjects of electricity and chemistry, which he realised would appeal to the air force. For five months he waited, working as a clerk in Melbourne, but the work was claustrophobic and Melbourne not to his liking so he returned to the rugged beauty of King Island. Life on the island had been pretty basic but as a child that was wonderful, even if there were occasions when you needed to outrun and outsmart a bull. On his RAAF application Buff wrote "farming" as his occupation – as it was for his father in Naracoopa, King Island – and waited for the inevitable disbelief concerning his name. He would explain that the family name was French and his father had changed it to "Cheese". Yes it was a little strange and to offer some levity Buff would relate that his sister Mary told people she, Buff, and a niece, "were the only cheeses to escape King Island without being eaten.[14] Buff was brought over to Victoria to join RAAF Somers and his technical qualifications saw him streamed into Wireless Operator/Air Gunner.

The day their elder son Buff left Elsie Cheese found her husband Arthur crying. He had served with the Australian army overseas during the last war and turned to his wife saying, "he doesn't know what he is in for, I do".[15] For Buff the war experience was just beginning. His training began with No 1 Wireless Air Gunners School, Ballarat, and six months of study. He found some of the theory hard and he sighed with relief when he qualified as a Wireless Operator in February 1941 and was drafted to do his gunnery course at Sydney's Evans Head. Air gunnery was exciting and he was awarded his Air Gunner's badge two months later. In May he embarked for Britain. The trainers tested him for night vision and wrote "above average" which was just as well because night raids were to become the norm. His training continued in a signals squadron at RAF Cranwell, Lincolnshire. On 17 August 1941 he received a "satisfactory". It was a blow to his self-respect. The next day he tested again and received a "good"; which he considered to be not good enough. On 19 August he scored an "excellent". He rested on his laurels and failed the following day. Consistency needed to be achieved and he did not fail again.

In October and November 1941 Buff Cheese was in Scotland patiently undergoing operational training, well perhaps not totally patient. His log book needed to be kept tidy and precise because at the end of each month it would be checked and signed by his Flight Commander. He was just pleased when, after what seemed ages, he could use red ink to highlight the exciting stuff, the "WAR OP" letters were very large. He was now in the twin-engine, long-range medium bomber, the Vickers Wellington. The aircraft may have been named in honour of the first Duke of Wellington but it was generally known by airmen as "Wimpy" after the "J Wellington Wimpy" character in the popular comic strip *Popeye*. Technical staff were quick to point out how robust the Wellingtons were, how the geodesic construction metal lattice structure offered terrific strength and meant that even after structural damage a Wimpy could keep flying. There were even stories of Wellingtons making it back to Britain with partially naked frames after the fabric had burnt off. It was something the young Tasmanian would prefer not to witness first hand. The technical people didn't like discussing the aircraft's vulnerability to attacking fighters. The bomber had a maximum speed of 235 mph (375 kph) at 15,500 ft (4,700 m). Wellingtons did not have self-sealing fuel tanks or enough defensive armament. It was best not to dwell on the vulnerability; Buff would just have to do his bit with the .303 Browning machine guns in the nose turret.

Sergeant Bill (Buff) Cheese (courtesy of Mary Cheese-Walker).

Over the next couple of months he flew with eight or so different pilots, some good, some not so. There were six different Wellingtons, some better than others. Buff practised "ZZ landings" (zero visibility, zero cloud base) and spent a lot of time at the wireless. Yet he preferred the other part of his classification as an Air Gunner and the surge of adrenalin it gave: "fired 800 rounds from front turret"; "tested all my equipment in the front turret". By the end of the March page he wrote in black 116.25 hours and in red 26.05 hours. He noted that he hoped to remain with the same pilot and crew as it was extremely unsettling to be thrown in with different crews.

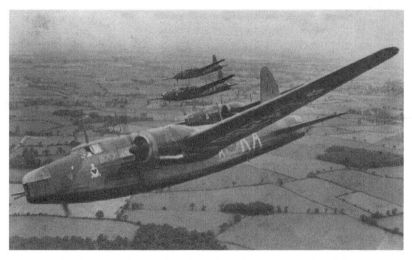

Vickers Wellington Bombers (courtesy Waldon family).

By April 1942 Buff was using more red ink than black in his log book. On the first day of the month he flew in aircraft Z1290, piloted by his Commanding Officer, Wing Commander Hubbard – it was such a buzz to fly with Hubbard. The four-and- a-half-hour operation was a success and the dockyards at Le Havre, France, suffered as a result. But the Wellington aircraft was frustrating and Buff was becoming impatient. On 5 April he wrote "dropped 12 x 250 lb (110 kg) bombs into sea owing to inability to identify Le Havre. Self in front turret. Fired 40 rounds test bursts into sea". On another day another operation, the same frustration: "jettisoned 3,000 lbs (1.35 tons) incendiaries into sea owing to failure of oxygen supply over Belgium – we never reached Dortmund, the target, self in front turret, fired 40 rounds in sea". On 8 April 1942 the crew needed to drop their bombs off the Dutch island of Terschelling because they had been unable to identify the target, Hamburg, due to low cloud and "gyro unserviceable".

But there was some success in that month. The crew bombed the docks and shipping at Le Havre and Buff watched the flash and smoke. The rear gunner became excited when he saw a German ME109. Fortunately the aircraft did not attack. Two days later Buff braced himself as the noise and acceleration enveloped him and the Wellington grudgingly lifted from the tarmac. Taking off with a full bomb load was always the most dangerous time and this night they were carrying 2,700 lbs (1.2 tons) of incendiaries destined to be dropped on Essen, Germany. Doug Hurditch was the pilot. Buff was in the nose turret. The intercom crackled with voices as the target was identified and there was a collective expelling of air as the bomb aimer called "bombs gone" and the course setting changed for home. Buff maintained his vigilance, searching the skies for fighters. The green pastures of England were a welcome sight and the body began to relax as Doug Hurditch dropped the aircraft wheels onto the tarmac. The propellers stuttered as engines were switched off. It was then that Buff noticed agitation among the ground crew. Z1344 had returned with its full bomb load, "bombs hung up without our knowing". His land legs seemed a little more wobbly than normal as they moved his body away from the aircraft and its deadly cargo. Hurditch rose immeasurably as a pilot in Buff's estimation and he hoped he would be crewed with Hurditch again, particularly if the bombs just happened to get hung up.

Operations were unsettling, and the crew tried not to dwell on the "what ifs". It could have been the stress or homesickness or a combination of both, but Buff wrote a seven-page letter home on 19 April and said more than he usually did. His mum sat down every Sunday and wrote to him; others too were generous with parcels of goodies and letters. He had not had a lot of time to write – what could he write anyway given the stern approach to mail censorship? He couldn't tell the family on King Island about his operations or all the emotions he felt during them. This war made a little less sense to him now and he no longer felt the loyalty for Britain which had motivated him previously. He had sent brief cables on a regular basis to let them know he was okay. Yorkshire seemed just that bit more dreary than usual on 19 April 1942. His mum had mentioned she would like to take a trip over to England again after the war, Buff wrote: "WHY???? What on earth do you see in this cursed country? Only God alone can tell Australians in this country why on earth the miserable dump wasn't evacuated centuries ago. ...I'd give my right arm to get out of it!"[16] He was struggling with his respect for all things British and the RAF. He watched while British airmen were commissioned and Australians were not. "The best men over here are still Sergeants and look like remaining as such forever, the way they run things in this racket. Don't think I'm talking about myself either. I can recognize plenty of far better men than I."[17]

Buff also felt slighted that pilots were commissioned but that there was a marked reluctance to commission other aircrew. "I'm in the wrong job for a start. I haven't seen a commissioned Wireless Operator/Air Gunner since I've been over here." There existed a perception on the part of the RAF that pilots were from a different class than other aircrew and this was reason enough not to commission non-pilots. Buff had also noticed that in 1942 many permanent RAF were not aircrew but involved in administration noting with exaggeration, "millions of winged wonders out of Orderly rooms etc. with commissions".

Similar summations were made by others. When Flight Lieutenant Ray Whitrod (407937), a former Adelaide policeman, who had entered the RAAF in February 1941, was posted to Britain he tried to make sense of the culture shock:

I'd grown up in Australia...where there wasn't so much inequality in the social classes as there was in England in wartime. I was a bit, I suppose, horrified sometimes by the distinction between sergeant aircrew and officer aircrew in the RAF. The sergeant aircrew got very little consideration and found it very hard to get commissions, whereas in the Australian and Canadian air forces your family background didn't matter so much – it was your personal skill as an aircrew operator plus your leadership ability that mattered.[18]

It was a little bewildering when you visited a nation you saw as the "motherland" and found yourself regarded as a lesser being. Flying Officer Lionel Rackley (414828) may have been a brash 20 year old when he arrived in England but it wasn't long before he locked horns with RAF officialdom:

> My flight commander was a thorough bastard. He was an RAF navigator. He didn't like pilots for a start, and I don't think he liked Australian pilots in particular. His reception was: 'How did you get shot up by flak? What the hell do you think they put windscreens in aeroplanes for? It's for bloody pilots to look out and see where the flak is'. I thought, 'Stuff you, boy.' ...I just gave him away after that.[19]

The attitudes were difficult given that the Aussies had volunteered to help Britain and the Empire but now nagging at the consciousness was the concern that their own country was directly under threat from the Japanese. Flight Lieutenant Peter Coldham (401908) was in England attached to RAF 156 Squadron. He eventually returned to Australia wearing a Distinguished Flying Cross and bar. He originally thought he had "a lasting affinity with, and love for, England". When he was stationed in England he realized his reaction to the English was more of a "patchwork quilt". "Some of them I didn't like at all; some were condescending to the colonial."[20]

Generally British non-military personnel were very welcoming and would share what they had with Australian airmen. There was a hospitality scheme called the Lady Frances Ryder Empire Scheme for Australians. English country folk provided homes for recreation for the forces. Airmen would put their names on a list and would be welcomed into family homes. Invariably these people would become second families and terribly important to the morale of Australian airmen. Buff brightened up when he was allowed leave to explore London and

Oxford. He visited family and friends and wrote of their wonderful welcome and care. He enjoyed comfortable houses and better food. His honest appraisal was never far away and he wrote of how he had been introduced to the son of family friends who was an army Second Lieutenant, who spoke with the "foul accent of some kind I have found peculiar to most Limey army officers". He wanted to speak of his crew and squadron but knew this would suffer the blackout of a censor's pen. His letter of 19 April 1942 closed, however, with the comment that "there have been dozens of rumours about our return to Australia but nothing definite yet". With Australia at war with Japan, the Australians based in Britain had begun to question why they were still there.

On 28 April 1942, with Sergeant Doug Hurditch in the skipper's seat, Buff's aircraft dropped incendiaries in the area of Kiel, Germany. In the front nose turret it was Buff's turn to get a little excited. "I saw a JU88 over Kiel; he did not see us." Once back at RAF Breighton the news was that Z1290, which had taken off with them for the raid on Kiel, had been shot down. Onboard was a crew of Aussies: Flight Sergeant Les Shephard (402885) a 25 year old from Wagga Wagga, New South Wales, who had enlisted in November 1940; the 28-year-old Pilot Officer Ralph Bond (402836) from Brisbane who had enlisted in November 1940; Sergeant John Carpender (404868) 29, from Brisbane; Sergeant Trevor McIlveen (402600) who was 33 and from Dubbo, NSW; Sergeant Bill Perroux (404661) 26, from Townsville; and Sergeant Johnny Cosgrove (408122) 25, a fellow Tasmanian from Launceston.[21] Buff had flown on Z1290 just days before. He had flown on Wellingtons piloted by Ralph Bond. He was on the Kiel operation. He tried not to think but you could not help but notice the empty beds. He visited family and friends away from base as often as he could and one of those friends wrote to Elsie Cheese that they were concerned how "depressed" Buff was now appearing.

During August 1941 research had shown that less than 10 per cent of bombs fell within five miles of the target. Nocturnal navigation was often deficient. Technical advances needed to be perfected to ensure accuracy and the bombing of military and industrial targets. But in 1942 Professor Frederick Lindemann, the chief scientific adviser to the British government, presented a paper to the British Cabinet recommending an escalation of the bombing campaign and the carpet bombing of German cities. His justification was because German bombing attacks on English cities, particularly on London, had intensified – the German air offensive had not spared civilians. He argued, that the inability of bomber crews to accurately attack targets rather than residential areas should therefore, no longer be of concern. Cabinet agreed and civilians were no longer exempt from the British bombing campaign.[22]

On 31 May 1942 Buff Cheese was with another pilot, an Englishman, RAF Flight Lieutenant Allan Holland. Buff figured he better keep his ideas about England to himself, at least until he found out what sort of bloke Holland was. Holland took them up on a test flight with dinghy and parachute drill, pretty boring really. The rest of the crew were Australians. Flight Sergeant Dudley Raymond Beinke (406136) was an orphan until taken into the home of Theodor Emil and Marie Antonia Beinke of Prospect, South Australia. Dudley had the palest of blue eyes which could be disconcerting until you got used to him. He had enlisted in August 1940 and was in the same intake as fellow South Australian Sergeant Thomas Lincoln Watkins (407308) and Buff. The three men had become mates through training and they realised how fortunate they were to be in the same crew and in a RAAF squadron. Sergeant Cliff Douglas (406349) was born in Albany, a jewel of a town clinging to the southern shores of Western Australia. He enlisted three months later than the other three Australians so received some ribbing about what had taken him so long to join up. That only worked until Victorian Sergeant Arthur Dansey (40080) good-naturedly lauded over them because he had been in since May 1940. And Arthur was counting, 17 operations gone, how many more? The men felt a special link not only because they were Australian but also because they had all been born in 1921.

It was the night of the first day of June 1942, just, because their Wellington took off from Breighton at 2321. From his position in the nose Buff looked at the dark unwelcoming North Sea less than 100 feet (30 metres) below. This time they had bombed their target Essen. Holland was moving the bomber around trying to avoid German anti-aircraft fire which spurted up from coastal installations on the Dutch coast. In mere seconds their world changed dramatically. There was a splintering of glass and metal and the cockpit controls shattered. Wireless Operator/ Air Gunner Cliff Douglas jerked as metal hit his thigh and foot. The port engine burst into flames and the crippled aircraft dived into the sea. The Wellington broke up as it hit the water and the rear of the aircraft sank immediately. The airmen struggled to the surface. They fought to get away from the fire blazing on top of the water, their heavy flying garb dragging against their under-inflated life jackets. There was no sign of Tom Watkins. They wondered if Tom, sitting in his rear gun turret, had been killed by enemy fire; they hoped in one way that he had because otherwise he had drowned as the bomber sank. Buff Cheese was dazed; he knew he was burnt and his body seemed unresponsive. He thought he would drown but a German "flak" boat arrived. Dudley Beinke was being supported by others and he appeared completely stunned. As men pulled him into the boat they realised Dudley had lost a leg and he died shortly after. Holland had a broken leg. Arthur Dansey was in great pain with a broken leg and shrapnel wounds. The toes on his left foot were dislocated.

The Danseys were worried. They had received no further news from the RAAF since that telegram arrived saying Arthur was "missing". The question "was Arthur dead?" hung heavy. A letter arrived from an RCAF friend of Arthur's, Flight Sergeant George Higgins, and the words leapt off the page: "He's safe and quite well except for a broken leg. I've had a strange feeling ever since he went missing that he was safe and when I got his letter yesterday, I could have cried I was so happy."[23]

There were tears shed in the Dansey home. Higgins wrote that Arthur had made light of being shot down in his usual Aussie manner and saying he was looking forward to the end of the war "when he could visit my wife and I in Canada, he'll certainly be made welcome as we Canadians have a great respect for all Australians, I guess we've got a lot in common".

Arthur Dansey senior forwarded a copy of the letter to the RAAF querying the "lack of official information" and suggesting officialdom "could expedite matters by letting me have my boy's internment camp no". Official confirmation came in November 1942: Arthur was still in Bergen hospital and the extent of his injuries were unknown. Dansey recovered sufficiently to be sent to a German POW camp and returned to Australia at war's end.

The dreaded telegram arrived at the Cheese King Island home. It was hard to avoid because Arthur Cheese was looking after the local post office. Buff was missing. Nothing further was received until a letter arrived via family in England. A copy was quickly wired to King Island. Buff was in hospital in Bergen, Holland, with Arthur Dansey and Cliff Douglas. The letter dated 17 June 1942 was dictated to a German orderly: "I won't go into all the details because there is only one way which I could have possibly got here. But please take the following news easily – I had to."[24]

Buff explained that he remembered nothing of the crash, had woken in hospital with "both my legs bandaged up and about ten stitches between my eyes, both ankles were broken". His face and head were swaddled because of burns, his right hand was severely bruised. After a couple of days medical staff "amputated my right leg from just below the knee". He attempted to write about where he was – it was a lovely place in woods – but sentences were cut out by German censors. Buff had just had his 21st birthday, on 13 July though there had been no celebration. He attempted to lighten the mood. "God alone knows when I will see you again, but if they keep on treating me as well…I will be well at the end of the war. …My face is practically unrecognisable but I am comfortable. Don't worry about me I'm all right and am learning German from Walter Kuntz my orderly."

He underestimated the extent of his injuries; they were too severe and Buff died on 20 July 1942. Family in England sent letters of condolence. They too were trying to accept the loss of a nephew who had been so full of life. "The only consolation is that he died gallantly in a noble cause and his life has not been thrown away", they wrote. It was difficult for those left behind on King Island to find consolation in those words, "noble cause" and a life not "thrown away". His sister Mary saw how hard her brother's death was on her father but "it was doubly hard on mother". For the Cheese family the legacy of World War II would continue. "They speak of a war to end all wars, what a heap of rubbish, it never ends", Mary Walker (née Cheese) would say in 2010.

The body of Tom Watkins was recovered from the River Schelde on 19 June 1942 and he was buried close to his mate Dudley Beinke in Flushing (Vlissingen) Northern Cemetery in Holland. In 1947 Thomas and Lena Watkins, of Keswick, South Australia, received a letter forwarded through a web of official channels. Miss Janny Van Der Meer, a 17 year old who lived in Flushing, had "adopted" the grave of their 20-year-old son. It would become a regular occurrence, Dutch honouring the graves of Australians – men who came from so far away. In 1947 Janny Van Der Meer sent a photo of Tom's grave and wanted the Watkins family to know she was "visiting the grave at regular times" and that it was a "peaceful piece of ground where their dear one has found his last resting place".[25]

The German anti-aircraft defences were dramatically strengthened during 1942. The searchlights and guns of the Kammhuber Line stretched along the entire enemy-held coast. A closely integrated network of ground-controlled interception boxes directed German fighters to British bombers as soon as they entered the area. Massive gun emplacements completed the enemy defence network. The Dutch coast was riddled with anti-aircraft gun emplacements. On the Dutch island of Terschelling a massive radar installation would prove formidable. Bunkers and anti-aircraft guns turned the small island into a German fortress. Bomber crews realised how much more dangerous it had become.

Ron Waldon and his crew of pilot John Keene, Wireless Operator/ Air Gunner Graham Berry and Air Gunners Doug Butterworth and Reg Biglands had also been busy. On 5 April 1942 Ron was onboard Wellington Z1323 with Squadron Leader Leighton to attack Le Havre. It was a pleasure to watch Leighton and his control of the airplane. Three days later the boys were back together with John Keene piloting the next attack on Le Havre. They were with Leighton again on 12 April to bomb Essen. John took the skipper's role on 14 April to bomb Le Havre and the next day against Dortmund. April was proving testing on stamina and nerves. On 17 April they undertook a six-hour operation

against Hamburg, followed by a few days leave, which were over too quickly. By the 22nd they were back in the air on a training flight. On the night of 29 April they bombed Kiel, an operation that took the crew 7 hours 35 minutes. Sergeant Les Shephard's team didn't return. Ron Waldon counted up his hours for April. In total 39.20 had been on bombing operations and his total operational tally was now 120 hours 15 seconds.

On 4 May 1942 Ron's crew were one of the 120 aircraft Bomber Command attack on the Daimler-Benz aircraft engine factories and the Bosch magneto works at Stuttgart. The weather was shocking and only 25 bombers pressed on to bomb the target. They needed to make amends and two days later they visited Stuttgart again. Ron and his crew released their bombs on target. The operation meant a flight time exceeding eight and a quarter hours – a long time to feel vulnerable. Upon returning to base they heard the news that Squadron Leader Gilbert, "A" Flight Commander, and his crew had been shot down.[26] "All members of the squadron felt the loss of this highly popular officer very keenly".[27] It was a shock. Gilbert's personality and abilities inspired all of 460 Squadron. "The loss of this superb airman was not only a tragedy for the squadron, but for the whole of Bomber Command".[28] Flying Officer William Joseph Kennedy (402362), a 26-year-old Sydneysider, another veteran, who had taken part in the squadron's first operation, was also shot down. Kennedy had stayed at the controls of his damaged Wellington giving his crew time to bale out.

Doubts crept into the minds of RAAF 460 aircrew – if such expert flyers like Gilbert and Kennedy could fall victim, surely they could also? On 8 May 1942 Ron and his crew joined seven other 460 crews as part of the 147 bomber attack on the Heinkel aircraft works at Warnemünde. No operational flying took place over the ensuing fortnight due to inclement weather over Europe and it was a welcome relief. Squadron Leader Leighton took some crews to RAF Linton-on-Ouse to meet British prime minister Churchill. Even more importantly, perhaps, was a visit to Breighton by the Australian prime minister John Curtin. Between 12 March 1942 and 28 August 1942, RAAF 460 Squadron attacked 69 targets and 26 crews were lost.

It was 26 May 1942 when Ron Waldon sent his parents a telegram, "Please don't worry", though clearly he was worried. His letters during the last month reflected deepening fatigue. He spoke of how "jolly tired" he was and thought more of "what it will be like" when he could "return to you folks at home – boy oh boy!" He had confidence in his crew, "Jack Keene – a really grand bloke"; his roommate was Wireless Operator Graham Berry, "another grand bloke"; "Front Gunner, Doug Butterworth he is from Queensland, again – a grand chap". Rear Gunner "Reg Biglands from South Aussie – all grand chaps". But the odds of returning from bombing operations seemed to be diminishing. In a letter written on 24 May 1942 he wrote: "Death in the air force is instantaneous and also remember if ever I should be posted as missing there is every possibility that I shall float to ground by chute and then I shall have a damned good attempt at evading the blasted Germans and escape back to England. Please do not worry." In the privacy of his room and his own thoughts Ron flicked ahead through empty pages in his log book, counting off the empty pages to where he believed the 35th operation, the end of a tour, would appear. He wrote "I'll be hellishishing lucky to reach this far" and closed the book.

Ron, Jack Keene, Doug Butterworth and Reg Biglands walked into the RAAF 460 Squadron briefing hut and took their seats with the other aircrew. It was difficult not to look relieved if earlier that day you discovered your crew wasn't expected to fly that night. Today, 2 June

1942, their crew was on the list to go. Doug Butterworth felt comfort in having these men beside him. "With the five-man Wellington bomber crew consisting of both officers and NCOs, the sense of comradeship engendered by facing the same risks to some extent cancelled the gap existing between the two levels."[29]

There was always a palpable excitement emanating from the gathered crews – excitement mixed with a generous dose of nervousness. This is what they were there for, to fly bombers into enemy territory, and throughout the period leading up to the operation and throughout the long hours of drumming aircraft engines they would suffer the full gambit of emotions. Eyes went to the huge map and the red marker. There were some targets which made the heart drop. Tonight it was Essen and that wasn't good. Essen was in the Ruhr Valley, better known by aircrew as "Happy Valley". A welcome of a solid blanket of anti-aircraft fire would greet aircrew on their arrival. Doug Butterworth thought "I have a score to settle with that hellhole". The RAAF 460 Commanding Officer arrived and the airmen rose to their feet. He told them to be seated and requested each skipper to acknowledge the presence of their crew. The meteorology officer gave a report of expected weather over the target area. A bright full moonlit night was perfect weather for bombing operations. It was also perfect weather for German fighters to identify and shoot down British bombers. The Intelligence Officer then gave a brief report on the target and bombing height in order to maximise damage. He added unnecessarily that heavy anti-aircraft flak and numerous enemy fighters would likely be encountered – crews knew Happy Valley all too well.

The crews silently filed out of the briefing room and walked to the parachute section to collect their flying kit and parachutes. Those not flying walked in and wished the others good luck and there was good natured banter in which they were referred to as "lucky bastards" by those preparing for take-off. There was the operational meal, scarce eggs and bacon. The lucky bastards then lined up along the airfield and waved and cheered as the crews given the responsibility to bomb Essen rumbled down the runway in their Wellingtons. The line of standing airmen willed each aircraft up into the sky because they knew all too well how dangerous take-off was. They watched each Wellington disappear into the darkness with a tinge of envy because for departing aircrew their waiting was at least temporarily over. They also tried not to wonder how many would return the following morning.

Graham Berry had been taken ill and his place was filled by RAF Wireless Operator/Air Gunner Sergeant Bill Kendall (1309012) from Birmingham.[30] You tried not to be superstitious but any change to your crew was unsettling. The beginning of the operation went exactly as it should. It was a bright moonlit night and if that wasn't nerve-racking enough, Jack Keene had been told to fly very low over the Dutch coast to make it more difficult for German fighters. Doug Butterworth watched "sandbanks and dinghies whipping in and out of view". "Bombs gone" sounded wonderful and Ron Waldon gave Jack Keene the course for home. Things changed suddenly – they were at a very low altitude – too low and the Wellington plunged into the water. Doug Butterworth knew his feet were caught in the wreckage and an inner voice told him to get his feet out of his flying boots. "The next thing I remembered was swimming upwards with lungs bursting." The turret had broken away from the main fuselage. Doug burst to the surface and released the air bottle of his flotation vest. He paddled towards Jack and Ron and all three believed their injuries were minor although they "were a pretty gruesome sight in the moonlight, with blood streaming everywhere". There was no sign of the other two crew members.

Doug was bleeding from cuts to his head. He felt down his legs, they were still there but not working the best – his right knee and left ankle were dislocated. Doug realised he needed to keep moving or the cold water would take effect. The others said they would swim also but in the darkness the men quickly lost track of each other. As the dawn colours enveloped Doug Butterworth exhaustion made him wonder if he could continue any further: "I had been in the water for about three hours and was at the end my tether". His senses were dull and the launch was nearly upon him when he became aware of its presence. Two German sailors hauled him into the boat and rubbed Doug's body vigorously to start the blood flowing. They gently put him into a bunk with an "outsize mug of straight cognac" and treated his lacerations. Doug was landed at a navy establishment on the Dutch coast and realised he was now a German prisoner-of-war. There was no sign of Jack or Ron.

The bodies of Jack Keene and Ron Waldon were washed ashore and buried in Flushing (Vlissingen) Northern Cemetery in Holland. Ron had no chance to "float to ground by chute..." – he had drowned in the North Sea and death had not been "instantaneous". They were buried between Dudley Beinke and Tom Watkins. These men, some not old enough to vote, now shared a cemetery with airmen of another war, flyers lionised in *Biggles* books. Sergeant Henry Mears Partridge of RAF 211 Squadron and Second Lieutenant Edward Corston Fletcher of RAF 214 Squadron flew those bi-planes which had filled the imagination of these who were now buried. Fletcher had been an 18-year-old Pilot of a Handley Page O/400 assigned to support ground forces on the Western Front and had been shot down on 22 August 1918. Partridge had been an Observer in a de Havilland DH.9 which ventured across the same dangerous expanse of sea from England, to bomb the Bruges Docks, on Zeebrugge Mole and Harbour and Ostend Docks and German submarines. His aircraft could carry just 150 tons of bombs. Partridge had been shot down on 22 August 1918 and died of his wounds. It seemed little had been learnt.

THREE

*"When it was dark I made my way
to this lone aircraft."*

Pilot Officer Allan F McSweyn, RAAF

Ada Keene cut out the obituary column from her Sydney newspaper and carefully glued it into the album she had religiously kept. Jack (John) had been good to send her so many photos – they were now even more treasured than before. She paused and ran her eyes over the newspaper portrait of Jack in his pilot's uniform. He was smiling broadly because life was exciting – she knew that thought should be past tense but she couldn't define it that way yet. The letter had arrived from the RAAF saying he was missing but there was still the chance he was a POW. With the war on, information was slow so she prayed he would be found alive. Then came that terrible letter which said German information was that Jack was buried in Flushing, Holland. She turned the pages and looked at the earlier images. There was one of Jack in civilian clothes striding down a Sydney street. One of those roving photographers had taken it and her son duly purchased a copy – she was so glad he did. There was a group shot of Jack and other Australian aircrew doing lifejacket drill on the ship over; they were all laughing and giving the thumbs up – young men leaving Australia for war too intent on the present than to consider the future. There were photos sent from Canada of Aussie boys and snow fights and trying to skate on a frozen pond. There was one of him with two classmates – Arch Honeyman (404549)[1] and Geoff Jackson (400414)[2] taken on course in May 1941 – neither would return home. A lovely photo of the Canadian couple named Heron who hosted Jack to some much enjoyed home-cooked meals. There were photos of his crew, Graham Berry, Doug Butterworth, Ron Waldon and Reg Biglands.

Pilot Officer John Keene's mother looked again at the obituary column. Her son was one of eight NSW RAAF boys whose portraits were featured. Pilot Officer Peter Forrest (412145), Pilot Officer James Trotter (402454), Pilot Officer Neville Kearney (403055), Sergeant Lewis Trunley (403610), Sergeant Robert Wells (403388), Sergeant Charles Butcher (403314) and Sergeant Herbert Warr (402582). They were all young men with such promising futures. Ada took little comfort in knowing the mothers of these RAAF boys were feeling the same pain. She would add three more items to the album. There would be the photo of the grave in The Netherlands and a simple white cross with "FO J.W.Keene, RAAF". A short letter with the crest of Buckingham Palace and the message: "The Queen and I offer you our heartfelt sympathy in your great sorrow. We pray that your country's gratitude for a life so nobly given in its service may bring you some measure of consolation. George R.I."

Ada Keene realised the King didn't sign the letter himself but that note was still important. She would place a public announcement in the Sydney newspaper to mark the anniversary of her son's death. "In sad but loving remembrance of a gallant young son, PO John Walter, RAAF, dearly loved youngest son of William Henry and Ada Keene and loved brother of Bill, of 133 Darley Road, Randwick, lost his life in air operations over Essen, Germany, June 3, 1942, aged 25 years. Sadly missed by a sorrowing mother, father and brother."

Britain's Bomber Command was established on 14 July 1936, its rationale provided by Italian air-power theorist General Giulio Douhet and his aphorism: "The bomber will always get through". Italy was now being attacked by British bombers. In the earliest phase his aphorism was true: prior to radar a bomber force reached its target barely hindered by opposing fighters. The British government saw bombers as a deterrent to war because they could inflict destruction and terror from afar. But this was overstated given the limited strategic capability of British bombers such as the Fairey Battle and the rules of engagement restricting targets to those deemed "acceptable".

In 1936 Bomber Command comprised three groups of regular RAF units, a total of 32 squadrons, plus No.6 Group, which consisted of 12 Auxiliary Air Force and Reserve squadrons. By September 1939, strength had expanded to 53 squadrons in six groups – some 370 aircraft, although only 33 squadrons were classified as operational. It was an inauspicious World War II debut when the day following the declaration of war, 15 Blenheims of No.2 Group and 14 Wellingtons of No.3 Group attempted to attack German warships. With rain and low cloud ten aircraft were unable to find the target and returned to base. One bomber dropped bombs on the Danish town of Esbjerg, "an error in navigation of some 110 miles (177 kilometres).[3] The remaining 15 aircraft crews attempted with courage to attack their target and at least three bombs landed on the battleship Admiral Scheer. Unfortunately the bombs did not detonate. Hits on the cruiser Emden caused little damage. Seven bombers were shot down. Bomber Command was ineffective and costly. Due to the neutrality of Belgium and The Netherlands British aircraft could not directly approach German targets thus stretching the range of aircraft like Bristol Blenheims, Handley Page Hampdens, and Armstrong Whitworth Whitleys. Between July and the end of December 1940, 330 aircraft and more than 1,400 men were lost to Bomber Command.[4] According to one summation RAF Bomber Command: "Flew many missions, lost men and aircraft but did virtually no damage, as most of the missions either failed to find their intended targets, or were limited to the dropping of leaflets rather than bombs."[5]

It was only after the battle of France that the British bombing campaign started in earnest. But aircrew were sent on daylight raids and aircraft and aircrew losses were huge. Bomber Command switched to night operations. When on 24 August 1940 German bombers dropped bombs on London, prime minister Winston Churchill ordered retaliation. The damage caused by the first raid on Berlin was minimal but it was motivation enough for Adolf Hitler to order a Blitz on British cities. Liverpool was bombed on 28, 29, 30 and 31st August. On 7 September 1940 attacks on the East End of London began. It was "total war" and an all-out endeavour to develop scientific means to defend against bombers and bigger and better bombers to overcome scientific means of defence.

The inability of bombers to bomb accurately encouraged the switch to carpet bombing and the new generation of heavyweight bombers, the Stirling, the Manchester and Halifax. The first began to join British squadrons in the second half of 1940. Initially production was slow and there were a myriad of technical faults. Flying Officer Sydney Douglas Marshall RAAF (402060) was one of the first pilots to take a Stirling on a bombing raid. It was an unusual place to find a former Sydney Telegraph yachting correspondent. His Stirling Mk1 was delivered to RAF 15 Squadron just the month before and it had 33.55 hours on the gauge when Marshall took off from RAF Wyton, Cambridgeshire, on 18 July 1941 to raid Wesel. It was the flight's intention to use cloud cover but with skies clearing quickly Marshall was instructed to return to base. The bomber was not heard from again. The bodies of four RAF crew were washed onto the Dutch coast, no trace was found of the New Zealander, or the Australian pilot.[6] Regardless of the endemic unreliability of the first heavy bombers British high command was impressed with the results of bombing operations – aircrew losses was just something to be expected.

A 128-page book titled *Bomber Command* was published by Britain's Air Ministry in mid-July 1941. It carried many glossy photographs of aircrew and their aircraft and outlined how successful the bombing campaign was. The book featured quotations intended to inspire – from the Book of Wisdom, chap. V, 21: "Then shall the right aiming thunderbolts go abroad; and from the clouds, as from a well-drawn bow, shall they fly to the mark."[7]

Aircrew were: "Brave yet cautious, cool yet daring"; "Gentlemen of the shade, minions of the moon"; the bomber was an: "Aloft incumbent on the dusky air". The book warned the British public not to succumb to

German propaganda: "The enemy has shown himself to be very skilful in covering up damage". The book did not warn to be mindful of British propaganda.

> Heavy damage was caused. ...Bombs had also fallen along that superb example of Prussian bad taste, the Sieges Allee...the heart of Berlin, was severely damaged. ...German experts appear to have miscalculated the penetrating power of a heavy bomb. ...Much more damage will be done before the war is over. ... As soon as German morale begins to wilt, victory will be in sight. ...nothing can prevent the achievement of air supremacy and therefore of victory. ...That day is approaching.

Embellished rhetoric compared bomber crews to those warriors: "Who each evening notched their dragon prows into the sun's red rim on the first voyage to Labrador" (the Golden Hind) or those brave souls: "Who stumbled with Scott from the South Pole". These men of Bomber Command had accomplished much in 21 months. "Their hearts are high." They were men who: "Have learnt skill and resource flying in aircraft which, when the war began, were the finest of their kind" and: "No chosen target can escape them. Our attack will go on, fierce because it is relentless, deadly because it is sure". As with all propaganda the book highlighted the bravery and resoluteness of the aircrew of Britain and the Dominions but not their vulnerability. Such towering prose would be sadly lacking at war's end. Propaganda and misinformation were synonymous of Bomber Command since the first phase of the war, from when on 14 December 1939, 23 Hampdens, twelve Wellingtons and seven Whitleys were sent to attack German shipping. German fighters shot down almost half the aircraft. The RAF could not admit such a defeat by the Luftwaffe and officially claimed bomber losses had been caused by anti aircraft fire.

While the Stirling bomber, with its 14,000 ft (4,200 m) ceiling was, "the first target of German anti-aircraft gunners and night-fighter pilots"[8], the Avro Manchester was a failure due to its under-developed, unreliable, under-powered engines. The early Halifax bombers had "alarming vices in the air and some Halifax crews were more frightened of their aircraft than of the enemy!"[9] There was always pride in one's own aircraft and once modifications were made to the Halifax it was spoken of as "a superb aircraft" and the crews who flew the Halifax Mark III "rated them equal to, if not better than, the Lancaster".[10] The Manchester was replaced by the Avro Lancaster. Its speed was 216 mph (348 k/h), with a top speed of 266 mph (428 k/h). The official ceiling was 22,000 ft (6,700 m) but crews would attest to flying the bomber higher. With a bombload of 14,000 lbs (6.3 tons) the Lancaster had a range of 1,660 miles (2,600 kilometres). It could be said that no other piece of British war machinery had such a profound impact on the outcome of the war in Europe as the Lancaster. Lancaster bombers would dominate Bomber Command and would drop around 60 per cent of total Bomber Command tonnage.[11] The heavy bomber carried a crew of seven: pilot, navigator, bomb-aimer, flight engineer, wireless operator and two air-gunners. No longer was there a second pilot and invariably the flight engineer or bomb-aimer sat in that seat during take-off and landing to assist the pilot with the throttles. Bigger bombers, more bombers, meant bigger crews and aircrew training programmes were yet again cranked up another level along with the expectation that the British Dominions would provide manpower.

RAAF selection boards quickly recognised the human needs of the air war. They favoured aircrew candidates who had a good education. Prior to the war those with education were likely to be university students, school teachers, journalists, public servants, and junior office workers in banks and large insurance and trading firms. Over 90 per cent of aircrew in 1940 had more than four years of secondary schooling at a time when leaving school prior to the beginning of secondary school was more common – the school leaving age was still 14. RAAF recruiters also preferred trainees who had demonstrated all-round abilities – educated volunteers who excelled at sport. "Gentlemen of the Dominions" headed at least one recruiting poster. Pilots needed to be able to fly the most modern aircraft in demanding and extreme circumstances but they also needed to be leaders who could captain a crew effectively, without external assistance. Navigators would face complex mathematical problems in stressful situations. Other aircrew were required to master exacting skills – to be able to operate radio and radar equipment and master Morse code; they needed to be men with quick reflexes who could shoot at rapidly moving targets. Given the overwhelming demand for aircrew places – in 1940 60,000 men applied for the first 4,000 places – RAAF recruiters could afford to be very selective.

John Cox was an energetic, enthusiastic 18 year old when he entered Sydney's RAAF Recruiting Office. He filled out the forms confident of his qualifications. He came from a comfortable middle class family, his father an engineer. His secondary education had been at North Sydney Boys High and he passed all but French for his Intermediate. He then enrolled in Hawkesbury Agriculture College. He was fit, with soccer and swimming being his sports of choice. The RAAF entered Cox at the beginning of February as a trainee pilot. Three months later at No.5 Elementary Flying School, Narromine, New South Wales, he was discharged, "Unlikely to become an efficient aircrew". John Cox would fight World War II dressed in army khaki.

The majority of the young men who applied for aircrew places envisioned themselves as pilots. They arrived at their state's Initial Training School anxious to proceed quickly through basic training to Elementary Flying Training School. No.1 Elementary Flying Training School was initially in Melbourne, before being relocated to Parafield, South Australia, and then to Tamworth, New South Wales. No.2 Elementary Flying Training School was at Archerfield, Queensland. No.3 Elementary Flying Training School was Essendon, Victoria; No.4 Elementary Flying Training School was Mascot, New South Wales; No.5 was Narromine, New South Wales; No.6 was Tamworth, New South Wales, No.7 was Western Junction, Tasmania; No.8 was Narrandera, New South Wales; No.9 was Cunderdin, Western Australia; No.10 was based at Temora, another New South Wales country town; No.11 was at Benalla, Victoria; and No.12 was at Bundaberg, Queensland, before relocating to Lowood, Queensland. Trainees were given 50 hours of basic aviation instruction, commonly on de Havilland Tiger Moths. Those who demonstrated prowess were then posted to Service Flying

Training School for advanced flight training. There were eight Service Flying Training Schools: Point Cook, Victoria (No.1), Forrest Hill, New South Wales (No.2), Amberley, Queensland (No.3), Geraldton, Western Australia, (No.4), Uranquinty, New South Wales (No.5), Mallala, South Australia (No.6), Deniliquin, New South Wales (No.7) and Bundaberg, Queensland (No.8).

It was largely believed that 'The pilot is considered the "King Pin", and the rest of the crew stooges. Therefore, all aircrew trainees are obsessed with the idea of becoming a pilot or nothing.'[12]

The immediate consequence of taking the very best of the best meant RAAF aircrew were of the highest calibre; the enduring consequence for Australia was a terrible loss of some of the most promising of a generation. The young Australian nation had lost so much human potential in World War I and now their sons were being killed in another European war. Flying Officer Winston David Love (402243) a Sydney University economics graduate; and Flight Officer William Kenneth Williams (401086) a Victorian with a First Class Honours degree in Economics, who had been awarded the Cobden medal, and a University of Melbourne Wyselaskie Scholarship in Mathematics, were killed when the bombers they were piloting were lost without trace in June 1942. Also killed in June 1942, was Melbourne University graduate and teacher, Flight Sergeant Hugh Rowell Brodie (400524). Brodie graduated with a Bachelor of Arts (Hons) with the Dwight Prize in History; and a Bachelor of Education. Prior to his death Brodie penned the following:

Almighty and all-loving power,
Short is the prayer I make of Thee;
I do not ask in battle hour
For any shield to cover me.
The vast unalterable way
From which the stars do not depart
May not be turned aside to stay
The bullet flying to my heart.
I seek no power to strike the foe;
I ask no petty victory here;

The enemy I hate I know
To thee is also dear.
But this I ask: be at my side
When death is flying through the sky.
Almighty God, who also died,
Teach me the way that I should die.[13]

Pilot Officer Frederick John Silk.

Pilot Officer Frederick John Silk (401676) was another Victorian teacher. Educated at Melbourne Boys' High School, in 1937, the 21 year old from Bayswater, became a student teacher at Chilwell Primary School, Newton, Victoria. His year at Melbourne Teacher's College was followed by stints at Belgrave, Carwarp, Ngallo, before enlisting in the RAAF in April 1941. He gained his wings in Canada, before arriving in England for advanced training. His father, too, had arrived in England on his way to war, in October 1916. A former market gardener, Private Frederick John Silk (6358), was a member of the 5th Battalion Australian Imperial Force. He proceeded to France in December 1916. During May and July 1917 Private Silk was admitted to hospital suffering from fever. It was a common complaint and he was discharged from hospital. Fred Silk rejoined the 5th Battalion in time to be involved in the British Flanders Offensive beginning on 31 July of that year. British and French forces attacked German defences along a 16-mile (26-kilometre) front east of Ypres. On 20 September following five days of German bombardment, two Australian divisions advanced – part of an assault by 11 British divisions along Westhoek Ridge, facing

Glencorse Wood, Belgium. Official War historian Charles Bean wrote of the battle: "So ended, with complete success, the first step in Haig's trial of true step-by-step tactics. ...The objectives being easily within the capacity of the troops".[14] Marshal Douglas Haig, 1st Earl Haig, commanded the British Expeditionary Force (BEF) from 1915 to the end of the World War I. Haig would be lauded by some as "The Master of the Field" and referred to by others as "The Butcher of the Somme". The "complete success" referred to by Charles Bean resulted in 21,000 Allied casualties, 5,000 of whom were Australians. It was thought Frederick Silk was buried, "about 300 yards [270 metres] southwest of Glencorse Wood". The 27-year-old Australian had no official grave and was one of 54,393 names enshrined on the Menin Gate, Ypres. Florence Silk signed for the package of her husband's Fred's "personal effects" in June 1918. Enclosed was a dictionary, a wallet, photos, nine coins, a purse, a pack of cards and the "lock of hair" of the son who was three months old when Fred enlisted, and two years old when he died.[15]

His son Pilot Officer Frederick John Silk fully expected to be posted to Bomber Command to fight over the same part of Europe as his father. It was a surprise to be posted to Cairo, Egypt, attached to the RAF's Desert Air Force, North Africa. Instead of Wellington or Lancaster bombers he proceeded into battle in the air in a Kittyhawk. In January 1943 Silk joined RAAF 450 Squadron. He excelled as a pilot and quickly notched up 43 dive-bombing operations and convoy protection sorties. The 44th operation was the 26 February 1943 bombing attack on Gabès, the preliminary to the final attack on Tunisia. Silk's Kittyhawk was attacked by Messerschmitts. Between June 1941 and May 1943 RAAF 450 Squadron lost 28 Kittyhawks and pilots. Silk was one of these. The 27-year-old pilot would have no known grave and his name would be engraved along with 11,869 others on the Alamein Memorial, Egypt. Like his father before him he was killed in war at the same age and had no known grave. Florence Silk would sign for another parcel of "personal effects" and as she aged it all made less and less sense.

Australian aircrew would rate as high as any in Bomber Command and demonstrate great skill under duress, but ability was but one factor in the staying alive equation. Reginald was an engineer living in the Brisbane suburb of Bulimba. He was perhaps best known as the inventor of the "Blunt Safety Cycle". Reg and wife Mary believed they were blessed -- with three sons and four daughters who took little time to excel. Malcolm James Larke Blunt, better known within the family as Tony, proved an excellent student at Brisbane Boys' Grammar School and in his final year he "stroked" for Grammar in the eight which won the keenly contested Great Public Schools Association of Queensland "Head of the River". Malcolm Blunt went on to graduate with a Bachelor of Economics from University of Queensland. When his eldest brother Rupert, a naval officer, was killed Tony enlisted in the RAAF in February 1941. At 2350 on 7 June 1942, Flight Officer Blunt piloted his RAF 150 Squadron Wellington towards Germany. He and his British crew were in the air less than an hour before being shot down by night-fighter pilot Oblt Ludwig Becker. The body of the Australian who had graduated with an economics degree washed ashore on the Dutch Island of Ameland.

The pride of a mother and wife; Lorna, Elsie, and William Mawdesley
(courtesy of John Mawdesley).

William (Bill) James Mawdesley was yet another Victorian teacher. Born in Picola in 1911 his reports as a student teacher in Shepparton, Victoria, in 1929 were favourable: "promises to be a very capable teacher". He enrolled at the Bendigo Teachers' College in 1931 for twelve months. Instructors wrote: "Is capable of very good work and seems fairly keen".[16] The next career step saw him head teacher at a school in Berringama, then Belleview, then Cannum. Bill proved "friendly and encouraging in personality" and his career became a whirlwind of Victorian country schools as a relief teacher: Lillimur, Mologa East, the Sisters, Talbot, Won Wron, Tintaldra, Nagamble and then Creswick North. In August 1940 he married Lorna Mitchell. Bill Mawdesley (401073) was selected quickly by the RAAF, commencing his training in June 1940. Prior to his posting to England he posed for a studio photo with his mother Elsie and wife Lorna. The expressions of pride were clearly visible.

In a letter from England, Bill wrote: "I haven't seen an enemy aircraft yet, but the sky is full of ours".[17] He felt there had been unnecessary delays in not allowing Australians to join operational squadrons and that Australian airmen should be given the option to return home: "It is particularly annoying for all of us who would like to get out East to have a crack at the Japs".[18]

On 1 June 1942 Pilot Officer Bill Mawdesley carefully eased Wellington R1266 into the air at 2305 from the aerodrome at RAF Pershore. His was one of the Operating Training Unit aircraft thrown into the mix to make up numbers for the Thousand Bomber strike on Essen. His crew consisted of an English Wireless Operator/Air Gunner and three Canadians. During the first hour of the following day the bomber was seen hurtling towards the ground and exploding on impact near Kerkdriel, Netherlands, on the bank of the River Maas. The body of Air Gunner Canadian Flight Sergeant Tom Norrie (R72641) was found with his parachute opened. The remaining airmen were trapped within the bomber, which was now deeply submerged in swampy ground.

In December 1942 Lorna Mawdesley wrote to Australia's Department

LEFT: *Alamein Memorial.* RIGHT: *Menin Gate.*

of Air Casualty Section. The only information she had received was the telegram advising that Bill was "missing". She intended to visit the Department in Melbourne in the hope that a personal visit may ascertain more news. Only then did further correspondence come from the British Ministry of Air. This indicated that "efforts to trace" Bill had "proved unavailing" and as there seemed so little "hope of finding him alive" further enquiry "must be abandoned". The Ministry wished to "complete" Bill's service affairs and "for official purposes to presume his death". Before these "necessary formalities" could be completed Lorna was "required to write a letter stating that no further news has been received from the missing member". After the war an RAF investigation reported: "Salvage of the wreckage is impracticable. ... The area in which the aircraft crashed is flooded at high tide, and, at other times, is completely waterlogged. There is now no visible trace of the wreckage." For the Mawdesley family there was no closure with the end of the war.

In April 1958, workmen from the nearby brick works were excavating for clay and discovered Wellington R1266. Lorna Mawdesley received a letter saying that the "remains of your husband and his three comrades" had been recovered. Unfortunately "it was not possible to establish individual identification" and the remains would be buried in a collective grave in Uden, Holland. There was little else authorities could add except: "Whilst it is realised this information may cause your further distress it is hoped the definite knowledge that your husband is laid to rest in a permanent war cemetery will bring you some comfort in your sorrow."[19]

Lorna Mawdesley wrote expressing her thanks: "Flight Officer Mawdesley was such a wonderful man and very dear to a closely united family. We shall be always grateful for what the Imperial War Graves Commission have done for us, something we were unable to do for ourselves, though longing to do so." It was another grave too far away. Buried in the same Dutch cemetery was a Lance Corporal of England's Royal Engineers. His name was John Mawdesley. They would have an eternity to work out the true spelling of the surname.

With Australia at war on many fronts, aircrew graduates found themselves dispatched to different parts of the world. Leading Aircraftsmen Ian MacPherson Ince (400028), Francis Norman (Frank) Meyer (290745) and Bob Aldridge (12404) stood beside their training aircraft at Cootamundra, New South Wales, to be photographed by a classmate. Ince was looking rather pensive, the course was demanding and there was the small issue of air sickness. It was not uncommon for aircrew recruits to wash out due to air sickness. The common saying was that "air sickness is just a state of mind", which as far as the sufferer was concerned was rubbish, the mind wasn't the problem, it was the stomach or stomach's contents which was problematic. Frank Meyer had a shy smile because he was having the time of his life since being accepted by the RAAF in February 1940 when he was only 18. He had been studying engineering and this worked to his advantage in gaining early entry.

LEFT: *Ince, Meyer, Aldridge at Cootamundra, NSW.*
RIGHT: *Meyer training at Parafield, South Australia.*

Frank Meyer left Western Australia to begin training with No.2 course at No.1 Service Flying Training School, Parafield, South Australia. On 6th May 1940 he was transferred to 21 Squadron at Laverton, Victoria, for pilot training. By 28 June 1940 he was commissioned as a Pilot Officer. Training continued at Point Cook, Victoria before continuing at Air Observer School at Cootamundra, New South Wales. He loved the adrenalin rush he got flying Gipsy and Tiger Moths, Wirraway, Avro Ansons, DH89 and Moth Minors. Some within his course weren't so fortunate. Accidents were not uncommon. Don Dodgshun (710) was accidentally killed at No 2 Service Flying Training School, RAAF Wagga Wagga, on 16 February 1941.

By September 1941, Mayer was keen to embark for the UK and the war but, for whatever reason, he was posted back to his home state, to Flying Training School at Geraldton; then the General Reconnaissance School, Laverton, Victoria. Finally he was transferred to an Operating Training Unit at Nhil, Victoria, to do conversion training on Lockheed Hudson bombers. Some of his friends, like Ian Ince were already with Bomber Command Europe. Ian was attached to RAAF 455 Squadron flying a Handley Page Hampden – a slightly weird looking aircraft but fast and manoeuvrable and known as the "fighting bomber". Frank was itching for that sort of experience and even his Commanding Officer noted on his record: "This officer has suffered from lack of opportunity to prove himself". Frank thought it surely could not be his age – he was now 20.

Frank Meyer.

On 19 January 1942 a more exotic posting materialized for Frank, to RAAF 13 Squadron at Laha, Ambon in the Maluku (Moluccas) Islands, in support of Gull Force. Australia was now at war with Japan and the enemy was advancing quickly. It was decided Ambon would be a strategic location because of its landing strip. A 1,100-strong Australian Army Gull Force was deployed along with Hudson Aircraft from 13 Squadron. Sadly the Japanese had been completely underestimated and it was too little too late. Through January Japanese bombing intensified destroying many Squadron 13 Hudsons. Flying in the face of heavy resistance, remaining aircraft conducted vital reconnaissance patrols to locate Japanese convoys. The order came to evacuate personnel to Darwin but there were not enough aircraft to carry them. Commanding Officer Wing Commander Ernest Scott and Flying Officer Frank Meyer were among those stranded on the island when three battalions of Japanese invaded. Dutch forces quickly capitulated. The Australians continued to resist. Two days later after a savage Japanese offensive, the final 300 or so Australians defending Laha airfield lay down their weapons. Between 2 and 20 February 1942 they were bayoneted, clubbed to death, or beheaded in four separate massacres and buried in mass graves. Their fate would not be discovered until after the war. On an operation to bomb Emden, Germany, on 21 January 1942, Sergeant Ian Ince was killed when his Hampden was shot down by a German night fighter. He was buried in Holland. Flight Sergeant Bob Aldridge survived the war.

Meyer having his Hudson refuelled, Ambon.

The Ruhr Valley and the city of Essen in particular, continued to be a principal target. It was a vast complex of coalmines, steel plants, power stations, factories and oil refineries imperative to German war production. Bomber Command was the only arm of the Allied war machine which could damage that production. The formidable German anti-aircraft blanket ensured this came at a high human cost. There were three Australians onboard an RAF 214 Squadron Wellington which took off from RAF Stradishall, Suffolk. Pilot Officer Eric William Cuthbert Creed (400581) was the pilot. From Melbourne, Creed was just 22 years old. The second pilot was 29-year-old Sergeant William Wykes Robey Norton (400885) the son of Wykes and Eva Norton of Armadale, Victoria. Sergeant Walter Irvine Christsen (404277) the 22-year-old Observer was a former clerk, studying accountancy, from Bundaberg, Queensland. Their Wellington was shot down at 2255 on 25 March over Vriezenveen, Holland by a fighter piloted by Oberleutnant Herbert Lutje. According to the local Dutch Resistance leader, Mijnheer Kruisinga: "The unfortunate crew of six had all been instantly killed by the smash. The lifeless remains were piously covered with blankets. ... Hundreds of people assembled...the six coffins were laid side by side in the south-west corner of the graveyard."[20]

In ceremonies that would be endemic throughout The Netherlands following the war, townspeople would gather to unveil memorials "in commemoration of those who gave their lives", like the Australians, Creed, Norton and Christsen. The Burgomaster (Mayor) of Vriezenveen would say: "Our thoughts go out to those Allied servicemen who fought for the freedom of our country and who found their last resting place in The Netherlands. By their deeds they show that freedom is a common aim of free peoples. We have our dead in common and as long as we keep alive this memory, there is no reason to despair in a new and better international society based on peace and justice." Photographs of the memorial and the graves were sent to the parents of the crew.

Flight Officer Donald McConachie (404109) who had been born in the semi-tropical climate of Nambour, Queensland, was the Observer on an RAF 83 Squadron Manchester which took off from RAF Scampton at 2045 on 25 March 1942. Donald studied Civil Engineering at Queensland University for two years before dropping out and returning to the country to become a jackaroo. He wrote "Grazier" as his occupation when he enlisted in May 1940. His bomber got only as far as the Dutch port of Antwerp before being shot down. The following night another man from rural Australia, Flight Officer Geoffrey Thomas Heard (400708) was the pilot of a Stirling which was shot down by a night fighter over Gendringen, Holland. He was the son of Walter and Ethel Heard of Willaura, Victoria. The same night, Pilot Sergeant Thomas Edward Parsons (403117) an Accountant from Sydney, and

Melbournian Sergeant Charles William Lawrence Pooley (400420) were part of the crew of an RAF 12 Squadron Wellington shot down by a night fighter at Monnickendam, The Netherlands. They had been good mates but their bodies washed ashore on separate parts of the Dutch Coast. Another RAF 12 crew flying this night to Essen included the 12 Squadron Commanding Officer, Wing Commander Albert Golding, RAF, Distinguished Flying Cross and bar. Second pilot to Golding was 23-year-old Australian Sergeant Finlay Donald McLeod (403431). McLeod, son of a Company Director, was an Assistant Manager of a Newcastle, New South Wales, firm. As good a pilot as the 12 Squadron Commanding Officer was, Golding could not win the contest with this particular German fighter and the Wellington crashed between Enkhuizen and Bovenkarspel. The crew consisting of three RAF, two Canadians and two Australians were buried together in Bergen General Cemetery, Holland.

Both RAF 12 bombers were shot down by Oberleutnant Prinz Egmont zur Lippe Weissenfeld. That Weissenfeld was an Austrian Prince is unlikely to have impressed the British crews. The fact that he was a fighter ace might well have.[21] A degree of respect existed between aviators even during their deadly game. The 12 Squadron bombers were his 20th and 21st "kills". At the time of his death in a flying accident on 22 March 1944 Weissenfeld was commanding the German night fighter 3rd group, and had claimed 45 British aircraft. He was buried next to another aristocratic German flying ace, Prinz Heinrich zu Sayn-Wittgenstein. At the time of his death on 21 January 1944 he was the Wing Commander of the 2nd group of the 2nd night flight wing, and was the highest-scoring night-fighter pilot. Sayn-Wittgenstein had flown 320 combat missions and was believed to have shot down 83 Allied aircraft. He would be ranked third by war's end. Sayn-Wittgenstein would be shot down by an RAF 141 Squadron Mosquito piloted by Flight Sergeant Desmond Byrne Snape (420071), a 20 year old from Sydney.

A month later however Snape and his Navigator, Canadian Flying Officer Ian (Rusty) Fowler, were again flying over The Netherlands when the temperature of their Mosquito starboard engine began to climb. Fifteen minutes later it began to seize up. Snape feathered the engine, rotating the propeller blades parallel to the airflow to reduce drag in an attempt to stop engine failure. An hour later the port engine began to vibrate badly. Snape ordered Fowler to bale out. The following day Fowler was taken by German soldiers to view his 20-year-old pilot's body – Snape's parachute was unopened. The Canadian would spend the rest of the war as a POW, but in June 1944 he managed to have a letter sent to Doris Snape:

> Des and I had flown together as a crew since July last year during which time he proved himself to be an outstanding pilot and a very popular figure in both the sergeants and officers mess. We had completed several missions and were detailed for operations again on the night of 24th February. Our kite got into difficulties over enemy territory and subsequently crashed in Holland, east of Groningen. There Des was buried by the citizens of the small town. I too, as his crew and roommate, keenly feel his loss.[22]

The two German aces would also be buried in Holland, in a cemetery in IJsselstein, Utrecht, where the bodies of 31,513 World War II German servicemen and 85 World War I German soldiers would remain. It was a deadly game in which there were no real victors and one which would leave a sad legacy in many countries.

Those who ordered RAF bomber operations referred to April and May 1942 as "a quiet spell"[23] yet there were many raids on Germany including the first Thousand Bomber raid. Leading up to that was a series of attacks on Stuttgart, none of which could be described as successful, and attacks on Boulogne, Le Havre, Poissy, Hanau, Hamburg, Warnemünde, Mannheim, Dortmund, Augsburg, Rostock, Kiel, Ostend, Gennevilliers, and several more trips to Essen. In this "quiet spell" 100 aircraft were lost and their crews either died, were injured or taken POW, including 29 RAAF aircrew killed and 11 taken POW. A minority escaped injury or evaded capture.

Throughout the war Bomber Command continued to drop mines along the occupied coastline to restrict and destroy German shipping.

Crews called it "gardening" but this was no innocuous hobby. With the coast strongly defended by anti-aircraft batteries and fighters this type of operation offered no respite from bombing operations. Flying Officer John Maloney (402376) eased his Hampden up from RAF Wigsley, Nottinghamshire, early in the evening of 2 April 1942 on another trip to lay mines. Maloney was from Wagga Wagga, a New South Wales town that would have continuing strong links with the RAAF. Onboard was Sergeant Calder Woodburn (400301) a farmer from Gunnedah, New South Wales, and a graduate of Dookie Agricultural College who enlisted on the same day as Maloney. Sergeant Horace Edward Rowley (402611) from Sydney married his sweetheart Joyce the month before he was shipped overseas and 21-year-old Flying Officer Harry Young (402629) who, like Rowley, enlisted in September 1940. Wireless contact was made at 2338 with their aircraft but then nothing. They were the first all-Australian Bomber Command crew to die.

On 6 April a crew lost en route to bomb Essen was from RAAF 455 Squadron. Their pilot, Londoner Sergeant Arthur Wincott, had an additional link with Australia given his mother's name was Matilda. Flying Officer Trevor Emlyn Roberts (400105) the Navigator was a 26-year-old dental mechanic, and the son of a Presbyterian Minister, the Reverend William Roberts of Victoria.[24] The Air Gunners were Sergeant Kenneth William McIlrath (400282), the 26-year-old son of William and Ethel of Nhill, Victoria. Sergeant Colin Gammie (402829), the Wireless Operator/Air Gunner was the 22-year-old son of Peter and Adeline Gammie from Marrickville in Sydney. Gammie was the least experienced. Unlike the rest of the crew who had flown 14 operations, this was just the 10th time he had participated in an air attack – it was a strange place to find an accountant. Their Hampden, airborne at 2355 from Wigsley, was attacked by a night-fighter piloted by Oblt Emil Woltersdorf, and crashed at 0413 south of the Dutch town of Zwolle, Holland.

It was a cruel twist that Scottish relatives of Colin's engineer father, Peter, cabled that they believed Colin was a POW. Peter wrote immediately to the Department of Air that "We are eagerly awaiting confirmation".[25] The ensuing months the Gammie family remained hopeful. Then the official

Amersfoort War Cemetery, The Netherlands.

letter came, "according to German information your son lost his life". The crew were buried at Amersfoort, a town 30 miles (50 km) south-east of Amsterdam, in cool and green woods and their families by chance or agreement engraved on each of the gravestones "Greater Love Hath No Man". The Gammie family added "He Died That We Might Live". By war's end there would be 142 British, 60 Canadian, 11 Australian, 13 New Zealand and 6 Polish airmen buried in these woods. Peter Gammie would travel to Holland to spend time at his son's graveside.[26]

The bombing campaign and carpet bombing in particular were unpopular and controversial within the British Parliament, even within the War Cabinet. Some continued to argue that Bomber Command should not be expanded. They cited the heavy casualties such as the raid of 7/8 November 1941 when 37 aircraft were lost in unfavourable weather. Supporters maintained that 392 bombers had taken off for Berlin that night and although only 93 aircraft reached the city and damage had been minimal, it was a morale triumph – and Bomber Command was still the only arm of the Allied war machine capable of taking the war to the enemy in Europe. But "the whole future of the RAF's strategic bombing campaign" continued to be debated at the highest level, "with ideas and views being forcefully exchanged between the War Cabinet, the Air Ministry and other interested parties".[27]

Initially Air Chief Marshal Sir John Steel headed Bomber Command. He was replaced by Air Chief Marshal Sir Edgar Ludlow-Hewitt in September 1937. After two and a half years he was succeeded on 3 April 1940 by Air Chief Marshal Sir Charles Portal. He was replaced by Air Marshal Sir Richard Peirse on 5 October 1940. On 22 February 1942 Peirse was removed after expressing concerns over casualty figures. The new Commander in Chief was Air Chief Marshall Sir Arthur Harris. Harris was a true believer and realised he needed to prove the worth of his command quickly. Immediately he was under pressure to justify the strategy and the massive resources being pumped into his command and to prove his own competence to lead Bomber Command.

On 30 May 1942 the first Thousand Bomber raid, in which more than 1,000 bomber aircraft took part in the same operation, codenamed "Operation Millennium" was launched on a German city.[28] Harris wanted his bomber force to attack Hamburg but a bad weather forecast shifted the choice to Cologne. Bombers took off from airfields all over England to drop 3,000 lbs (1,455 tons) of bombs, two-thirds of which were incendiaries. This was the first time that the tactic to be known as "bomber stream" was used, and it would remain the standard of Bomber Command operations for the next two years. It was believed that a large, densely packed stream of bombers would travel through the German night air defence system, known as the Kammhuber line, overwhelming it. Advances in British radar and the relatively new GEE navigational system allowed bombers to fly at the same height, on the same route, and at the same time. GEE was a radio-pulse system that allowed a navigator to fix his position by signals from three transmitting British stations. Bomber stream effectively meant saturation bombing and the devastation was extensive: 600 acres (240 hectares) of city were devastated; 250 factories, including those involved in creating war machines such as the Gottfried Hagen factory, the Humboldt-Deutz submarine engine works, and the Nippes railway workshops.[29] In total, 486 Germans were killed, approximately 5,000 injured and another 45,000 were "bombed out" when 3,330 houses were destroyed and 7,000 damaged in the 12,000 fires that raged through the city. Of those that took part 52 British bombers crashed and their crews were killed, injured or became POW. A new phase of the war had commenced.

The crew of one of the Thousand Bombers was made up of James (Jim) Donn-Patterson, Canadian Pilot Sergeant William Ross Campbell (R/86418) from Winnipeg, a 21-year-old former clerk; and four other Australians: Sergeant Ronald Arthur Broodbank (405256) 24, Sergeant George Frederick Bolton (401412) 27, and 26-year-old Sergeant Michael Lotherington Glenton-Wright (404913). Jim Donn-Patterson epitomised the handsome man dressed in blue who stared down from RAAF recruiting posters with an air of confidence blended with a rakish disregard for danger. He proved to be a reasonable school student and obtained his New South Wales Intermediate Certificate, but he could never entertain the prospect of taking his education further. His youngest brother Rod Donn-Patterson remembers "Jim was Dad's favourite...[they] had a really close relationship". "Dad was a building contractor so Jim went into carpentry." Outside of work Jim was never happier than when he was out in the Australian sunshine. The outdoors life, physicality and a sense of adventure defined who he was. The family home was close to the wonderful beaches of the New South Wales coastal haven of Coffs Harbour. He loved the beach and the surf and became a champion surf lifesaver. Rod recalls: "They didn't have the gear they have today. The buoys they would take out to help someone stay afloat were kerosene tins. They (lifesavers) would fix them up themselves and paint them bright colours."

In 1938 Jim was captain of the Coffs Harbour Surf Life Saving Club and won most of the events. He had captained the Coffs National Championship team in 1935–36. Rod was seven when he last saw his hero brother accomplish physical feats on a Coffs Harbour beach and in the surf which crashed onto white sands.

> One of my strongest memories was me playing on the sand making a sand castle. Jim came running up the beach, pat me on the head and said 'How you going mate?' I can't help but wonder what might have been if Jim had not died. I still have Jim's school reports. He could have done anything. One of his Principals wrote 'Jim could do anything that he put his mind to'.

LEFT: *James Donn-Patterson.* RIGHT: *Coffs Harbour Rescue and Resuscitation (R&R) National Championship Team W Johnstone, D Riding, J Pollock, J Donn-Patterson, E Franklin, A C Bastian, J Lawler.*

Jim was 24 when he filled out the RAAF enlistment papers on 9 December 1940 and entered as Aircrew (pilot). The initial training saw Jim re-mustered as Observer and by July 1941 he was on a passenger train crossing the Rocky Mountains – he most definitely was not in Coffs Harbour any more. EATS Observer training was taxing and it was slightly humorous that Jim had failed Geography when he sat for his Intermediate Certificate. Fortunately he passed Mathematics A and B which together with his carpentry skills meant he found the dead reckonings easier than certain classmates. Six months later Sergeant James Donn-Patterson (403132) was on a ship bound for the UK and more training.

In the RAF OTU he crewed up with a 21-year-old Canadian Pilot Sergeant William Ross Campbell (R/86418) from Winnipeg a former clerk; and four other Australians: Sergeant Ronald Arthur Broodbank (405256) 24, Sergeant George Frederick Bolton (401412) 27, and 26-year-old Sergeant Michael Lotherington Glenton-Wright (404913). It was unusual to have two RAAF crew with double-barrelled names, but whereas Jim was an Aussie through and through, the 26-year-old Wireless Operator/Air Gunner was a "toff". Sergeant Michael Lotherington Glenton-Wright's name would have categorized him as such, and his clipped English accent reinforced it. Born in Tonbridge, England, and schooled in Surrey, Glenton-Wright had always been a restless man. Under "Occupation" he wrote "Private Income". Asked for more detail he wrote "Motor trade (sales); motor racing (5 years)". He had spent time with The King's Shropshire Light Infantry when in England and even undertook a ten-month wireless course at RAF Cranwell. None of that really worked out so he emigrated to Queensland to become a "Stud Breeder". When war broke out he enlisted in the RAAF and by 14 November 1941 he was back in the land of his birth.

The Rear Gunner, Ron Broodbank, also had an unusual background. Born in Cooktown, Queensland, his family moved to the small island of Samarai at the top of the eastern point of New Guinea. His father Arthur Broodbank was a carpenter and built a grand house for wife Effie and their five children there. Samarai was small enough to walk around in 20 minutes and had a history of being home to pearl traders, gold miners, drifters, and plantation managers seeking a brief relief from isolation. It was a mecca, according to legend, for wild parties.

The school there only took students to grade six so Ron was sent to boarding school, to Mt Carmel College, Charters Towers, and then St Teresa's Agricultural College, Abergowrie, in the district of Ingham. At a nudge over 6 feet (1.8 metres) tall he enjoyed many sports and outdoor activities such as sailing and fishing. His much younger brother Eric only remembered him from Christmas holidays: "As a fairly tall young lad who used to carry me around on his shoulders. ...I have always felt sad that...I did not get to spend much time with him."

Ron Broodbank failed Animal Husbandry and at the time of his enlistment in February 1941 he was a Hardware Salesman. Ron was bored as there were very few opportunities for challenging jobs for young people in the Townsville district, so when the war started in Europe he was quick to enlist in the RAAF.[30] Seven months later he was a qualified Air Gunner and two months after that he was in the UK.

George Bolton was born in Corowa, a town nestled in a gentle bend of the Murray River. He attended Corowa High School and successfully completed his Intermediate and Leaving Certificates by 1930. Studies in accountancy ensued and by the time he married Nancye in St John's Church, Toorak, in July 1940, he was a production manager with Dunlop Rubber Company. Enlistment in February 1941 saw him mustered as a Wireless Operator/Air Gunner. After completing his eight months training in Australia he shipped overseas to the UK and he was a dad.

The crew never made it to an operational squadron. Caught up in the hurly burly of the first Thousand Bombing Raid the 23 OTU crew was despatched to Cologne in an elderly Wellington to make up aircraft numbers, one of 25 OTU aircraft and 127 trainee aircrew, who would not return from the first Thousand Bomber raid. The bomber carrying the Canadian pilot and four Australians was shot down at 0114 over the Dutch town of Gravendeel by a German night fighter piloted by Feldwebel Gerhard Herzog. A Dutch Air Warden was standing outside in the cool evening air speaking with the local policeman when a burning

Sergeant Donn-Patterson.

aircraft came in their direction. They watched as the German fighter continued to fire on the bomber until it crashed and flames devoured the wreck.

The Broodbank family were living with war on all fronts. As the Japanese advanced they were evacuated to Australia. The grand house Arthur had built on Samarai was burnt to the ground – a casualty of the Allied scorched earth policy. Upon receipt of the official letter announcing the disappearance of his eldest son, Ben Donn-Patterson wrote that he and wife Janet "during this anxious time" hoped soon "to hear good news about Jimmie in the very near future". There was no good news and by November the crew were declared "dead". After the war Arthur and Effie Broadbank were advised that the remains of their eldest son Ron were found to have been buried in Rotterdam (Crooswijk) General Cemetery, The Netherlands. Eventually the RAAF advised the Donn-Patterson family that whilst the bodies of Sergeants Broadbank and Johnston were "recovered from the wreckage by the Germans, and interred", all efforts to "establish whether the bodies of your son and the remaining two crew members were ever recovered, have proven unsuccessful". They were spared the blunt language used by RAF investigators who simply advised the RAAF that: "No bodies or fragments of bodies found. As parts of aircraft were scattered over radius of 2,900 feet (900 metres) may be assumed occupants were blown to atoms."

Rod Donn-Patterson said their father Ben "took it really hard when Jim was killed. As they say, 'it was a quick kick in the teeth'". Doug Riding and Ernie Franklin, fellow crew members of Coffs Harbour 1935–36 National Championship Rescue and Resuscitation team would also die in World War II.

A Movietone newsreel was shown in cinemas after the 31 May 1942 raid. Air Chief Marshall Harris is shown in grainy black and white speaking to aircrews from behind his desk: "Press home your attack. If you succeed you will have delivered the most devastating blow against the very vitals of the enemy, let him have it right on the chin". With music intended to stir patriotism the newsreel showed bombers taking off and returning and a voice which atones: "In Cologne and again at

Essen, Germany has felt the growing might of the Royal Air Force". The cameras return to Air Marshall Harris:

> That is just the beginning, let the Nazis take good note of the western horizon...when the storm bursts over Germany they will look back...as a man caught in the blast of a hurricane looks back to the gentle zephyrs of last summer. There are a lot of people who say that bombing can never win a war. Well my answer to that is it has never been tried yet and we shall see.

Harris needed to prove the worth of the statement, one he made constantly in discussions with prime minister Churchill and the War Cabinet. He was convinced Bomber Command would win the war and he pushed for another Thousand Bomber raid to convince some of the sceptics requesting that it be soon so that the British prime minister and his government could take pride in such a demonstration of air power and because the Americans were about to join the air war over Europe.

Allan Francis McSweyn was said to have: "Qualities of keenness, determination and persistence".[31] He also showed great enthusiasm, and was the fifth New South Welshman accepted for Empire Air Training. Allan McSweyn's trainee pilot's course of 40 would exemplify a typical pilot's class. By the end of the war 12 of his class would be dead – half in flying accidents; another seven would become POWs. The accidents were commonly caused by the haste to qualify trainees and their use of very inferior aircraft. Like that of other recruits Allan McSweyn's training took place in Australia, Canada and Scotland, where he was posted to RAF 115 Squadron.

Piloting a Wellington bomber on a routine attack on Hamburg was supposed to be a five-hour operation; but the journey McSweyn took was anything but routine and it would be two years and three months before he returned to England. Approaching the target the Wellington was lit up by a cone of searchlights. McSweyn pushed the bomber into evasive action but flak hit the starboard engine and it began to overheat. The 22-year-old Pilot Officer was determined to continue on and from

10,000 ft (3,000 m) the bombs were dropped onto the target.

He pulled the Wellington around and set off for England. Again the bomber was caught in the cone created by searchlights. This time there was no anti-aircraft fire. McSweyn knew this meant one thing – night fighters. Seconds later there was a shout over the intercom from the rear gunner and a burst of gunfire raked along the Wellington. The cockpit windows were shattered and the radio was destroyed. The rear gunner returned fire and the attacking German Heinkel 113 was aflame and earth bound. A Messerschmitt 110 continued the attack, pouring cannon-fire into the British bomber. The Wellington's damaged starboard engine burst into flames and set alight the tailplane fabric. Two crew members were wounded and both gun turrets were now out of action. Another Messerschmitt began its attack. McSweyn struggled to hold the aircraft steady and ordered his crew to bale out. He made his way to the open escape hatch and his attention was diverted to the starboard wing. The fabric was totally burnt off and the metal was melting, "what was that story about Wellingtons making it back to Britain with partially naked frames after the fabric had burnt off?" There was a loud explosion and the wing fell off. The Australian didn't remember leaving what was left of the aircraft.

His landing in a farm paddock was remarkably soft and fortunate. After burying his parachute Allan McSweyn cautiously moved in the direction of where his crew should have landed. Gradually they gathered together and found the wounded rear gunner. Sergeant Gill had landed in a tree and either due to fear or disorientation he released his parachute and fell 40 feet (12 metres) to the ground. His back was broken. A local doctor was persuaded to give him medical attention but Gill died the next day. His crew shook hands, wished each other good luck and set off on separate journeys. McSweyn hid when he saw a German soldier approach on a bicycle, lean it against a wall and enter a house. The minutes ticked by. The RAAF pilot crept up to the farmhouse and "borrowed" the bike. "I cycled for the rest of the night in a southerly direction", which was hard on his feet given that his flying boots had been blown off during the unscheduled exit from the aircraft. During the next two days McSweyn remained hidden and at night he cycled the roads of Holland, trying to work out what could be done when he eventually reached ocean. Into view came "a German fighter station with many, Messerschmitt 110s". Hiding in underbrush the next day he quietly observed "an isolated one (aircraft) near the boundary fence".[32] That would do nicely the Australian decided and when night came he would simply "borrow" a Messerschmitt and fly back to England. "When it was dark I made my way to this lone aircraft."

FOUR

"I had a little difficulty crossing the canal"

Pilot Officer Charles Roland Lark.

Allan McSweyn had commenced his elementary flight training at Narromine on 27 June 1940. He proved an exemplary student pilot and embarked for Canada on 5 September 1940. He passed out as a pilot on 22 November 1940. With training completed in Canada he arrived in England on Christmas Day; yet another young Australian getting to grips with snow and ice, England, English manners and habits, learning how to fly operations and hopefully stay alive. Posted to RAF 115 Squadron on 11 April 1941, his operational duties were brief – he and his crew were shot down on 30 June 1941. There was time to assess the 14 operations of his Bomber Command career in the immediate aftermath as he cycled roads at night and spent the days hidden and attempting to sleep. His body was weary and starved of replenishment and having crashed near Bremen in the German heartland the natives were definitely not friendly.

It was the fourth day since Wellington R1509 plummeted to earth and McSweyn waited patiently in the undergrowth observing the movements on a German fighter air base. He had decided "his aircraft" was the one furthest from the huts. Conveniently the Messerschmitt was re-fuelled and re-armed during the afternoon. As night darkened the sky, hunger

Sergeant Allan McSweyn (courtesy McSweyn Family).

and thirst were forgotten as adrenalin coursed through his veins. With no one visible on the airfield he crept carefully forward and climbed into the aircraft. Quickly trying to familiarise himself with the strange controls, his heart pounded as the engine began to turn over – nothing. Again the engine turned over but still would not fire. The thought, the prayer, the plea – "let it start this time!". There was a shout and German ground staff began to run in his direction. Once more he turned the engine over, once more it did not fire, and he now looked down the barrels of German small arms.

His body was pulled from the aircraft and the German voices were shrill – the Australian understood none of the shouts but they likely had something to do with trying to steal a German fighter. McSweyn knew not what would be his fate as he was shoved towards a large hut – at least he had evaded the enemy for four days. His immediate fate was better than expected; "I was allowed a bath and a shave and given a very comfortable pair of boots plus, of course, food and drink".[1] Apparently he had over primed the Messerschmitt engine and he vowed that next time he would be more careful. It was then over to the officers mess to meet the pilots. Although he wondered which "one of them had shot me down" the mess was similar to any RAF mess and so too the pilots; "the same age of men, all keen on flying". "They asked why I had left Australia to fight for the British. The unanimous opinion was that Germany, with Britain, should be fighting the Russians and not each other."

The following morning he was taken to Luftwaffe Headquarters in Bremen for the perfunctory interrogation. It was 4 July 1941 and after two hours the Australian was taken to Hamburg for further interrogation. McSweyn was not yet overly concerned because whilst in Luftwaffe hands the treatment would be humane. He was then placed under guard on a train – destination unknown. An RAF Squadron Leader joined him and although their freedom was severely impeded, beer and sandwiches ensured the night trip was a pleasant one. Next stop was Dulag Luft transit camp, Frankfurt. This time the interrogation was more exacting and it was a relief when finally allowed into the camp proper. There was one glitch, three of his crew were in the camp and although the Australian pilot had kept strictly to his name, rank and official number during interrogations, his crew: "Were so pleased and surprised to see me that they shouted "Hello Skipper thought you had bought it!" Of course the Germans then knew when and where I had been shot down."[2]

On 9 July he was sent to Oflag IX at Spangenberg, near Kassel. The moat surrounding the 1315 castle was dry but to discourage escape attempts the Germans filled the moat with wild boar. Yet McSweyn was determined to escape. In April with a New Zealand Squadron Leader he; "ran a rope from a gate on the castle wall and we climbed over the side to the side of the drawbridge". They had chosen a rainy night but the sentry still dutifully came out of the watch house and sighted the New Zealander. McSweyn scrambled back to his hut without being seen. His fellow Anzac received seven days in the cells; "so escape number two had also failed".[3]

At the beginning of October 1941 he was transferred to Oflag VIB, three miles (five kilometres) from the Warburg railway station. For the first time McSweyn was sharing POW accommodation with British Army officers. Camp conditions were not good so he decided it was time to leave. The Australian was admitted to a British escape plan. Ladders were constructed. Plans were hatched to interfere with the electricity supply at the time the ladders were slung against the high fence. One team of eleven and three of ten were rehearsed. Their faces blackened, they waited for the planned diversion to begin and for the electricity to be cut – it was 2230 on the night of 30 August 1942. McSweyn realised the likelihood of his making it out of the camp was slim given he had been placed at the rear of a team. Like clockwork the diversion begun and the camp was thrown into darkness. POWs ran with their ladders and flung themselves at the fence. Three teams successfully made their way over to safety, one did not. McSweyn was caught, "after two hours of freedom"[4] and escape attempt three had failed.

His next attempt at escape was a tunnelling scheme, which was swiftly curtailed when he was transferred, along with 800 POWs, to Oflag XXIB, at Schubin, Poland. Yet, no sooner had McSweyn stowed his small bundle of belongings than he volunteered to assist in digging an escape tunnel. This escape attempt continued to be dug for five months until the Germans became suspicious, the number of guards was doubled and additional floodlights set up. Mines were laid between the huts and the wire. The senior British Officer forbade any escape attempt due to the likely loss of life.

The Australian suggested another ladder escape attempt. On a dark stormy night 20 prisoners ran to the wire perimeter and threw lines intended to fuse the electrified fence. Unfortunately the searchlights were "on a different circuit". POWs were made to stand outside their barracks from 2200 to 0800 while guards trashed their huts. Allan McSweyn had begun to lose count of his escape attempts, so he began to dig another tunnel. This tunnel was discovered after only two body lengths. In the ensuing months he paid great attention to every detail of his camp and captors – there had to be a way out!

Rumours circulated that air force personnel were to be removed to Stalag Luft III at Sagan, in the German province of Lower Silesia (now Zagan, Poland) 100 miles (160 kilometres) southeast of Berlin. Luft III was a Luftwaffe-run camp which meant treatment would be far better than in other POW camps. "The German Luftwaffe was the cream of the German forces. All the educated men were in the Luftwaffe".[5] The

Germans believed it was the same in British air forces. It was thought aircrew would make valuable hostages. Luft III was designed to make escape extremely difficult, particularly by means of tunnelling. Eventually the camp would become famous for two of the greatest POW escape stories, "The Great Escape" and "The Wooden Horse", but in April 1943 Allan McSweyn believed German propaganda.

He approached Scottish orderly, Private John McDiarmid of the Seaforth Highlanders, asking if he would change identities. The transfer to Luft III went ahead with both men assuming the other's persona complete with false identity cards. For McDiarmid his treatment as an RAAF officer would be far superior to any treatment he would receive as an army Private. For three months McSweyn worked as an orderly and then began to act belligerently. The senior British Officer, Group Captain Kellett, privy to the conspiracy, suggested a change of camp for the "troublemaker" McDiarmid. The Germans quickly agreed and McSweyn, aka McDiarmid, was on his way to an army camp of around 10,000 POWs, Stalag VIIIB, at Lamsdorf. En route the Australian promoted himself to Corporal – if you were a Private you were made to work, if you were an NCO you could volunteer to undertake specific duties. "I volunteered to go out with a party digging potatoes on a farm". During his first work parties the observation was that few guards accompanied the group, so on 19 September 1943, "I just walked away from the farm". The following day he contacted Polish workers and was given a bicycle. He cycled by night and hid during the daylight hours. He had been in this position before, perhaps this time he could escape for good!

Allan McSweyn had been peddling a bike and walking for five nights now and could smell the sea – he had made the Baltic Polish city of Danzig. Arriving at the quay was such a relief. He befriended some French workers and they provided him with identification papers. There was a small Swedish boat tied up so the Australian pilot crept aboard and hid in the coal bunker. There was relief as the boat got underway. Allan McSweyn dared hope; "I thought I was safe" – he was not. After less than ten minutes; "a launch came alongside and three or four Germans with dogs, came aboard". He would never know who had given him up but it was difficult to condemn people caught up in desperate times. "They started to search the ship calling out in English for me to come out".[6] He stayed hidden hoping against hope that this was just a random search – it wasn't. The Germans threw tear gas canisters into the bunker and McSweyn had no option but to come out, his eyes streaming. "They manhandled me in rather a rough manner, and when I arrived back at Lamsdorf I was given ten days' solitary confinement on a bread and water diet."

Allan McSweyn had plenty of time to think about how many times he had attempted escape – was it five or six? Five if you didn't include the tunnel senior British officers ordered POWs not to use. Ten days gave him plenty of time to think whether he would give up trying to escape – in truth that took less than half the first day, the remaining nine and a half days was spent devising his next escape plan. Allan McSweyn dared believe that next time he might really be free.

Air Chief Marshal Harris

Bomber Command Commander-in-Chief Arthur Harris would have liked Hamburg to have been the city visited by his next Thousand Bomber raid but Churchill favoured Essen and that fact together with favourable weather conditions meant Essen was the target on the night of 1/2 June 1942. Only 956 aircraft could take off and despite the favourable weather forecast the target was difficult to find. Essen suffered minimal damage and bombs were dropped on a dozen other towns in the Ruhr valley. Thirty one bombers did not return.

Plans were immediately in play for another Thousand Bomber

operation for the latter part of June. Harris had introduced his "principle of concentration and the increased incendiary bombs".[7] No longer would the bomber force be diminished by numerous attacks over several hours, there would now commonly be a concentrated bombing attack on one target for a duration of two hours or less.

As Harris and his staff huddled over the map of Germany conferring on which city would face the next Thousand Bomber fury, bombing operations continued. Over the next three weeks "a staggering total of 126 aircraft" and their crews were lost.[8] It would not have comforted those who pulled on their leather flying helmets and wrestled heavily laden bombers into the skies over the British Isles to know that the first week in June 1942 was but the mid-point of World War II. Aircrew were also fortunately unaware that 77 per cent of Bomber Command's casualties were still to come.[9] Essen was revisited by 195 aircraft on 2/3 June and again on 5/6 June, the drumming of 180 British bombers would be heard in the skies above the city. The German seaport of Emden was visited by 233 aircraft on 6/7 June. Essen was again attacked on 8/9 June by 170 bombers, followed by another raid by 106 on 16/17 June. Emden was bombed repeatedly on the nights of June 19, 20, and 22 by a total of 611 aircraft.[10]

Bremen had first been bombed on the night of 17 May 1940 when 24 Whitleys attacked oil installations. Next it was RAF 15 Squadron Wellingtons on 21 December 1940. During the first days of 1941 three raids hit the Bremen aircraft factory. These were followed up by more raids in March and July, then January and April 1942. On 3 June 1942, 170 aircraft attacked the city.[11] Bremen was to be the target for the RAF's third Thousand Bomber raid, and the night would be 25/26 June. The need for such an assault would be debated later but Bomber Command had become a victim of its own propaganda. In July 1941 the book Bomber Command reported: "That German morale has suffered is without question, that it will go on to suffer is quite certain, that it is fast cracking under the strain is, however, not yet true. What the future holds no one can foretell. But it must not be forgotten that the attacks delivered by Bomber Command are steadily increasing in weight and severity."[12]

Every aircraft that could fly was utilised for "Operation Millennium Two". Mosquitoes and Bostons from 2 Group were included although their crews had only previously conducted daylight raids. The Admiralty agreed to release Coastal Command, then changed their mind, then acquiesced after Churchill intervened. Even five Army Co-operation Command aircraft were thrown into the mix. The final aircraft count in the attack on Bremen was 1,067, making this the largest British bombing raid.

A band of cloud cloaked the target area reducing the effectiveness of the attack. Officially the raid was listed as of "limited success" and that success was due to the navigation system Gee, which enabled the leading crews to start fires, to guide those following to the target. The plan to destroy the Focke-Wulf factory and shipyards "was not successful".[13] The Germans claimed 52 bombers were destroyed this June night, the British would admit to 50 aircraft or 4.9 per cent.[14] This however did not include Coastal Command aircraft. In the earlier Thousand Bomber raid, on Cologne 40 aircraft or 3.8 per cent of the force had been lost. Bremen approached the 5 per cent Air Marshal Harris had expected but the loss of 50–55 bombers and their crews was well short of the 100 bombers Churchill deemed "acceptable".[15]

The largest raid conducted by Bomber Command had resulted in the largest loss of aircrew. This was, in part, due to Harris ordering the involvement of OTUs to make up numbers. OTU crews were commonly aircrew trainees with a few seasoned instructors. More importantly OTUs operated older aircraft such as Whitleys and Wellingtons retired from frontline operations. Australian Don Charlwood was undergoing observer training with No 27 OTU out of Lichfield, Staffordshire. He heard men discussing "a flap" a term commonly used for a major attack because "everyone got into a 'flap' thinking and preparing for it. Furthermore, this was "a full moon do", a Thousand Bomber raid when "every kite that can fly is sent". Charlwood was pleased he wasn't going, but walked out into the darkness to watch aircraft preparing to take off. Two of his RAF instructors didn't notice their student, and one said to the other; "Can't say I'm sorry not to be on tonight. These Wimps (Wellingtons) have had their time". His companion replied;

"Yes, I don't even like them on cross countries (training flights which remained in British air space)".[16] The Bremen raid involved a distance of 200 miles greater than that needed to fly to Essen and Cologne, and on those raids, older aircraft had been pushed to capacity. On the attack on Bremen, 23 of the 198 participating OTU Whitleys and Wellingtons, and their crews, were shot down or crashed, a loss of 11.6 per cent.[17]

Australians killed in OTUs on the 25/26 June, aircrew who were still undergoing operational training, included; Sergeant Eric Douglas Williams (402687), Sergeant Thomas Stanislaus Gaffney (405441), Sergeant Robert George Ashley Brathwaite (403312), Flying Officer Gordon Richard Lind (400229), and Flight Sergeant Ian Frank McManus (404056). Sergeant Williams, aged 24, of Glenbrook, NSW, grew up with the spectacular Blue Mountains National Park as a backdrop. Williams completed four years at Parramatta High and followed his father into the insurance business. He was small and light in stature and hoped this would not hinder RAAF opportunities – it didn't and he qualified as a pilot in June 1941. Tom Gaffney, 33, husband of Josephine, was an assistant chemist with Mt Isa Mines prior to enlistment. With two years' engineering from the University of Queensland and two years industrial chemistry from Brisbane Technical College, he was quickly mustered as an Observer. Robert Brathwaite, was a 27-year-old Sydney Barrister. Gordon Lind, a 23-year-old former audit clerk from Mont Albert, Victoria, also mustered as an Observer. Ian McManus (404056), a Queenslander, was a 24-year-old pilot. For McManus there may have been a moment of realisation that his luck had run out because on 16 May 1941 his crew made a forced landing in Portugal and were interned. Diplomatic intervention saw them released and returned to England.

Also from 27 OTU, a Wellington crew whose pilot was a 21-year-old Canadian, Pilot Officer Thomas Fraser Lamb from Sault Ste Marie, Ontario. His crew were Australians. Sergeant James Bruce Mathers (403940) was 29 and a former student of Scots College and North Sydney Boys High. He graduated from University of Sydney and was a survey draughtsman with Department of Works in his native Sydney. This made him a natural selection for Observer Training. Sergeant Neville Holt Cox (405174) 21, was a former student of Brisbane State

High and graduate of University of Queensland. In December 1941 he qualified as an Observer. Sergeant Kenneth Hastings Poynting (403786) a 23-year-old Wireless Operator/Air Gunner from Sydney's Bellevue Hill, was educated at Sydney Boys High and business college, prior to commencing work as an advertising copywriter.

When RAAF recruiters received the enlistment papers of James Murray Synnott (400442) there were possibly a few raised eyebrows. His address was St Kilda, at a time when this Melbourne suburb had a reputation for "parlours" and "ladies of the night". Synnott listed no next of kin but, given he was educated at the prestigious Anglican Church's Brighton Grammar, had a benefactor during his informative years. The 25 year old noted his occupation as parlour coach driver. Sergeant Synnott had only qualified as an Air Gunner in February 1942. He and his crew had just finished their training and were proceeding on well earned leave prior to being posted to an "operational squadron", when they were recalled to make up numbers for "Millennium Two". They never made it to their "operational squadron", had they done so they may have had a better aircraft than one of the very first Wellingtons built. Remarkably they made it to Bremen before being shot down by a night fighter.

Ruby Poynting would write to the RAAF asking for further information about her son's last operation: "It is not necessary to tell what this means to his sister and myself. But I feel that I should know exactly what has happened?"

Sergeant James Mathews' father, Robert, had been in touch with Ruby Poynting and the Cox family as well as exchanging correspondence with the Lambs in Canada. They were all asking how and why. He implored the RAAF to offer any information because "this would afford us some consolation". But the RAAF had no information, they were an organisation that had relinquished control over personnel who wore their insignia but were attached to British Bomber Command.

Nor was it just OTUs expected to fly older bombers to make up numbers. The twin engine Manchester I, was never popular mainly due to the, "chronic unreliability of its two under-developed Rolls-Royce Vulture engines".[18] A batch of Manchesters were ordered in

July 1937 and delivered between August 1940 and November 1941. Manchester L 7471 belonging to RAF 50 Squadron was given to a RAAF crew for an operation on Emden on 6 June 1942. It was unusual for an all RAAF crew to be part of an RAF Squadron. The starboard engine gave trouble immediately after leaving the target and then cut out. The pilot, Flying Officer Argyle Donald Beatty (403104) from Sydney, tried to feather the airscrew as the bomber dropped to sea level. Beatty pulled the aircraft up to 300 feet (90 metres) but the strain was too great on the port engine and the Manchester crashed nose first into the sea. The second pilot, 22-year-old Pilot Officer Ronald Garnet Burton (403856) from Millthorpe, NSW, smashed forward into the instrument panel and went down with the Manchester. Beatty was pulled onboard the dinghy suffering from a fractured skull. The Navigator, Flight Lieutenant Frederic William Robert Allen (400362) had a fractured hip; first Wireless Operator/Air Gunner Sergeant Ronald Gibson Buchanan (404646) a 25 year old from North Queensland; second Wireless Operator/Air Gunner Sydneysider, Sergeant Alan Frederick Scanlan (402615) 20; Air Gunners, 29-year-old Sergeant Arthur Campbell Tebbutt (402472) from Sydney, and Sergeant Ronald Frank Davies (400342) 26, from Melbourne, all had minor injuries. A German seaplane landed and picked up the survivors. The 22-year-old Argyle Beatty never recovered and died on 10 September 1942. His crew spent long and testing years as German POWs. Not until 1948 did the final official letter arrive at the Burton's Millthorpe home. The years had taken their toll and Bill was no longer able to acknowledge receipt. Clara put pen to paper – the couple had waited since 1942 to learn the fate of their sons. Petty Officer Eric Samuel Burton, RAN, was a member of the commissioning crew of HMAS *Perth*. He was still on the Australian cruiser when it became: "the last-minute pawn in a belated attempt to appease the Dutch. Those who dictated British Dutch East Indies strategy, due to arrogance or ignorance, or a combination of both, completely misjudged the capability of the Japanese and had forsaken Perth and crew to a hapless fate."[19]

HMAS *Perth* was sunk in the Battle of Sunda Strait. There was little news of the crew's fate until after the war. Fewer than half the

681 survived the battle and a further 106 died as Japanese POWs. Only 214 Perth crew came home and Petty Officer Eric Burton was not one of them. One a sailor and one a pilot, Clara wrote: "It grieves me very much when I think two of my darling sons were lost at sea and no burial for either...our great loss."

Another RAF 50 Squadron Manchester I delivered early in the war was damaged in a heavy landing in March 1942. Manchester L7289 was repaired and considered airworthy. Sometimes there appeared to be strength to the rumour about it being a case of who you were as to who received the "clapped out" aircraft.[20] It was given to a crew who in the previous war would have been referred to as "Anzacs". The pilot was Sergeant John Charles Roy, a 21-year-old Kiwi from the tiny town of Gore in his nation's Southland (Murihiku). This was his second operation as the Captain. The other six crew members were Aussies: Sergeant Jasper Stormond Peters (12419), Sergeant Robert Leslie Hugall (406318), Sergeant Lawrence Chase Thompson (402622), Sergeant James William Lindsay (403194), Sergeant Edgar Griffiths Johnson (403813), and Sergeant Neil Malcolm Hardy (404903).

Peters was a 27 year old born in the small rural Upper Hunter Valley town Merriwa, a name derived from the Aboriginal term for 'grass seeds', before his family moved to the Blue Mountains town of Blayney. Peters was working as Blayney Municipality Assistant Shire Clerk when he enlisted. The RAAF mustered him as a "Clerk General". Peters badgered authorities until he was re-mustered for pilot training. Reports from his instructors were very mixed: "Very aggressive type"; "Asks questions until satisfied"; "Good type all round, average results", "Landing Poor, does not look around enough". At the end of his flying training Jasper Peters scored 541.75 out of 750 and they gave him his wings. For the Thousand Bomber Raid on Bremen Peters was the second pilot for just the third time on an elderly Manchester.

Bob Hugall was a year older than Peters. Born in the West Australian Margaret River township of Pingelly, by 1940, he and wife Freda lived close to his nation's most famous beach, Bondi. Lawrence Thompson was 29 and had an even more exotic place of birth and residence than the others, hailing from Lord Howe Island. It was certainly a cultural change for a farmer from an island off the NSW coast, who gave his religion as "Seventh Day Adventist". He had completed the only formal education available on the Lord Howe from age six to 15. He came to Sydney to enlist in Australia's air force. Twenty-three-year-old Jim Lindsay believed he had no other choice but to enlist given he was born in Edinburgh, Scotland. His family had migrated to Sydney but by September 1941 the former Rotary Machinist with Associated News was back in the land of his birth. Ed Johnson, 22, from the Sydney suburb of Collaroy, was schooled at Knox Grammar and was a Bank Clerk with the Commercial Bank of Sydney. Neil Hardy wrote everywhere he could on his RAAF application, even in the borders, and attached additional information. The 20 year old who lived on the rich-soiled Darling Downs, impressed upon the selectors that he was made of the right stuff. He had completed his education at Toowoomba Grammar where he played rugby in the school's first 15. He studied accountancy before his employment as a clerk with a Toowoomba Foundry and although he was entered as a general clerk in the RAAF he was "very eager" to be accepted as aircrew.

It would never be known if it was the "chronic unreliability" of the Manchester I engines which caused the death of the crew of six Australians and a New Zealander. The explosion was so great that only the remains of Hardy and Peters could be identified, and then only by way of an identity disc and a laundry name tag. What remained of the rest of the crew was buried in a joint grave with two RAF flyers who crashed the same night. After the war they would join more than 2,200 allies in Germany's Becklingen War Cemetery, chosen for its hillside position overlooking Luneburg Heath, where Field-Marshal Montgomery accepted the German surrender from Admiral Doenitz on 4 May 1945. In June 1942 a surrender was a very long way off and many would never see the day.

Another Manchester resulted in the death of other Australian, Alfred Fisher Peters, a respected Commercial Bank representative in Blayney, NSW. The community supported the Peters family, particularly Jasper's mother, Esther Catherine Peters, as best they could. The deaths of young men in this war would profoundly affect small communities

The joint grave of the crew of Manchester L7289.

throughout Australia for it was these which could least afford to lose their potential. Even the most stoic supporter of the British Empire could not help but be concerned. On Friday 2 October 1942 Blayney District's Lyndhurst Shire Chronicle included two references to Jasper Peters. Under "Methodist Notes":

We deeply sympathise with the Peters family and particularly Mrs Peters. ...Jasper has been missing since June, and though the International Red Cross Society has sought information no news has been available. Hence the presumption that another gallant lad has sacrificed his life for his loved ones and Empire. We sincerely wish for Mrs Peters and her family God's sustaining grace in their time of sad loss.

In the "Personal" page there was news of the "Patriotic Branch Meeting" whereby the Chairman, a Mr R H Clark:

made sympathetic reference to the loss of two young Blayney airmen, Jasper Peters and Douglas Lovejoy,[21] two gallant lads, he said, who had given their lives in the cause of the Empire. The sympathy of the meeting was expressed by all standing in silence for a few moments, and the Secretary was directed to write to the relatives of each airman.

Belief in the British Empire was severely tested during 1942. The might of the British Navy and its ability to protect the East and Australia sank with HM ships *Repulse* and *Prince of Wales*. Singapore, the "impregnable fortress", the "Guardian of the East", had proved to be a farce with the swift capitulation of British forces. Australia had been bombed and the Japanese advance was seemingly impossible to stem. Britain, the British Empire, was nowhere to be seen.

The mother of Jasper's crew member, Sergeant Ed Johnson, wrote to the RAAF in February 1943, explaining a friend in England had elicited information from the British Red Cross that Ed was officially dead and was buried in Germany. Ruth Johnson thought that it should be understood "what a shock the news of his having been buried in Germany has given me, having had no word of this from your Department". The RAAF Casualty Section reply was brief, acknowledging the information was correct and that: "It is greatly regretted that this news has not been conveyed to you earlier but it has been delayed in transit".

In total, 244 aircrew were lost to Bomber Command during the Bremen Thousand bomber raid, 198 were killed and 46 became German POWs. In addition, a large number of German citizens were made homeless and 85 were killed, but yet again aircrew had suffered most. When the BBC broadcast that over a thousand bombers were involved it was judged to be a propaganda bluff. Air Chief Marshal Harris was now nicknamed Bomber Harris and his eyes were on a bigger picture. Harris believed Bomber Command had achieved much and had shown what could be accomplished if given the aircraft and men to fly them. Churchill agreed, and this would ensure the rapid production of bombers and radar navigational aids; and the development of more efficient bombs and bomb sights. The second half of 1942 would be spent devising new tactics. Additional squadrons were needed to wage the air war and pressure was brought to bear on the Dominions to recruit even more aircrew and train them faster.

The next major attack in the second half of the war was yet again against Bremen the night of 2/3 July; of the 325 bombers despatched "265 aircraft claimed to have bombed in good visibility" but likely outside the city.[22] Five Germans were believed killed; four small industrial firms, around 1,000 houses, three cranes, and seven ships were damaged.[23] The price paid in British aircrew was yet again not commensurate with the damage caused to Germany's war machine. Thirteen bombers which flew out of British airspace were lost. Other than one RAF 10 Squadron Halifax and a Blenheim Bomber intruder from RAF 18 Squadron, the remaining eleven lost were all older aircraft – Stirlings, Wellingtons and Hampdens. The 13 were piloted by three RAF, two Canadians, two Poles, and eight Australians.

Sergeant Ernest Joseph Lawer (404344) a 21-year-old student from Stanthorpe, Queensland, was the captain of the Halifax. Lawer had actually enlisted as a Wireless Operator and failed a Morse code test in March 1940. The following August the former Warwick High graduate, son of an Engine Driver, made his father proud by beginning his pilot's training. Contact was lost with Lawer's Halifax when the bomber crashed into the sea off the Dutch coast. Flight Sergeant Ian Clarke Dunn (404927) was born in Laidley, Queensland, and was another graduate of University of Queensland. Following graduation with a Bachelor of Arts degree he studied theology at Emmanuel College, to become a Minister of Religion. The controls of a bomber was a strange place to find a man of God. His RAF 12 Squadron Wellington was shot down over Holland by a night fighter. Dunn was killed as were his RAF Navigator and RAF Rear Gunner. The remaining two RAF crew members became POWs.

Sergeant Douglas Wilberforce Spooner (404553) was pilot of an RAF 103 Squadron Wellington. Although born in Edithvale, Victoria, Spooner called Innisfail, Queensland, home. The former Shipping Clerk had been awarded a Distinguished Flying Medal for an operation on the night of 10 January 1942 when he was second pilot of a Wellington bomber. As the approach was made on Wilhelmshaven at a height of 15,000 feet (4,500 metres), the aircraft was subjected to intense flak. When over the target a reconnaissance flare stowed in the rear of the bomb compartment became detached and set fire to the fabric and wooden floor of the beam gun seat. The fire spread rapidly. Spooner moved back through blinding acrid smoke to attempt to extinguish the flames. He then brought portable oxygen to the suffocating Wireless Operator. Coned by searchlights the Wimpy again came under heavy anti-aircraft gunfire. The Captain ordered the crew to bale out. Four crew members did so but Spooner chose to continue extinguishing the fire and seeing this, his Skipper went back to the controls. Although suffering acutely from fumes and having suffered slight burns, with the fire out Spooner returned to the cockpit. He and his Captain changed roles and with the skipper navigating the Australian flew the Wellington back to England. His squadron recommended him for the Victoria Cross. The recommendation was not accepted by the RAF hierarchy although it was noted that Spooner had upheld "the reputation of the Australians as being 'Non-Quitters'". On the night of 2/3 of July the 25-year-old Spooner took off on his ninth operation as Captain. The Wellington he was piloting was attacked at 0130 by a night fighter over the Dutch town of Sage and Spooner was killed instantly.

Pilot Officer Peter Richard Vincent Sullivan (403385) was from the NSW country town of Gundagai. He was skipper of an RAF 109 Squadron Special Duties Wellington carrying experimental equipment to conduct a wireless test. Sullivan and four of his RAF crew became statistics of night fighter ace Oblt Egmont Prinz zur Lippe Weissenfeld. Pilot Officer Archie Thomas Little (402821) was quite at home during his elementary flight training because he trained at his home town of Narrandera, NSW, No 8 EFTS. Just the same it was quite a career change for the baker who worked in his parents Narrandera business. He was awarded his wings and disembarked in the UK in July 1941. Pilot Officer Little, a squadron mate of Doug Spooner was on his tenth operation as skipper of a RAF 103 Wellington, which crashed near the German border on the night of 2/3 July 1942. His RAF navigator became a POW, but 28-year-old Little and the rest of his RAF crew were buried in the land of the enemy. Mary Little would write: "The loss of my son is a terrible blow as his father died after Arch had gone to England". She politely asked if his personal effects could be sent to her: "I would be very grateful as I feel sure he would have left a letter to comfort me also many photos".

Of the eight Australian pilots who died during the 2/3 July attack on Bremen, six flew RAF squadron bombers and two were members of RAAF 460 Squadron. RAAF 460 crews were establishing an admirable reputation for their squadron. They were also proving to be very Australian by adding levity to the frightfully serious business of bombing. Practice bombing exercises were conducted at a range close to Breighton. RAAF 460 pilots decided to dive bomb "their lumbering old Wellingtons" from 1,000 feet (300 metres) at the target when senior RAF authority was not attentive. "This ludicrous sport flourished unhindered...until one day, one crew's aim was not so good and their bombs fell amongst chickens and stock of an irate local farmer who cursed all Australians, disputing their ancestry without exception and the air force in general."[24] The farmer was appeased with a tidy financial compensation from the British Air Ministry which then ordered a stop to "this unauthorised form of aerial sport".

Sergeant Alexander Frederick Whittick (404844) joined as a 20 year old. His family were well-known merchants in the tropical city of Cairns, Queensland, and he was learning the family business after studying accountancy. Whittick was anxious the RAAF thought he a proper gentleman arguing his one traffic offence, "incorrect parking Cairns, January 1940," was wrong and he had spent 6/- (60c) in costs contesting the 10/- ($1) fine. His pilot training over, he was posted to RAF 460 on 28 May 1942. Sergeant Jack Douglas Hancocks (401237) was the 22-year-old son of Bill and Violet Hancocks of Kew, Victoria, and the Wireless Operator/Air Gunner; Sergeant Allan Edwin McCrae (406444) 25, was a Metallurgist with Kalgoorlie Central Eastern Goldfields before he enlisted in December 1940. He was a bit of a wild lad mining sometimes had that affect on men. On several occasions he incurred the wrath of his RAAF superiors by going Absent Without Leave and enjoying beer a little too excessively. This resulted in extra duty, loss of pay and finally 120 days detention. Despite the recalcitrant behaviour McCrae qualified as a rear gunner.

It was unusual at this stage of the war to have two seasoned POs in a rookie crew. Pilot Officer Charles Roland Lark (403409) was a 24-year-old Observer from the Sydney suburb of Chatswood who had enlisted in January 1941. The 29-year-old Navigator was Pilot Officer Albert Ernest William Webb (406272) who had enlisted from Perth in October 1940 but had been born in Canterbury, England. He was filling in from 31 OTU. There seemed to be added pressure for the new boys to measure up in a hurry. This was particularly the case for Alex Whittick, a Sergeant Pilot and the bomber captain. Commissioned aircrew lived and ate in different quarters and tended to socialise with other officers – none of this was great for crew cohesion. The new kids on the block were just pleased that Webb and Lark were Australian at least.

It was the middle of the night when Whittick and crew took off from Breighton. Out of seemingly nowhere German fighters flashed up from beneath releasing a barrage of fire. Pilot Officer Lark "fell to the floor wounded". Lark called to the pilot and navigator but there was no reply. The Wireless Operator, Hancocks, moved to free Lark from "entanglements". According to Lark, Hancocks then "climbed over the main spar and disappeared into the cabin" to check on other crew members. The Wellington was burning in several places and was diving out of control".[25] A bullet had gone through Lark's right eye, another through the left chest area and another in his right thigh. "A cannon shell made a couple of ugly holes in my right shoulder." Being "too weak to pull out the oxygen tube" Lark took off his helmet, "stumbled somehow back to the mid-opening (losing my boots)"and baled out. One of his parachute harness clips was broken but the other held and he landed in water. Unable to release himself from the parachute because of his injuries it filled with the wind and dragged him further away from land. The parachute then filled full of water and began to drag him under. There was that last cry from deep inside as water filled his mouth. With his one good arm he jerked at the harness and it finally came loose – the parachute descended to the bottom as he floated to the surface. Unable to swim he rolled onto his back and with one good leg and one good arm, unfortunately both on the same side, he pushed towards the shore. It took more than two and a half hours before he made landfall. After a short rest somehow he summoned up the energy to haul himself to his feet. Hobbling towards where he thought houses would be he came upon a canal – this was Holland after all. Lark would state later, "I had a little difficulty crossing the canal. The first house I came to they refused me admission, but the people in the second house were very kind". He would remain in a Dutch hospital for seven weeks after his right eye was removed. Dutch medical staff refused to surrender him to the Germans until they could no longer.

Charlie Lark was the only member of his crew to escape as the bomber crashed into the large lake in central Netherlands and sank immediately. The lake was shallow at just 16–19 feet (5–6 metres) in depth. During the war, seven Allied bombers would crash into the lake but in 1947 it was decided not to attempt to recover the aircraft or their crews. The report said "The possibility of recovering from the Ijesselmeer is problematic".[26] Pilot Officer Webb had been supporting his mother widowed by the previous war. Ellen Webb struggled when informed her son was "missing". The news in September confirming "killed in action" proved devastating, Ellen Webb suffered a paralysing stroke and died soon after.

So many of those who called themselves sons of Australia were living adrenalin- filled lives. So many of their exploits would rival any of the *Boys Own Adventures* books they had excitedly read. Many made the adventures of *Biggles* pale by comparison. Flight Sergeant Arthur Maxwell Johnston (404784) was born in Mount Molloy, Queensland, an historic mining and timber town North West of Cairns. He had done well to be accepted as aircrew (Pilot) in November 1940 given he could not boast of a private school and university education unlike so many other applicants. He was a graduate of Technical College. Under the question concerning Higher Education he wrote "have only studied practical sawmilling". He was manager of his father's sawmills and decided that should be enough. Under the question on religion he simply wrote "never christened" and for his father's nationality he wrote "born in Iceland". Recruiting officers saw something in this 25 year old from North Queensland, and he was offered the opportunity to prove he could fly. In June 1941 he was awarded his wings. He was in England when the Japanese declared war and Johnston immediately decided the battle to protect Australia was more important than the battle to protect the UK. He wrote to his Commanding Officer requesting a transfer back to Australia so he could serve as a pilot at an Australian base. His letter was passed further up the chain of command and Johnston was told his duty was to win this battle first. Unhappy with this decision Johnston reacted against RAF code of conduct. In April 1942 he was placed on charges by two different RAF police corporals. The first charge was for "Not carrying a respirator (anti-gas) when walking out in uniform". The second charge was "Having all the buttons of his blue service greatcoat unfastened". A third charge was "Having both hands in his trouser pockets". For these he was officially "Reprimanded".

Flight Sergeant Arthur Johnston was the skipper of a Wellington IV which took off from Breighton at 2327 on the 2 July 1942. His crew was Australian. Sergeant Darryl Downing (407709) the Second Pilot was still very young. The 20 year old was from Lameroo, a South Australian town close to the Victorian border. He was a former student of Prince Alfred College, had undertaken a commerce course at the University of Adelaide. While studying accountancy he worked as a clerk in a chartered accountant's office. Of solid build the 20-year-old Downing was a first division boxer. Sergeant David August Radke (405139) a 22-year-old printer's assistant from Beenleigh, Queensland, was the Wireless Operator. Sergeant Maxwell Joseph Andrew Wyllie (405001) was the 26-year-old Observer. Of Scottish parents Wyllie completed his secondary education at St Joseph's College, Brisbane, and then he too studied accountancy. Wyllie wrote 'grocer' on his application form and was re-mustered when he washed out in flight training. Sergeant William James Taylor (407775) the 27-year-old Wireless Operator/Air Gunner was another South Australian, from Port Pirie, and yet another studying accountancy while working as a clerk. Sergeant William Gerald Reed (402479) made this crew one of many accountants. The 22 year old from Melbourne was now a Bomber Command Air Gunner.

Johnstone and his crew had barely survived an operation against Bremen when the main plane, rear turret, and starboard engine of their Wellington were hit by flak. Days later, on 2 July the flight to the target was reasonably uneventful, other than the ubiquitous flak spurting up from below, bursting like deadly firecrackers all around the Wellington. Over the intercom Sergeant Bill Taylor called "bombs gone" and Sergeant Max Wyllie then gave their skipper the course for base. At 0235 on 3 July they received a direct hit from anti-aircraft fire. Johnston was killed and the body of the second pilot 20-year-old Darryl

Downing, was found with his parachute unopened. Bill Taylor baled out and fell to a grisly death onto high tension wires. Reed's parachute unfurled so rapidly his shoulder was dislocated. He, Radke, and Wyllie were quickly rounded up by enemy soldiers.

Max Wyllie and an English POW made an escape from Stalag VIIIB. They were dressed in civilian clothes and under cover of night they followed a railway line they hoped would take them to neutral territory. It was shortly after midnight on 22 April 1943 when a voice came from out of the darkness ordering them to stop. Turning around slowly they faced a policeman and a man in civilian clothes demanding identification papers. They had none other than their POW identity discs. According to Englishman Joseph Terry: "The policeman drew his revolver and became very excited. He showed the identity discs to the civilian, all the time becoming more excited and shouting to us in German, little or none of which we understood."[27]

The two Allies began to raise their hands as ordered, their minds working overtime on how to extract themselves from this predicament. The policeman was becoming increasingly agitated and suddenly fired his gun. It happened so unexpectedly the Englishman couldn't believe what was taking place: "Wyllie grasped his body and gasped "Oh!". Wyllie stood for a few seconds, after which his leg appeared to collapse, causing him to spin around and stagger a few paces. The policeman then fired another shot and Wyllie gasped and fell to the ground."

Terry was shocked but it was clear the policeman shouting "Vic" and "waving his revolver" around wanted him to attempt an escape "so that he could shoot at me". He stood perfectly still with arms raised. The Australian was not dead; "I could hear groans". Terry wasn't sure how but he lost consciousness. When he was returned to a POW camp Terry made a statement and the policeman who killed the unarmed Wyllie at point blank range was eventually identified as Chief Patrol Leader Alfred Gebauer.

Wyllie's family in Australia was told that he "died in a POW camp in Germany". On his record the words "shot while attempting to escape from POW camp" were written. Clearly both were incorrect – Wyllie had already escaped from the POW camp when he was shot. In a December

1943 letter to RAAF Headquarters in London, the British War Office decided that; "credence would be given to the testimony of a German policeman" in a German Court over that of an escaped British POW. It was believed; "it is important to confine our protests to those cases in which our grounds of complaint are strongest". The Germans had, it was argued; "been reasonable" in "cases of violent deaths, and if we complain in all such cases they may discontinue the present practice". The War Office ordained; "In these circumstances we hope your government will agree that no further diplomatic action should be taken". The Australian government again acquiesced to British authority. Officially Max Wyllie was recorded as; "shot while attempting to escape" – only Joseph Terry would dispute the verdict. Following the end of hostilities Allied authorities would discover enormous crimes against humanity committed by the NAZI regime and the murder of RAAF Sergeant Max Wyllie was forgotten. In time he would be posthumously awarded a Mentioned in Despatches, and his mother Ellen received the "small gold cross" her son wore around his neck.

Wyllie's Air Gunner, Sergeant Bill Reed, attempted his first escape, from Stalag VIIIB on 20 September 1942 but failed. He changed identities with an Army Private and was sent on 7 April 1943 to work in a German stone quarry. The next escape came on 17 April with another POW. Hiding from German soldiers in the mulling crowd they boarded a train. Upon reaching Stettin (Szczecin, Poland) on the 20 April they found the city in the midst of a British air raid. How ironic to die in an air attack wrought by their own! With so many forced labourers in the district it was possible to move around head down and unchallenged but they were unable to procure food. Proceeding to the dock area they stowed onboard a Swedish coaler. If they could at least reach Stockholm and were then interned this would be superior fate – perhaps they might even fall into the hands of the Underground.

Less than two days later a German search patrol came onboard and at gunpoint the POWs were pushed ashore and handed over to the Gestapo. The next days according to Reed were, "very bad". Reed was taken to Berlin and thrown into solitary confinement for seven days. It was then he learnt that Wyllie had been executed. It left a sinking feeling deep in his gut, but he vowed he would continue trying to escape – it was a mixture of his overwhelming desire to be free, and the sweetheart he was engaged to back in the British Isles. On 1 July he changed identities again and attached himself to a railroad maintenance working party. Using his few Red Cross foodstuffs and cigarettes, Reed traded with Polish and Czech workers for clothes and money. On 27 July he climbed onto a passing train and the next days drained every human reserve.

By 1 August the South Australian was again in Stettin. Again he crept onboard a Swedish boat and then another and then another. On the first two boats the crew may well have known of his presence but turned a blind eye. On the third, the Swedish steamer *Hanna*, the first mate turned him over to German authorities. It was 5 August 1943 and Reed had been free ten days. This time his treatment as a prisoner of the Gestapo was even worse. He could write only of it; "17 days of solitary confinement and all the extras". What was left of the RAAF Air Gunner was returned to Stalag VIIIB and admitted to hospital for a stay of eight weeks for "malnutrition and other injuries". Released back into the POW camp, Reed "Took up work on escape committee". His fourth escape attempt ended on 9 May 1944 when the Germans discovered the tunnel he was digging. Reed was sent to work in the coal mine. He wrote "bad conditions" that were in no way in keeping with "the Geneva Convention". The next notation committed to paper was: "Two men shot escaping 12 May". This was still not a deterrent and by 11 July, carrying forged identification papers, Reed was on the run again. Arriving in Stettin two days later, he stowed away on another Swedish coaler. Finally he escaped and on arrival in Stockholm he was handed over to an Ally Naval Attaché and then the British Consul.

Upon the outbreak of World War II, prime minister Robert Menzies instituted conscription for militia operating in Australia and her territories. All unmarried men aged 21 and over were required to attend three months of compulsory military training. Certain occupations such as engineers, munitions workers, coal miners, were "reserved", exempt from military service. The Defence Act conscripted militia for home service. The next step was national conscription but during World War I there had been two plebiscites, in 1916 and 1917, on conscription and it had divided the nation. Never before had Australians witnessed such vitriol and it became blatantly clear to the Australian Parliament that the people they represented did not want their youth drafted into the military and sent to the battlefields of Europe.

In 1941, John Curtin was elected prime minister of a Labor government. In World War I he had been a staunch opponent of conscription, but this war was huge and its shadow was creeping closer to Australia. Rumours were rife that conscription was inevitable, women had already begun to take on work previously undertaken only by men and for the first time in Australian history there was even talk of the formation of women's auxiliaries for the nation's armed forces. Already some Australian companies had enacted their own style of conscription. Dennys, a Geelong wool-broking company, required every single male employee of military age to apply to enlist in return for guaranteed employment upon completion of military service.

Sgt John O'Brien.

Sergeant John Ormond O'Brien (403876) was born in the leafy Sydney suburb of Gordon in 1919. His father Eric, a successful businessman, sent John to the Cranbrook School a prestigious centre of education founded in 1918 by a group of businessmen and the Anglican Church. The son was to follow the father in business so one of the subjects John studied for his Intermediate Certificate was business principles. He then studied with the Real Estate Institute of New South Wales and commenced work as a clerk then real estate salesman. Life was pleasant and John enjoyed "yachting, cricket, football, tennis, swimming and rifle shooting".[28] Military service had not been a family tradition and around the dinner table discussion seemed to raise almost as many objections to joining as it did to signing up.

With some background in yachting the RAN could have been a viable option for John O'Brien but this lacked appeal. World War I digger stories had been committed to the national psyche and were horrific, so he similarly ruled out joining the Army. The RAAF still had a certain mystique – the wonder of flight a definite frontier charm. John O'Brien was an impressionable eleven year old when on 9 June 1928 Charles Kingsford Smith and Charles Ulm touched down on Eagle Farm airfield, Brisbane, in the Fokker F.VII/3m monoplane, the *Southern Cross*, after the first successful Trans-Pacific crossing. Their amazing 83 hours flying time to cover the 7,388 miles (11,822 kilometres) from Oakland, California, via landings in Hawaii and Fiji, was an unparalleled accomplishment of navigation and endurance. Like so many of his nation's youth John watched enthralled by the shuddering black and white cinema newsreel of the monoplane landing and "Smithy" and Ulm being interviewed. Like so many of his peers he dared to dream.

John O'Brien applied for RAAF entry at 21, the age that no longer required parental consent and became RAAF 403876 on 4 March 1941. Within two months he was undergoing Elementary Flying School Training and excelled. By 26 April he was a Leading Aircraftsman (LAC) mustered Aircrew II (P). In July John returned home on embarkation leave to familiar haunts in which he was now less at ease than in civilian life. He had changed and social chit chat with civilian friends seemed futile. He missed training for war as well as fellow RAAF aircrew trainees who he had known for less time but seemingly knew them better. Farewells were awkward – he didn't know if he was going away for a short time or would never return. Relatives tried desperately to avoid that subject as well as direct eye contact. He tried not to show how eager he was to just board the troopship moored in Sydney Harbour and get on with this amazing journey.

Training in Moncton, New Brunswick, Canada, was fun and testing at the same time. It was late summer and John O'Brien couldn't imagine training here in winter when there was 8–12 inches (20–30 centimetres) of snow on the ground, or when the snow was mixed with freezing rain. By the time he embarked for the United Kingdom the first snow had fallen. He had been awarded his flying badge, sewn on his sergeant stripes, and the level of anticipation had risen another notch. It was 24 February 1942 when he joined 14 OTU. Staying alive seemed to be the priority now – in 1942, 14 OTU would lose eleven aircraft in operations and 28 in non-operational flights. Overall Bomber OTU and flight losses for 1942 would amount to 633 aircraft. The total for 1940–42 would come to 1,204.[29]

Crews would form crews at OTUs; "a rather bewildered milling herd of aircrew formed themselves into crews by a process of natural selection".[30] Being a pilot ,John O'Brien was in the best position because he selected his crew; but it was essential that his knowledge and instincts were good. Other trainees hoped a pilot would approach them, and as bands of men gathered as crews, they hoped like mad they would not be the last to be chosen. The mêlée boarded on chaos as close to a hundred men lingered over tea and sticky buns to make decisions which would affect their future. It was because these were life and death decisions that there could be no arbitrary selection process. Aircrew needed to believe others they teamed up with was their choice because each crew member would make a vital contribution to their survival. Most went into the assembly with some idea of who would be there. They had heard rumours of the expertise or otherwise of certain pilots being able to land an aircraft without breaking it. Pilots had heard of the expertise or lack of, whispered about certain wireless operators, rear gunners, and navigators; perhaps of personal foibles. For some, nationality was the most important criteria.

It was May 1942 when John O'Brien and his crew were posted to RAF 49 Squadron. When the war began RAF 49 Squadron crews were flying Hampdens from Scampton, Lincolnshire, and in April 1940, helped inaugurate the RAF's sea-mining campaign. Crews then began to be sent on bombing operations, as well as dropping mines, and in August 1940, pilot, Flight Lieutenant Rab Learoyd, RAF, won the first Bomber Command Victoria Cross, for his part in a low-level attack on the Dortmund-Ems Canal. Learoyd was a legend in this squadron and other pilots wondered if they would be as brave under duress.

John O'Brien's crew included three RAF blokes. Second pilot, RAF Sergeant Charles Edward Goldring (657308) was a 22 year old from Essex; the two RAF gunners were Sergeant Alexander Garos (778783) and Sergeant Neville John Rogers (778781), who had voyaged from Nyasaland, Africa (now Malawi), to enlist. John had chosen fellow Aussies to make up the remainder of the seven man crew. Sergeant Keith Allen (401359) came from Melbourne, and being 30, was the old man in aircrew terms. Educated at Wesley College he was fit and strong having played representative rugby, tennis, and swimming, as well as been involved in water polo, squash, and golf. In the non-sporting hours he was an accountant and the RAAF trained him to be an Observer.

Sergeant Harrington (Harry) Price (402539), 27, who was born in Musselbrook, New South Wales but educated at Newington College, Sydney, was an auditor and shipping clerk prior to his enlistment in September 1940. He had crashed a Tiger Moth in training at Tamworth. The enquiry found that he had allowed "the aircraft to stall during a side-slip at too low a height to affect recovery". The aircraft was a wreck and Price sustained a "contused wound under the right eye, abrasion of left elbow, abrasion of left leg, abrasion of right thigh, and mental shock". Although it was believed his injuries would not have "permanent ill-effects nor impair his future efficiency as an Officer or an airman", and, "training action be taken to improve the flying technique of L.A.C. Price", he was re-mustered away from direct aircraft handling duties and qualified as a Wireless Operator/ Air Gunner. 21-year-old Sergeant Terence Francis Breen McKenna (405162) added his own international background. His dark good looks he inherited from his mother, Mary Ligoria of Port Moresby, and not his father Joseph Bernard McKenna. He was just 19 when he enlisted in July 1940 and still a student at Brisbane's St Joseph's Christian Brothers College, better known as "Nudgee". He was just shy of completing his University qualifying when the RAAF accepted this model student and outstanding sportsman, who not only represented Nudgee in 1st cricket and 1st football teams but had been selected for both the Combined GPS Football and Cricket teams.

Unfortunately the timing of their arrival in Bomber Command was not good. Firstly, they were caught up in the Thousand-Bomber raids of Cologne and Essen. Worst still, was that while RAF 49 had recently converted from Hampdens, crews were now flying Manchester bombers for a period of around two months until Lancasters arrived. Manchester I L7387 was an aircraft built in 1940 and had a chequered career. The previous year with a different squadron L7387 was bounced on a heavy landing, when the pilot opened the throttles too quickly and choked both engines resulting in the under-carriage collapsing. It was repaired and sent to another squadron. In April L7387 was landed diagonally in front of road crossing before becoming airborne again and the starboard rudder struck ground. Repaired again, it was sent to RAF 49 as an interim bomber. It was believed L7387 had a total of 220.30 hours when assigned to Sergeant John O'Brien and his crew on the night of 20 June 1942. They took off from Scampton at 2330 as part of a search and rescue party for nine crews who had not returned the previous night from Emden. Night fighters and anti-aircraft batteries made no allowance for aircraft looking for downed crews, a bomber was a bomber. It was believed Manchester L7387 crashed somewhere off the Dutch Frisian Islands.

The initial telegram was delivered to Harrington Price's father so Winifred Smith heard the news second hand. She was upset that Harry was missing and she was upset she had not been informed. In a letter to the RAAF, Winifred expressed her feelings, Harry: "Had lived with me since a baby and he knew no other mother but me (His mother asked me when she was dying to take him). I educated, clothed and fed him and loved him as my own. When he joined the air force, he had to give the name of his father, but whom he seldom if ever sees. His father is my brother."

The RAAF added Winifred's name to the next of kin list and there was no escape from the firsthand news. An urgent telegram on 12 December advised: "Sgt L.H.W. Price now classified missing believed killed in action" – this time they had his initials correct. Such telegrams Post Master General staff hated to deliver – they believed there should have been a more sympathetic way of breaking dreadful news than simply sending a family a telegram. Two days later an official letter, confirmation that Harry, "previously reported missing, is now reported missing but believed to have lost his life on the 20 June 1942". On 25 January another telegram: "Deeply regret to inform you that it has now been presumed for official purposes that the death of your nephew, Sergeant Harrington Warren Price, occurred on 20 June 1942". A gravestone bearing Harry Price's name would forever stand on the Dutch island of Schiermonnikoog. Winnifred Smith thanked authorities for photos of the grave which "I shall value" and she also received a letter from Dutchman Mr Van der Werff "saying he would always tend the grave", which "was wonderful".[31]

The body of Terry McKenna was washed up on the shores of Sweden and was buried in Kviberg Cemetery. Kviberg was testament to not only the legacy of war but the evolution of war. Sixty eight graves were from World War I, casualties of the 1916 Battle of Jutland when the navies of Britain and Germany endeavoured to blast each other into submission. Dreadnoughts and lesser ships thundered away at each other until 14 British and eleven German ships had been sunk. Opposing Admirals claimed victory but 6,094 British and 2,551 German officers and sailors had been killed. Of the 68 who washed ashore and were buried in Kviberg, 30 would simply have the gravestone epitaph "Sailor of the Great War". In World War II taking the war to the enemy acquired a new guise. By the end of this war the remains of 46 young airmen would be buried here at Kviberg, eleven of whom would be inscribed Unknown Airman of the 1939–45 War.

Eric O'Brien wrote to the RAAF – he was getting conflicting messages because he had received the telegram that John was missing but his son's name had not appeared in the print media. The RAAF apologised for "inadvertently omitting your son's name", but the lack of information and miscommunication continued. Eric O'Brien asked the RAAF for any details concerning his son's last flight but was told such information was classified. Then through the mail came a letter from Sergeant Russell Lloyd Cumberland, RAAF, (403644). Russ had trained and travelled with John since Narrandera days. "We became very friendly, especially since arriving in England and spent a good deal of our spare time together". John was in his opinion "one of the cheeriest persons I had ever met". Russ Cumberland tried to assure the O'Briens that "John was happy and really did enjoy flying". At the same time he was himself struggling with the bitter reality of war; "I have lost a number of my friends, but I feel the loss of Johnnie greatly". Eric O'Brien wrote thanking Cumberland and hoped to hear more of John's last days from the 24-year-old pilot from Goulburn, but Cumberland, too, would soon die.

John O'Brien's family received a letter from the RAAF telling them their son's body had been buried on Schiermonnikoog, an island off the Dutch Coast. The body was buried originally as "J.E. Mond, RCAF, 54038" but subsequent enquiry revealed that there was no J.E. Mond serving with the RCAF nor was there any member of the RAF named Mond missing. The puzzle was believed resolved when it was decided the "Ormond" part of John Ormond O'Brien's name had been "misread by the Germans" and the number 54038 was in fact 403876. It was a grave too far away but to have John laid to rest somewhere was comforting. In 1951 the Australian Ambassador to The Netherlands visited Schiermonnikoog and sent the O'Brien family photographs of "where your late son is laid to rest". In 1954 a dozen years after the death of their only son, yet another official letter arrived. RAF investigators had made "an error" – John was not buried in a cemetery on Schiermonnikoog after all, it was now believed the dead airman was an RAF 142 Squadron Observer, with the surname Emond. John O'Brien's body was never found.

FIVE

*"They were your boys, now they are ours
and we shall take care of them."*

Andries Meijer

Few Australians could say where the town of Yarrabandai was, not even if the names of towns within a radius of 30 miles (50 kilometers) were provided, like Monomie, Ootha, Warroo, Derriwong, Bedgerebong, Gunningbland, Borambil, Nelungaloo, Kadungle, Brolgan, Bundaburra or Wowingragong. It sounded more like an indigenous conversation particularly as Sergeant Rawdon Hume Middleton (402745) could enunciate them perfectly. If those who had asked where he was from still looked none the wiser he could say "Alloway". The sheep station near Bogan Gate in the Gilgandra district his father managed was north of West Wyalong, northwest of Forbes, west of Parkes, east of Condobolin. If they still looked puzzled he could just say, New South Wales. Those tongue-twisting towns Rawdon Middleton knew very well – he had traversed them often enough on horseback, as a jackaroo, as a spirited boy and man with a quest for excitement and travel. Perhaps adventure was in the genes because the middle name he carried was in honour of his great uncle, the explorer, Hamilton Hume. Although he was born in Sydney in July 1916 his family moved to the property when he was a child. He finished his education in the High School at Dubbo.

At 5ft 11 in (1.8m) and of solid build Rawdon was very competitive at sports and set himself high standards. He loved the vast open spaces, the dry plains that hugged every horizon of his part of the country.

He was called Rawdon at home but once in the RAAF from October 1940 he was called Ron. Being mustered as Aircrew (Pilot) was exactly what he wanted and his flight training commenced at Narromine in December 1940. By March 1941 he was in Canada, by September the UK, and October 42 he was attached to RAF 23 OTU. He was seen as "an earnest, plodding pupil. All he did was thorough, though unspectacular"[1] and perhaps because of this Middleton found himself posted to different RAF squadrons. It may also have been because he appeared uncomfortable with his duties in Bomber Command. One English author described Middleton as a pilot who: "Brooded a lot on the German bombing of unprotected cities, and followed a common trait among out-back Australians in being inclined to bouts of melancholy."[2]

For this "quiet, unassuming chap"[3] the frequent postings may have been a little unsettling but Rawdon Middleton knew that time spent as a second pilot would result in his eventually being made skipper in his own right, and there was some excitement along the way.

LEFT: *Pilot Officer Rawdon Hume Middleton.*
RIGHT: *Leading Aircraftsman Rawdon (Ron) Middleton in training.*

On 6 April 1942 he was second pilot to RAF Flight Lieutenant M R Evans. The Stirling crew of seven plus an additional trainee realised it could be a difficult night because the target was Essen. Take off from Lakenheath, Suffolk, at 0037 was routine, but that changed as soon as the bomber was over Holland. The Messerschmitt attacked and gunfire ripped into the British aircraft damaging the starboard wing. They weaved and the British gunners fired as rapidly as they could. The German fighter broke off. Evans and Middleton struggled to keep their aircraft in the air. With one engine out they were steadily losing height. The decision was made to jettison the bombload and change course for England. It was such a relief to begin their approach into an English airfield. As the aircraft touched down at 0446 the undercarriage collapsed. Other than racing pulses and bruising the crew gave thanks to whatever lucky talisman or deity they believed in.

By July 1942 Sergeant Rawdon Middleton was allowed to choose his own crew. His first operation as skipper on the night of 31 July 1942 was not the debut he hoped for – with the bomber's rear turret unserviceable the crew returned to base. Quickly however the Australian with the Errol Flynn or Tyrone Power looks began to make a reputation as a first class aviator and bomber captain. His three gunners elected to continue flying even though they had completed their tour of 30 operations. His wireless operator said Middleton was: "About the most modest chap I've ever met, and one of the best-looking. He was so efficient".[4] Middleton enjoyed flying the Stirling because due to the thick wing it could invariably out-turn night fighters. The downside was that the same thick wing resulted in a low ceiling, commonly 12,000 ft (4,000 m). Raids on Italy necessitated flying through the Alps rather than over so not only was there the difficult terrain to master but the aircraft was also an easier target for anti-aircraft fire. Middleton had already witnessed the upside of flying a Stirling first hand and survived – he hoped he wouldn't suffer the Alps scenario.

Flight Lieutenant Doug Hurditch (402862) the pilot who impressed Buff Cheese so much by landing with full bomb load without loss of life was shot down on 8 June 1942 during an operation to attack Essen, his Wellington (Z1412) yet another victim of Happy Valley. One crew member was killed but Hurditch and others became POWs. Hurditch would survive the war and continue an illustrious RAAF career. He joined as a 19 year old from Leeton, New South Wales, in November 1940 and would retire an Air Vice Marshal on 19 March 1975, his 54th birthday. RAAF 460 Flight Commander Squadron Leader Leighton who had signed the pages of the log book belonging to Buff Cheese died on the night of 25 /26 July 1942 on an operation to bomb Duisburg. With him were RAAF Sergeant Laurence James Sams (407834) an Englishman who migrated to Adelaide and Sergeant William George Taylor (6201) from the Brisbane suburb of Indooroopilly. They were buried in Germany's Reichswald War Cemetery. Sergeant Clarence Frederick Sinclair (405219), from the New South Wales town of Wilberforce, and Brisbane's Sergeant Raphael Sherman (404804) were taken POW.

On 4 July 1776 the new American Congress signed the Declaration of Independence affirming that the 13 American colonies at war with Great Britain to wrest themselves from British governance were henceforth: "Absolved from all Allegiance to the British Crown, and that all political connection between them (American colonies) and the State of Great Britain." The irony of, 4 July 1942, could not be ignored because it was the first time crews from the United States 15 Bomber Squadron (Light) participated in a bombing mission over Europe. Descendants of those who forced Britain to cede the American colonies were now resisting German forces on behalf of Britain. American airmen attached to RAF 226 Squadron for operational low level day bombing training attacked four Dutch airfields. Six of the American-built Boston bombers had American crews and two were shot down. A week later six more teamed up with RAF 226 for an attack against Abbeville, France. In August, the 15th Bombardment Squadron received its own aircraft, former RAF Bostons and A-20s from the United States. The squadron flew a number of missions with Bomber Command and in October was transferred to United States Twelfth Air Force for support of Allied landings in North Africa.

The blend of uniforms in the titanic struggle in the air continued to broaden and for men from the United States who believed their nation should have been involved in the war in Europe earlier, it was confirmation of their duty with other nations. Prior to 1942 American volunteers travelled to Canada and the United Kingdom to enlist. The intercom onboard a Halifax from RCAF 405 Squadron carried an interesting blend of accents. The Captain, of Halifax W1113 which took off to bomb Bremen on 29 June 1942 from Pocklington, Yorkshire, was 22-year-old Australian, Flight Sergeant Henry (Harry) Adolphus Chinn, (402223) RAAF. The standard crew of seven in his bomber was joined by a trainee. Sergeant William Jessup Harrell (R/83419), the second pilot, wore a Canadian insignia but hailed from Eastman, Georgia, USA. Warrant Officer James (Sammy) William Bell (648880) the 28-year-old Observer was from New Brunswick, Canada. RAF Sergeant Alexander Simpson (571779) at 21 seemed too young to be the aircraft Flight Engineer. For some reason engineers commonly came from Scotland and Alex Simpson was no exception. His parents' names epitomised Scottish pride – Alexander Stewart Simpson and Annie Campbell Macadam Simpson lived in Saltcoats, Ayrshire, Scotland. Sergeant Walter Beare (1284966) RAF, was the Wireless Operator/Air Gunner who had a dash of Irish blood. Flight Sergeant Winston James Dickinson (R/84563) RCAF, was actually a 25 year old who came from Houlton, Maine, USA. RAF Sergeant Reginald Thomas Adams (759300) 21, the Rear Gunner, was from Wiltshire, England. Sergeant Paul Oneson (R/56246) RCAF, the 26-year-old Wireless Operator/Air Gunner, was from Quebec, that most French of Canadian provinces.

Life had not been easy for the Chinn family, for Henry, Violet and their four children. The effects of the Great Depression impacted on their town of Gunnedah, New South Wales, as it did throughout Australia, but for this family it was all the more difficult when Violet died in 1930. Roy was 13, Harry was nine, and Richard six. Much of the family care now fell on their 16-year-old sister Maisie while father Henry endeavoured to provide for his now one-parent family. Harry impressed everyone he came in contact with. "Even tempered, of cheerful disposition and a keen sense of humour" was the description offered by brother Richard, "Harry was my role model". Harry completed high school, having been a prefect and school representative in athletics and rugby league. Harry Chinn was determined to rise above the stringencies of the time and in 1937 convinced the proprietor of a local Gunnedah garage to take him on as a trainee automotive mechanic. The following year Harry moved to Sydney to become an Assistant Engineer at the Excelsior Supply

Company. Love blossomed and he became engaged. A war intervened and Harry enlisted on 22 July 1940.

During his pilot's training at Tamworth Harry made the trip west to Gunnedah. At the time Richard was finishing high school and wanted to know everything about flying a Tiger Moth. In 2011 Richard would recall "his description of the take-off and landing, demonstrated with the aid of a Staedtler pencil, stays with me to this day". By late November 1941 Harry was in England and his mood was more cautious when he wrote to his younger brother:

> I expect you are still eager to join up in the RAAF. Just take my advice son, I don't wish to be selfish, but please forget such acts. I know it's hard and they need fellows to do their little bit but there are thousands of others a darn sight more eligible than you who should be doing their bit...these days heroes are many and consequently easily forgotten.

Harry knew on the uninitiated his advice might fall "on deaf ears" so he added "please...don't be a wireless/air gunner unless as a last resort. I say be a pilot-observer".

Another letter arrived in February 1942. "I expect that trying to get into the air force is like winning a State Lottery. It's the pick of the bunch". Harry was concerned for Richard's welfare, but also his country: "You're a true Aussie fighting for a grand country". By the time the letter arrived Richard had been in the army for several months. He had enlisted in the RAAF after his 18th birthday and was told he would begin training within weeks. Whilst awaiting Richard was called up for military service and placed in a machine gun company about to deploy overseas. The letter from the RAAF instructing Richard to report for duty arrived but the army refused to release him and Richard left for New Guinea.

Harry Chinn and his crew had already had a close call during an operation to bomb Dortmund on the night of 14 April 1942. Their RCAF 405 Wellington was struck by flak and limped back to England. Such was the damage that Chinn ordered the crew to bale out over

Hampshire. All survived and immediately became members of "The Caterpillar Club", membership was restricted to those who survived a bale out over land. The pin emblazoned with a caterpillar could never be worn with uniform but it was a novel badge of pride within the ranks of those who flew.

The Caterpillar Club badge.

Left to right: Pickard, Francis, Wood, Bell and Chinn
(courtesy Richard Chinn).

Perhaps the most famous World War II bomber crewman involved with the The Caterpillar Club was one who was denied membership. RAF Flight Sergeant Nicholas Alkemade was a Lancaster tail gunner. On 24 March 1944 the 21 year old was a member of a RAF 115 Squadron

Lancaster crew. On the return trip from bombing Berlin the Lancaster was attacked by a German fighter. The burning bomber began to spiral downwards. With his parachute destroyed by fire Alkemade opted to jump rather than burn to death. His fall from 18,000 feet (5,500 metres) was broken by pine trees and he fell into deep snow. The Rear Gunner survived; his only injury was a sprained leg. Four members of his crew died. To be a member of The Caterpillar Club you had to have baled out with a parachute – there was no criteria for anyone leaving an aircraft without a parachute at 18,000 feet (5,500 metres) and living to tell the tale!

"The Goldfish Club" was formed in World War II in recognition of airmen who parachuted from their damaged aircraft into water. Each member was presented with an embroidered badge. The production of metallic-embroidered badges was prohibited in World War II and all cloth was severely rationed. When news of the club and its elite membership appeared in the British media, the public donated old formal evening wear so the badges could be fashioned with silk embroidery upon black cloth. The badge was worn by aircrew under the flap of their left hand uniform pocket flap so as not to incur a charge for not wearing regulation uniform.

On 29 June 1942 the RCAF 405 Halifax skippered by the 22-year-old Flight Sergeant Harry Chinn, RAAF, flew over the Dutch coast en route to Bremen. Harry and his crew were fatigued. There had been a lot of operations of late: 2 June the target had been Essen; 6 June it was Emden; on 8 June Essen again. Added to that, there had been engine trouble. A few days leave was gratefully received. On 16 June the crew attacked Bonn; 19 June it was Emden and the following night Emden again, and two nights later yet again Emden. On 25 and 27 June Bremen was targeted. Harry was meticulous and thorough yet he had not had the energy to keep his flying log book properly notated – he promised to bring it up to date after his next operation.

The flak was particularly deadly the night of 29 June 1942 and the night fighters unseen until too late. In total 14 bombers were shot out of the sky including the Halifax skippered by Harry Chinn. Harry and his crew of eight were buried with veneration in the Dutch Reform

Churchyard in the village of Noordwolde in Weststellingwerf province. The church had existed since the middle ages and was extended in 1400 and again in the 19th century. Those who preached in this beautiful but modest church were humble men bent on improving the lot of the villagers – it is not difficult to believe the bomber crew of five nationalities would have been comfortable with such a principle. In early autumn 2009 the graves were resplendent with carefully cultivated red and white flowers.

Andries Meijer was a boy when the bomber crashed close to his village and what was left of the crew brought to this churchyard. Life under German occupation was harsh. Atrocities occurred in Noordwolde and Andries has been unable to forget and forgive. Men were taken away to labour camps never to return and there was torture and death of those suspected of belonging to the Dutch underground. There were reprisals too, if villagers were believed guilty of harbouring Allied airmen – five Dutch lives for one harboured ally was a common ratio and vengeance was swift. The Australian, Canadian, American, English and Scottish crew who died on 29 June 1942 represented all that was just in life when villagers felt powerless. Over a lifetime Andries has cared for the graves of this crew who gave their lives in a battle he interprets as one to free the Dutch people. With the help of Bart and Marten Dragtsma and the then Burgemeester, Remco Heite, Andries ensured a memorial

Chinn crew graves in the Dutch Reform Churchyard,
Noordwolde, and Andries Meijer.

was placed where their bomber came to a fiery end. There is another imposing memorial behind the church with the names of the crew on one side, those taken as slave labour on another, and villagers who were killed on yet another. There is a flat memorial stone on a grave beside those of the crew. It is engraved "Thomas H. Verdenius". Andries explains: "He was the local doctor and in the underground. The Gestapo put him in jail. He was uncertain he could withstand the torture without giving others up so he smashed his eye glasses and cut his wrists. It was decided to bury him near the boys (the Allied crew)."

Contact with generations of relatives has survived seven decades since that night in 1942, and they are made to feel very welcome. Crew birthdays and the anniversary of the crash of the Halifax are observed. Andries organises a ceremony attended by Dutch military, a band, schoolchildren and the public here on 4 May each year to observe Remembrance Day. Throughout The Netherlands at 2000 on 4 May the nation pauses. All public and private transport is stopped for two minutes of silence and radio and television broadcast the various ceremonies between the hours of 1900 and 2030. The following day, 5 May, the Dutch celebrate the liberation of their nation from German occupation. To a word of thanks for looking after the graves of the Harry Chinn crew, Andries, without reservation says: "They were your boys, now they are ours and we shall take care of them".

Pilot Officer Henry (Harry) Adolphus Chinn.

Harry's brother Richard was serving with the Australian Army in New Guinea when Harry was reported missing. His parents' generation was one which seldom expressed emotion and struggled to discuss freely, but Richard believes that when his family heard Harry was killed: "It must have been as searing for them as it was for me, even though I probably had a soldier's attitude towards the possibility/probability of 'getting the chop'."

On reflection Richard recalls his own feelings as "disbelief, dismay and anger". It was ironic that Harry was so concerned that Richard not be subjected to combat as a member of the army yet "Harry died, I survived". In 1946 their father Henry received a letter from Mw Verdenius-Bense, the widow of the Noorwolde doctor who was leader of the local Underground and who was buried close to the crew. She described the crash of Harry's Halifax and the crew's final resting place – such was the link forged by war, between Dutch and Australian. Richard would discover after the war that the correct family surname was not Chinn but Echin and he would visit Noorwolde three times. At the age of 87 he would like "one more visit" to Noorwolde and his brother who lies in a grave too far away, "we shall see how I am holding".

For Thomas and Margaret Oneson of Dorval, Quebec, the parents of Sergeant Paul Patrick Augustus Oneson (RCAF), the 26-year-old Wireless Operator/Air Gunner in Harry Echin's (Chinn's) crew, the war dealt another cruel blow. Their misery deepened dramatically when their 20-year-old son, Martin Joseph Oneson, RCAF, was killed in training in September 1945. RAF Sergeant Cyril Wood the Wireless Operator/Air Gunner with Harry when they became members of "The Caterpillar Club" had been ill the night of 29 June and now his regular crew was no more. A month later, Cyril Wood was killed with another RAF 405 crew.

On the last night of July 1942 Air Marshall "Bomber" Harris ordered a raid by 600 bombers against Dusseldorf. "In many respects this operation was typical of what in 1943 became a common event... to reduce the industrial capacity of Germany's industrial heartland."[5] Again Harris used OTUs to make up numbers and again relatively inexperienced crews flying older aircraft suffered most from the relentless German defence. Twelve Australian airmen died this night which was foreseen as being "typical" for the rest of 1942 and for 1943, two became POWs, two Australians evaded capture.

One 27 OTU crew with a New Zealand skipper, Flying Officer Mervyn George McNeil (40239), 25, from Auckland, and five Australians, were given an original Wellington to fly. Flying Officer Arthur Frederick Richard Nash (406576) 27, was a pilot from the Perth suburb of Subiaco. Sergeant Owen Morgan (405450), 27 was the Observer. He was born in Gayndah, Queensland, a town located on the twisting Burnett River. Gayndah proudly wore the mantle of the state's oldest town and had the river been deeper it may well have been Queensland's capital. As it was, the name was indigenous for "thunder" or "place of scrub", no one was quite sure. Owen prided himself in his strong, beautiful penmanship which may well have led him to his career as a cadet draughtsman. He had been working his way up the ladder, pegger out in the Main Roads construction works; then chairman of a survey party; and then Assistant to the Officer-in-charge of Main Roads, in the city of Charleville.

Sergeant Charles Henry Robert McKee (411031) 21, was the Wireless Operator/Air Gunner of this 27 OTU crew. After leaving school the boy from Sydney worked as a telegram messenger; then a junior clerk before becoming a postman. He enlisted on 31st March 1941 and embarked on 20 May for overseas service. The Rear Gunner was Sergeant Clifford Douglas Luedeke (406809) 20, born in Albany, the pretty town with a magnificent view of the Great Australian Bight. Sergeant John Daniel O'Halloran (403991) 32, from Tamworth, NSW, was the Bomb Aimer. The former Christian Brothers, Tamworth, student had always stood out from his peers. When he enlisted on the last day of March 1941 he was a solicitor, proctor, and attorney of the Supreme Court. The Australians had bonded so closely as a crew this man of the law was willing to jeopardise his reputation and RAAF record, by joining the others on an unauthorised run ashore which ended up with severe headaches and severe reprimands for being AWOL for nearly three days. Fines, and loss of pay accompanied the official RAF reprimands but these Australians from different states and different backgrounds, had shared a very memorable time together. Ten days later they were sent in an old Wellington to bomb Dusseldorf. They never made it back, and would remain together in the Huldenberg village churchyard, 15 miles (24 km) from Brussels, Belgium, testament to the terrible sacrifice being made by the neighbouring southern hemisphere dominions.

Ronald Evennett Pearce (403034) was not aware he had been promoted Pilot Officer four weeks earlier when he took off in an RCAF 405 Halifax on the last night of July. He belonged to one nation's air force but was in the charge of another and attached to yet another nation's squadron and things took a while to wind their way through all the red tape. He still wore his flight sergeant stripes when at 0305 the first morning in August his bomber crashed in Belgium. The rear gunner was dead on impact and another crewman would die shortly after. The remaining five took off in different directions. Before long four would be POWs but the Australian refused to be caught. Pilot Officer Ron Pearce had been born on the north side of Sydney harbour. He was an engineering draughtsman when he enlisted in December 1940 at 21 and was mustered six months later as an Air Gunner. The Australian defied the odds to link up with the Underground who guided him to Gibraltar on 8 September and he was back safely in England a week later. He continued to serve and was with No.12 OTU as a Flight Lieutenant when he left the RAAF in January 1946.

Geoffrey Silva (402258) was wearing his Pilot Officer rank when the bomber he was piloting was shot down by two night fighters and crashed at 0400 on the first morning of August. He had certainly drawn the short straw when given a 24 OTU Whitley carrying one 500 lb (quarter ton) bomb to drop on Dusseldorf. Born in Inverell, New South Wales, in March 1916, he enlisted in July 1940, aged 24. As a weaver with a carpet company and with no flying experience Silva was not expected to pass elementary flying school but he did. By 1942 he was in England and his salary was now supporting his widowed mother Amy. On the morning of 1 August Silva saw his RAF rear gunner was dead and with the remaining two RAF crew members was quickly hidden by members of the Belgian Underground. Taken to Brussels they came under the shelter of Elizabeth Marie Eulalie Helene, the eldest daughter of Prince Albert de Ligne, and moved frequently between safe houses along the "Comet line". On 15 August the disguised British airmen were taken by train to France. From there they were guided to Spain. The icy water of the River Bidassoa had to be crossed but within a week they were on their way from Madrid to Gibraltar and then England.

At Buckingham Palace on 15 December 1942, King George VI presented Pilot Officer Geoffrey Silva, RAAF, with a Distinguished Flying Cross. The Australian was then posted to Coastal Command to fly a Catalina with RAF 210 Squadron. On 13 June 1943 he and his crew set off on a patrol in the Bay of Biscay and did not return. Squadron aircraft were instructed to look for signs of the downed Catalina or a dinghy. The Commanding Officer hoped the crew "may have put down near a ship, friendly or otherwise, and have been picked up". There was no trace of the aircraft or crew. Amy Silva put pen to paper in December 1943 and in a letter to the RAAF she wrote: "would it become necessary to immediately presume that my son is dead!" Geoffrey had escaped last time perhaps he had again, "If it is at all possible to delay doing so I would ask you to hold it in abeyance". With the passing of another couple of months she agreed to accept his personal effects. Like other families, when the only son died, a family ceased to exist with the death of parents. In 1979 the RAAF received a letter from a member of the public living in South Australia who had come across some personal effects belonging to a Pilot Officer Geoffrey Silva – he wished to return these to the family. The RAAF advised there had been no contact with Amy Silva since 1949.

Pressure was brought to bear on Air Marshal Harris until he agreed "freshman" crews would now only be sent to close-range, lightly defended targets on the French coast. He was less happy when forced to release six more squadrons, including one Lancaster squadron, to Coastal Command to fight the omnipresent German U-boats which were wreaking havoc on convoys bearing badly needed supplies and men to the United Kingdom. Morale within Bomber Command had been surprisingly high and some believed Harris himself was directly responsible for this. It could also be suggested that this was due to the men themselves. This was unusual military service. Rarely had men formed into such small units as bomber crews. A crew was a tight band of brothers, men who over months, even years, spent seven, eight hours together in a cramped small space on the most exacting operations.

They became more familiar with each other's personality traits and human foibles than they were with those of their own siblings. Shared experiences welded them even more into a team – they depended on each other to stay alive and only men at the pointy end of Bomber Command understood the anxiety, the exhilaration, and the fear. Crew members would forever hold a very special place in their lives.

The full gambit of emotions would have been felt by an RAF 7 Squadron crew which included three Australians, and took off on the night of 26 July on a raid which was described as "probably a full maximum effort for the regular Bomber Command squadrons".[6] No OTUs on this operation but the attack was on Hamburg, a very long journey for a Stirling bomber on an operation marred by cloud and ice. In total 403 aircraft took part and bombing results were claimed to have been good; "823 houses were destroyed and more than 5,000 damaged...14,000 people bombed out. 337 people were killed and 1,027 injured".[7] Aircraft losses were heavy at 7.2 per cent.

The first emotion felt by the 7 Squadron crew may well have been disappointment or even anguish with regards to aircraft, their Stirling had a chequered history – even on the last operation engine trouble and shortage of fuel meant the crew barely made it back to England. They were airborne at 2250 from Oakington, Cambridgeshire. Onboard were four members of the RAF; the pilot was Flight Lieutenant J N Harris; the Flight Engineer was Sergeant A J Roberts, the Middle Upper Gunner was Sergeant E E Blythe and Sergeant W C P Harfoot was the Navigator. Also three Australians: Flying Officer Douglas Percy Leigo (401069) 28, who lived in Ballarat, Victoria, was the Bomb Aimer; Wireless Operator/Air Gunner Sergeant Robert Charles Stewart-Moore (405426) 20, a former Brisbane Clerk; and the Rear Gunner was Sergeant James Humphrey Caldwell (407637). Two among them could truly be called intellectuals. Sergeant William Charles Percival Harfoot, RAF, was an Oxford University graduate with first class honours in classics and was teaching before the war. Flying Officer Douglas Percy Leigo was also a scholar of some distinction, and the 28 year old was teaching at Mt Mercer, Victoria, before his world was turned upside down.

On the run into the target strong searchlights made night turn into day. As soon as the bombs were released Harris dropped altitude turned the aircraft to follow the river Elbe to the coast. They were immediately buffeted by heavy flak which damaged the elevators and shattered the rear turret killing Caldwell. Bright searchlights again coned the descending bomber before it "struck the water, bounced and nosed down into the river, disintegrating". Harris, Stewart-Moore, Blythe, and Roberts, escaped the flooding fuselage. Because of their position in the aircraft the two intellectuals trained as Observers, stood no chance of escape. Leigo at his position in the front turret was likely killed on impact. Similarly Harfoot, probably severely injured, could not escape the sinking plane. Harris observed three coffins being taken away the following day and while the survivors now faced years of captivity they at least had the hope of going home – eventually.

The standard official letters were sent to the Australian next-of-kin advising them that the crew were "missing" but that it remained possible that the crew had escaped and further information would be passed on as soon as the RAAF received it. Doug Leigo's mother Mary wrote that her family "have received private advice by cable from a relative in England, that he was killed in the crash". The RAAF replied that they now had received such confirmation. The family of Sergeant Caldwell a South Australian milkman, who had just celebrated his 28th birthday, were told he was buried in a Dutch cemetery close to the crash site. In 1950 they were advised that this information had been incorrect, that the Stirling had crashed into quicksand, authorities had decided "in the circumstances salvage was impossible" and three bodies would remain with their bomber.

Authorities informed the Leigo and Caldwell families that: "It is proposed to commemorate your son by including his name on a memorial which will be erected at a later date by the Imperial War Graves Commission, to the memory of those deceased members who have no known grave."

The Air Forces Memorial would eventually be erected at Runnymede, in the English county of Surrey. The large impressive sculpture would display engraved glass and painted ceilings. It would list the 20,331 names of airmen who served in Bomber, Fighter, Coastal, Transport, Flying Training and Maintenance with the Royal Air Force who had "no known grave". For the Leigo and Caldwell families it was a strange and sad situation – they knew where the bodies of their sons lay. While it was an honour to have James's name engraved on such a huge memorial in England, his family felt more comforted to have his name also engraved on the roll of honour in their town of Kimba, South Australia, a small town midway between Kyancutta and Port August with a heart large enough to declare itself "midway across Australia".

In the latter part of 1942 and the first months of 1943 morale amongst bomber men dropped. Whilst the first Thousand Bomber raid on Cologne had buoyed their spirits, the later Thousand Bomber raids had not been successful and these were followed by a "disappointing run of raids on targets in the Ruhr".[8] Aircrew losses increased. Despite the resolve and bravery of aircrew, for every successful operation, "there were two or three failures"[9]. By August 1942 the casualty rate was 4.3 per cent, and by the end of the year it was 4.6 per cent. It was impossible not to notice the empty bunks, the personal effects being packed up and removed and the subdued mood in the mess. It was not hard to do the math and figure the chances of surviving a tour were not good. For Bomber Command administrators who worked closely with these figures of death they realised, "a loss rate exceeding 4 per cent would lead to the eventual decline of the force". If aircrew consistently did not survive their first tour there would be a vacuum of experience and leadership. The early Halifax bombers experienced "serious technical difficulties" and between March and August 1942 no fewer than 109 were lost from 1,770 sorties, which meant a casualty rate of 6.2 per cent.[10] Halifax squadrons, 10, 35, 76, 78, 102, 158 and 405 suffered such a morale dip that the whole Halifax force was rested from operations for almost a month.

For some the rest period did not come soon enough. Halifax W1215 belonging to RAF 158 Squadron took off on the night of 5 August to attack Bochum in the German heartland – it would be yet another seven to eight hours flying time. The Captain was RAAF Pilot Officer Clive Henry Phillips (402539) and the Observer was RAAF Pilot Officer

Lesley (Lee) Vincent Harvey (400239). War meant lives took very unexpected turns. In November 1940, Clive Phillips was a pastoralist in the Queensland Cloncurry region, and then he was accepted by the RAAF as "aircrew (Pilot)". When the pilot trainee departed Sydney for overseas service in February 1941 little did he suspect that on the other side of the world he would marry an English girl before the end of the year. Born in Swan Hill, Victoria, Lee Harvey was a Clerk with the Melbourne Branch of the firm Ballarat Trustees. He was only 18 when he began Observer training in July 1940 with no inkling that by August 1942, three days after his 21st birthday, he would be a German POW.

The relationship between pilot and navigator needed to be particularly strong – for other crew to remain confident. This crew was fortunate, their skipper and navigator spoke the same language even if the rest of them didn't always understand some of the Aussie jargon. What was of great importance was that the two Australians relayed professional mutual respect and were obviously good mates. Together since 22 OTU days, Lee was a witness at Clive's marriage to his English bride Dorothy the following November. The crew believed they were as efficient as any other when they took off on the 5 August. With the bombs dropped on the target Clive Phillips turned the Halifax for home. There was gunfire and flashes and the bomber burst into flames. Phillips told his crew to prepare to bale but the voice of Rear Gunner RAF Pilot Officer John Edwin Marshall (117005) crackled over the intercom. He was wounded badly and would be unable to parachute to safety. Crew hesitated and the voice of Phillips was more assertive this time. As five obeyed his order Phillips was left in the cockpit with the rear gunner at the other end of the burning plane. In that split second the man who two years earlier had been a Cloncurry pastoralist decided to crash land in an attempt to save the life of his rear gunner. Before the Halifax began to lose altitude the bomber suffered structural failure, plunged into the ground, and exploded. Lee Harvey was taken POW and wrote to his friend's wife of just months. He hoped it would be of some consolation to know: "Clive's coolness no doubt saved the lives of five of us. He tried to land the aircraft as the rear gunner was wounded. I regarded Clive as my best friend. Please accept the sympathies of myself and the rest of the crew for your great loss. It is difficult to tell how much we admire Clive's action that night."

Bomber Command had been using "raid leaders" to improve the target finding capacity. There were arguments for a Target Finding Force (TFF) consisting of above-average crews flying ahead of the main bomber force. Harris opposed the idea, preferring that the most experienced remain in their squadrons to inspire and encourage newer crews. As 1942 entered its final season Harris was ordered to prepare a TFF. Now there was resistance from the British treasury who were opposed to selected aircrew being promoted by one rank to compensate for the additional danger. By 11 August 1942 all objections were finally overcome and the Pathfinder Force, which would become a legendary arm of the air war, was instigated.

The aviator appointed to lead the Pathfinder Force (PFF), was Australian, Wing Commander Donald Clifford Tyndal Bennett. Donald Bennett was the youngest son of a grazier of the rich soils in the district of Toowoomba, Queensland. Enlisting in the RAAF in 1930 as a 20 year old, he followed the only available route for experience and promotion, and transferred to the RAF. Bennett developed a passion for precise navigation. In 1935, he opted for greater adventure and left the RAF for the nascent world of commercial aviation and Imperial Airlines. For five years he broke long-distance records and pioneered air-to-air refuelling. In 1938 Bennett flew the experimental Mercury-Maia composite flying boat and was awarded the Oswald Watt Gold Medal for the feat. With the outbreak of World War II he re-entered the RAF and was tasked to form the Elementary Air Navigation School at Eastbourne, to train observers. In December 1941 Wing Commander Bennett took over the command of RAF 77 Squadron. When 77 Squadron was transferred to Coastal Command Bennett became Commanding Officer of RAF 10 Squadron. Bennett would continue to inspire – when shot down leading a raid on the battleship Tirpitz he evaded capture and escaped through Sweden. For this he received the DSO in June 1942. A month later he was given the difficult task of organising the "Pathfinder Force". During 1943 Bennett would be promoted to Air Vice Marshal, the youngest to be appointed to the rank. It has been suggested that whilst Bennett was respected he was not well liked – there were those who "didn't like this aloof young Australian and criticised Harris's choice".[11] The dislike stemmed "from some senior officers in the RAF: no doubt some of these individuals resented Bennett" because he was junior to many. At the end of the war he would be the only bomber group commander not knighted. Cynics would suggest it was due to the nationality of his birth but Donald Bennett felt more British than Australian and remained in England after RAF retirement. Although his term was brief he became a British Member of Parliament. He died in England, on 15 September 1986, Battle of Britain Day, at age 76.

It was suggested that in 1942 the Pathfinder Force had "a hotchpotch beginning".[12] Bennett was initially given four squadrons, one from each of the groups, operating four different types of bombers. With Bennett at the helm by April 1945, this had grown to 19 squadrons equipped with Mosquitos and Lancasters. Air crew volunteering for the PFF had to have undertaken at least 30 operational sorties. From them the very best were chosen. Their duties offered the most adrenalin charged operations and also resulted in the most casualties. Initially there were no special "bombs" with which Pathfinders could mark the target and this was done with flares. Within weeks however a "target marking bomb" was produced which made a distinctive coloured burn at or near the target to guide the main bomber force. They were called "Pink Pansies" and though some references were less than polite, bomber crew would be forever grateful for this brilliant burst of pink and the brave men responsible.

Observers were commonly, although not always, "scrubbed" from the pilot stream for their inability to "reach the required standard" – usually as a result of lack of confidence, poor night vision, being unco-ordinated or other reasons. Some were unhappy with what they saw initially as a demotion, but as time progressed, most warmed to their new mustering when they realised how vital they were to a crew and an operation. There were many pre-flight duties to be performed after briefing, a myriad of items to be checked prior to takeoff. In flight the observer kept the aircraft on course; had to obtain a "course fix" every three minutes, plot it, pass the "fix" to the plotter every six minutes for the calculation of the ETA (Estimated Time Arrival) on target. Wind velocity and direction needed to be calculated every 20 minutes, and the pilot given the course and speed changes required to get to turning points and the target on time. It took meticulous timing to fulfil the bombing operation, to avoid heavily defended positions, and to find the shortest route home. He could never relax and spent his time on complicated mathematical problems. If blind bombing was necessary the observer set the bomb switches to drop the flares and bombs at proper intervals.

Henry Hume Turnbull.

Raymond de Champfleur Darken.

Stephen Falcon Scott McCullagh.

Donald Ernest Cameron Charlwood.

The Observer sat at a narrow table with barely enough room for his charts. Under the table a mass of protruding electrical connections effectively prevented any straightening of legs for many hours. With the advent of the heavies, Bomber Command at last realised that an observer was responsible for too much -- front gunner, navigator and bomb aimer. It was extremely difficult to move from a brightly lit plotting chart to the darkened area of the bomb sight. Their multifarious duties were finally reduced in April 1942 when the observer was split into the categories of navigator and air bomber/bomb aimer; and more air gunners added with the advent of heavy bombers.

Flying Officer Henry Hume Turnbull (418211) was the son of a Toorak medical doctor and was studying at university when he enlisted on 25 April 1942. Wearing his "O" half wing, Turnbull expected to be posted to heavy bombers. Instead Turnbull found himself with RAAF 461 Squadron flying in Sunderlands. Introduced in 1938 the Flying Boat carrying a ton of bombs and depth charges proved useful in the destruction of U-Boats. The German nickname for the Sunderland was the Fliegendes Stachelschwein (Flying Porcupine) because of the prominent protruding antennae, and the aircraft's defensive firepower. One aviation specialist referred to the Sunderland as "when attacked the plane was almost impregnable"[13] In October 1944 Turnbull's pilot was Australian Flight Lieutenant Herbert Marshall Godsall (429427), a 31-year-old Toowoomba solicitor married to Margaret with a two-year-old daughter Eleanor. Wireless Operator/Air Gunner was Warrant Officer Percival Richard Criddle (417621) who had been a clerk with Dalgety & Co., Naracoorte, South Australia. The crew were killed when their aircraft was attacked by not one but three ME110s and the Sunderland crashed into the sea. Turnbull and Criddle were both 21.

Aircraftsman, later Flying Officer Stephen Falcon Scott McCullagh (403754) was born in the green and pretty US city of Seattle, Washington, before settling on Sydney's North Shore. A clerk with the AMP Society before enlisting in March 1941, he was posted as a Navigator to RAAF 460. He and his crew took off in Lancaster ED391 on the night of 29/30 March 1943 to bomb Berlin. ED391 was shot down by a night fighter and the crew were buried in the Dutch Village of Hardenberg. AC, later Flight Sergeant Raymond De Champfleur Darken (411096) was born in Parkes. The 26 year old was a teacher prior to enlistment and expected to wear the "O" half wing until his badge was changed to "N". His Lancaster was shot down by anti-aircraft fire during an attack on

Essen on the night of the 21/22 January 1943. Also onboard were two other Australians, Sergeant John Charles Dangerfield (407965) from Adelaide, and Sergeant Francis Alexander Kevin Gallagher (403464) of Sydney. Their remains would stay in Germany in Reichswald Forest War Cemetery.

Flight Lieutenant Donald Ernest Cameron Charlwood (408794) was born in Melbourne in September 1915. He tried his hand at several occupations but most enduring was his love of writing and his short stories and articles supplemented his wages. Unlike some of his fellow aircrew trainees he was hoping he wouldn't be considered for pilot. He survived the initial six week Initial Training Scheme (ITS) course at Somers, Victoria, and with classmates faced the Category Selection Committee. "Many of those confident of becoming pilots faced bitter disappointment". Charlwood "hoped to be a navigator" and was pleased when so selected. He was soon on the ship to Canada and in his Observer Class of 25 "there were at least seven scrubbed pilots". His was EATS Course 35 of the EATS No.2 Air Observers Training School. For six months he applied himself to the difficult courses and completed around 160 hours flying. Twenty of his course qualified as navigators and he would name them the "Twenty Men" .

Like Don Charlwood, observer/navigators were; "inclined to be quiet, reserved types: considered the least warlike of the aircrew members". For outwardly exuberant, red blooded Aussie boys this description may not have been popular but they soon realised how difficult both their training and bomber duties were. They also heard quickly of navigational errors which led to death, like the first crash involving a RAAF 460 crew following its formation in mid November 1941. It was a training exercise and Wellington Z1327 set off from Breighton at 1920 for a night cross country heading for Peterborough and Harwell. Returning to base the aircraft strayed from its track and while descending crashed into a cottage and nearby woods and burst into flames, at Farnley Tyas, SSE of Huddersfield Yorkshire. Onboard was a crew of six – including two Australians, both Air Gunners, Sergeant Robert Litchfield Tresidder (402894) 26, from Melbourne and New South Welshman Sergeant James Henry Ware (402897) 24, from Sydney. They were buried in a quintessential English churchyard, the 13th century All Saint's in Holme-Upon-Spalding Moor, Yorkshire. In time another house would be built where the Wellington crashed – it would be called Phoenix Cottage.

Wallace Martin and Arthur Hoyle were two such Aussie boys, both re-mustered from the pilot stream, one not entirely happy with the transition, one was; one would survive the war and one would not. Arthur Hoyle couldn't wait until he was old enough to join them. He would be a "daring young pilot" he told himself. He was studying at university to be a teacher and was "overwhelmed by excitement" the day he entered the RAAF. "I looked on joining the RAAF as possibly the greatest adventure of my life...which indeed it turned out to be".[14] His ideal of being a pilot altered. The selection board decided that as he was a university student, "thought to be academic", he should enter as a navigator. It took little convincing before Arthur decided that "the most interesting job in aircrew belonged to the navigator". He was sent to Cootamundra to join No.1 Air Observers' School. He found the course exacting and it wasn't the mathematics which tripped him up but the "mania for smartness" and immaculate uniform kit demanded by the Commanding Officer. It was standard practice for trainees to be less than respectful of their commanding officers but this was particularly the case of young men preparing themselves for war when viewing permanent RAAF officers who had not seen action.

Arthur Hoyle found that although he enjoyed studying navigation:

Navigation was still far from being an exact science. After learning to do dead reckoning plots on the ground – the so-called "dry swims" – we were finally allowed to get airborne to practise it in the air. ...I had coped on the ground, but...after all, the aircraft could not stop still while I caught up with my plotting. I might get lost and be humiliated.[15]

He need not to have worried because he was so busy his anxiety was forgotten and his confidence rose as his ability to find the towns, which were turning points on the triangular routes, increased enough not to have to suffer "the sneers of the bored pilots who only wished to go off to war". The progression to night flying did however increase the pressure. Always in the back of his mind was the doubt that he would be good enough to apply his expertise in war conditions, at night, over Europe.

His awe of the aged Avro Ansons had waned, not only did they not "exactly leap into the air", the twin engine wooden monoplane was very underpowered, not to mention the laborious 141 turns it took to wind up the retractable undercarriage. "As a machine of war, I cannot imagine that it frightened anyone". Then there was "an incident". On his next trip in the Anson, the aircraft seemed even slower than normal. The pilot unfortunately chose to continue. At some point Hoyle felt fear and the thought "we're going to prang" was unavoidable. The aircraft hit a sloping bank, started to climb, stalled and nosed down straight into the ground. There was much tearing and crunching and the engines ripped off as the Anson disintegrated. Here in Cootamundra in July 1942, "thousands of miles from the battle zone" he received a "war wound" when his head hit the radio. Though a little embarrassed Hoyle hoped it would be the last he would receive.

Now promoted to the lofty heights of Leading Aircraftsman, there was a propeller on his sleeve and his pay increased from six to ten shillings per day (45 to 76 cents). "I would liked to have been a dashing young airman" but as he neither drank or smoked and "hardly knew a girl", he wasn't quite sure how to begin. Next he was sent to Evans Head on the New South Wales central coast for bomb aimer training. Training aircraft was now the single-engine, and elderly light bomber, Fairey Battle trainer. The Bomb Aimer trainee was required to lie on his belly mid-aircraft trying to judge the release point for the practice bomb. This required hanging precariously, over a large hole which once housed an underbelly gun. With very little of the body actually in contact with the airplane there were some fairly scary moments. Hoyle survived and was delighted he wasn't one of those who had released the bomb sight instead of the bomb. Even so he admitted he was "never more than a slightly below average bomb aimer – a fact which caused me little worry".[16]

Next came gunnery training which made him affirm again why he really, really, just wanted to be a navigator – and perhaps why he should never completely trust a pilot. Aloft at 4,000 feet (1,220 metres) awaiting the drogue to shoot at, the pilot became bored and decided to break off into aerobatics without telling the two trainee gunners. While turning into the loop Hoyle realised his body was not actually attached to the aircraft in any form and due to the centrifugal force he was upside down. The pilot then rolled the aircraft at the top of the loop. It was at this stage that the trainee who had worshipped aircraft as a 15 year old questioned that faith; "I popped out of the aircraft like a cork out of a bottle, desperately clutching the coaming with my fingers". His right leg from the knee down was wedged inside the aircraft – the rest of him was not. With the wind tearing at his body his fingers began to lose their grip on the aluminium. As the terror became numbing the aircraft turned right way up and he fell back into the Fairey Battle. The face of the other trainee was ashen and the two teenagers clung together until the aircraft landed and with wobbly knees they crept out "too shaken to abuse the pilot".

Soon the 19 year old was in Parkes flying in Ansons again studying astro navigation, "trying to catch elusive stars in the sextant bubble". There seemed hardly time for a thought about "taking an active part in the war". It was October 1942, Arthur Hoyle had just turned 20, and proudly sewed on his Observer's half wing and Sergeant's chevrons. He felt very pleased with himself as he walked down the streets of Sydney thinking about his friends in the Sydney University Regiment. Those who referred to him in tones of derision as a "Brylcreem boy" or a "Blue Orchid", who had not volunteered for overseas service, were conscripted, turned into an anti-aircraft unit, and sent to Meruke, New Guinea. Hoyle waited anxiously for his posting. Being steeped in British history since early childhood he wanted to be based in England and was elated when those orders arrived. "With no real idea of what the future was to hold I went home, full of excitement, to tell my parents. It was truly harrowing for them. Well educated by the horrific casualties of World War I, they had no illusions that they might be saying goodbye to me forever."[17]

Unlike Hoyle, Wallace Martin was a country boy. He grew up on the family property Splitter's Creek near Murrurundi in the Upper Hunter Shire, of New South Wales. When the rain fall was good and the Page's River ran it was a most beautiful part of Australia. Splitter's Creek was surrounded by the beautiful blues and greens of the mountains of the Liverpool Range. Wallace was a middle child of a family of six children but with a different personality than his sibling. His mother, Mary Martin, tried hard to hide her favouritism for him. Wallace was particularly close to older sister Heather. With just around a year between them they rode to school on the same horse until old enough to have their own. Wallace was wonderful with horses. Some called him the "horse whisperer". He was a gentle man with a sense of humour and love of the adventure of life and became a member of the district's militia 16th Light Horse Regiment. It was however, flying that grabbed his attention. Wallace wrote "grazier" by the question of "Trade or Profession?" on his RAAF application. He thought he was at a disadvantage because he believed the air force preferred men who had flown or at least had operated equipment rather than horses. He was told he would have to wait and the waiting list was long.

Grazier, Wallace Martin from Murrurundi, received notification that he was to report for recruit training on 19 August 1940 and he became RAAF 402450. He would have liked to be a pilot but was mustered as an Observer. Martin saw a good bit of Australia as his courses came and went. Mallala, South Australia, was where he soon found himself. This was large dry plain country, wheat country, "very dusty in dry weather and the mud sticks to everything".[18] He yearned for the colours of Splitter's Creek. Wallace and a couple of mates would get into Adelaide on leave – three days off every fortnight. They had very little money so were pleased that funds raised by the School Children's Patriotic Fund resulted in accommodation called "The Cheer up Hut" which was "comfortable". "Adelaide is a nice place and has some beautiful parks and creeks running through them". If he stood with his eyes closed and listened to the water he could almost feel at home. Wallace hired a row boat and managed some time on the Torrens River. His course was held up by wet weather and he was itching to get flying again. "I had 85 hours flying at Temora in Tiger Moths, they are better than the Ansons we will be flying here, you can't do acrobatics in these and that was the best part of the flying at Temora, we had to be able to do all the acrobatics solo at Temora. Flying upside down, loops, spins, slow rolls off the top of the spin, some of the chaps didn't like it much, but it will do me."

By April 1941 he was onboard ship heading for Canada – and the trip seemed to be taking forever! It took a lot to make Wallace Martin lose his sense of humour but he wrote home how "unpleasant lying in bed with a couple of dreadfully sick men in your cabin" was, even if you realised how fortunate you were not to suffer sea sickness. Like Australian aircrew trainees before and after him, Wallace was enthralled with the "lovely scenery...great long gorges...beautiful fir trees and pines drooping with feet of snow" as his train crawled up through the Canadian Rockies. Quickly he was in a faster tempo, caught up in the concentrated navigator's course "there is a terrific lot of study...a terribly hard course at Edmonton". Subjects like "Dead Reckoning, Magnetism, Compasses, Instruments Navigation, Photography, Metrology Maths, Reconnaissance Morse" took care of the six one-hour lectures during the day and another two hours at night. To fight the cold they were given "bearskin overalls to wear under our flying suits". He thought of his brothers Jack and Bruce and wrote: "Get a pilot's course or nothing... the observer's course is far too tough", particularly as they, "both loathe maths". He thought of his mother who had spent her life raising six children and working hard to keep the farm going, and asked his sister, Heather, if she could check with Australian Customs on how much duty he would need to pay if he purchased a "silver fox fur" for their mother Mary. Wallace was counting the days until he could sew on his wing with its distinctive "O" – "three months all going well!" and then perhaps, "a commission in four months". From there it was to Mossbank, to study Bombing and Gunnery for five weeks. There were around 1,200 trainees in camp which was a few too many for this country boy, "the living is not so good". He was happy with his progress and entirely infected by the flying bug "Well! I have got quite into the way of this flying business". In Fairey Battles, "it is a thrill diving at the target at 260 mph (418 k/h), the ground just jumps up at you". He already had 81 hours flying time and expected another 40 hours before he was finished at Mossbank. It was fun to dive on "prairie wolves and chase them across the prairies about 30 yards (27 metres) above the ground", sometimes they would pass them and the aircraft's slipstream "knocks them over". Sons commonly wrote excitedly of adrenalin-charged adventures to their mothers, unaware that such evoked very different emotions, and in this Mary was no exception. So, too, the news that Wallace was destined for a "bomber squadron" and perhaps a few trips as a "co-pilot".

Wallace described the snow in Canada as simply amazing, but after a while the chill began to take its toll and the first signs of spring were very welcome: "There are thousands of pussy willow and fir trees beginning to shoot". His departure for the UK was now much closer and he believed he was totally prepared it would take him even further away than "Splitters Creek". Photos sent from home made him, "homesick when I saw all the old scenery of home", and he particularly missed his horse "Toby". He wondered if "Toby" would be "worn-out...by the time I get back or I will be too old to ride him". Wallace even found himself thinking how it was "strange here not seeing any sheep". With four other country boys he entered a team in a local horse show, in which they rode against the Canadian army. Wallace, as captain of the team, was delighted that the Aussie boys won the competition even on horses which were far inferior than those they "were used to riding at home". Wallace admitted: "It would be great to get back for a couple of days to see the old Hunter in its bloom".

His mind was nonetheless never far from the war and flying. He had warmed to his mustering, navigation: "I think piloting a bomber on a long trip would be a very uninteresting and monotonous event". In the letters to his father John, there was still an element of bravado, something missing in his letters to his mother. About to board the ship which would take him across the Atlantic he wrote: "Dad, we will make Germany pay for all that they have given so far and they shall pay damn dear". At the same time he acknowledged that this war had put the family sons in uniform and his father was working much harder: "How are things running at home Dad? You want to take them easy old chap and don't worry over anything these days as life is too short now and one never knows what is ahead. I think that you should get rid of a few of your worries by selling out and getting a small comfortable place somewhere."

Finally Wallace was on his way to England and marvelled about the "cosmopolitan lot" of men on the ship. He was soon on an OTU and the possibility of not coming home entered his mind though he tried to gloss over this as best he could. "I will cable you for the first 'Hun' I get. Of course if the cable doesn't come you will understand that the boot is on the other foot". His letters now focussed on the seriousness of war how: "Quite a number of those boys that I introduced you to have gone west...it is very sad but we must expect to lose a few and it is just too bad for some of us."

Wallace had bonded with Allan Thomas Gell, nicknamed Jelly. The two men helped each other through basic training and Wallace took Allan home to meet the family – there was an immediate connection between Allan and Wallace's favourite sister Heather. She had grown up very pleasingly since they shared a horse. Allan and Heather began to correspond and although Wallace gave his mate a hard time over it he was quietly very pleased. Both were country lads although Allan's home district of Cunnamulla, Queensland, was very different from the Hunter region. They travelled around the world and helped each other through the tougher courses and spent rare free time together. Both were sent to different squadrons which disappointed.

LEFT: *Wallace and Heather Martin.* RIGHT: *Observer Wallace Martin.*

In February 1942 Sergeant Allan Gell (402440) wrote to the Martin family: "I have not heard from Wallace for about three weeks, and am getting worried". Allan was already weary from many night bombing operations and had lost too many classmates. He wondered if his increasing sense of doom had not got the best of him. But Wallace had indeed been involved in another "crack up" and was in hospital. Not wishing to worry his family Wallace told everyone well after the event and made light of being "shot up over France". He failed to mention the injury which nearly resulted in the amputation of his leg. Being one of the early bomber airmen like Allan Gell, Wallace was suffering from fatigue and concerned about the "invasion" of Australia. "I really wish that I was at home now to lend a hand but the work I am on here now I hope will benefit us indirectly."

Mates continued to die; "Most of the old brigade have been bumped off...I am now the only Aussie on the squadron". He felt frustrated by the lack of progress and the loss of life, becoming increasingly angry: "This government is like ours, pretty sleepy". Wallace struggled to understand how what he and other Australians were doing in Bomber Command, simply appeared expected, almost taken for granted. "I think they will fully realise the importance of our country to the Empire". Perhaps then, "we may get a little more consideration". It was upsetting, a mate from Murrurundi, Sergeant Roger Bede Murphy (403143) a fellow grazier, never made it out of training with 23 OTU, "killed in a flying accident on 3 January 1942". The first Roger's wife heard of her husband's death, was a telegram telling her: "The funeral of your husband took place at 3 pm on the 9 January 1942 at Pershore Cemetery, Worcestershire". Wallace would take a photo of "Roger's grave to send home". On the same night-flying exercise was another Australian, 20-year-old Sergeant Bernard Bradley Connell (403041) from Sydney, was also killed. In an almost off-hand manner Wallace finished one letter home abruptly with "my pal" 21-year-old Sergeant John Shannon (404264) from Nebo, near Mackay, Queensland, who was flying with a 6 OTU crew, "was hit with flak while carrying a land mine and they all blew up".[19]

Night raids were held up by bad weather so Wallace and his crew were sent out on daylight operations when "one gets his share of opposition". His existence defied explanation – how could his family living peacefully on a Murrurundi farm understand – and yet he knew he could never put it into words. His language had to be forever guarded for fear of worrying his mother in particular. "This is a marvellous experience for anyone who can survive". He admitted that this "marvellous experience" resulted in his drinking much heavier which in turn resulted in a "terrible headache" the following morning. His wellbeing changed for the better when he was invited to spend his leave with the Jeffrey Family on their Scottish farm. "Had one grand time... Gee I did enjoy my leave". Not only was it a relief to get away from stressful duty, to be on a working farm again, but it became especially enjoyable when his hostess introduced Wallace to her niece. The initial shyness between the two was brief and the Australian Navigator simply decided this Scottish lass was meant for him. The letters and phone calls were many, Wallace felt invigorated and now looked to the future. "Jess is 18 years old quite a tall girl, good looking, has a wonderful personality". This war was so still a rollercoaster, full of exhilaration and adrenalin and Wallace admitted: "Despite the fact that my nerves are a little shaken I still get a great kick out of the ops but would certainly like a change to night raids again."

But now he looked forward to getting away from the base as quickly as he could to meet up with Jessie whenever she too was off duty. It was the most surreal setting for romance, a few hours snatched from a war like none other. There was time spent together in bomb shelters as German aircraft attempted to destroy the British war machine and the spirit of those sheltering in Britain. Then Wallace would return to base and fly across the English Channel to bomb cities in an attempt to destroy the German war machine and the spirit of those sheltering within.

SIX

*Although my son is believed killed...I still hope
that he is coming back.*

Abi Olive Keats

The world was changing rapidly. On 7 December 1941 the Australian prime minister, John Curtin, had announced in a nationwide broadcast: "Men and women of Australia. We are at war with Japan. This is the gravest hour of our history. We Australians have imperishable traditions. We shall maintain them. We shall vindicate them. We shall hold this country and keep it as a citadel for the British-speaking race and as a place where civilisation will persist."

On 19 February 1942, Darwin, the most northern capital, suffered the first and the largest single attack by a foreign power against Australia, and would be known as "Australia's Pearl Harbour". Some 240 Japanese aircraft attacked the city's airfields and shipping in Darwin's harbour. In this and a second attack that day, 252 military personnel and civilians died. On 3 March Broome, in Western Australia, was strafed and 88 died. Over the following months Japanese aircraft attacked many towns in northern Australia including Port Hedland, Wyndham and Derby in Western Australia. Darwin and another Northern Territory town, Katherine, were also subjected to air attacks, as were Mossman and Townsville in Queensland, and Horn Island in the Torres Strait.

On 31 May 1942 Japanese midget submarines released their torpedoes in Sydney Harbour and 21 sailors died. Eight days later it was the NSW port of Newcastle. In total, 80 sailors were killed in submarine attacks on shipping along the NSW coast over the next month.

In January 1942, the Australian government formed the Directorate, later renamed, The Commission of Manpower, to oversee the composition and direction of Australia's human resources. On 19 February 1943, the Defence (Citizen Military Forces) Act was passed, which allowed conscripted military men to fight in areas of South East Asia south of the equator. Although manpower control and conscription challenged national tradition, Australians accepted it was now the duty of every citizen to defend their country or support those who did. The burgeoning military forces created dire labour shortages. Women took up the shortfall moving into factories and other vital industries. Australians were issued identification cards with name and address of employer – curiously age and marital status were included on those of the nation's women. The Women's Australian Auxiliary Air Force (WAAAF); the Australian Women's Army Service (AWAS) and the Women's Royal Australian Naval Service (WRANS) were formed, and women in uniform took over military support positions to free men for front line service.

A great deal had changed since Hilda Ludlow listened to prime minister Robert Menzies' announcement in September 1939 that Australia was at war in Europe and like most of her generation, wondered how it would change lives. Blackouts, censorship, food rationing and petrol rationing were introduced. Industry began to concentrate on war production. It was nonetheless the increasing number of killed and missing that made war more of a reality. Growing up, Hilda Ludlow had been keen on John Mackay whose parents owned the corner store in her Brisbane riverside suburb of Toowong. John Mackay and his mate Tom Freeman put their names down for the RAAF early but needed to wait for training programmes to speed up. Tom Freeman, a gentle quiet man of six feet (1.8 metres), was accepted in July 1940. He had been studying X-ray Engineering for three years and that impressed recruiters. During flight training he excelled. By March 1941 he was a Flight Sergeant pilot and departed for the United Kingdom the following month. Tom had a natural prowess for fighters and by July 1941 had completed 170 hours on Spitfires and 19 hours on Hurricanes. John Mackay was accepted by the RAAF in June 1941 and delighted in making it through pilot training at Temora and Wagga Wagga in NSW. Sadly, in August 1942, the month he was promoted to Pilot Officer and embarked for the UK, his mother Elsie died of cancer.

Max Norris was impatient, his personal future looked bright as he and Hilda made wedding plans, but Max was in Queensland's 61st Battalion, the Cameron Highlands, and plans to deploy the regiment overseas were still indefinite. Finally Max was released from both the army and the Commonwealth Bank and accepted by the RAAF in August 1942. Even with the optimism of youth it was difficult for Hilda not to worry. Her patriotic sentiments had strengthened with the enemy at the gate of Australia; and she was proud to have a fiancé and close male friends serving with the RAAF, though there seemed to be an inordinate number of youthful faces in air force uniform featured in the obituary columns of *The Courier Mail* and this was just one state's daily newspaper. The true losses were far worse than she could have imagined and as with so many of her generation and that of their parents, the death of men in RAAF blue would soon bring personal grief.

As the momentum of RAF Bomber Command operations increased, more and more Australians died. On 20 August 1942 alone the RAAF Casualty Section received a cable with 174 names of RAAF bomber aircrew who had been killed or taken POW. The section struggled to keep up and invariably did not. Australians had been in the thick of the bombing of Duisburg on 6/7 August. Five types of aircraft took part in the 216-strong force, with the loss of nine and their crews. Of the three Stirling Is; the Hampden I, three Halifax and two Wellingtons[1], which did not return, Australians were on four. One of the Stirling's was skippered by a New Zealander. The entire crew were killed, including the Tail Gunner, 26-year-old Sergeant Samuel Leach Hore (401217), who signed on in his native Melbourne on 4 January 1941 "for the duration of the war and a period of 12 months thereafter". Sergeant

Hore posted from 20 OTU to RAF 7 Squadron on 29 July 1942, and died just eight days later. His mother Rita asked for more information, any information which would help her understand the circumstances of her son's death. Due to censorship and lack of RAF communication the Casualty Section could offer nothing further than that Samuel was killed in an operation over Germany and marked the file: "All available details as known to this department were conveyed to next-of-kin". Rita Hore was unaware that Bomber Command Commander-in-Chief, Arthur Harris had complained to the Ministry of Aircraft Production about the Stirling bomber; "it's murder, plain murder to send young men out to die in an aircraft like that".[2] In 1951 she received a photograph of a simple white cross bearing her son's name.

Sergeant Karl Hugo Eklund (404887) was a 21 year old from Brisbane who was the pilot of a Hampden shot down over the North Sea on 24 February 1942. His family struggled with his death and the lack of information. Hugo Eklund wrote asking what was the type of aircraft his son was flying in? Was Karl alone? If not alone what were the names of those with him? Where was he flying? The questions were normal for a father who had lost his son. The answer came three weeks later and was brief – most of the information could not be provided – there was a war on. In December 1942 some of Karl's effects arrived at the Eklund home. Hugo wrote enquiring of the rest. Months later the RAAF Casualty Section sent Karl's identity disc without explanation – perhaps none was needed.

The family of Gilbert Carrington Keats (407794) owned property near Orroroo north of South Australia's Port Augusta. He had graduated from University of Adelaide in Law and was an Articled Clerk in his father's law firm. His father, 2nd Lieutenant Frederick Phillips Keats, had been a member of the 17th Australian (South Australian Mounted Rifles) Light Horse. Frederick did not share his son's eagerness to enlist a month after war was declared in Europe. Gilbert attempted to sway his father arguing that the new way of war, in the air, was safer than World War I trench warfare, and submitted his enlistment papers to be a RAAF Gunner. His father was unwell and Gilbert withdrew from the RAAF trainee list citing "domestic" reasons. He tried to be patient but expressed concern that if he did not join soon the war might be over. Gilbert re-applied and was accepted for pilot training.

On the night of 2 July 1942 Sergeant Gilbert Keats was the pilot skipper of a RAF 12 Squadron Wellington tasked to bomb Bremen. He had just received news that his father had died. With the bombs gone they were on their way back to Binbrook when attacked by a Ju 88. With no starboard engine Keats struggled to keep the aircraft aloft. Steadily losing height Keats succeeded in making the English coast and force-landed near the town of Cromer, Norfolk. His British crew acclaimed their 25-year-old pilot's ability.

On the night of 13/14 July the crew took off to bomb Duisburg. On the return flight they struck a storm bank. With "weather very bad with frequent electric storms rendering wireless reception bad" Keats made for the closest airfield, the North Weald fighter base.[3] Dodging manmade hazards the Australian overshot the airfield but brought the Wellington to a stop with minor bumps and bruises to himself and crew. His Commanding Officer believed Keats could not be blamed for "crashing" the Wellington. The report concluded that although still fairly inexperienced Keats was "full of guts and determination" and "unmoved" by the two recent operational mishaps.

On 6/7 August the operation was yet again, the Ruhr Valley city of Duisburg. It would not be third-time lucky – a German night fighter destroyed any chance of the Wellington and crew returning. Having lost her husband in June, Abi Olive Keats was ill-prepared to accept her only son had been killed. RAAF officialdom wished to close his file and needed acknowledgement. Abi Olive was in no such haste: "Although my son is believed killed, have I got to have his affairs fixed up? I still hope that he is coming back." She tried not to accept the truth until October 1943 when she admitted defeat. She then wrote again to the RAAF seeking copies of official letters: "I am sorry to trouble you for I know you are very busy but unfortunately owing to the fact that I couldn't bear the notices to be about I burnt all the notices sent me by your office in connection with the death of my beloved son."[4]

In civilian life, Robert (Bob) Wilson Baxter, was a Bank Clerk, a very respectable but not the most exciting of careers. Then a war came and he enlisted in the RAAF in October 1940, writing "Air Crew" as his preference. Bob Baxter wondered how he would react in combat, would he instinctively respond under great stress, and in dangerous situations, and would he come close to the gung ho hero popularised by Hollywood? Operational life for Bob Baxter officially commenced, with RAF 150 in October 1941 though in reality it occurred when he was with 21 OTU from 26 July 1941. By May 1942 he was a seasoned veteran, yet still only 24.

On 5 May he was the Captain of a Wellington and an all RAF crew that took off at 2235 to bomb Stuttgart. The bomber was hit by anti-aircraft fire over the target damaging the port engine. Baxter used all of his training and operational experience to maintain height. Once the English coast was in sight his wireless operator radioed the urgent need to make an emergency landing. The closest airfield was not prepared and in the semi-darkness Baxter failed to see an unlit obstruction. The Wellington collided and burst into flames. Baxter and other crew scrambled free of the burning wreck but quickly realised the wireless operator was missing. Ammunition and pyrotechnics exploded as the flames intensified. Baxter ran back into the blazing fuselage to find the wireless operator trapped in the lower escape hatch. He bashed and kicked at buckled metal until he could pull the injured crewman free and drag him away just before the fuel tanks exploded. The Australian sustained extensive second degree burns to his face, feet and hands and was taken to hospital. The Bank Clerk born in Ballarat, Victoria, was awarded the George Medal for gallantry for "unselfish heroism displayed which undoubtedly saved the life of a comrade". After extensive treatment Baxter re-joined the squadron on 13 July. On 7 August 1942 Flight Sergeant Bob Baxter was again skipper of a Wellington which lifted off at 0040 to bomb Duisburg. Just after gaining height the bomber twisted, plummeted into the ground and burst into flames – this time there was no escape.

RAF Bomber Command would officially record that the 6/7 August attack on Duisburg was the last of five raids over three weeks on the German city, of which, "only one had resulted in significant industrial damage". On this last attack "Most of the bombs fell in open country west of the target". It was believed "18 buildings destroyed, 66 seriously damaged and 24 people killed".[5] Nine bombers were lost on this last raid, 37 aircrew died with yet further airmen injured or becoming POWs.

An aircrew first tour of duty consisted of 30 operations. After a short rest, aircrew were expected to undertake a second tour of 20 operations. Aircrew who wished to remain operational after a second tour could continue, but officially no crew would be asked to continue after that number. Often, however, there was crew peer-pressure to continue. By the second part of 1942, operational fatigue became an issue.

One of the participating bombers in the 6/7 August Duisburg attack was an RAF 158 Squadron Halifax piloted by RAAF Flight Lieutenant Jeffrey Peter Meurisse Haydon (402352). Also onboard was Victorian, Observer, Flying Officer Ivan Henry Davies (400528) a company director in his former life. The RAAF had curiously chosen to record on Haydon's October 1940 application that his family were living in the Royal Military College, "Duntroon, ACT, in the state of NSW". Haydon was working as a public servant in Canberra, ACT, which really wasn't part of NSW. Two months into RAAF training he married Clarice and she saw him embark for the UK the following May. On 7 August the Halifax lifted into the air at 0029 loaded with bombs and the 1,512 gallons (5,725 litres) of fuel needed to last for seven to eight hours flying time. Flak pierced the bomber and as a blaze took hold Haydon ordered his crew to bale out. There had been practice at a landlocked tower on how to leave an aircraft but it was very different when leaving a blazing bomber and falling into an unfamiliar environment. Twenty-three-year-old New Zealander, Sergeant Will Gray (405484), did not reply to Haydon's call and the Australian skipper realised the rear gunner was unlikely to have survived the attack. As he pulled himself towards the escape hatch Haydon saw that his 22-year-old RAF Wireless Operator/Air Gunner, Sergeant Harry Huddless (10150628), was dead. Haydon threw himself into cold empty space. His descent was rapid and panic clawed at his gut. Thoughts were confused before the drilled reaction kicked in and the ripcord was pulled. There was an urgent jerk skywards as the canopy filled, hugging the blackness. The view downwards was no less terrifying.

Observer, Flying Officer Davies, managed to evade capture and after months with the Underground made it back to Britain.[6] Haydon was also fortunate as he landed near the home of Belgian Martin Jansen who quickly took him into hiding, and then into the hands of the "Comet Escape and Evasion organisation". Haydon was escorted through Spain to Gibraltar. A Royal Navy ship returned him to England and Haydon was posted as an instructor to a conversion unit. Things did not go well and it was decided to repatriate him to Australia. The confidential report said "his conduct is exemplary at all times. When physically recovered from the effects of his operational tour" he would be capable of undertaking "any allotted task". His Commanding Officer concurred, Haydon while obviously "operationally tired" still "retained the characteristics of a good officer". Jeffrey Haydon was struggling with his combat experience, two dead crew, whom, as skipper, he felt responsible for, but also the news that his younger brother, 26-year-old Private Malcolm Raynor Meurisse Haydon (NX687), serving with the 2nd/20th Australian Infantry Battalion, had been killed in action in a war on the other side of the world. The pilot disembarked at Sydney on 22 January 1944 to be greeted by a pleased but grieving family.

Flight Lieutenant Jeffrey Peter Meurisse Haydon, DFC, RAAF.

Haydon wore the DFC which came with the citation: "This officer has displayed great gallantry and determination in attacking targets in enemy occupied territory" – he should have had nothing more to prove but was posted to Northern Australia. Haydon flew another 373.55 hours but was not recommended for promotion and was simply graded "average" by another Commanding Officer. Many more Australian aircrew would return tired, unsettled and sickened by their experience, to an Australia which could not understand, and an Australian-based RAAF which did not either.

RAAF 460 Squadron was suffering the loss of too many. One Halifax, one Lancaster and 30 Wellingtons were lost to 460 during 1942. In August alone five aircraft and their crews did not return; on the night of 4/5 while "gardening" a crew were killed; 9/10 a crew against Osnabruck; 12/13 a crew against Mainz; 27/28 against Kassel two crews; against Saarbrucken on 28/29 another crew.

The small island state of Tasmania claimed 58 of the 106 Australians named "Viney" who served with the Australian military forces in World War II. Flight Sergeant Cyril (Kim) Charles Viney (408139) may have been related to a number of them. Educated in Hobart he tried several jobs to find his fit: radio mechanic, haulage worker, stockman, draughtsman, cotton grader, before he turned to farming. He enlisted in the RAAF on 3 January 1941 and left wife Betty and new daughter Margaret for overseas training and service. After so many occupations and restlessness he revelled in his duties as a Pilot Captain with RAAF 460. He was 27 and his choice of crew was a tad unusual, not the average crew in age and with more impressive educational qualifications than his own.

Sergeant Horatio Irwin Munckton (405133) was educated at the prestigious Queensland boys' school of Ipswich Grammar. His chosen occupation was however not one commonly boasted about by Ipswich Grammar Alumni. Munckton never imagined himself emulating Douglas Fairbanks Hollywood feats, he was a gentle soul who enjoyed being a shop assistant and window dresser. When the war began he was torn, so joined the 1st Cavalry Field Ambulance. Only he understood why he switched to RAAF aircrew and became a Bomb Aimer. Sergeant Warren Wallace Jarrett (411451) was the Observer. A studious man, Jarrett was 30 and a NSW school teacher. The Wireless Operator/ Air Gunner, Sergeant Colin Hugh MacKenzie Smith (411397), came from Sydney and at 31 was partly responsible for the crew being called "greybeards". Sergeant Henry Thomas Augustus Turner (403158) at

23 helped a little in that respect but he also was a teacher, somewhat unusual for a Tail Gunner and further consolidated the image of this crew as being unusually erudite.

The Wellington took off at 2007 from Breighton, one of 306 bombers to attack Henschel aircraft factories in Kassel, on 27/28 August – 10.1 per cent of the force would not return. Viney's Wellington and crew stood no chance when attacked at 14,000 feet (4,270 metres) by three enemy fighters. With the port petrol tanks damaged, fuel quickly emptied; the hydraulic and control column were shot away, as was the intercom. Munckton was standing beside Viney and the pilot turned quickly and jerked his thumb downwards. Munckton struggled to the hatch to bale as the bomber dived towards the ground. At only 1,500 feet (458 metres) he tumbled from the aircraft but upon landing he was arrested by a Dutch policeman. German authorities informed the Australian that three bodies were found in his crashed Wellington and one was outside. It was Irwin Munckton's 23rd birthday and he would spend the remainder of the war as a German POW. He wrote to the Viney family that Kim: "had every chance of getting out himself but evidently tried to get the remainder of our crew out first and I believe they were still in the plane when it crashed."

Another RAAF 460 crew which failed to return from an attack on Osnabruck on the night of 9 /10 August 1942 was skippered by Flight Sergeant James (Sandy) Alexander Finlay (403175) from a Scone, NSW, farming family. Life was never easy on the land and personal tragedy caused them further heartache. When James was very young he and his younger brother found a box of matches. It was just childish curiosity but the ensuing blaze caused great damage to the Finlay homestead and more importantly Sandy received bad burns and his younger brother died. The significance of the situation was confusing for a four year old, but having recovered from his injuries Sandy seemed intent on getting the maximum out of every minute of every day. He studied hard at Sydney's The King's School, finding chemistry, mathematics and physics more to his liking than languages. Sandy returned to work the family property, grew to be a strapping six feet and was an excellent horseman; from polo to rodeo, his skill frequently on show.

His occupation on RAAF enlistment on 9 December 1940 was jackaroo, perhaps not the most obvious training for pilot but his understanding of machinery from tractors to "windmill engines" was. Sergeant Finlay, (403175), resplendent in his RAAF uniform with gold wings over the left pocket, departed for the war in Europe on 20 May 1941.

The 29 year old like his fellow RAAF 460 pilot Kim Viney, felt confident he had chosen a good crew, three Aussie boys and a New Zealander because there seemed to be a familiar military tradition involved. Flight Sergeant Stephen Bryan Goord (39099) 28, was a Wireless Operator/Air Gunner, in the New Zealand Air Force. He held his own even if outnumbered by Aussies. That was the odd thing about people from these two southern dominions. They were seriously competitive with each other but should another nationality oppose either they would find they had committed an offence against both nationalities. The Air Gunner was Sergeant Kevin Argyle Smith (402832) 27, husband of Hilda and father to two-year-old Sonya. He worked as a stock and station clerk in Casino, NSW, until he decided to open his own barber shop tobacconist. The Bomb Aimer was 23-year-old Sergeant Nicholas Dan (403561). Educated at Sydney Tech High School and Wollongong College, he had played representative rugby league. Dan worked at an iron and steel firm at Port Kembla. Observer, Sergeant Robert Allan Ponton (401080) 29, from the shipwreck coast city of Warrnambool, Victoria, loved machines and had managed a car sales business. The five would remain together in the south-eastern corner of a cemetery in the village of Hengelo, The Netherlands, as always the New Zealander among the Australians.

Operations did not diminish with the onset of autumn. Bombing results had improved since 1941 but it was still "freely acknowledged that a good deal of the effort being put into the campaign was being wasted."[7] Furthermore Luftwaffe expertise had continued to improve. Sixty years on, with the beginning of another century, each military member "killed in action" would be mourned publicly by those who ordered them to war, and the nation to which their remains were returned. In 1942 and the ensuing three years the dead were too numerous to be afforded singular commemoration, and their bodies never came home. Between

1 July and the 31 December 1942, 247 RAAF Bomber Command Europe airmen were "killed in action" and 34 became POWs.

On the night of 10 September 1942, 479 bombers lifted off from English airfields into clear sky – destination, Dusseldorf. For the first time the Pathfinder Force successfully marked the target area with "Pink Pansies". These were delivered in converted 4,000 lb (1,800 kg) bomb casings, (each Pink Pansy weighed 2,800 lb/1270 kg).[8] The blaze of pink was truly a sight for sore eyes and rapidly becoming the favourite colour of Australian aircrew, other than RAAF blue. Results were far more accurate and it was believed 52 industrial firms were forced to cease production for varying lengths of time. Intelligence reports included the statistics that 132 people living in Dusseldorf were killed and a further 116 people were still "missing" two days later. The same report included the statistics that 178 aircrew were killed and a further 19 became German POWs – 7.1 per cent of the force was lost. More heavy bombers coming on line meant larger payloads, larger crews, and more aircrew killed in action.

The raid against Duisburg was not successful and Gee had not resulted in improved results: "It is probable that between one half and three quarters of the bombs dropped at night were not even hitting the cities designated as targets."

Thirteen Australians were killed. As bad as this was, 16 men were lost to New Zealand and 50 Canadians would never return to their homeland. In total, 16 training unit bombers were destroyed. Two 26 OTU Wellingtons were piloted by Australians. Sergeant Creighton Carlyle Ogilvie (403599) was from a pastoralist family of Gunnedah, NSW. He was 23 and had enlisted 14 months earlier. His classmate, 25-year-old Sergeant Alexander Irvine Lewis Downs (403565) from Sydney, died in another Wellington. Sergeant Lloyd Watson Thomas (402282), also from Sydney, was just 20 and his RAF 61 Squadron Lancaster pilot was even younger, the 19-year-old Flight Sergeant Frank Hobson, RAF. Flight Sergeant John Hamilton Woodford (400187) from St Kilda, Victoria, was the Air Gunner on an RAF 78 Squadron Halifax shot down on the Dusseldorf raid. An RAF 106 Squadron Lancaster which also crashed in the city's precincts had two Australians onboard. The Pilot was Sergeant Alfred Geoffrey Smith (407688) 24, from Pinnaroo, SA. His Wireless Operator/Air Gunner was Sergeant Ray Douglas McPherson (401244) 25, from Donald, Victoria.

Two RAAF 460 Wellingtons also failed to return. Sergeant James Christopher Pearson (404941) was the skipper of one elderly bomber which turned back due to engine trouble. The Queenslander tried to fly the bomber as long as he could to give his crew an opportunity to survive. The Wellington ran out of height and plunged into the sea 15 miles (24 kilometres) off the English coast and shy of the closest airfield at Cromer, Norfolk. Pearson from Sydney is believed to have drowned, so too the 30-year-old Victorian Rear Gunner Sergeant John Howard Murphy (408194); and Pilot Officer Eric Cliffe Parton (411102) the 28-year-old Wireless Operator/Air Gunner. The Reverend Arthur Parton wrote to the RAAF from his Katoomba parish thanking them for the "efficient and kindly way" Eric's effects were retrieved from England; "We are glad to receive the goods, but they give a sad finality to our gallant son's passing". Sergeant Lawrence Matthew John Evans (407735) from York, Western Australia, the Bomb Aimer, escaped the crash with bruises and exposure and would continue to fly to war's end. Sergeant Ronald William Lawton (406599) another West Australian, would also, and discharge in 1945 as a Flight Lieutenant with a DFC and Bar.

There were no survivors from the second RAAF 460 Wellington. Flight Sergeant John Alexander Bryden (404601) 26, was the Pilot. The air war was a great leveller; it brought men from very different backgrounds and threw them into a very small space where they were totally dependent on each other for long, exhausting hours. Bryden's crew was no exception. John Bryden was a fruit grower from Queensland's richly soiled Warwick district. With titian-coloured hair and "sandy, red complexion" he, of course, answered to the nickname "Blue". His interest in religion strengthened as he searched for answers during a war and thumbed through a bible, two copies of the New Testament, as well as books entitled, *A Man's Religion* and *Is God Dead.*

Sergeant Keith John Danks-Brown (404403) from Sydney's north shore was also 26 but his background could not have been more different. He studied English and elocution with Miss E Pope, Neutral Bay, and attended the Wentworth Business College. Prior to enlistment as an Air Gunner he was an advertising executive and then newspaper photographer with Brisbane's *Courier Mail*. He excelled at the less than common sports of skating and diving. Danks-Brown had already been seriously injured in a crash caused by "adverse weather and error of judgement on part of pilot", so he was pleased to transfer to this crew. Sergeant Albert Ernest Brown (403105) had hoped to gain his pilot's wings but was deemed to be better suited for Bomb Aimer duties. After leaving NSW country's Wellington High, he worked as a motor car parts storeman. Sergeant James Kevin King (406980) 24, was the son of the station master at Western Australia's Midland Junction. Air Gunner Sergeant Terence Claude Harris (406453) the 20-year-old son of a Perth building contractor had been a little wild as a teenager and landed up in The Children's Court. It was a wake-up call and he turned his life around by going to night school, finishing his leaving certificate, and landing a position as a clerk with J H Wilberforce & Co.

This group of men who in peace would be unlikely to meet, and even less likely to share common interests, needed to bond as a crew. They journeyed to an English pub to share an ale or two, or three. Unfortunately they lost track of time and where they actually were. All were placed on report for being Absent Without Leave (AWOL). "Severely reprimanded", was written on their service records and "loss of pay" added to the physical discomfort which accompanied over indulgence. Bryden's mother, Martha, wrote to the RAAF asking for the addresses of the families of her son's crew – she felt that the solidarity shared by the Australian airmen may also console families who "anxiously awaited some information regarding my son and his mates". When the news came it was "a shock".

Ellie Harris, mother of the 20-year-old Air Gunner, was not ready to accept Terry's belongings and the circumstances caused her to put pen to paper. She was away from her home and was hurt and annoyed that the case of "my late son's personal belongings...was dumped on the landing" and found late at night on her return. She believed they could have been stolen and more care was needed as such belongings "mean a great deal to parents". She and other Bryden crew parents would need to find comfort in the official statement that their sons were buried in "very beautiful garden".

On occasion, the RAF struggled to adapt to the incredibly rapid pace of wartime expansion. Clashes between pre-war RAF officers and those enlisted to fight an air war, were inevitable. The fact that the RAF chose to label World War II entry personnel as separate, (RAFVR), was indicative of an entrenched belief that there should be an almost class system between RAFVR and "real" RAF. Pre-war RAF could not help but be bothered on occasion by the less formal attitudes and behaviour of those of the Royal Air Force Volunteer Reserve (RAFVR). War volunteers "hostilities only personnel" were less inclined to follow regimental exactness, spit and polish. They also shouldered most of Bomber Command operational responsibilities. This divide was complicated by air forces of the dominions. Thousands of Australians, New Zealanders, and Canadians arrived, eager recruits of the air war, mostly anxious to learn and serve, but they were young men with the normal arrogance and often misguided confidence of youth. They were indeed fighting for King and country but they had left their families and homes, come a long way, and were doing some very dangerous stuff. They truly admired seasoned RAF aircrew instructors, men who quietly went about their serious jobs in their battered caps and faded DFM and DFC ribbons. There was great respect for those who maintained their aircraft; and the amazing air force men and women who drove tractors which tugged trolleys laden with bombs to tarmacs; and armourers who loaded and armed bombs deep in the bellies of aircraft. There was nonetheless, a degree of contempt for "wingless wonders", RAF administrators who were overzealous with rules, pomp and circumstance and who seemed not to appreciate the service and sacrifice of dominion airmen. Rules were needed and service discipline maintained but at the end of the day all that seemed inconsequential for aircrew who night after night silently climbed up into their bombers knowing that the odds of their returning were increasingly against them.

On route to Duisburg on 7 August 1942 Flight Sergeant Edward Keith Forbes Brasher (404949) 25, from Brisbane, was piloting a RAAF

460 Wellington when it was attacked by a Ju-88. Cannon and machine-gun fire seriously damaged the bomber and RAAF Wireless Operator/ Air Gunner Sergeant James Lowrie Forrest (401688) was wounded. As the fighter dived in for another attack, the Rear Gunner RAAF Flight Sergeant Keith Campbell Bennett (407992) fired an accurate, long burst, into the nose of the German fighter. The Ju-88 made a sharp climbing turn, stalled, and enveloped in flames, crashed. It was a wonderful result for Bennett who had been admonished by RAF authorities whilst with 27 OTU for: "Causing damage to Wellington aircraft by failing to securely lock the doors of the rear turret thereby causing loss of one turret door."

He was fined 10/– "towards the cost of replacement". His skipper on the Duisburg raid, Ed Brasher, managed to just about fly the wings off the badly damaged Wellington to get the bomber and his crew back to England. Unable to close the bomb doors or lower the undercarriage Brasher belly landed what was left of the Wellington with no loss of life. Brasher received an immediate DFM – Bennett's skill went unrewarded. Whilst aircraft pilot/skippers were traditionally recognised ahead of other crew, in Bennett's case the misdemeanour highlighted on his paperwork counted against him regardless that the loss of a turret door paled by comparison with the loss of an aircraft and crew.

On the night of 13/14 September Brasher, Bennett and their crew took off to bomb Bremen. This time German defences proved lethal. Edward Brasher was buried in the small Dutch village of Sage. With him were most of his crew: Sergeant William John Carr Monk (403793) an accountant from Sydney; Sergeant Douglas Westbury Johnson (403139), a 25-year-old former salesman from Maitland, NSW; and Johnson's navigator classmate, Sergeant Alistair Dalton Crowther (411007) 31, from Wyong, NSW, former school teacher, and 1st grade rugby player. The remains of the 22-year-old Flight Sergeant Keith Campbell Bennett (407992), a graduate of Adelaide High School, and proven Rear Gunner, would rest in Germany's Rheinberg War Cemetery. Wireless Operator/Air Gunner Sergeant James Lowrie Forrest (401688) from Mildura, NSW, was injured but made it back to England. Forrest was returned to duty, joined another crew and was killed on 9 April 1943.

Like so many parents those of Sergeant Alistair Dalton Crowther (411007) clung to the hope that their son would be found alive. Following a letter from the RAAF these hopes were extinguished and they struggled with the reality: "That you fear that all hope of finding our son alive must be abandoned. We have been buoyed up with the thoughts that may be he might be a prisoner of war: but your letter I am afraid does away with that thought." Fate was fickle, Brasher and crew were the last RAAF 460 Wellington bomber casualties. The squadron commenced a conversion programme to Halifax bombers but before coming operational again Lancasters replaced the Halifaxes.

Flying Officer Raymond Edward Norton Butcher (406638) from Armadale, Western Australia, was killed during the last hour of 21 September 1942 when his Wellington was attacked by a German fighter while "gardening". The RAF 101 Squadron aircraft had taken off from Stradishall, Suffolk, at 1941 and was at 4,000 ft (1,200 m) when it was raked from the rear to the cockpit. Butcher being the rear gunner was the most exposed and the first killed. His Pilot was Squadron Leader Victor Roberton Paterson, DFC, RAF, but experience on this occasion counted for little against a skilled German night fighter pilot. The RAF Wireless Operator/Air Gunner Flight Sergeant Edwin John Rowe (648115) was also killed whilst the remainder of the crew, Canadian Observer Pilot Officer C H Mitchell and New Zealand Wireless Operator/Air Gunner G L Otter baled out and were interned in Denmark for the remainder of the war. Ray Butcher had enlisted on 3 March 1941. His squadron operational life was just three months. The crew represented the four air forces, the four nations, making the largest contribution and sacrificing the most aircrew to Bomber Command. RAF 101 lost another Wellington on 21 September and converted to Lancasters.

As a spellbound 15 year old, Arthur Hoyle enjoyed celebrations for the 150th anniversary of Australian white settlement in Sydney's Centennial Park. A flight of three Avro Ansons in vee formation flew low over the crowd: "Painted silver, with the sun reflecting from the canopies and the red, white and blue roundels of the RAAF". Hoyle entered the RAAF with the same starry-eyed awe and optimism.

He approached his navigator studies with the same enthusiasm and was delighted when he was posted to England. "I had to pinch myself to believe that I was actually in London! Here was the Haymarket, there was Pall Mall!" London was still a "glamorous place in the dying days of 1942".[9] Like all Australian aircrew he found himself in the seaside resort of Bournemouth for three months attending lectures impatiently waiting "to get on with the war". Hoyle continued to see the humorous side of some military traditions.

Arthur Hoyle.

Every Sunday was church parade. Those who were determinedly Christian went off to their respective churches. The heathen remainder were then taken on a route march around the town. The column, in ranks of three, stepped out bravely but, as soon as it turned a corner, the last two or three ranks melted away. By the time the column had travelled half a mile there were often only the first two or three ranks still marching behind the officer.[10]

Arthur Hoyle was then sent to the Midlands and again marked time. Like those who came before him "boredom soon set in". After what seemed an eternity to a 20 year old he was posted to Air Observers' School at Bobbington in Shropshire and he was back yet again training on Ansons. Now he was yearning to crew something a lot larger, faster, and more lethal. At last he was posted to 27 OTU at Lichfield, West Midlands, and his "first step towards becoming part of an operational crew". Hoyle was unsure if he would end up on a light bomber such as the Mosquito and a crew of two; on a medium bomber, like the Wellington with a crew of five, or as part of the seven-man heavy-bomber crew and flying a Stirling, Halifax or Lancaster.

He lacked confidence in his ability and finding the "way around a darkened Europe". He knew no one and wondered if he would ever find a crew, but was pleased when he was approached by a pilot from the notoriously hot mining town of Marble Bar, Western Australia. "He seemed pleasant and I hoped he could fly well". With the formation of the crew there was a great deal of flight training, every available hour spent on "circuits and bumps", but not for Hoyle. "Navigators, as befitting their 'academic status' spent most of their time plotting 'dry swims'". A classroom and northern hemisphere meteorology and stars, meant Hoyle could not bond well with the remainder of the crew who were flying together. What was more he did not drink and "was shy with girls" so neither was he part of the standard off-duty practices of "local pubs or pursuing the members of the WAAF on the station" – this was not going as he envisaged. Next came flying cross-country, by day and by night. The pilot struggled with night landings even after additional tuition. The decision was made for the crew to be broken up which was unsettling. This Australian pilot was killed during a bombing raid in 1944.

Hoyle was much relieved when he was approached by not one pilot but two. It was decision time. "I rejected the second crew because they drank too much and I knew that a lot of alcohol and survival were likely to be incompatible." To some the judgment may have appeared harsh but Hoyle now realised what once appeared purely as an exciting adventure, was shrouded in black. He took no pleasure in the news a few months later when this crew was killed.

Sergeant Arthur Hoyle (420884) settled into a crew captained by "a young, blond, good looking Australian jackaroo from Hay in the Riverina of NSW named Bob Wade".[11] This crew had needed to shed its navigator because he was unable to navigate in the air. The crew was made up of four Australians and an English Rear Gunner. They were a mixed bunch of men, a couple Hoyle found likeable, a couple he did not. The fact that he refused to go to either The Salt Box or The Dog and Partridge pubs worked against him. In the air nonetheless there was mutual respect, particularly for the captain. From Wellingtons the crew graduated to the Halifax Mark II. These were unpopular as their stall characteristics killed many inexperienced crews. "We survived the Halifaxes and then, on a blissful day in October we graduated to Lancasters".[12] For the navigator the "Lanc" was a great improvement over the "Wimpy". Whereas the Wellington was cramped and the smells of oil and coolant penetrated the oxygen mask and caused airsickness, in the Lancaster it was almost wonderful: "I sat at a bench on the port side of the aircraft with the plotting table in front of me and with the various electronic instruments facing. As well, I had a repeater compass, an altimeter and a repeater airspeed indicator while the table was lit by an anglepoise lamp."

At the conversion unit they picked up an English Engineer and an Australian Middle Upper Gunner. Hoyle was ashamed to admit he was disappointed to hear the Allies were crushing Italian resistance and that the Italians may soon seek an armistice. "Perhaps the war would be over very soon and all my training would have been for nothing". He had trained for two years and the 21 year old was disappointed at the prospect of seeing "the great adventure end".[13] Hoyle was elated when the crew was posted to RAAF 460 and described the arrival at the squadron's Binbrook base as a "happy day". But like so many others he would soon refer to what had been "the great adventure", as "the furnace of war". Soon he would appreciate how naive he had been "because I had almost no idea or understanding of what it is like to live in the immediate presence of death".[14]

Hoyle didn't know the men others mentioned in quiet reverent tones but the monopoly of such talk made an impact. RAAF 460 Squadron had lost a lot of good men. On 19 September 1942 alone, eight airmen were lost on a conversion training flight and, yes, it was a Halifax II. There was some experience in this crew of Australians and one Englishman so it could not help but affect the confidence of junior aircrew. Sergeant James Thomas Sutton (404860) from Brisbane and Sergeant Sidney Arthur Solomons (403079) from Sydney had enlisted on the same day, 9 December 1940. Sergeant Frederick Raymond Keyes (401220) born in the pretty NSW town of Bundanoon, had enlisted a month later. Sergeant Allan Ralph Morant (400931), from Melbourne was in as early as 11 November 1940. Pilot Officer Harry Sutton Brander (403658) came from Newcastle. Sergeant Frank Elliott Bishop (416113) had moved from Broken Hill to Adelaide and enlisted in March 1941. Corporal William John Ronald Hazelton (22126) was born in Brisbane in March 1920. It was not clear if the "stall characteristics" resulted in the crashing of Halifax DT481 but the seven Australians onboard were buried and would remain in Binbrook's (St Mary) Churchyard while the body of RAF Sergeant Arthur Joseph Betteridge (1138925) was taken home to Walton upon Trent.

In October 1942 a new chapter began in World War II. For two years Allied forces struggled to gain and hold position in North Africa. Italian resistance was fortified by ever-increasing German forces commanded by General Erwin Rommel. He faced an equally stubborn and efficient Commander, General Bernard Law Montgomery and his British 8th Army. A new offensive commenced on the evening of 23 October as British artillery erupted. The bombardment, the like of which "had not been witnessed since the major battles of the First World War"[15] continued unrelenting for a week. This was the prelude of "Operation Torch" the British-American invasion of French North Africa. On 8 November Montgomery's forces and those commanded by US Lieutenant General Dwight D Eisenhower attacked from numerous fronts. The offensive was the beginning of the end of Axis power in North Africa.

For Bomber Command Operation Torch further diversified strategic attention. Italian commercial and industrial facilities in Milano, Genova and Torino were targeted. On the night of 22/23 October a daring raid of 112 Lancasters from 5 Group with Pathfinders bombed Genoa to coincide with the opening of the Eighth Army El Alamein offensive. Although carrying only 180 tons of bombs, heavy damage was caused. A "Lanc" flown by Sergeant Russell Lloyd Cumberland (403644) RAAF, almost became the first statistic of Operation Torch. During the outward journey the port outer engine cut out. Ten minutes later the engine burst into flames. The Australian pilot feathered the airscrew. Cumberland's crew breathed a sigh of relief when through the skill of their pilot the fire was extinguished. With bombload intact the crew returned to Skellingthorpe.

Cheating death brought forth a range of uncomfortable emotions. Russ Cumberland had written to the family of his classmate RAAF Sergeant John Ormond O'Brien (403876) when John was killed on 20 June 1942.[16] He was also struggling with the bitter reality of war. Cumberland was the youngest of three boys of Arthur and Alice of "Wyvern" a property in the prime sheep country around Goulburn, NSW. He realised he was ill-suited to life on the land and from an early age applied himself to his studies. School rugby provided a healthy diversion as did representative cricket and swimming and the combination of scholastic and sporting ability resulted in his becoming Goulburn High School captain in grade six. His attention had always been stirred by life outside Goulburn – so much to see, learn, and involve oneself in. This enthusiasm for life saw Russ take a gap six months off school to work as a Telegraph Messenger. He returned to complete his Leaving Certificate and was delighted when taken on as a Cadet Journalist with the Goulburn Penny Post. This new occupation encompassed the variety he thrived on and he looked forward to joining a larger newspaper and travelling.[17]

Travelling came with a different emphasis and Russell Cumberland left Goulburn and Australia to join a war in Europe. He may have been surprised when offered a re-muster in February to Pilot, but he certainly didn't have to be asked twice – what could be more exciting? After training at Narrandera he embarked for Canada on 16 August 1941 and then travelled to England. During time with 14 OTU and August 1942 Lancaster conversion course he gathered a crew. There were four RAF Sergeants; Walter Scott (949357) was the Flight Engineer; John James Glendinning (991158) was Wireless Operator/Air Gunner; Frank Adey (1332609) and John St Bernard Fern (1277501) were the Air Gunners. Cumberland chose 24-year-old Sergeant James Temple Philpot (403532) from Lithgow as Navigator and Sergeant Stanley Alfred Gregg (404420) a 23 year old from Brisbane as his Bomb Aimer.

Jim Philpot was the third child and only son of John and Millicent. They named their son in honour of John's younger brother, Second

Sergeant James Temple Philpot (courtesy Gwenda Stanbridge).

Lieutenant James Temple Philpot, 3rd Battalion AIF, who died of wounds received at Pozieres, the Somme, France, on 25 July 1916. He was 21. The younger James Temple Philpot was born in Lithgow, NSW – his father was manager of the Hermitage colliery. Five years later there was a move to Wollongong, New South Wales, on John's appointment as manager of the Mount Pleasant Colliery. The Methodist Church played a large part in family life, and Jim kept busy with his schooling, violin lessons and swimming. His first three years at Wollongong High School was followed in 1934 with entry to Newington College, Sydney. He proved a valuable student for Newington, a "good all-rounder in swimming, athletics, tennis and cricket, as well as rowing in GPS regattas".[18] Jim was destined to follow a family tradition in the coal mining industry. His grandfather, William Thompson Philpot, was manager of the Lithgow Valley Colliery and upon his retirement, Jim's father John moved back to Lithgow to take up the position. Jim Philpot joined the staff of the Hermitage colliery, Lithgow, as assistant surveyor. He studied surveying at the Lithgow Technical College and became very involved in town life; establishing a lifesaving group at the local swimming hole and was much in demand as a violinist. War came and Jim enlisted in the RAAF.

By September 1941 the Cumberland crew was with RAF 50 Squadron. Genoa was again the target for a raid on the night of 23/24 October by 122 bombers from 3 and 4 Groups. Reports concerning the raid's success were mixed as thick cloud cover resulted in most of the bombs being dropped on the town of Savona instead. Five crews were lost and five more crash-landed in England with some injuries and loss of life. Less than 48 hours after their abrupt but safe return from the Genoa operation, the Cumberland crew were onboard another Lancaster headed for Milano. This was another risky daylight raid by 88 Group 5 Lancasters and due to the distance to the Italian city there would be no fighter escort. The raid was very unexpected and warning sirens only sounded after the first bombs fell. Five British aircrews were killed – one was the Cumberland crew. It was just Russell Cumberland's 3rd operation as Skipper. Lancaster R5691 was hit by anti-aircraft fire. Cumberland and his crew decided not to abandon their bomber and turned for England – and, they very nearly made it. It is not known if the damaged plane fell, easy target to either anti-aircraft fire from emplacements in France, enemy fighter, or the British bomber suffered catastrophic failure. Wayne Cumberland would say of his uncle and crew: "We will never know what actions the crew took in getting their aircraft so close to home, or if any were wounded or killed before they crashed."

Two bodies washed ashore, the Australian Skipper and his Australian Navigator, James Philpot. They would be finally buried in Bayeux War Cemetery, Normandy. The town of Bayeux would be the first French town of importance liberated. But the Allied invasion of 6 June 1944 was still a long way off and too many Australian airmen with Bomber Command Europe would never see the day. It would be following the invasion that the Cumberland family in Goulburn would receive another reminder of their son and brother. The bodies of British aircrew were brought to the Grand Hospital, Caen, France. The Mother Superior would treat them with the utmost reverence and ensure they had a Christian funeral. She found Russell's cigarette lighter and hid it from the Germans. Upon liberation she would hand over a cache of belongings to Allied authorities. John and Millie Philpot had lost their only son. By a strange twist of fate their daughter, Dorothy, who had also been living in the Goulburn district, with her husband and 10-month-old son, had died in October also, the year before. It was of no comfort to John Philpot that his only son, Sergeant James Temple Philpot, RAAF, lay in a French war grave like the brother he had named him after.

The night of the death of the Cumberland crew the Operation Torch bombing offensive continued with another visit to Milano by 71 aircraft from 1 and 3 Groups – 8.5 per cent of the force was lost. The next Italian raid came on the night of the 6/7 November. It involved 72 Lancasters from 5 Group and the Pathfinders. Again the results were mixed and four crews were killed. Another operation against Genoa the following night had more success but for Bomber Command Operation Torch had exposed problems. Italian resistance was not the cause of lost bombers and crews as much as aircrew fatigue and weather. Operation times of ten hours or more combined with very difficult weather conditions had not been foreseen by those in authority. Upon returning to their Waddington airfield two RAF 9 Squadron Lancasters collided in the early morning of 8 November killing both crews; another three bombers ran out of fuel. Italian operations were halted while the situation was assessed and instead 213 aircraft bombed Hamburg on 9/10 November.

On the nights of 13/14 and 15/16 November two operations were conducted against Genoa with no aircraft lost. Torino, Italy, was visited on the night of 18/19 by 77 aircraft, with the Fiat works the main target. Again bombing took place on Torino on the night of 20/21 – six aircraft crashed but the force of 232 inflicted significant damage. The Operation Torch Bomber Command offensive was coming to an end with the last raid operated against Torino on 29/30 November. In that raid 29 Stirlings and 7 Lancasters of 3 Group plus Pathfinders were dispatched. Three aircraft crashed with the loss of two crews. For one RAAF Flight Sergeant the trip would be both exciting and unusual – insofar as the RAF 35 Squadron Halifax returned to England without him. Frank Edward Solway became RAAF 403457 on 6 January 1941. Life had not been easy for the Solway family particularly when Francis Solway Snr could no longer work as a miner. Frank left Cessnock High school after his Intermediate to help with the family subsistence but work was hard to find. With the help of his bicycle, muscles honed by numerous sports, and enthusiasm, he started his "own business" delivering newspapers. Frank had enthusiasm and energy to burn and was a young man in a hurry. He was still 18 when he enlisted. Whilst completing his Wireless Operator/Air Gunner training in Britain he married Elizabeth – he was still 19. Elizabeth was mid-term in her pregnancy when Frank was on operations with RAF 15 Squadron – he would be 20 when the next Francis Solway was born in February 1943. Flight Sergeant Solway (403457) would not see his son until he was two years old.

The pilot of Solway's RAF 35 Squadron Halifax which took off to drop a load of high explosives and flares on Torino on the night of 18/19 November was very experienced. At 30, Basil Vernon Robinson, RAF, was a Wing Commander with DSO, DFC, after his name. Two of his crew were RAF and three were RCAF. The enthusiastic Wireless Operator/Air Gunner was the Aussie Solway. Torino was reached and the bomb load released. Shortly after a fire broke out in the bomb bay, caused by an extremely powerful flare – designed to light up Torino – had hung up. Flames spread quickly and the bomber filled with smoke. A "violent explosion" ensued. The bomb bay doors were re-opened and the crew prayed the flare would dislodge. It failed to do so and the fire continued to spread. The Halifax was aflame yet only 1,500 feet (460 metres) below were snow capped mountains. The aircraft was losing height and Robinson believed it would crash into the peaks – he ordered his crew to bale out. One by one bodies fell into the night below and canopies burst open. Robinson began to follow when he realised the fire had been extinguished by the rush of cold air through the escape hatch. Returning to the cockpit Robinson flew the Halifax back to England where he crash landed with no injury to himself. The three Canadians escaped but Frank Solway and the two RAF crew members spent the remainder of the war as German POWs. Solway had left Australia on 22 February 1941 and arrived home on 9 September 1945 – it had been a very long war and the youthful exuberance had waned. His skipper, Basil Robinson, was promoted to Group Captain (G/C) at 31 and had DSO, DFC and Bar, and the Air Force Cross (AFC) after his name, but Robinson was killed over Berlin on 24 August 1943.

On the night of 28/29 November 1942, Pilot Officer Rawdon Hume Middleton (402745) and his crew were also tasked to raid the Fiat works in Torino. The Pathfinders were a little slow this night and Middleton dropped the RAF 149 Squadron Stirling I down to 2,000 ft (610 m) and made three runs across the city to establish the exact position of the target.

Ironically, the previous August, Middleton had been asked to join the Pathfinders. He and his crew flew as Pathfinders on a raid on Nuremberg. Upon their return his superior officer informed him that whilst Middleton was welcome to remain a Pathfinder pilot, his navigator was not up to the required standard and would therefore be posted with other Middleton crew members to another squadron. The Australian refused the posting, choosing to remain with his crew at RAF 149. In turn, his three gunners elected to continue flying even though they had completed their tour of 30 operations.

As Middleton released the Stirling's brakes and jockeyed for position with six other Stirlings on Lakenheath airfield at 1814 the night of 28 November, Middleton was comfortable with his decision. This was his 29th operation and he was exactly where he needed to be. His crew were all RAF and a truly mixed band of brothers. Second pilot was Flight Sergeant L A Hyder a former student from Glasgow. The navigator he believed in enough to leave the Pathfinders for was 32-year-old RAF Flying Officer George Reicher Royde (118604) a London Lawyer. The Wireless Operator/Air Gunner was Pilot Officer N E Skinner from Yorkshire. Middle Upper Gunner was Flight Sergeant D Cameron a former Gamekeeper. The Engineer was Sergeant J E Jeffery from Dorset, and the Rear Gunner was Sergeant H W Gough, a garage hand in his pre-war life. Sergeant John William Mackie (994362) the Front Gunner, was a 30 year old from Scotland's Clackmannanshire pretty much as difficult to pronounce as those towns of Middleton's youth a world away.

The green light for take-off came from the airfield control pilot in his runway caravan and Middleton opened the throttles. Hours later the heavily laden bomber was barely able to climb over the Alps. Visibility was poor and only by screwing up their eyes could the two pilots distinguish the mountain peaks which lurched out of the pitch black all around the aircraft. Fuel consumption was excessive and four of the RAF 149 seven Stirlings turned back for England. Middleton spoke to his crew and decided to press on. Flak spurted up from anti-aircraft guns below destroying metal, fabric, and human bodies. Middleton, his second pilot and the wireless operator were all wounded when a shell splinter burst in the cockpit. Middleton lost consciousness and as a result the bomber plummeted towards the mountainous terrain. Hyder, the second pilot, struggled with the controls and at 800 feet (245 metres) pulled the aircraft out of its deadly descent. House roofs were visible and only when at 1,500 feet (460 metres) again were the bombs jettisoned. The Stirling bucked as it was hit over and over again. Middleton was bleeding badly from shrapnel wounds to his chest and legs and where his right eye had been there was now a gaping bony hole. In terrific pain he took the controls and in a wheezing voice ordered the second pilot back to the rest bunk to have his wounds dressed. Hyder insisted on then returning to the cockpit.

Speaking in little more than a gasp the Australian pilot told those onboard that he was determined to get them back to England rather than have them become prisoners of war. He instructed the crew to jettison everything they could to lighten the load. For four hours the badly wounded pilots flew the bomber, the shattered windscreen exposing them to an icy blast. Middleton would have realised how serious his injuries were and how unlikely it would be for him to be able to bale out. As his badly damaged plane reached the French coast the Stirling was coned by a dozen searchlights, more anti-aircraft fire filled the sky. Middleton could do little to avoid the danger as the Stirling was buffeted by hits to both wings – how it was still flying none of the crew knew and the same could be said for their captain. The English coast came into sight and never had it looked so welcoming. With only five minutes of fuel remaining and the bomber at 600 feet (183 metres) Middleton changed course to fly parallel to the coast and ordered the crew to bale. Sergeants Jeffrey and Mackie were either too wounded or hesitated too long. The Front Gunner, John Mackie helped the wounded Second Pilot to the escape hatch and placing Hyder's hand on to the "D" ring of his parachute assisted him out of the aircraft. Middleton was barely conscious but pointed his bomber back out to sea rather than have it crash on an English town. At 0255 the Stirling, twisted and bent, and out of fuel, finally gave up its struggle and crashed

The funeral of Pilot Officer Rawdon Hume Middleton, VC, RAAF.

into the sea. The bodies of the Jeffrey and Mackie were found the next day, their parachutes had been opened but they had landed too far from the Kent coast and drowned. Hyder, Royde, Cameron and Skinner survived. Rawdon Middleton's body was not recovered from the ocean until 1 February 1943. His Wireless Operator reflected later: "No-one will ever know what was going on in Middleton's mind in those last few moments...During the return home there were many opportunities for us to abandon the aircraft over France, and for Middleton to live. But he preferred that we, his crew, and the aircraft of which he was Captain, should not fall into enemy hands. That was the kind of man he was."[19] The RAAF Pilot from the difficult to pronounce town and district was awarded a Victoria Cross, on 15 January 1943, with the citation: "His devotion to duty in the face of overwhelming odds is unsurpassed in the annals of the Royal Air Force". The RAAF had its first Victoria Cross, won by an aviator who had inspired his crew with "heroism of a high order". Following a full military funeral Rawdon Hume Middleton was buried in Suffolk, England, a landscape very different to his own. In time, his personal effects would return to Australia and be reverently cared for in a museum in the small town of Trundle, a town on the wide brown plains of NSW and in time a school in Parkes, NSW, would be named in his honour.

SEVEN

"All being well! We may be all home for next Xmas –
Wishful thinking!!! I really can't see this mess being
cleared up in one year."

Flight Lieutenant Wallace Martin

Wallace Martin had already lost too many friends and now another boy from Scone, "I was so sorry to hear of poor old Sandy Finlay's luck – one never knows these days in this racket!!" He paused and then continued his letter home; "by all the laws of averages we should never have come through ourselves". Wallace had just completed a three week "Bombing Leaders Course" which involved "quite a deal of study but made the grade with 72.5 per cent. Wallace was to be promoted to Flight Lieutenant and was to receive the DFC, "a 'gong' which is something new for old Murrurundi"; the thought brought a smile and he knew how proud his family would be – Jess was already thinking about what she would wear to Buckingham Palace for the award ceremony. On 15 September Wallace had navigated the lead aircraft on the attack on the whaling factory ship Solglint in Cherbourg harbour. The ship was set on fire and gutted. The DFC citation read: "Although the attack was executed in the face of heavy anti-aircraft fire, the ship received severe damage, and was later seen partially submerged. Martin's accurate bombing, contributed in a large measure to the success attained. Some days later, he participated in a low level bombing attack on a factory. His skilful navigation has resulted in the location of two dinghies on the sea, in consequence of which seven lives were saved. He has displayed skill and determination of the highest order."

The DFC was awarded for operations in the third week of September when he was celebrating his 23rd birthday, which made for "quite an interesting memory". Better still he had just returned from "8 real smashing days leave" with Jess, "we had a really grand time". It was thoughts of the future that sustained him in the present. "I am sure you will like Jess as she is a really swell girl – is not the 'fancy' type and has plenty of common sense". Yes, he had asked Jess to marry him and she had said yes. "We have not yet decided when we shall arrange our wedding but maybe soon!!!" Jessie Jeffrey had agreed to travel around the world, to come to Australia and live as the wife of a Grazier, in the region around Scone which Wallace enthusiastically described as the most beautiful in his nation.

Wallace was pleased to hear Allan Gell had been promoted to Pilot Officer because "this living as an officer is pretty good". Wallace had survived an entire tour of operations and realised how lucky that was. He had been flying beside other bombers which were blown out of the sky, like that of Sergeant Jack Connelly (402566). "I saw it happen and really didn't think he had a chance". At least Jack had survived but "is now a prisoner of war". He and Jelly "were about the lone raiders" left from his class.

Wallace was now RAAF 464 Squadron Bombing Leader, though he believed it was as much to do with his being the last man standing as it was to his prowess as a navigator. He had survived a tour but just after his 23rd birthday in September 1942 his aircraft crashed leaving him with quite severe head and internal injuries. While hospitalized there was little else to do but look out of his hospital window and think. When well enough to write letters again to his younger brother and sister he struggled to sound optimistic. "The wireless is good company and I listen to all the BBC broadcasts". There was a great deal of news on the war against the Japanese, "the boys seem to be holding their own in New Guinea". His latest bomber "crack up" and extended stay in hospital had knocked his confidence, he was no longer the naive youngster anxious to go to war, who believed "we will make Germany pay for all that they have given so far and they shall pay dam dear". He no longer believed the propaganda; "the Germans I think are still far from broken".

Wallace could not help but think of all the mates he had lost. "I have not been really 100 per cent since my crack-up as I kind of have had the jitters...it will eventually wear off as time goes on". He wanted to marry Jess and craved a future for them both. He also wanted to go home. "The winter is creeping on here now and we have had our first touch of snow...I wish that I could see some of the good old Aussie sun – we go for weeks on end here and very seldom see the sun."

Wallace called it "melancholy" or "jitters"; in 1942 Post Traumatic Stress Disorder (PTSD) was unknown. The Australian knew he needed to shake what ailed him or he would be labelled "lacking moral fibre". A tour, a DFC, promotion after promotion, several major crashes meant nothing – you were only as good as your next flight. "I hope that I can only see the affair through to get back and see you all again" he wrote to those who would not judge. Finally out of hospital, he was sent to Feltwell Airfield to continue his recuperation; "the rest will do me quite a lot of good especially after this last crash". Some of the emotions he was having weren't easy to overcome; "I seem to be a real 'Jonah' as regards accidents and have had no end of them since I came to this country". Wallace felt almost certain just that bit more rest would "settle my nerves". He attempted to convince himself and those at "Splitters Creek": "All being well! We may be all home for next Xmas". The reality was that he knew this to be impossible, "Wishful thinking!!! I really can't see this mess being cleared up in one year". It was best to keep his mind on the approaching Christmas period when he would spend precious leave with Jess. Wallace had organised "a grand flat" for when they were to be married on his next leave. "I am sure that we shall be very happy – we are looking forward to the war ending now and to get back home".

A call came from RAF 21 Squadron – a volunteer navigator was needed to make up numbers so that an RAF Ventura crew could join operation "Operation Oyster" one of the most ambitious raids mounted by No 2 Group – on the Philips Factory in Eindhoven, Holland. Deliveries of the American twin-engine Ventura had begun in late May 1942. Early reports from RAF 21 Squadron "were none too promising and in many respects. ... Frustrating technical problems delayed its debut on operations until mid November".[1] By this time four Venturas had been lost and two others had suffered training accidents and were written off. Regardless of concerns about the aircraft it was decided 47 would fly to Eindhoven.

Murrurundi's Wallace Martin was on "rest leave" at RAF Feltwell, thinking of Christmas with Jess and getting married, but felt obligated to volunteer when the Ventura "Operation Oyster" operation was short of a navigator. Another operation may prove to himself and others that the label "lack of moral fibre" was in no way appropriate. It was the night of the 6 December 1942 and No 2 Group would suffer its highest casualties in a single operation since the outbreak of war. The weather was bad. One Ventura was seen to crash in the Dutch countryside, another damaged by ground fire and turned back for England. As the ground fire ceased thousands of startled sea birds rose "into the path of the bombers". The aircraft were battered by winged bodies – metal dinted and windscreens shattered. Official Bomber Command would report that the bombing was accurate and "radio equipment severely disrupted for the next six months".[2] Also reported was that "around 150 Dutch citizens were believed killed" and that "the object of 'Oyster' (was) accomplished. ...Ten Venturas, five Bostons and a Mosquito joined the list of aircraft destroyed".[3] This report failed to mention 40 aircrew were killed, seven became POWs and five were injured. RAAF Sergeant Farquharson Proctor (8063) a 21 year old from Melbourne; 27-year-old Sergeant Mervyn Lionel Vivian Hass (414026) from Oakey, Queensland, were among the dead. Sergeant Stanley Charles Moss (408513) from Melbourne and five days shy of his 21st, became a POW, as did Sergeant Frederick George Lindsay (411921) 25, from Sydney.

Ventura AE940 from RAF 21 Squadron, and its crew of four which included Flight Lieutenant Wallace Martin, DFC, RAAF, took off at 1120. The flight maintained a low altitude trajectory to cross the Dutch coast. The prescribed route might have concerned Wallace as it crossed an enemy emergency landing ground. At this point the flak increased dramatically and it was very accurate. The Ventura piloted by the NZ487 Squadron OC, Wing Commander Seavill, blew up. Another aircraft was hit, the crew jettisoned the bombload and turned back to base. Yet another British bomber was hit. The flak over Eindhoven was intense – guns mounted on the roof of the Philips radio valve factory were firing a deadly blanket into the sky. Two more Ventura bombers were hit and crashed into the target area. RAF 21 Squadron Ventura AE940 was one of these. The crew, including Wallace Martin, were killed instantly.

LEFT: *Flight Lieutenant Wallace Martin, DFC, RAAF.*
RIGHT: *Wallace Martin's grave in Eindhoven, The Netherlands.*

Allan Gell was deeply upset when he heard his best friend had been killed – Wallace was not even supposed to be back flying yet. Pilot Officer Allan Thomas Gell (402440) was killed a month later, on 8 January 1943. Like Wallace his grave was across the world and beyond the means of his parents, Hugh and Mary, to ever visit. They could but see his name engraved on a World War II memorial plaque in their home town of Cunnamulla.

For Mary Martin life would never be the same, she had six children of whom she was proud. Mary had pretended she had no favourite, but she did and Wallace was hers. First that awful telegram in officious language; "Flight Lieutenant Martin is reported missing", then another, "presumed to have lost his life". Wallace had sent photographs in November 1942 and Mary had been alarmed how her son "had aged greatly". She could not understand why Wallace had been sent to "Feltwell Airfield to recuperate after suffering severe head and internal injuries", but was then sent on the 6 December raid.

The following year Mary Martin wrote to the RAAF, concerning an Australian newspaper report, about: "A man about 37 years old (our boy would be 27) who was an amnesia victim and patient in Sainte Foye La Grande Hospital in Bordeaux, France." The man was found in July 1943 by a band of escaping French POWs. "Fearing German reprisals, the prisoners or Frenchmen, stripped him of his British flying overalls, (and) took him to France". Mary wondered if this could be her lost son. She wrote again, enclosing precious photographs of Wallace to help with identification and then offered the suggestion that the mention of his RAAF nickname "Hoot" might jar a memory in the patient now in the French hospital. Mary was grasping at the slightest chance that there had just been some terrible mistake. "I feel a bit inclined to think and have had premonitions that he is still alive, suffering from loss of memory. ...please don't regard me as being ridiculous." She concluded her letter with; "I earnestly pray that you will get in touch with the hospital mentioned and see whether it is our son". The authorities advised that the man in question was shown to be a fraud and had been jailed.

Final acceptance brought with it a great deal of pain. Like the Gell family, the Martins struggled on the land, they did not have the finances required to cover the huge expense of international travel. Mary longed to see her son's grave. For some reason Wallace's grave was not photographed by the Imperial War Graves Commission and Mary Martin was informed those "responsible for photographing of graves of servicemen buried in Europe, have been withdrawn". The Department of Air "enclosed an order form" for "a service provided" by the British Legion, London, through which Mary could apply for a photograph to be taken – she just had to ensure she enclosed the correct monetary "amounts...in sterling". The British Empire was responsible for the death of her son but she needed to pay in British currency for a photograph of his grave.

Mary Martin became ill, a decade later she died, and running the

Martin home full of young people, and come shearing season, a great many more, was left to Heather the sister who would ride with Wallace on a horse far too big. Heather at 92 still living on the family farm relates her favourite memory. She was five and Wallace four, they were sent to collect the eggs from the chook house. Wallace could not say "Heather" just yet, only "Hattie". As Heather went through the chook gate she let it shut. Wallace called "Hattie open gate". "He had his arms full of eggs, for some reason I didn't react straight away so I received an egg in the back of the head".

In January 1943, the British prime minister, Winston Churchill, the American President, Franklin D Roosevelt, and their principal advisers, met in Casablanca to consider the future direction of the war. The decision was made that nothing less than an unconditional Axis surrender would be accepted. A year earlier this was unthinkable but since the Americans had joined the war there had been six months of greater Allied successes. The leaders agreed that whilst a cross channel invasion could not yet be considered there would be an invasion of Italy. A second front would occur in France to assist a Russian advance. Discussion took place on the Allied bombing campaign and there was disagreement between the British and US on the conduct of the air war. Britain had been subjected to sustained German bombing of its cities and citizens, the US had not. US hierarchy favoured the destruction of the German military, industrial and economic systems; the British and particularly Air Chief Marshal Arthur "Bomber" Harris, believed the bombing campaign should encompass German cities. It would not be until May that there would be general agreement on the overall framework, codenamed "Pointblank", for a combined Bombing Offensive against Germany. Harris interpreted the framework as giving approval for the attack on any German industrial city of 100,000 inhabitants or more – it would take a little longer before those in charge of the US Eighth Air Force to agree. A zone map of cities, based on aerial photographs, was prepared and in the years to follow the world would witness destructive power as never before.

Two revolutionary aids, Oboe and H2S were introduced into service. Oboe utilised signals transmitted from ground stations and these enabled Pathfinder aircraft to mark their target in all but the very worst weather. Initial trials resulted in a myriad of technical problems. Modifications enhanced performance though intermittent signal interference continued. Oboe's range restricted it to the Ruhr but aircrew were pleased with any aid which assisted them to penetrate the glare of searchlights, decoy lighting systems and industrial haze protecting many Happy Valley targets. H2S was an airborne device less accurate than Oboe but the rough radar map of the ground over which the bomber was flying was very useful and there were no range restrictions.

Nonetheless German night defences had reached formidable new levels by early 1943 and Airborne Interception-equipped night fighters exacted an increasingly heavy toll particularly during deep penetration raids into the Reich. Bomber losses rose rapidly during January even though operations were reduced by winter weather. For Australian aircrew of Bomber Command, 1943 started in the same way as 1942 had finished. It was difficult not to waver in faith. You needed to believe in what you were doing; you were comforted by the ability and comradeship of those serving with you and hoped this was enough; and prayed this horrible mess would be over very soon.

The real experience and tragedy of aircrew was misunderstood and unappreciated by the general public in Britain and elsewhere – it was deemed not good for morale to feature reality. Invariably there was very little difference in the patriotic message imbued in cinematic films and the more blatant propaganda of the newsreels.

The films of 1942 did not reflect the reality of air war.

At the same time, films released for general consumption included such fare as Captains of the Clouds; starring James Cagney as a Canadian bush pilot motivated by a Winston Churchill speech to enlist in the Royal Canadian Air Force. *Desperate Journey* was straight out of Hollywood. Australian actor Errol Flynn, the consummate hero, played a member of an RAF bomber crew that was shot down. He went on to outsmart his Nazi pursuers and fly a captured British aircraft back to England. Flynn would be aided in this feat by the American member of the crew, played by actor Ronald Reagan, who would become better known for his political career than for this film role. *One of Our Aircraft is Missing!* commences with the destruction of RAF Wellington bomber "B for Bertie". The crew bale out over The Netherlands and are helped to escape through occupied territory by gallant members of the Dutch resistance.[4] There is not a ruffled male hairstyle in sight, and the downed flyers wear perfectly clean, tailored RAF dress uniforms, as they are welcomed into the homes of Dutch citizens who appear prosperous and cheerful. *Mrs Miniver*, the story of a stoic middle class English family caught up in the World War II German bombing and whose elder son was in the RAF; would win the 1943 academy award for best film. The closest the media came to an honest interpretation was a broadcast by journalist and BBC broadcaster, Richard Dimbleby.

Dimbleby would fly 20 raids as a RAF Observer and on 17 January 1943 he was on his way to Berlin in a Lancaster captained by the Commanding Officer of RAF 106 Squadron, Wing Commander Guy Gibson, DSO, DFC, RAF. The first raid against Berlin had taken place on the night of 25 August 1940 when 95 bombers were despatched to bomb Tempelhof Airport. The 590 miles (950 kilometres) between England and the German capital was an extreme range for bombers. Another raid against Berlin took place on 7/8 November 1941 and out of 160 RAF aircraft 12.5 per cent – 20 were lost.

Harris never lost his fascination with bombing Berlin and by 1943 he had the heavy bombers he needed: "We can wreck Berlin from end to end if the United States Army Air Force will come in on it. It will cost between 400–500 aircraft. It will cost Germany the war".[5] Two probing Berlin operations were staged in January 1943 and although "Losses were disproportionately high with 23 bombers missing and two others written off in crashes"[6] it would not deter those who sent others into the air war. Between mid-1943 and March 1944 the "The Battle for Berlin" would cost RAF Bomber Command more than 500 aircraft and take the lives of 2,690 men with another 1,000 becoming POWs.

On the night of 16 /17 January 1943, 201 aircraft were sent to Berlin. It was the first time in 14 months and Harris provided the dynamic rhetoric: "Tonight you are going to the Big City. You will have the opportunity to light a fire in the belly of the enemy that will burn his black heart out."[7] For the first time purpose-designed Target Indicators rather than modified incendiaries were used. Target Indicators were now red pyrotechnic added to a basic marker mixture of benzol, rubber and phosphorus and one 25 lb (11 kg) Target Indicator could light up a radius of 300 feet (90 metres). The results of this raid on Berlin were nonetheless disappointing. The range was beyond Gee and Oboe and the technological faults were still to be eliminated from H2S. "The Big City" was covered by heavy cloud – damage was minimal. The only redeeming feature of the operation was that the German anti-radar system malfunctioned and subsequently only one British bomber and crew were lost.

Within a day another 170 bombers took off for Berlin to hit the Daimler-Benz factory and BMW aero-engine factory at Spandau. The route was the same and this time German defences were ready. Broadcaster Richard Dimbleby was in a RAF 106 Squadron Lancaster: "The flak was hot but it has been hotter...For me it was a pretty hair-raising experience and I was glad when it was over, though I wouldn't have missed it for the world. ...We knew well enough when we were approaching Berlin. There was a complete ring of powerful searchlights waving and crossing." Considering the crews who flew this and other operations the journalist broadcast the words: "Night after night they've been out over one of the hottest parts of Germany returning to eat, drink and sleep before going out again. That's their life, and I can promise you it's hard, tiring and dangerous."[8] Whether Dimbleby was caught in the propaganda net or just bowing to the power of the censor he offered the words "We saw no night fighters...nor did any of the flak on the homeward journey come anywhere near us". He was truly blessed because German night fighters did find the bomber stream. In total, 19 Lancasters and three Halifaxes were lost that night, a terrible 11.2 per cent of the force; 135 aircrew were killed, including 14 Australians, and more were taken POW.

Berlin stretched men and machine to the limit and beyond. The flight was around nine hours fifteen minutes in duration – a very long time physically and psychologically to be cooped up in cramped quarters with adrenalin coursing through your veins and no reprieve from constant vigilance. Bombers took off under moonlight and returned to see the wonderful colours of dawn break. Though the white cliffs of Dover were welcome the aircraft still needed to be landed safely. As one RAAF 460 crew approached England after their Berlin raid on the morning of 17 January, they knew it was touch and go with the fuel gauge on the black line. The crew of Lancaster R4816 with one exception, were Australian. The Pilot was Sergeant William (Bill) Murray Wendon (403389), who called Sydney home although he was born in England. He had just celebrated his 22nd birthday. As he nursed the Lancaster over English countryside trying to return to the RAAF 460 home airfield he realised they simply had no fuel left and ordered his crew to abandon the bomber – at least he had got them back safely even if the same could not be said about the Lanc. Men fell from the doomed bomber, canopies opened above them carrying the crew earth-bound. In a familiar landscape they tugged on deflated parachutes and began to count heads – Wendon, the 24-year-old Sydneysider; Sergeant Alastair Kennedy (403619) 24, a bloke born in Stirlingshire, Scotland, but who moved to Sydney; Sergeant Ronald Gordon Wynn (408605) 25, the Middle Upper Gunner from Geelong, Victoria; 21-year-old Rear Gunner Sergeant Alexander Clive Johnston (404684), who was born in Tenterfield, NSW; Sergeant Gordon Alexander Williams, (411082) 24, the Wireless Operator/Air Gunner from the Blue Mountains; the 22-year-old RAF Engineer, Sergeant Clarence Askham (936478) from Yorkshire. One was missing RAAF Sergeant Dudley Anstruther Corfe (411124). His body was found, his parachute had never opened. The 29-year-old Navigator, son of Dr Anstruther and Bertha Corfe of the NSW inland town of Inverell, had left the bomber with his helmet still on his head and his intercom radio leads became entangled with his parachute lines. Corfe, a man of great potential, Melbourne University graduate in Arts/Law, was buried in Bubwith (All Saints) Churchyard, England. In a week's time he would be joined in the churchyard by another RAAF 460 Australian, Flight Lieutenant John Howard Kearns (400804) 33, from Ballarat, Vic, and husband to Elizabeth.

There was little respite for Bill Wendon's crew, little time to mourn their popular navigator. They were assigned another Navigator, 24-year-old RAAF Flight Sergeant Evan Seaforth MacKenzie (403146), from the cold weather NSW town of Guyra. It was a very small world given the Wireless Operator/Air Gunner, Gordon Williams, came from Black Mountain, almost spitting distance from Guyra. Flight Sergeant Neville Ray Mason (404987) from the central Queensland coast town of Yeppoon joined the crew as Bomb Aimer. Disappointingly the crew was transferred to RAF 156 – which was unusual for an almost exclusively Aussie crew. Wendon had been one of the original 460 Squadron aircrew and his expertise would be missed. Neville Mason was doubly disappointed to leave RAAF 460 because his twin brother, Flight Sergeant Norman Talbot Mason (404975) also served with 460 Squadron. The boys not only looked alike but had done pretty much everything together, same schooling at Rockhampton High, and had both participated in swimming and lifesaving. It was no surprise that the twins enlisted the same day and both undertook Observer training.

Flight Sergeant Norman Mason was killed on Australian Day 1943, on a raid against Lorient, north-western France. His RAAF 460 Squadron crew consisted of pilot and captain, Sergeant Harold Bruce Oliver (403368) from Armidale; Flight Sergeant Edmund Joseph Austin (405618) from Brisbane; Sergeant Gordon Robert Sedger (403701) from Lithgow; Flight Sergeant Edwin Atholwood Day (403913) from Adelaide; Sergeant Stanley James Matthews (14444) of Sydney; and 21-year-old RAF Engineer, Sergeant John Robert Brierley (1499412) from Lancashire. The men of RAAF 460 mourned the crew and tried to appreciate the impact of Norman Mason's death on Neville Mason but how did you come to grips with the death of a twin?

On 12 May 1943 Sergeant Bill Wendon's crew, which had been re-assigned to RAF 156, took off to bomb Duisburg, Germany, and did not return. This time only Williams survived to become a POW. Bert and Winnifred Mason of Yeppon, Queensland, had lost a future and both their 22-year-old twin sons, Neville and Norman, in less than four months. The district of Rockhampton and Yeppon had lost the potential of two men who would likely have added much. The family were "further distressed" when during a radio "Morning Bulletin" it was reported "Flight Sergeant N R Mason took part in a bombing attack on Mannheim". Norman had been killed four months earlier. Emotions were running high as the family and their friends mourned. Local Deputy Public Curator, Mr M J McMahon, was indignant, "there must be definitely something wrong somewhere". He pointed out that the RAAF had initially got the twins confused and advised the wrong twin had been killed in January 1943. Next they had sent telegrams and letters to the Mason parents care of the wrong address and as a result Neville's death was published before the Masons received official advice. Finally a radio broadcast which included the name of a son killed months before. "For the sake of the relatives and friends of these boys", Deputy Public Curator McMahon pointed out the errors needed to be eliminated. The response from the Department of Air was that "this local authority has overstepped his authority" and their Minister would speak to his Minister.

It was not uncommon for brothers to join the RAAF. To many a youth his big brother was a hero in a glamorous uniform on the cutting edge of the adventure of war – magnificent men in their flying machines. Fred Borrett joined the RAAF Reserve when war was declared and was one of the first to pester the RAAF for enlistment to defend the British Empire – his name was after all Frederick Britain Borrett. He was nonetheless born and bred in Western Australian. Although Fred did not excel at school his solid build enabled him to do well at sports and he was a natural leader at Perth Boys' School and then Perth Modern School. His gregarious nature boded well with his chosen career as a radio announcer on Radio Perth. Entry into the RAAF as a "trainee (pilot)" occurred in May 1940. Fred was not entirely a natural and managed only "Satisfactory" during training – perhaps he was fortunate the early demand placed on the RAAF by the RAF was for young pilots. He arrived home on embarkation leave resplendent in air force blue and gold wings. Younger brother Arnold was suitably impressed. The boys were teenagers when their father died, consequently Fred was the main role model in Arnold's life.

Arnold Harvey Borrett filled out his RAAF application form in September 1940 with a flourish accentuating anything and everything he believed might give him an edge in selection in this highly competitive race. He wrote "Yes" to the question "Of pure European descent?" Arnold even wrote beside the nationality question of his parents "Father Australian (South Australia)" and "Mother Australian (New South Wales)", with his own "Place of Birth: Kalgoorlie, Western Australia" it might look just that much more "Australian" having three states represented in the first paragraph. It was certainly unusual given that it was standard practice for applicants to write "British" and his family had migrated from England around 1844. The 23-year-old Arnold was a model applicant, of solid build, fit and strong from swimming and tennis; well educated with some technical college training; and even some security clearance due to being a public servant in the Department

Back row left to right: Frederick, 19 and Arnold, 16.
Front row left to right: Stuart, 14 and Carmen, 15.

of Treasury. He was already serving with the militia, the 13th Field Coy., Royal Australian Engineers. It was the last day of March 1941 however before Arnold was told to report to Pearce, Western Australia. He was disappointed when mustered as an Air Gunner – he would have liked to be a pilot like Fred, at least he was finally in the game.

For Leading Aircraftsman Arnold Borrett (406769) the first serious training was at the Wireless and Gunnery school at Ballarat. He was cranky when a misdemeanour was added to his record for being "responsible for lights burning after a general order for lights out had been given by the hut Non-commissioned Officer" (NCO). Arnold decided his hut NCO was one of those pedantic types more interested in following the fine letter of regulations than in fighting the war. This bloke was only a Corporal, was 31, but had only joined the air force a couple of months before himself – he would likely never see actual action. Arnold was found guilty, and received five days extra duty. He had been scoring "very good" and now they scribbled "satisfactory" on his RAAF service card. Time at No.2 Bombing and Gunnery School, Port Pirie, SA went quickly – perhaps there was something to be said for being an air gunner, the training was shorter. Arnold realised he would have months of overseas operational and conversion training but he was hoping he and Fred might serve in the same squadron, or even the same crew given Fred was a pilot and skipper. Less than a year after he enlisted Sergeant Arnold Borrett embarked from Melbourne for the UK, less than a year later he would be dead.

Flight Sergeant Frederick Britain Borrett (402104) found himself not in the green, misty English or Scottish countryside but in the hot harsh Middle East, attached to RAF 11 Squadron, which had been sent to Aden, Egypt, as the war in the Mediterranean intensified. Instead of flying Stirling, Wellingtons, or Halifax bombers, Fred found himself flying the Bristol Blenheim monoplane as part of the RAF Aircraft Delivery Unit (ADU). The Blenheim was all-metal, with two, Bristol Mercury VIII air-cooled radial engines, capable of 840 hp (627 kW). Armament comprised of two .303 in (7.7 mm) machine guns and the Blenheim carried a 1,000 lb (454 kg) bombload. Originally the aircraft was fast – capable of 285 mph (459 k/m), but as heavier equipment

Frederick Britain Borrett.   *Arnold Harvey Borrett.*

was installed and AXIS fighters modernized the speed advantage was eclipsed. The Blenheim would nonetheless play an important role in the North African campaign through a combination of "astute reconnaissance and well-planned bomber operations".[9] Some pilots believed them fun to fly but others found them challenging. Fred Borrett was one of those not entirely comfortable with this light bomber. In January 1942 he was injured in a crash, and spent three weeks in hospital with lacerations and a hand wound. Emily Borrett received the telegram from Dept of Air – they had her son's name wrong, Cedric instead of Frederick – one would think that they could at least get his name right. She now had two of her three sons in bombers and it was difficult not to worry.

Fred was happy with his all Aussie crew. The Blenheim could only fit three. The Navigator was Sergeant Robert Fordell Henderson (405192) 22, from the Brisbane suburb of Toowong. He was a top RAAF trainee attaining second place at Initial Training School and finishing top of his Air Observer's School with a distinguished pass. The Wireless Operator/Air Gunner was Flight Sergeant John Alexander Bowditch (403523), a 26-year-old former mixed business manager from the tiny Riverina town of Talmalmo via Albury, who enlisted on 6 January 1941. On 19 August 1942, the Australian crew took off on an exercise from Lagos. Their Blenheim was seven miles north of the Nigerian town of Oshogbo, Nigeria, it was 0900 but a squall approached over the horizon. Radios crackled as the flight leader instructed Blenheim crews to return to base. There was no response from Fred Borrett and his aircraft disappeared into turbulence and heavy rain. What was left of the Blenheim and its crew would be eventually found. They were declared dead from "multiple injuries and burns". The telegram was awful: "Deeply regret to inform you that your son…is reported to have lost his life as result of aircraft accident in Middle East on 19th August 1942. The Air Board join with the Air Ministry in expressing profound sympathy in your sad Bereavement." After the word "son" a different name was simply typed in, three households, one in Brisbane, one in Perth and one in the Riverina, received the telegram they had prayed they would never receive and somehow it seemed worse because the crash was deemed "accidental".

Bob Henderson's parents would receive a letter from a RAAF official which included: "Your son's instructors found him keen, energetic and conscientious. He at all times went about his work cheerfully and with quiet efficiency". Blanche Henderson answered the letter with "He was a son to be proud of". Emily Eliza Borrett was told; "Your son was unable to keep control of the aircraft when caught in the squall". The three Australians were buried in a small cemetery in Oshogbo. In successive communications the name of the Nigerian town was spelt differently – this was 1942 when few Australians could place the African nation on a world map. In the official notification the department also got her son's name wrong "(402104) Sergeant/Pilot Bonett Frederick Britain". Later still, in 2011, the nation's archives compounded the error and his entry appears as "Cedric Borrett".

Sergeant Arnold Borrett (406769) was told his brother Fred was missing while he was with 20 OTU. The adventure had paled with reality and what he had lost. To his sister Carmen, he wrote: "I hope that this year will see the end of the war and then for the grand reunion of our family. There will be two missing though. That will spoil it quite a lot. However we have the consolation of knowing that both Dad and Fred are together and even though they are in body far away at least they are very near to us in spirit."[10]

Arnold continued to train for operations and was posted to RAF 15 Squadron on 6 February 1943. His operational career lasted less than a fortnight. On 19 February 1943 he and his crew were sent to bomb

Wilhelmshaven. Arnold had teamed up with a New Zealand pilot, Flying Officer Bernard Verdum Crawford (414256). Also in the crew was a Canadian Navigator, Flying Officer Clarence Roy Long (J/11238), three RAF, and another Australian, former Hurlstone Agricultural College student and now Middle Upper Gunner, Flight Sergeant Charles John Jay Wellesley, (405370). The Stirling I bomber was an easy target for a night fighter piloted by Oblt Jabs less than two hours after takeoff. Bodies of crew washed ashore separately along the Dutch coast.

Emily Borrett was advised Arnold was missing on 23 February. In an effort to dampen the shock the RAAF added: "Recollecting the bereavement you have already had in the loss of your son Flight Sergeant Frederick Britain Borrett, I trust that any further news received will be good news. Permit me to extend to you the sincere sympathy of the Department in the anxiety you are suffering."

Emily Borrett felt the weight of grief that her sons, 25 and 27 years, had been killed overseas. Her youngest and remaining son Stuart Donnin Borrett had enlisted in the RAN rather than the RAAF at the beginning of 1941 and trained as a telegraphist. Due to the death of his brothers he applied for a compassionate discharge but was denied. He served on corvettes and survived the war.

In June 1948 Emily Borrett was advised that the body of her son Arnold had been "recovered from the sea near Texel Island and he was buried in a small private cemetery in sand dunes on the island of Schiermonigkoog. Who in Australia would know where Schiermonigkoog was? Emily now had one son buried on a small windswept island, the most northerly of the Frisian Islands lying 6¾ miles (11 km) off the Dutch Coast and a son buried in Nigeria, West Africa: she would never have an opportunity to visit either grave. Emily wrote to the Department of Air asking particulars of the vicinity of Fred's grave, if she could perhaps have a photo and if his burial place was receiving any care. The return letter advised her "Ogbomosha is situated 125 miles north-east of Lagos", again the town name was incorrect – Frederick Borrett was buried in Oshogbo, not Ogbomosho. Emily was told she would need to write to the UK, to the "Imperial Grave Commission" for further details. On the matter of the photograph she needed to "appreciate the magnitude of this work" as well as the remoteness of the location and therefore "some time may elapse before a photograph" would be available.

Frederick Borrett buried on Oshogbo, Nigeria.

To lose one son was devastating to lose two sons meant sadness few could imagine. Sometimes it also meant a family ceased to exist. Kenneth John Winterbon was the son of a successful businessman and land owner in Essex. His life was comfortable and privileged until World War I. He enlisted to fight the enemy of the British Empire and

Arnold Borrett buried on the island of Schiermonnikoog, The Netherlands.

his pleasant outlook on life was wrenched away on the battlefields of France. The stain on the soul left by such war service eased when he met and married Hilda Constance Watson. Hilda was charming, cultured, musical and educated. She spoke several languages and had been a Governess to the children of Kaiser Wilhelm II. She had accompanied the family on a trip to Russia where they stayed with the Czar.

The light left Emily's eyes.

Their first son, John Trevor, was born in 1921 and Brian Kenneth, their second, was born in 1924. The gloom from World War I made the rainy grey English days harder to endure and the family decided to begin another life in Australia. Kenneth's brothers Arthur and George were already in Australia when the family boarded the SS *Orvieto* in 1927. They settled in a suburb on the north shore of Sydney Harbour. The magnificence of the harbour and the splendour of ships moving through its waters, bearing the flags of exotic countries, encouraged John's restlessness. Desperate for adventure rather than the class room he was delighted to be taken on as a Deck Boy with an Australian cargo line.[11]

A larger adventure arrived and the 19-year-old John persuaded Hilda to sign first his army enlistment papers and then his RAAF ones in 1940. He applied to be considered as a "fitter (motor transport driver)". Never did he believe he would be considered for aircrew but the RAF needed pilots so a pilot he became. By August 1942 he was back in the land of his birth. After further training he arrived at RAF 101 Squadron in April 1943 but a month later he was transferred to RAF 156.

Brian and John Winterbon.

Brian impatiently marked time until his 18th birthday. His elder brother was a RAAF pilot and Brian couldn't wait to try to emulate heroic feats more part of the imagination than reality. Hilda signed the consent form and Brian donned the baggy trainee uniform on 5 November 1942. He had hoped to be a pilot like John but the RAAF judged Brian more suited in intellect and persuasion for Observer. Brian was still training when the news came that his brother was "missing in action, believed killed".

On the night of 21 June 1943, 705 aircraft took off to raid Krefeld. In total, 2,306 tons of bombs were dropped burning out the centre of the city. The next night a force of 557 aircraft severely damaged Mulheim. On the night of 24 June the target for 630 British aircraft was Wuppertal. Aircraft losses for the three targets were 6.2 per cent, 6.3 per cent and 5.4 per cent respectively,[12] of airmen "losses were grievous 113 crews missing".[13]

On 22 June 1943 Flight Sergeant John Winterbon (413469) eased his Lancaster into the summer sky at 2307 to bomb Mulheim. A night fighter attacked the RAF 156 bomber with an Australian pilot and the Lancaster crashed at 0210 near Maarn (Utrecht). The Squadron Commanding Officer wrote to Kenneth and Hilda Winterbon expressing his sympathy for their anxiety but that "quite a fair proportion of our flying personnel who are reported missing...have managed to make a safe descent by parachute". He added that it was likely that John and his crew "gave a good account of themselves under whatever circumstances prevented them from bringing their aircraft back". John Winterbon and his crew, average age 22, were buried in the cemetery in the woods, Amersfoort, The Netherlands.[14]

Flight Sergeant Brian Winterbon (429254) assumed he would join his brother in the European war – instead he joined a war in the Pacific. He was the Navigator of Catalina A24-53 tasked to lay mines off Dutch Borneo. The Catalina had nine onboard; Flight Sergeant D G Abbey (410135) was the Captain and first pilot, and Flying Officer F K Robinson (402544) was the Second Pilot. Also onboard were two Wireless Operator/Air Gunners; two Flight Engineers, a Fitter and an Armourer.[15] To lay the mines in the bay the Catalina was low and vulnerable, ground fire broke out. Before they could gain altitude they were hit, with mines still onboard the Catalina exploded and disappeared into the bay. Flight Sergeant Brian Kenneth Winterbon (429254) was only 19. Kenneth and Hilda Winterbon received another telegram, this one saying Brian was missing. The Pacific war was still raging, and there was no further news. In some ways having no definite confirmation was worse than knowing Brian had been killed – in some ways it wasn't. The letter sent to the next of kin read; "I regret to inform you that no further news of your son has been received. With the cessation of hostilities against Japan and the re-occupation of Japanese held territory, it is hoped that more definite information concerning the fate of missing members will soon be obtained."

Mr R L Van Kralinger a Dutch member of the Salvation Army and Japanese POW, would recall how exhilarated he was to catch sight of an Allied aircraft. When a Japanese convoy entered Balipapan Bay the next day: "It was a great delight to see how the ships were struck by explosion and either sank or were set on fire". The Japanese brought the bodies of the Catalina crew ashore and ordered POWs to bury them. According to Van Kralinger: "One of us picked flowers that were put on the graves...I made a short speech and had us stand to attention. We were surprised the Japs allowed us to do so." Life would be lonelier for Kenneth and Hilda Winterbon, there was no real solace when the war ended. Kenneth who survived one World War but lost his sons in another, died in 1962. Hilda wished she had never signed the military consent forms and died in 1971.

RAAF Observer Don Charlwood looked around at his RAF 103 Squadron peers in the Sergeants mess. They were due to leave on another operation. The waiting was hard. Aircrew sat slumped in well worn armchairs, some read, others wrote letters; some spoke in subdued tones, some preferred not to speak at all. Charlwood referred to their expression as "contemptuous serenity", the sullen manifestation of men about to face another test of their courage and conviction, the look of men about to face death yet again.

It was a January night in 1943 and a worn recording of "Tristesse" played on the gramophone. This haunting song seemed now part of the mess ritual during the waiting – it would be a melody those still alive by war's end never wished to hear again. Charlwood wondered who would not come back this night or the next night, and with a new sense of urgency he returned to the letter he was writing to a home he had not seen for nearly 17 months: "Once again it scarcely seems possible that we will leave this room with its chairs and fire, for the grey miles of the North Sea, then Germany."[16]

Charlwood believed Observers "tended more to seriousness than the men they flew with," Charlwood certainly did.[17] Of course there was always the exception to the rule. Classmate Sergeant Edward (Blue) Roy Freeman (408678) RAAF, was known for his high spirits and lack of reverence. He would be mentioned in the British House of Commons, cited as an example "of poor colonial behaviour", because while intoxicated the 19 year old set fire to a Land Army cottage on display in Trafalgar Square.[18] Freeman faced a Court Martial in April 1943 but was acquitted.

Charlwood often contemplated his No 35 Observer Course, a group of raw but enthusiastic aircrew recruits who commenced their Canadian training on 10 October 1941. They had left Sydney in September 1941 onboard the SS *Monterey* on an amazing adventure. Friendships were quickly made. Charlwood and Robert Maxwell Bryant (411748) would not have met if not for the war. Bryant was a 20-year-old student from the NSW country town of Cowra. Charlwood was a 26 year old from Melbourne who had tried his hand at several occupations, whose love of writing and short stories and articles supplemented his wages. Bryant was described by his Cowra High School headmaster in glowing terms, as someone who made "maximum use of his undoubtedly high ability". Bryant was an excellent student who achieved the highest Intermediate results in the school and during his Leaving Certificate years "was a most successful House Captain last year, and was appointed Boys' School Captain at the beginning of this year".

He has carried out his duties with thoroughness and tact and attained a degree of respect from his fellow pupils almost equal to that of a teacher. His relations with the staff have also been excellent. He won the prize for sportsmanship and leadership at the end of this year – an honour thoroughly deserved. I feel quite confident in recommending him as I feel sure that he will do well in whatever walk of life he takes.[19]

Bryant chose his "walk of life" but then a war altered the future and the RAAF recruiting train rolled into Cowra in 1940. Bryant enthusiastically filled out enlistment papers writing "Have passed Law Examinations". A reference from a Cowra solicitor included the comment: "Mr Bryant is highly esteemed in this district as a very fine type of young man". Max Bryant applied to be a pilot. At Initial Training School he wrote in his log that he now understood "the petrol and oil systems of the Tiger Moth aircraft" and that "the safe endurance of this aircraft (is) 2 hours 15 minutes". The ability to master theory was not enough and Max was re-mustered as Navigator. Trainee pilots and navigators remained at the Initial Training School for eight weeks preliminary training on a salary of 9/- per day (90 cents) whereas Wireless Operator/Air Gunner pay rate was 5/6d per day (56 cents) until they completed their course and then received 9/-.

It was the intelligent repartee which saw Charlwood and Bryant become firm friends on the ship to North America. Max Bryant was fascinated by all he saw and all he heard. Food was the first marvel because this was an American merchant ship and the food seemed endless and for a country lad there were so many new taste sensations:

Breakfast: boiled salmon bellies with melted butter. Fried or boiled ham or bacon and eggs. Poached or scrambled eggs with asparagus tips. Boiled or hash brown pots. Cold buffet roast beef, ox tongue, York ham, roast lamb rolls, spiced buns, hotcakes breakfast rolls, preserves many.

Dinner: smoked salmon; canapé of minced chicken; sliced eggs and tomato with Russian sauce. Consommé with barley or cream of seafood madras. Grilled halibut steak, anchovy butter. Larded beef tenderloin with Madeira sauce; boiled chicken with rice mare hale; string beans, buttered carrots, Hawaiian poi. Walnut cake, cantaloupe, sherbet, strawberry blancmange. Pimiento, Brie, Neufchatel, fresh fruit in season, demitasse.

Diary entries exuded Max Bryant's interest in the fascinating new world opening to this latest class of aircrew recruits from the land down under. It was so cosmopolitan – straight out of the movies almost, he was in America for a World Heavyweight Title Fight: "Joe Louis successfully defended his heavyweight title for the 19th time a TKO over Lou Nova in the sixth round of their 15 round bout in New York."

In New York he went to The Ethel Barrymore Theatre, to see the musical Best Foot Forward, and then to the Radio City Music Hall to see "America's greatest revue". A billboard read; "Thru these Portals pass the most beautiful girls in the world". "Thru" may have been spelled differently but Max was most impressed to see the "very leggy" show girls who were "very scantily clad" – he was a long way from Cowra, NSW.

Charlwood and Bryant sat with the other 23 Australians of No 35 Observers Course at No 2 Air Observer and No 16 Elementary Flying Training School, Edmonton, Alberta, Canada, for their official photo. Clearly the photographer was more interested in the formal and regimented look than the more relaxed look reflective of the nation from which they hailed. Each was given a copy and it is easy to imagine what comments were forthcoming about the seriousness of the faces and the perfectly well-ordered crossed legs.

Within a month Bannister and O'Sullivan had failed early tests

Edmonton, Canada. 1941. Left to right, back row: Colin Cherrill Cooper (405395), Guy Bamford Herring (411783), John MacKenzie Oberlin Harris (408129), Wilfred Gordon Burrows (411739); Harold Theodore Waddell (412217), Joseph Albert Turnbull (411555), Thomas John James Cunliffe (411127), Robert Maxwell Bryant (411748). Middle row: Colin McDowell Miller (401848), Donald Ernest Cameron Charlwood (408794), Edward Freeman (408678), Ronald Wheatley (412053), Rupert Theodore Bannister (411475), George Joseph O'Sullivan (408699), Ian Victor Heatley (405310), George Bruce Loder (412160), Ronald Pender Bowen Anzac Pender (411517). Front row: Owen Barton Lloyd (412155), Thomas Hector. McNeill (405381), Harold John Alfred Wright (405611), Harold James Barker (405288), John Sidney Braithwaite (411479), Keith Robert Webber (411562), John Irvine Gordon (412218), William Roy Kenneth Charlton (411121). (Australian War Memorial)

and returned to Australia. Lloyd broke a leg and was repatriated. Guy Herring and Jack Harris required further training. Don Charlwood henceforth named the successful graduates who sewed the half wing with a large "O" above their left pocket, the Twenty Men. They shipped off to England with no real inkling of what lay ahead. All too soon their number diminished.

During OTU Don Charlwood was confronted by West Australian pilot, Sergeant Geoff Maddern (406601), "a rather short, untidy" man who had a rather contemptuous regard for RAF spit and polish. Maddern asked Charlwood if he would join his Wellington crew. While Maddern may have had a distinct lack of regard for RAF uniform standards, most would refer to Maddern as "the personification of courage". Charlwood did not hesitate joining the Western Australian's crew. Rear Gunner was an English Sergeant from Nottingham: Arthur Browett, chose to be as out of touch with RAF uniform regulations as Maddern and went by the nickname "Shag". The Bomb Aimer was Ted Batten. The last to join the crew was a Wireless Operator/Air Gunner from NSW, Sergeant Reginald Maxwell (Max) Burcher (411440) an "impetuous youngster" who "had the restlessness of a caged tiger".[20]

On their first trip aloft the crew were a "planeload of bewildered individuals" most of whom questioned simultaneously and frequently Charlwood's navigational ability. The by now flustered Observer remembered an insightful tip from his instructor about not allowing other crew to rattle you and if they did a navigator should simply pull out his intercom plug. Charlwood did so and then returned the bomber and the "bewildered individuals" to base in a timely fashion.

Posted to RAF 103 meant crew changes. Don Charlwood and Geoff Maddern stayed together, the Engineer was Welshman, Doug Richards. The Middle Upper Gunner was Frank Holmes. As the various members of the crew demonstrated their own prowess mutual respect and confidence grew. They bonded together also during non-operational hours, invariably over a beer or more.

Don Charlwood roomed with classmate Harold John Alfred Wright (405611) who was the "untidiest, most generous, least promising-looking man among us. He was a Queenslander and spoke "with a pronounced Australian accent". The 21-year-old Wright was a former draughtsman. During his time in England Charlwood noticed Wright's Australian accent became even more pronounced – it was a pride thing. Wright carried in his kit bag other items to remind him and others of his origins, such as an Australian army slouch hat. He also fixed a boomerang above the head of his bunk on which he would notate his operations. He believed the boomerang would "bring me back" to Australia. The strength of the boomerang proved worthy although Wright needed more than a single boomerang on which to notate his operations. He would complete 28 operations with RAF 103 Squadron and a further 50 with RAF 156. Wright would return to Brisbane with a DFC and bar and a DFM – and be pretty unfazed by it all.

It was September 1942 and Charlwood's crew was operational. As the RAF 103 bombers queued for take-off Max Bryant, who had been visiting Charlwood, watched from the edge of the airfield, Maddern released the brakes and "they came thundering up the runway, lumbering heavily lifting off at the end".[21] Take-off with a full bomb load was very dangerous and Max Bryant was pleased to see the Maddern/Charlwood bomber disappear on the horizon. He returned his attention to those left. The second last bomber was in the charge of 21-year-old West Australian pilot Sergeant William John Percival Fletcher (406476), a former student of Fremantle Boys' High and Christ Church Grammar, who had been employed as a Shipping Clerk. Also onboard was 26-year-old Wireless Operator/Air Gunner Sergeant James Gordon Milne (408774) a farmer from Tatura, Victoria. The Navigator was classmate 30-year-old Sergeant Joseph Albert Turnbull (411555) from NSW, perhaps the most vociferous and rubicund among the Twenty Men. The bomber barely made it off the ground before Fletcher pulled the Wimpy into a steep turn as the port engine began to falter. Bryant could but watch as the bomber crashed "suddenly the [wingtip] light dashed straight into the ground". Flames leapt skyward before the deadly cargo ignited in bright flashes ending the lives of the men within. It was horrific to witness knowing that in that inferno was a mate, other Australians, other aircrew.[22] It was particularly eerie as Joe Turnbull had told Don Charlwood that he would be dead inside a week, and he was. The crew were buried in Fradley (St Stephen's) Churchyard, Staffordshire – by war's end 24 of the 35 World War II remains buried there were Australian.

Charlwood acknowledged that he was a typical Observer which, at times, could be a curse, because the thoughts and questions never really went away. It was January 1943 and RAF 103 crews were told they would be operational the following night. Sleep this night did not come for Charlwood as his heart pounded and a "long succession of thoughts moved with leaden feet across my mind". This was one of two occasions that Bomber Command morale was low. When the briefing room doors closed Charlwood felt that familiar knot in the stomach. He hoped it was an Italian target – "Italian targets weren't considered worthy of a bomb painted on the aircraft's nose",[23] instead an ice-cream cone was painted on the nose of the bomber on the completion of the operation. When the target was revealed it was no ice-cream cone, the target was Essen. Charlwood the serious Observer yet again noticed the stony resolute expressions of other aircrew, how there was now:

> Something ugly in the room; something grotesque. However much one may read of war and train for war, it is not until the unbelievable moments before action that reality suddenly strangles one. We were about to kill people we had never seen. And they would attempt to kill us. I felt an urgent need to think, even though I knew that all my thinking of the past three years had failed to clarify my mind. ...To kill and to be killed. Why was this, again? Freedom: yes that was it; for freedom. Whose freedom? Freedom for what?[24]

Geoff Maddern nudged his thoughtful Observer and Charlwood wrote down the meteorology officer's assessment for this night and target notes. They were to fly at a height which was supposed to be too high for light flak and too low for heavy flak and night fighters. Maddern left immediately in the hope of booking "a good kite. 'R Robert' is about the best of a poor lot". Ground crew liked the brash Australian so his crew was confident he would indeed be assigned the best bomber available. Charlwood noticed how the mood in the room "changed swiftly to something elating but strangely unpleasant, as though suddenly we had been stripped to spiritual nakedness". Happy Valley had that sort of affect on aircrew, a bugger of a place to attack. On the bus to the aircraft Charlwood felt "a sudden paralysis", he felt like a man in a dream who wanted to "run away". Nonetheless, he was "rooted to where he stood", a feeling which lasted until take-off.

Bomb Aimer Sergeant John (Jack) Vincent Conlon (411084) enlisted in March 1941 and embarked overseas in July the same year.

From the inner Sydney suburb of Glebe Point and a product of De La Salle College, he enrolled in the Sydney University Regiment and was undergoing high school teacher training at Christian Brothers Lewisham. After OTU he posted to RAF 12 Squadron, then RAAF 460. Now he was a Bomb Aimer on a Lancaster. It was another operation, tonight, 23/24 January 1943 they were on their way to Dusseldorf and the nerves were overcome by getting on with the job. Conlon edged past the pilot and made his way forward. Their skipper, considered one of the best, was popular RAAF 460 "A" Flight Commander, RAF Squadron Leader Richard Bentley Osborn (74686), DSO, DFC.

Conlon had a quick look at the bombsight and at the computing mechanism on the right of it. He glanced to the left at the bomb selector switches and those governing the tail and nose fuse-settings. Next he looked at the bomb-distributor mechanism and selector arm.[25] His head was into the task ahead, loads of responsibility, lots of precision required – on his shoulders the success of the bombing run. He crawled further forward and moved upwards into the front turret to examine the two .303 Browning machine guns and ready and loaded ammo trays, giving a silent thank you to the ground crew and armourers who likely stood now watching on the verge of the take-off area – they had again done their duties well. Conlon's brain was racing as he worked through the mental check list. He examined the oxygen connector and intercom socket – communication was so important between himself and his Skipper as they approached the target area. He had come to the end of his check list so dropped down into the fuselage again and crawled back through the bomb-aimer's compartment.

Sergeant Ivor Hayes the RAF Flight Engineer was checking his equipment and barred the way – some vulgar pleasantries and the Englishman moved to let Conlon past – this bloke was certainly learning the Aussie lingo. Conlon asked Wireless Operator/Air Gunner Sergeant Phillip Andrew Martin (406441) if he would come aft with him to check the photo-flash housing. Martin was acquainted with his photo-flash task but a double check never went astray and it was good to be kept busy prior to take-off. Martin was a 22-year-old Western Australian, from Northam, on the banks of the Avon River, about 90 or so minutes from Perth. One of Martin's duties was to release the flash manually if it didn't leave the aircraft when the bombs were dropped to ensure a good photo over the target.

There was nothing else to do until they were well in the air so Conlon settled down. Thoughts of the WAAF (Women's Auxiliary Air Force) member he was seeing brought a smile to his face: she was a great girl and was going to help him buy a ring for his sister. Conlon had been saving for some time and now had enough to buy the ring, a 21st birthday gift. He may need to think about saving for another ring if this romantic relationship kept getting better, another slight smile – she liked that he was a good classical violinist, something he took some teasing about from his 460 Squadron peers, or those who could not play an instrument. Conlon found playing the violin took his mind off more serious duties. Some days he wondered why he had volunteered! It was a strange feeling because if he were told he could just walk away from this operation and his crew, he wouldn't be able to do it.

In the crew was his "great friend" the Rear Gunner Pilot Officer Stuartson (Stewie) Charles Methven (400391). Stewie was born in Suva, Fiji after his parents Ruby Iris and Stuartson Collard Methven moved from London to the South Pacific. The family then moved to Melbourne. Stewie enlisted in August 1940 and had struggled with the news that his younger brother Captain John Malcolm Methven (VX48690) 23, of the 2/23 Australian Infantry Battalion, had been killed on 22 July 1942, and was buried in El Alamein War Cemetery, Egypt. The Observer was another Australian, Flying Officer Harold (Bing) Leonard Edward Longworth (403620) from Maitland, NSW, a former Commonwealth Bank Teller. This was his 14th trip, still less than half way through a tour – in some ways it rushed past in a blur, in others it seemed to take forever. The Middle Upper Gunner was Sergeant Ronald Arthur Brown (401812) RAAF, a 21-year-old former clerk from Northcote, Victoria.

The Skipper gave the thumbs-up to the two ground crew operating the starter mechanism and first the port-inner engine and then the starboard-inner burst into life. The starboard-outer Merlin engine roared followed by the port-outer. Osborn tested the magnetos of the Merlins, did a check-round of the crew over the intercom, and eased the Lancaster around. They waited until another Lanc took off and their bomber, "C Charlie", edged forward. It was a little unsettling that their regular kite was "J-Johnny" but the mechanics were still working on the Lancaster, so they were assigned the third Lancaster delivered to the Squadron. They tried not to think that the first two, "A" and "B", had been destroyed with their crews in the unwelcome skies over occupied Europe. A green Aldis light and Osborn swung "C Charlie" onto the runway. Another green, maximum pressure was applied to the brakes with help from Hayes. Osborn opened all four throttles as wide as they would go. The bomber was shuddering with anticipation, and as the Skipper released the brakes the Lancaster raced forward. It seemed like they would run out of airfield but ever the consummate pilot Osborn eased back on the control column and the Lancaster lifted up and off, as they said in the movies, "into the wild blue yonder". The undercarriage came up and the crew put on their oxygen masks at 5,000 feet (1,525 metres). At around 8,000 feet (2,440 metres) they set course for Dusseldorf. The bomber stream was small, only 80 Lancasters and three Mosquitos, and with complete cloud cover visibility was not good.

Those who were used to flying in a Lancaster would not wish to fly any other bomber: four Rolls-Royce Merlin engines; height 19½ ft (5.9 m); length 68 ft (21 m); wing span 102 ft (31 m); cruising speed 216 mph (348 k/h); maximum speed 266 mph (428 k/h); ceiling 20,000 ft (6100 m); bomb load 14,000 lbs (6.3 tons) (with fuel for 1,660 miles/2,670 km); twin .303 Brownings in front turret and mid-upper turret; four in rear turret – quite a bird. Jack Conlon preferred his position to that of his mate Stewie Methven. "Tail End Charlie" was the name they gave the Rear Gunner, because they were seated in the rear turret in the unheated, most isolated position in bomber. The Rear Gunner commonly did not see another member of his crew once in his turret, until the aircraft returned to base, often some nine, ten, hours after take-off. Conlon figured you needed to be a particular personality to be a Rear Gunner, and Stewie Methven was that sort of bloke.

As RAAF 460 "C Charlie" approached the target the cloud thickened even more, at least there was minimal flak, but still, bombing accuracy would not occur this night. Jack Conlon lay prone on the floor of the nose dome his view through the large transparent Perspex as good a front on view as any. The controls of the bombsight headlay in front, the bombsight computer was on his left and the release selectors on the right.

LEFT: *Sergeant John (Jack) Vincent Conlon.* RIGHT: *Bomb Aimer.*

He was all concentration, speaking in deliberate tone to his skipper to hold the bomber level, the bomb bay doors open. With no visual on the target when they reached the Estimated Time of Arrival his right thumb pressed hard on the button, better known as the "tit" and called into the intercom "bombs gone". The standing order was that no bombs were to be brought back from Germany. Osborn closed the bomb bay doors. Conlon's job was not yet done, taking the Aldis lamp he shone the light up into the bay. Stories of fused bombs being hung up were legendary.

Jack Conlon breathed a sigh of relief and returned to his nose turret and the .303 Brownings. The machine guns were unlikely to be used as night-fighters very rarely attacked from the front. It had been common for fighters to attack from below until they worked out that such a manoeuvre took out the fighter as well when there was a full bomb load so it was preferred to attack from behind or above. "C Charlie" was cruising along at 12,000 feet (3,660 metres) – they were just over the Zuiderzee, the shallow bay of the North Sea off the Dutch coast, and Jack Conlon's mind was just at that point of thinking about the next date with his Waaf when a cacophony of noise and flashes invaded his senses. His skipper was in all sorts of trouble: "There were flashes and bangs in the cockpit and an almighty thump on my left upper arm and my hand disappeared from the wheel. A deafening roaring noise filled the cockpit, the roar of the slip-stream in the gaping holes along the belly of our plane."[26]

Wireless Operator/Air Gunner, Martin, offered an Australian description "It was like someone running a stick on an empty galvanised-iron tank".[27] The gunners were firing as the fighter swooped, cannon fire shattered fuselage and Brown felt sharp pain as cannon shell fragments entered his right leg below the calf, breaking bones in his right ankle. The main fuel tank between the two starboard engines was ablaze and a sheet of flames streamed back towards the tail plane. Osborn was shocked by the speed of the attack and tried to speak into the intercom but it was dead – they were over the North Sea in mid-winter. The fighter attacked again, Osborn banked and turned the Lancaster sharply to port. With only one hand Osborn was flying by instinct now and by "the seat of my pants".[28] With a badly shattered left arm the Pilot continued to struggle with the controls as the earth loomed up. He let go of the control column for a moment, clasping it between his knees and cut the engine throttles with his only good hand. They were skimming along the ground, no flaps down, wheels up, "I already had more than enough to do without trying to lower these with one hand". The nose of the bomber reared up, hit the ground abruptly, and slithered to a halt. Osborn shouted "everybody out".

Hayes was there, Martin, Longworth, and the wounded Brown – no Conlon or Methven. The rear of the Lancaster was a blaze and they could not get near. Hayes had seen Jack Conlon ready to bale out through the nose hatch. The hatch was only 2½ ft (0.75 m) square and as you were about to exit you were facing aft with your feet placed close together on the front edge – there was no way Jack could have seen how close they were to the ground. The survivors were quickly taken prisoner. The Germans found Jack Conlon's body the next day, his parachute still closed on his chest – he had baled when his aircraft was only 30 feet (9 metres) off the ground. Osborn received extensive medical attention but his arm injury was incapacitating enough for the Squadron Leader to be repatriated prior to the end of the war. The Australians Longworth, Martin, Brown and RAF Sergeant Hayes remained POWs. The two "great friends" were not as fortunate. Stewie Methven died endeavouring to fight off the fighter, his position the most vulnerable. German gunfire likely caused a loss of hydraulic power making it impossible for Stewie to save himself before fire engulfed the rear of the aircraft. His crew hoped their Rear Gunner had been killed outright by gun fire. In June Ruby Methven wrote to the Dept of Air asking for any news of "our darling son". The same day her husband wrote a letter to the captured and hospitalised Osborn: "We feel we know you very well, our precious Stuart frequently spoke of you in his letters...of your many kindnesses to him and to quote his own words, he used to say you were the best skipper in the Air Force."

Michael Sylvester and Mary Matilda Conlon, now living in Orange, NSW, would take some small pleasure in knowing Jack was finally buried in Gaasterland (Bakhuizen) Roman Catholic Cemetery, in Grave 12, Row 24, next to his mate Stewie Methven.

EIGHT

"Our planes become our shrouds."

Flight Sergeant James Patrick Galligan

The European bombing campaign entered another decisive offensive from March 1943 with the Battle of the Ruhr. Sir Arthur Harris would call the months between the spring of 1943 and the spring of 1944 his "main offensive".[1] The Ruhr valley was a vast web-like complex of industry sprawled from the banks of the Rhine between Dusseldorf and Wesel. Within lay centres such as, Bottrop, Dortmund, Bochum, Duisburg, Gelsenkirchen, Duisburg, Essen, Hagen, Hamm, Recklinghausen, Krefeld, and Sterkrade. Whilst he firmly believed to destroy Berlin would bring Nazi Germany to capitulate, he realised the tactical importance of the Ruhr. There had been numerous attacks on Happy Valley and many aircrew killed, but the damage inflicted had been disappointing because the low lying country between Holland and Belgium lay obscured by an industrial haze, making precision bombing difficult. The Ruhr was ringed by searchlight and Flak batteries. Radar stations along the Dutch and Belgium coasts provided a mesh of warning posts and the numerous airfields provided safe harbour for the large night-fighter force.

The Ruhr nonetheless was the very heart of German war industry and it needed to be destroyed. Forty three operations would be launched against the Ruhr between March and July 1943 and approximately 34,000 tons of bombs dropped on cities and their industry. These raids would severely hamper German war industry. German steel production fell by 200,000 tons. Between July 1943 and March 1944 German production of aircraft was severely impeded.[2] From March 1943 Bomber Command was all powerful, from the opening of The Battle of the Ruhr around 600 bombers were available and at the peak of the campaign, around 800 aircraft could participate, four fifths of these were four-engine heavies.[3] The Pathfinder squadrons played a major role – Oboe beams would guide Mosquito Pathfinders to targets. Day weather reconnaissance aircraft greatly assisted operation preparation and the United States 8th Air Force would mean the Ruhr had little respite during the daylight hours. But, The Battle of the Ruhr would come at enormous human cost.

Media banner headlines such as; "Bomber Command has severely hampered German war industry", were trumpeted far and wide throughout the Allied world, the media would not however offer the startling statistics concerning loss of life within Bomber Command. On the first night of The Battle of the Ruhr, 5/6 March, 75 British airmen were dead although the operation against Essen was deemed "most successful with the principal objective, Krupps, damaged on a scale never previously achieved".[4] Within a week Essen was visited again and 127 airmen were killed and 24 became POWs, such casualties were to be commonplace as the offensive continued.

The demands on aircrew continued to grow and flying six operations a week was no longer unusual by 1943. Harris never lost his fascination for Berlin and on the night of 29/30 March despatched 329 aircraft to attack the German capital – the weather conditions were difficult and bombing accuracy suffered. In total, 21 aircraft – 6.4 per cent were lost; 203 aircrew were killed and 24 became POW. The families of these crews could never have envisaged what would occur and how their lives too would be changed forever.

This operation and the young men tasked with fulfilling the huge and dangerous duty were typical for early 1943. The 21-year-old pilot/ skipper of RAAF 460 Lancaster ED391 was Flight Sergeant David

Harold Victor Charlick (416322) from Adelaide. Charlick started flying bombers before he was old enough to vote. Now 21, he could almost be called a veteran carrying a great responsibility on his shoulders. Charlick had chosen as his Navigator Flying Officer Thomas Hector McNeill (405381) a 25 year old born in Gympie, and now from the Brisbane suburb of Milton. As a classmate of Don Charlwood he was one of the Twenty Men. The Bomb Aimer was Flight Sergeant Eric Neil Cooper (403502), a 23-year old from the pretty New South Wales seaside resort of Kiama. Before the war Cooper was a Coles store manager studying law and accountancy and determined to continue his studies and rise further in the retail management sector. Cooper was the sort of candidate the RAAF sought, someone who had demonstrated "all-round interests, with a mechanical bent".[5]

So too was the Rear Gunner, RAAF Flight Sergeant Gordon Vivian Hampton (408578). Hampton was a 22-year old from the Melbourne suburb of Caulfield. After an education at Melbourne Grammar and Melbourne Technical College he applied to join the RAAF as a pilot, but was rejected. He worked as a clerk with a firm of shipping and customs agents until war offered him another opportunity for RAAF service and he opted for the accelerated Air Gunner training. At No.1 Wireless Air Gunners School, Ballarat, Hampton was charged for being "sighted unshaven at 0745 hours" with "Conduct to the prejudice of good order and Air Force discipline". For this he was given two days punishment.

The Engineer was as per usual RAF, Sergeant Percy Perry (980250); the other Air Gunner was also RAF, Sergeant William Patrick Delany Chapman (1316314). The Wireless Operator/Air Gunner was Flying Officer Francis (Frank) James Falkenmire (411445) 26, from the rural town of Tamworth, New South Wales. Frank studied at Armidale Teachers College before becoming a surveyor's assistant in the beautiful Barrington Tops region. He was one of seven brothers and had a sister. His father, George Falkenmire served with the Australian Light Horse during World War I so it seemed natural that his sons should follow his example regardless of any misgivings George may have harboured. Of the other Falkenmire sons and brothers, 23-year-old Bruce (NX140928) and Geoffrey (NX125968) joined the army. Kenneth (S9632) waited impatiently until July 1944 before he enlisted in the Royal Australian Navy aged 17. Alex being a member of the NSW police force remained in that role.

Lancaster ED391 climbed laboriously into the night sky departing at 2145 from RAAF 460 base, Breighton, the night of 29/30 March 1943, bound for Berlin. It was fully loaded with fuel and bombs on what was the crew's seventh operation. The description offered by Flying Officer (later Flight Lieutenant) Frank Falkenmire illustrates well what was a common aircrew experience:

> We were travelling home in just about 10/10ths cloud, and I heard the Rear Gunner say 'Look Out' and then I heard cannon fire hit us along the floor of the fuselage. The machine nosed over and then dived. I heard nothing from the Captain whom I fear must have been killed immediately. I do not know if anyone else was hit. I put on my parachute and then was thrown to the roof; my reaction was to pull the ripcord. This dragged me out of the machine. I landed practically within 50 feet (15 metres) of the wreckage. The aircraft was burning very furiously with its nose in the ground. I was very dazed but I think it exploded. I ran over to the machine where I saw four bodies, all dead. The Germans told me that besides the four people found dead, two others were still in the machine. I am sorry to have to report that all my crew were killed. ...Would you please convey to the parents and relatives of the deceased sincere sympathy?

Lancaster ED391 was shot down by Lt August Geiger, III, and crashed at 0446. Charlick, McNeill, Cooper, Hampton, Perry and Chapman would remain in a cemetery in Lichtenvoords, The Netherlands. They would keep company with an RAF crew from RAF 106 also shot down by Geiger that night, and other aircrew shot down earlier. Ages carved into gravestones read; 22, 21, 22, 25, 20, 24, 20, 22, 26, 27, 19, 26, 19, 20, 21.

The shock was too great for Anne McNeill. She refused to believe her son was "missing, believed dead" and when the confirmation was sent by the RAAF she could only reply: "Why do you have to keep harping about something you don't know the first thing about. I would have you know my son is not dead. ...If that's your best efforts please do nothing, time will work out its solution."

Falkenmire would spend the remainder of the war as a POW. From Stalag Luft III he sent a message to Anne McNeill, "Tom was my best friend. We always promised each other to write to the parents of the other if one survived". Although this would be confirmation it doubtless was not the resolution Anne McNeill sought. Falkenmire would return to Armidale, NSW, the image of his dead crew would stay with him forever, as would the inevitable question, "why not me". The graves of his crew would be cared for by the people of Lichtenvoorde, who would continue to commemorate the 23 Allied airmen aircrew buried in their town, because "these men died for our liberation and it is our duty never to forget their offering for Liberty and Justice".

Flying Officer Frank Falkenmire (courtesy Falkenmire family).

Another 460 Squadron Lancaster shot down that night by Uffz Christian Koltringer was piloted by 28-year-old Flight Lieutenant Kenneth Hugh Grenfell (403735). Kenneth Grenfell was born in the Gilbert Islands but enlisted from Sydney. His Commanding Officer wrote of him; "very keen and willing. Particularly keen to get on to operations". He had recently married an English girl named Mabel from Durham, England. Other Australians in his crew included the Wireless Operator/Air Gunner Flight Sergeant Phillip (Pip) Wesley Dunn (411010) 22, from Watson's Bay, Sydney. The Navigator was Flying Officer Stephen Falcon Scott

McCullagh (403754) 29. He had been born in the green and serene town of Seattle, USA, before calling Sydney's Neutral Bay home. Strangely Air Gunner Flight Sergeant Robert Potter (406680) 31, from Perth, Western Australia, had the very American middle name of "Lincoln". These men went to their deaths knowing that Potter and their RAF Gunner Sergeant Sidney Webb (955673) 26, from Worcestershire, shot down the night fighter and killed its pilot. The crew attempted to bale out but the Lancaster was too low and their parachutes never opened.

During March and April operations were also ordered against widespread geographic regions from Stettin in the Baltic, to Turin in Italy, to Plzen in Czechoslovakia, to the German city of Munich, and the losses made grim reading. In total, 327 aircraft attacked the Skoda armaments factory in Plzen on the night of 16/17 April 1943. The trip of approximately ten hours and 40 minutes taxed crews to the limit. An asylum was mistaken for the target and bombed. The general comment was "missed by miles" and only six crews "brought back bombing photographs which were within 3 miles of the real target".[6] Two hundred German soldiers encamped near the asylum building were believed killed. The mistake was grievous but made all the worse by the Luftwaffe finding the bomber stream and shooting down 36 crews, 11 per cent of the force, including four Canadian 408 Squadron Halifaxes. The same night 18 bombers failed to return from a raid against Mannheim. Fifty four aircraft (8.9 per cent) were lost making this the greatest loss in the history of Bomber Command – it exceeded the 50 aircraft lost on the June 1942 Thousand Bomber raid on Bremen. And the losses continued, on 20/21 April of the 339 aircraft despatched against Stettin 6.2 per cent of the force did not return.[7]

Daisy Hewitt received one of those telegrams which caused a sudden inhale of breath and tears – her son Kenneth Hemsley Hewitt was dead. He was now buried in Bradley St Mary and All Saints Churchyard, Staffordshire, England. She had friends within her Brisbane suburb of Toowong, whose sons had been killed in combat, and she had tried to prepare for the same, but now she struggled with the words "accidental death". It was nearly a month before she could put pen to paper and write: "I would be grateful for further information regarding the accident".

Sergeant Ken Hewitt (414237) had boarded a 27 OTU Wellington bomber on 14 April 1943. His crew included two other Australians, Air Bomber Sergeant Clem Buckeridge (414196) 22, from Bundamba in the Ipswich region of Queensland, and Air Gunner Sergeant Donald Ross Grant (413307) a 22 year old from Goulburn, NSW. They were due to take off on a cross country flight at just before 2200 when their 19-year-old pilot/skipper, RAF Sergeant Roger Crook (1320902), told Ken Hewitt to leave the aircraft and contact 'C' Flight Office to enquire as to the whereabouts of his (Ken's) Bomber Code book. Hewitt alighted from the aircraft through the main hatch. The Wellington engines had just started the warm-up sequence and the Australian navigator due to misdirection, bad luck, or lack of concentration, walked into the port propeller blade suffering a "glancing blow" to the forehead. Crook "switched off the engines and contacted Flying Control". Daisy Hewitt needed to know whether "my son suffered at all and how long he lingered". His death was deemed "accidental" but he was still a casualty of the air war. Daisy Hewitt may have received a "killed in combat" telegram just two months later.

Sergeant Roger Crook's crew were given another navigator and to the delight of Air Gunner Don Grant, it was Flight Sergeant Stanley Joseph Marriage (420697) who hailed from the same home town of Goulburn. Marriage was older than most, at 31, and a former Railway Porter. He was married to Annie and had a daughter named Jill. Don Grant had been a Railway Refreshment Room Buffet Car Attendant and had the same employer – it was indeed a small world that Marriage and Grant should find themselves in the same seven-man Lancaster crew. After OTU they were posted to RAAF 460. The grim Bomber Command axiom was that the first five and last five ops in a tour were the most dangerous; the first five due to inexperience, and the last five because of over-confidence or perhaps even nervousness. The Crook crew were to reinforce the axiom. On their third operation, an attack on Oberhausen on the night of 14 June 1943, Sergeant James Rupert Morrison (14824), from Hamilton, Vic, described how he heard Clem Buckeridge exclaim; "I cannot open the hatch" before the aircraft "blew up" and Morrison found himself in "mid air" – he was the only survivor and became a

POW. In the attack against Oberhausen out of a force of 197 Lancasters and six Mosquitos, 17 Lancasters or 8.4 per cent were lost. This included three from RAAF 460 – 14 Australians were killed.

RAAF 460 moved from Breighton to Binbrook on 14 May. Aircrew and maintenance personnel flew in Lancasters; and others were transported by Airspeed Horsa gliders. Binbrook was situated on top of the highest part of Lincolnshire and would prove bitterly cold with the full blast of North Sea winds. The quarters and catering were nonetheless superior. In keeping with the disrespect Australian air crew had for "Penguins" – non-flying RAF officers -- the presence of Base Headquarters at Binbrook caused a plethora of less than polite comments, and HQ would forever be referred to as "Bullshit Castle". This particular group of RAF administrators, described as "rather overbearing people", quickly antagonised the newly arrived Australian aircrew with their practice of reserving two mess tables for themselves while aircrew queued for meals.[8] This practice was quickly curtailed by the Australians and henceforth the "Penguins" had to queue as well. For the men of RAAF 460 Squadron Breighton held a lot of memories, not least of all of mates who never returned.

The village folk would no longer hear the massed revelry of their Australian guests during their off-duty moments and in turn it was a period of reflection for the squadron personnel whose stay in these surroundings had been such a happy one. The people of Breighton looked upon them as their protégé, and were grieved at their losses, and tolerant of their pranks.[9] It is said that the two Breighton pubs, the Black Swan and the Seven Sisters, popular watering holes for Australian aircrew, never recovered financially with the departure of RAAF 460 Squadron.

Dortmund was the target on the night of 4 May, the first for RAAF 460 out of their new base. News of the previous day's operation had begun to filter through and was unsettling. Twelve Venturas of New Zealand 487 Squadron had been dispatched to attack a power station on the outskirts of Amsterdam. One aircraft with a mechanical fault returned early. Unbeknown was that there was a meeting of German fighter pilots being held at Schiphol airfield, Amsterdam. Within minutes of the Venturas crossing the Dutch Coast, 69 German fighters were in the air. There wasn't even a proper battle before nine Venturas were shot down, one badly damaged, turned back to England. One Ventura flown by Squadron Leader Leonard Henry Trent, DFC, RNZAF, continued on and bombed the target, before it too was shot down. Trent and his navigator became POWs and following the war Trent was awarded a Victoria Cross. The shocking statistic of 61 per cent of an attacking force was one that Bomber Command would never wish to be repeated. The Australians were concerned to hear so many New Zealanders had been killed.

On 4/5 May 1943 a force of 596 aircraft were sent to bomb Dortmund the largest "non-Thousand Bomber raid" of the war, 31 aircraft, 5.2 per cent, were lost. Included was a 460 Squadron Lancaster flown by Flight Sergeant Desmond Nelson Jaekel (416680). Born in Pinnaroo, South Australia, Desmond's father was a storekeeper in Beverly, South Australia, which may be why Desmond studied accountancy and was an invoice clerk with Fowler Grocers. Desmond Jaekel had just turned 18 when he entered the RAAF and was married to Marie, with a son Robert Desmond. With good looks and a fast wit Desmond Jaekel had already fitted more than most people into his short life. As the Pilot of a Lancaster he was still only 19 when he was shot out of the sky.

Flight Sergeant Desmond Jaekel.   *Flight Sergeant William Williams.*

Jaekel's crew was all Australian with exception of the Engineer, RAF Sergeant William James Turpin (1476394), and this was their first operation. Flying Officer Sidney Michael Russ (414506) 32, wore an Australian tunic but his parents lived in England. Flight Sergeant William Williams (405597) 26, was a Mt Isa Mines, mining engineer; 23-year-old Air Gunner Flight Sergeant John Lawrence Barry (20047) was educated at St Joseph's College, Glen Innes, NSW, and worked as a shop assistant before securing clerical work. From NSW came Flight Sergeant Alan Hilton (412139) 22, from Kurri Kurri, and Flight Sergeant Eugene John Candish (412479) from Wallsend. Candish, a former student of Maitland Boys High and Newcastle Technical College, where he studied "motor construction" until employed as a "garage assistant". With the exception of Sidney Russ, very young men ordered to attack a very fortified German target. Elsie Jaekel would write:

> May I, broken-hearted mother of Flight Sergeant Desmond Nelson Jaekel, ask you some questions? I would like to know if any of the crew are known to be alive, would it be possible for me to have the addresses of the parents or wives of the crew? ...is it the usual thing for 19 year olds to do such a job...it is cruel that such young boys are sent so far from home. He spent his 19th birthday on the way to England, he complained bitterly of homesickness.

A friend of Bill Williams also wrote for information because "Bill was the only child, so you can imagine what his mother is feeling like".

It is estimated more than 1,000 night fighters were deployed to defend Germany by the first half of 1943.[10] During the following year anti-aircraft (AA) defences became increasingly lethal. An estimated 900,000 German personnel manned AA guns and it is believed around another million were committed to the clearance of wreckage from bombing raids. No fewer than 8,875 x 3.465 in (88 mm) guns, as well as a smaller number of larger calibre weapons, were trained on the skies over German occupied territory. These were complemented by about 25,000 x 0.79 in (20 mm) and 1.46 in (37 mm) light flak guns. According to one expert: "The '88' was arguably the war's best piece of artillery and was both an effective AA weapon and a potent battlefield tank destroyer".[11] Supporters of the British Bombing campaign argued that: "This diversion of weapons and manpower to the defence of Germany was Bomber Command's greatest contribution to Allied victory".[12]

On 12/13 May 1943, 572 aircraft bombed Duisburg. The operation was deemed the most successful yet on the German port but 5.9 per cent of the bomber force and their crews did not return. The next night 442 aircraft were sent to bomb Bochum and 168 raided Plzen and 5.3 per cent were lost. With the onset of summer and better weather the tempo of operations rose yet again. The first days of June 1943 provided a brief reprieve with poor weather conditions, but it was all too brief and the following months would be deadly indeed. On 12 June 22, RAAF 460 Lancasters joined a bomber force of 503 aircraft in an attack against the German city of Bocum.

Onboard one RAAF 460 Lancaster was Flight Sergeant David Crawford Paterson Lundie (412986) DFC. David was the third eldest in a large family of six sons and one daughter. Parents, Andrew and Mary Lundie were both children of Scottish emigrants. They encouraged their children to study hard, and worship regularly at the Eastwood, Sydney, Presbyterian Church. Andrew Lundie taught the classics, Latin and Ancient Greek, at Sydney's Fort Street Boys' High School, so his sons attended Fort Street. David, was a social, happy, youth with a wide circle of friends. On every occasion possible he would borrow his father's 1926 Chevrolet to take friends out. The Chevrolet was given the name the "Lundibus". There was much for Andrew and Mary to give thanks for as Alex, Andie, David, Jack, Jim, and twins Jean and Doug, matured into impressive young Australians – a war would change this forever as an idyllic lifestyle was thrown into uncertainty and emotional upheaval. Andie, Jack and David enlisted in the RAAF and all too quickly they were overseas. Andie was RAAF ground crew in Malaya as the Japanese advanced quickly. Jack was a Flying Officer with a Kittyhawk Squadron in New Guinea. Twenty-year-old David was a Navigator attached to a bomber squadron flying in the skies above occupied Europe. Andie and Jack would survive, David would not.

On 12 June, Flight Sergeant David Crawford Paterson Lundie (412986) carefully plotted the course to Bochum for Lancaster W4316 and his crew. His Skipper was RAF Sergeant Ronald Oliver Vaughan (1388329) 22, from Middlesex. The RAF Engineer, Sergeant Leonard

Frederick Charles Day (1433929) 20, was from Hampshire; and the 19-year-old RAF Wireless Operator/Air Gunner was Sergeant Dennis Arthur Thomas (1336716) from Sussex. The RAF AB was Flying Officer Charles William Ross Young (132851) 27, of West Lothian. The Rear Gunner was 20-year-old RAAF Flight Sergeant Andrew Gordon (409404) from Melbourne. The Canadian Middle Upper Gunner, Sergeant John (Jake) Cornish, had already been traumatised. In April he was a member of RAF Sergeant Roger Crook's No.27 OTU Wellington crew, when 21-year-old Australian Navigator, Sergeant Ken Hewitt (414237), was killed by a propeller blade. Cornish changed crews.

These aircrew aged 20, 22, 20, 19, 27, 20, and 20, had joined 460 from training just a fortnight earlier and were on just their third operation. They were not aware that a German fighter had been alerted to their presence by a radar station. Cannon fire raked the bottom of the Lancaster, and according to Jake Cornish, "there was a large explosion... everything was on fire". The order for abandon aircraft came across the intercom and Cornish climbed down from his turret and opened the doors of the rear turret to assist Andrew Gordon. He found nothing, "he must have been blown off". Cornish baled but was knocked out by part of the aircraft. His unconsciousness was fortunately brief but then he found his chute was tangled with his intercom cord. Had there been time to reflect Cornish could well have found it all too much; he had a bullet in the left leg, a toe torn off the right foot, and a badly burnt face. Instinctively he grabbed his knife and cut away the cord. Once on land he realised he was the lucky one, the only member of his crew to survive to become a German POW. He would also learn his original crew, with RAF Skipper Roger Crook, which included, Australians, Sergeant Clem Buckeridge, Sergeant Don Grant, and Flight Sergeant Stanley Joseph Marriage, were killed just two nights later, on 14 June, also on their third operation.

Andrew Gordon's mother, Violet, wrote to RAAF 460 asking that the parcels of food stuffs and knitted garments she had sent Andrew and which were still in transit not be returned to her, she would rather have them "given to his squadron...or am I asking too much". She apologised for not having written earlier but she "had not given up hope of his return". It was easier for mothers to express their emotions than for fathers. Andrew Lundie felt anger and struggled to contain this. "It is now 13 months since my son was killed, but none of his personal belongings have yet been forwarded to me and yet I think ample time has elapsed for that."

David Lundie.

Andrew Lundie, in the solitude of his study, would write a poem to a son killed in war, which included:

> Me thought, my son, that you on that black night...
> And Australs dreaming of their sunny home,
> Had crossed the Ruhr and flown to Dusseldorf...
> Then on the Ruhr, bristling with Hitler's might.
> You rained down bombs to vindicate man's right
> But alas, your short allotted span,
> Which twenty years ago you just began,
> Is ended now, and life's brief web is spun
> Your spirit, hope, your courage still live on...
> You'll be commissioned in God's Heav'n of Love;
> Then flying planes bedecked with filmy wings
> You'll look adown upon these worthless things
> And wonder why men fight till wizened and old
> And ramble and scrape and gamble for gold.[13]

Twenty-two-year-old Sergeant Lindsay Oliver Howard Upjohn (411972), former student of Sydney's Scots College, and Union Bank

Clerk, was the captain, but only Australian, on an RAAF 466 Squadron Wellington which took off at 2226 on the 29 May to bomb Wuppertal, Germany. The night fighter came from nowhere and RAF Rear Gunner Flight Sergeant Frank Hay (1023216), DFM, was killed. The controls were shot to pieces and the Wellington was on fire. Upjohn gave the bale order and RAF Sergeants Paterson, Garfield and Napier answered. Upjohn remembered pulling his parachute's rip cord at around 8,000 ft (2,400 m) and the canopy opening above him. There was no way he could avoid the trees. He released the harness and dropped to the ground, on this occasion it was good to be 6 ft (1.8 m) tall, he had less distance to fall. Somehow he had lost his boots. Upjohn began to walk through Dutch countryside, stealing some clogs from outside a small hut. Unused to the wooden footwear, progress was rather laborious. Later he was "accosted" by a civilian who appeared "very friendly" and gestured to Upjohn to follow. Shortly later he was in German custody.

On the night of 22 June 1943, Flight Sergeant Edwin Alfred Sims (413676) from Sydney, was the skipper and only Aussie in a RAF 77 Halifax detailed to bomb Mulheim, Germany. JD213 took off at 2329 and nothing more was heard. It was not just Australians attached to RAAF squadrons who were taking the war to Germany but those, like Edwin Sims, aircrew who called themselves the "Odd Bods", around 80 per cent of Australians attached to Bomber Command, were attached to RAF squadrons. At the outbreak of war Canada had endeavoured to retain some control over their airmen within the then, "British Commonwealth Air Training Plan", authorities from New Zealand and Australia did not. Canada insisted that Article XV was included in the agreement. This decreed that airmen would be: "Identified with their respective Dominions, either by the method of organising Dominion units and formations, or in some other way, such methods to be agreed upon."

The British government and RAF were reluctant for dominion squadrons to have any autonomy for fear that command unity would be destroyed by different practices and administration. It could also lead to dominion governments jeopardizing fundamental strategic aims decided in London which maintained the safety of Britain was paramount to the interests of the Dominions. The Canadian government remained resolute on the implementation of Article XV and by the beginning of 1943 Canada had formed its own bomber group with 19 squadrons. Australian prime minister Robert Menzies declared in Parliament that he and his government would where possible, "preserve the Australian character and identity of any air force which goes abroad"[14] but this would prove to be pure rhetoric. Menzies and his government did not hold the British government to Article XV and the creation of 18 Australian squadrons by May 1942. Only eight RAAF squadrons would be created and not all of these would be part of Bomber Command, Europe, or subsist throughout the war.

RAAF 455 was formed at Williamstown, NSW, in 23 May 1941 and originally consisted of ground staff. While they awaited passage to England, RAAF 455 was formed on 6 June 1941, at Swinderby, Lincolnshire, as part of No.5 Group. The squadron did not receive its first aircraft (Hampdens) until 10 July and the operational debut, delayed due to lack of RAF ground crew, was not flown until 29 August 1941. On 27 April 1942, RAAF 455 was transferred to Coastal Command. Between June 1941 and April 1942 whilst 455 operated within Bomber Command there were 67 fatalities, of whom 25 were Australian. The squadron converted to Beaufighters December 1943 to February 1944. Between April 1942 and May 1945, 84 squadron personnel died, 66 were Australian.

RAAF 458 was also formed at Williamstown, NSW, on 8 July 1941. In early August 37 airmen sailed for the UK. The Squadron was established in Britain on 25 August at, Holme-on-Spalding Moor, Yorkshire, and commenced operations with Bomber Command on 20 October 1941. Although reputed to have been deemed one of most functional in any bomber group, RAAF 458 was withdrawn from Bomber Command at the end of January 1942, to be relocated to the Middle East. At this time the squadron had 24 fatalities, 13 of whom were Australian. Following the transfer 458 personnel were dispersed to RAF Squadrons and not reunited until the first day of September 1942. Their primary role was henceforth to attack enemy shipping in the Mediterranean and did not undertake conventional bombing again until August 1944, in support of the Allied invasion. They were then relocated to Gibraltar in January 1945.

The third RAAF Squadron was 460 formed on 15 November 1942 and equipped with Wellington aircraft. Originally 460 was part of No.8 Group, but upon its move to Breighton, Yorkshire, it joined No.1 Group and began operations on 12 March. In mid-May 1943, RAAF 460 moved to Binbrook, Lincolnshire, where it remained based until disbanded in October 1945. After briefly converting to Halifaxes, 460 Squadron was equipped with Lancasters in October 1942 and Lancaster operations began the next month. In June 1943, 27 Lancasters were despatched to bomb, setting a Bomber Command Squadron record. Two months later, 460 became the first Bomber Command squadron to fly a 1,000 sorties in Lancasters. The last operation was when 24 aircraft destroyed Hitler's mountain retreat at Berchtesgarden, Germany. World War II operational sorties numbered around 6,264, at the human cost of around 1,000. Lancasters, W4783, known as "G for George", would undertake 90 operations and would return to Australia at war's end to be a major exhibit in the Australian War Memorial.

RAAF 462 came into being on 7 September 1942 but not in Bomber Command, Europe, but in the Middle East. In early 1944 the squadron became RAF 614 and Australian personnel transferred to RAAF Squadrons in England. On 12 August 1943, No 462 RAAF Squadron re-formed at Driffield, Yorkshire, as a heavy-bomber squadron in No.4 Group flying Halifax bombers. Only a quarter of personnel were RAAF and requests that more Australian personnel be posted fell on deaf ears. On 3 March 1944, RAAF No 462 Squadron, was redesignated No 614 Squadron.

RAF 463 Squadron, RAAF was formed from "C Flight" of 467 Squadron RAAF at Waddington, Lincolnshire, on 25 November 1943 and six of the aircraft despatched to bomb Berlin the following day did not return. Equipped with Lancasters 463 was part of 5 Group. Its first Commanding Officer was Squadron Leader Rollo Kingsford-Smith (381), nephew of the famous Australian aviator, Sir Charles Kingsford-Smith. The squadron's last operation was flown on 25 April 1945, although on the 6 May 1945 twelve RAAF 463 Lancaster crews had the rewarding opportunity of flying 236 ex POWs back to England. In total, 393 RAAF 463 airmen would die, of whom 226 were Australian.

RAAF 464 Squadron was formed at Feltwell, Norfolk, on 1 September 1942, as a light day-bomber squadron with No.2 Group, equipped with Lockheed Ventura aircraft, popularly called "flying pigs", because of their porcine type bodies. From July 1943, 464 was converted to Mosquitos but was also transferred from Bomber Command to the Second Tactical Air Force and remained with Fighter Command until disbanding in September 1945. The last operation was flown on 24 April 1945 when twelves aircraft were sent to strafe and bomb a number of targets – two failed to return.

RAAF 466 was formed at Driffield, Yorkshire, on 15 October 1942, as a medium-bomber squadron. Equipped with Wellington bombers it was under the control of No.4 Group. In December 1942 the Squadron moved to Leconfield but returned to Driffield in June 1944. The first operation was mine-laying on 13 January 1943. Halifax IIIs replaced Wellingtons and personnel would conduct a further 170 raids against 92 different targets before the end of hostilities. On 25 April 1945 the squadron flew its last operation, attacking German defences on the island of Wangerooge. On 7 May 1945, 466 was transferred to Transport Command.

RAAF 467 was formed at Scampton, Lincolnshire, on 7 November 1942, as a heavy-bomber squadron in No.5 Group. Later that month the squadron moved to Bottesford, Leicestershire. A year later it returned to Lincolnshire, and based at Waddington, for the rest of the war. Equipped with Lancasters, the squadron took part in all the major Bomber Command campaigns against Germany and German-occupied Europe as well as attacks in support of "Operation Overlord" the Allied invasion of Western Europe. RAAF 467 also returned liberated POWs to England and was disbanded on 30 September 1945. One of the most famous Lancasters in Bomber Command belonged to 467; R5868, "S for Sugar", which survived 137 operations, and was subsequently moved to RAF Museum, Hendon.

Pilot Officer Charles Rowland Williams (405224) was not impressed with being stuck in the English seaside resort of Bournemouth. As a result of the Australian government's acquiescence the majority of RAAF aircrew found themselves fighting a war in Europe attached to non-RAAF squadrons. "I am still waiting for my posting, and only hope it is not going to be much longer as I am sick of this idleness here, and will feel much better when I start the job properly."[15] He had come around the world, given up life in the Queensland outback, trained, and been set to fight a war and then – nothing! Being raised on the large Queensland sheep station "Telemon" on the banks of the Flinders River, near Hughenden had been exciting and as a boy he had been encouraged to stretch the boundaries of life. It was a very physical lifestyle even more so because Charlie's father Horace, was a keen sportsman, and ensured a tennis court and cricket pitch were constructed adjacent to the homestead. As a consequence sons Doug and Charlie distinguished themselves when sent to board at Townsville Grammar School. Charlie proved a good student with technical leanings. He became fascinated with wireless and telegraph. When he left school in 1926 and returned to the property he began to build wireless receivers – it seemed ever more important to keep in touch with the world. Not all was well in the distant world beyond the sheep station. First, massive amounts of money were wiped off the New York stock exchange, and the repercussions reverberated around the world. By 1932 the Australian economy had collapsed. As the world recession deepened, unemployment stood at around 30 per cent. Farmers walked off their properties when no one could afford their produce. The good life as the Williams family had known it was no longer. They moved to another property outside Hughenden. "Bannockburn" offered a dim, drab, reflection of their previous life and Horace and his sons worked very hard for very little return. Charlie had dreamed of joining the nation's air force but his enlistment application came to nothing. The RAAF, as with Australia's navy and army, faced new harsh financial stringencies: "There was no chance of an unknown boy from the bush even being considered for selection in the handful of cadets who trained at Point Cook, near Melbourne, at the other end of the continent.[16]" War resolved the dilemma, and by February 1942, Charlie Williams was shivering in an English winter.

It was such a relief when his Bournemouth sojourn ended and he joined 14 OTU in April 1942. Pilot Officer Charlie Williams was now flying in Hampdens, which as far as Wireless Operator/Air Gunners were concerned, "are the most uncomfortable thing ever invented".[17] But flying continued to bring him great joy and he remained enthusiastic, picking up additional flights whenever he could. Sometimes the cross-country trips came with added excitement. With one pilot undertaking his first solo trip there was "quite a bit of excitement...he made three attempts at the first landing and nearly landed on top of another plane".[18] Charlie was pulled out of training to fly as a Hampden Rear Gunner to make up numbers in the first Thousand Bomber raid on Cologne and it was plain scary. Charlie had not practised gunnery since Evans Head, and had never flown as a Hampden gunner. Added to that he had fewer than six hours night flying. In the frigid night air of the exposed canopy Charlie thought he would freeze. He tried not to think of how German fighter pilots liked to kill the Rear Gunner first and how the slow Hampden was such an easy target. He wrote that he had "a lively time" and survived. After seven hours in the air he was exhausted. Sleep did not come when he finally got to bed at 0800. "Several of the lads I knew well did not return. ...tonight I will be in it again, do not feel very keen as I am very tired, and will be a wreck physical and nervous, by tomorrow."[19]

He was then called upon to participate in the next Thousand Bomber raid, on Bremen but at least this time he was a Wireless Operator/Air Gunner. Between the two Charlie was back to his training, broken only by the occasional funeral. "One of our planes crashed...and the whole crew were killed (including) two Australians". The Spartan conditions at Salby, North Yorkshire, was something he could have done without, "there is no running water and all our water is brought in a bucket", furthermore, "the messing arrangements are bad and the food poor".[20] Two years after he had joined up his training was over and as he packed his kit he hoped, "I will be able to do my job as well as those who have gone before me".[21] In July 1942 there was no Australian squadron to be posted to so he was sent to RAF 61, his RAAF blue uniform making him feel different but at the same time proud. He was delighted to fly in Lancasters and his crew except for a Canadian Bomb Aimer were RAF. Even though Charlie found operational flights demanding and exhausting he retained the delight in taking to the air – this is where he was supposed to be.

The months slid by, it was a time of huge concentration and Charlie tried to keep his mind on the task at hand and not on the "danger and death around him". On average, "about every second operation one of the eight to ten crews which took off became casualties".[22] RAF 61 attrition rate meant that the likelihood of Charlie finishing his 30 operations was somewhere in the vicinity of 22 per cent. Making the situation more unsettling was that his pilot, upon finishing his tour ,was sent to an OTU as an instructor. Charlie and four of his crew were sent back to a conversion unit to find another. His nerves were unsettled and this was reflected in his letters home, "hard to find anything decent to read...am now reading rubbish"; "I do not go out very much as there is not much pleasure being out these cold foggy nights"; it would not be long, "before the first snow starts, how I dread the thought of winter here"; "have not had any mail all the week".[23] It would have been better to have kept operational flying – he just wanted to complete his tour of 30 operations or 200 hours, and finding another pilot meant he was held up three weeks. Finally a pilot, and what was more, he was a New Zealander – the next best thing to an Aussie. Of course, the new pilot had to continue practicing circuits and bumps (take-off, circle of the field, and land), incredibly unsatisfying for his more seasoned crew. One bump was solid – they had run into another Lancaster. Finally, he was able to report the new pilot had "come good". The flying he still found challenging, but the lustre of the adventure of war had worn off and with Christmas came the inevitable thoughts of home. Charlie struggled to get into the Christmas mood and in the end decided not to send presents: "I hope that I will be able to make it up next Xmas, for I hope that by that time the war will be over and I will be back in Australia."[24]

Another year and the tempo of operations continued to increase as well as the number of friends killed. Charlie had taken to morbidly marking below the faces on his course photo with "KIA" (killed in action). On 12 March 1943 he wrote: "My first operational tour is gradually drawing to an end as I now have done 22 trips for 138 hours. So only have 52 hours or eight trips to go and I will not be sorry to finish and have a rest as the strain is beginning to tell."[25] But then the bad news – there were insufficient aircrew to allow men to finish operational service after just one tour. It came as rather a shock to be told the requirement was now for an additional tour of 20. Charlie decided to leave his crew and though it "may not be wise" join an Australian pilot with a similar number of operations and go to a newly created RAF squadron. His belief was that this squadron looked like it would have a faster operational impetus which, in turn, meant he would complete his duty quicker and "have a much better chance of being sent home" sooner.

Flying Officer Charlie Williams joined the newly created RAF 617. His Australian pilot was Flight Lieutenant Robert Norman (Norm) Barlow (401899), DFC, from the Melbourne suburb of Carlton. He, like Charlie, was experienced and older, 31. He enlisted in 1941 whereas his brother Alexander Arthur Barlow (250159) was career RAAF and by May 1943 was a Wing Commander at 6 SFTS, Mallala, South Australia.

The ages of the crew were as mixed as their nationalities; two Australians, a Canadian gunner, and four from the British Isles, ranging in age from 18-year-old RAF Rear Gunner Sergeant Jack Robert George Liddell (1338282), from Somerset, England, to Charlie who was now 34. There was little Charlie could tell his family in Hughenden about his new training and the highly secret duties assigned his squadron. RAF 617 was commanded by the legendary Guy Gibson. A Wing Commander at 23, a veteran of more than 170 operations, who would ultimately be awarded the Victorian Cross, DSO and bar, DFC and Bar, and be killed on an operation on 19 September 1944, aged 26. Hand-picked crews from 5 Group were trained for six weeks for their special operations. Their Lancasters would each carry one "bouncing bomb" designed by Barnes Wallis. The mission was to cause catastrophic flooding by breaching dams, which would destroy factories, infrastructure such as railways and bridges, but most significantly affect hydro-electric power for Ruhr armaments production.

Charles Rowland Williams.

Flying Officer Charles Rowland Williams and his Dam Busters crew.

The drum-like bomb would be dropped at the low altitude of 60 ft (18 m) at a speed of 220 mph (350 k/h). It would then skip along the surface of the water and explode against a dam wall. Their campaign commenced on the night of 16/17 May 1943 with "Operation Chastise". The Mohne and Eder Dams were successfully breached, but of the 19 aircraft participating, eight were shot down and of their 56 aircrew, 53 were killed, three became POWs. Lancaster ED927 crashed after colliding with high tension wires. The crew included two Australians, a Canadian and four RAF – the Wireless Operator/Air Gunner, was Flying Officer Charlie Williams from Hughenden. Further remarkable operations would be undertaken by those now referred to as the "Dam Busters" and the crews of RAF 617 would be awarded many decorations. The citation of the DFC awarded to Flying Officer Charles Williams, described how he had undertaken, "numerous successful sorties" while demonstrating "technical ability in the air...of the highest order" and that his "quiet efficiency" had "greatly influenced his crew."

Flight Sergeant Henry (Harry) John Krohn (34017) was 19 when he joined the air force on the last day of September 1940. He actually had pestered the RAAF since war was declared. The son of Gilgandra, NSW, store keepers, Arthur and Evelyn, Harry had been working as a Dental Mechanic since leaving school. He was not sure what that would qualify him for but he just wanted to get into RAAF uniform. Before the last day of the next September he was designated "Airman Pilot" and was in England by November 1942, another of those getting cranky while waiting in Bournemouth. Being ill-tempered was not something Harry did often – he was better known for his easy grin and sense of humour. Not even his RAAF mug shots could extinguish the sparkle in his eyes. Instructors were suitably impressed, one wrote, "Cool and determined, with team spirit". Harry was almost too nice, one instructor applauded the fact that he instilled "passenger confidence" with his "very youthful" attitude, but felt his pupil needed to develop more "power of command" – Harry saw himself as one of the blokes and needed some work to become an aircraft captain. No instructor could fault him on his enthusiasm.

Flight Sergeant Henry (Harry) John Krohn.

On the night of 21 June 1943, Harry was the second pilot on an RAF 35 Squadron Halifax which took off at 2312 to bomb Krefeld, Germany. His skipper was a New Zealander, Flying Officer Bill Hickson and the other crew were three RAF and two Canadians. This was a seasoned crew that had been with the Pathfinders for five months. With typical enthusiasm, Harry asked if he could come along for the experience, so Hickson agreed to his being second pilot. It was a moonlit night, the shortest of the year, and about ten minutes from the target they were attacked by a night fighter flown by Major Gunther Radusch. It happened quickly and Bill Hickson tried to take evasive action but the port inner engine burst into flames. The New Zealander feathered the engine before pushing the extinguisher button, but nothing happened. With the fire burning fiercely he ordered the crew to abandon the Halifax. Unbeknown to the skipper was that the Rear Gunner was already dead. As they jumped there was an explosion and the bomber disintegrated. Harry Krohn baled out at a good height but his parachute didn't open. His mother struggled with his death, she turned to her Catholic religion and would often "say a prayer for Harry".

The Galligan family was another deeply affected by war. They were typical of those who travelled from County Cork, Ireland, gambling on a better life in a country they knew so little about and on the other side of the world. After a sea journey that must have felt like an eternity for those who sailed in steerage, they alighted in Queensland

Dennis, Bill, Ted, Pat (courtesy Galligan family).

for a life so entirely different. The lush and rich soils of the Darling Downs beckoned and they settled on a farm near Pittsworth. Another generation and John Patrick Galligan joined the Queensland police force. He and his wife Emma Theresa revelled in a life which evolved around Roman Catholicism, family and hard work. They were living in Childers when their eldest son Edwin (Ted) Richard was born in 1916. Next came William John in 1917. A son Jack died in infancy. Patrick James was born in Imbil, Queensland, in time for Christmas 1921. Finally a daughter, Mary Ellen (Ellie) born in 1919, and another son, Denis Vincent, completed the family in 1924.

Police postings required the family to move to different districts. Consequently Patrick (Pat) James was educated at a number of schools, Convent School, Gordonvale; then Ayr; then Christian Bros, Maryborough, and finally Sacred Bros., Douglas Park, NSW. He proved an excellent student, a talented athlete, but it was his artistic abilities for which he was most accredited. He wrote poetry from an early age, played the piano and began to compose his own music, and his paintings were created with flare. Pat's many talents and itinerant life as a policeman's son, made him restless, although he realised how fortunate he was to be able to continue his education. The Depression meant his older brothers needed to leave school earlier to help support the extended Galligan family. Ted turned to shearing and William (Bill) worked at a number of physically taxing jobs such as droving cattle on his cousin's farm, and working in a timber yard, before being able to follow his father into the police force.

Upon leaving school with his Leaving Certificate Pat remained uncertain about his future – initially considering the priesthood. For whatever reason he moved away from this career choice and worked on a dairy farm for six months. Clearly he was not cut out for life as a farmer. His father John was by now a Police Inspector stationed in Cloncurry, so Pat began work as a Stores Clerk with Mount Isa Mines. This was not exactly thrilling for a 20 year old who was full of life, and like so many of his generation, the opportunity for overseas travel and promise of excitement were the catalyst to enlisting on 1 February 1942, the day after his eldest brother, Ted. The mustering of Gunner surprised no one, particularly as elder brother Ted was also an Air Gunner; and being attached to Squadron 44 (Rhodesia) and the only Australian in his crew, seemed just that more exotic.[26] Eighteen-year-old Denis Vincent Galligan (425298) enlisted in the RAAF in September the same year. Ellie would defy the RAAF family tradition and enlist in the Australian Women's Army Service (AWAS) in 1943.

On 28 June 1943 Lancaster ED307 of 44 (Rhodesia) Squadron, took off to attack Cologne. Flight Sergeant Patrick James Galligan (425298) and his crew had been with the Squadron a mere four days, and this was their first operation. Pat was the Rear Gunner and his pilot skipper at the opposite end of the bomber was RAF Sergeant Charles Vernon Leslie Hulbert (1334066). Between them were five members of the RAF.[27] At 0254 on 29 June, Lancaster ED307 was shot out of the sky by a night fighter flown by Major Gunter Radusch, and the aircraft crashed and exploded into Dutch countryside near Eindhoven. Parts of the Lancaster were spread over a large area, the farthest away pieces being an engine and a tail piece which lay on a road. Dutch Special Constables approached the blazing wreck but the ferocity of the flames forced them back. On later examination they found, "three completely charred bodies in the cockpit", then "three completely charred bodies lay in the immediate vicinity", while further away, "another part of a body which had been torn open and of which various parts lay in amongst pine trees". The RAAF was misinformed and the initial letter sent to Pat's parents said their 21-year-old son "had been lost while on an operational flight in the Middle East". John Galligan wrote to authorities; "Amongst his effects were several poems written by him which I am most anxious to get as early as possible". His parents were spared the grisly details that there was little left of their son and his crew, just "a small amount of charred remains and ashes. ...a piece of clothing...a neck band of a shirt" and a pair of "flying boots size 8".

For the Galligan family the pain was not yet over. Flight Sergeant Ted Galligan (425149) was flying with an RAF 623 Stirling crew tasked to bomb Berlin on the night of 31 August/1 September 1943. Ted was likely impressed that on this operation 623 Squadron Commanding Officer, the distinguished 28-year-old RAF pilot, Wing Commander Edwin John Little (37573), DFC, MID, three times mentioned in despatches, had decided to fly their aircraft this operation. The crew's regular pilot, Flight Sergeant Oliver James Tanner (414170), a 20-year-old storeman clerk with the Shell Co, in the Queensland coastal town of Bundaberg, was second pilot. The remainder of the crew were RAF.[28] The target was cloud covered, only seven out of the twelve Oboe Mosquitos reached the target, and only six dropped their markers, and seven minutes late. The bomber force did release a significant attack but Stirling EE 949 was hit by flak on the outward journey, crashed and disintegrated. There was little left of the crew to bury and only Tanner and RAF Sergeant Alfred John Henry Millin (1097417), the Middle Upper Gunner, would have graves. This operation demonstrated the vulnerability of Stirling bombers on extended operations and they would never again be included in a raid on Berlin.

For the Galligan family this awareness came too late. John and Emma Galligan were again spared the grisly details that it was "assumed the aircraft exploded and they (the crew) were blown to pieces". The Galligan family had paid dearly in this war. The RAAF would restrict the service of RAAF LAC Denis Vincent Galligan (429405). He would undertake a short stint in Papua New Guinea late in the war and would discharge in December 1945. Denis went on to become a barrister, QC, and solicitor general for Queensland. He would be awarded the Member of the Order of Australia (AM). Bill Galligan would serve in the Queensland Police throughout the war, retire a superintendent, and be awarded the Police Medal. Their sister, corporal Mary Ellen Galligan (QX53363) would discharge from the AWAS in January 1947. She would then work in a clerical position in the public service and never marry.

Pat's poems about, "his strong religious faith, his love of the Australian bush, and, possibly, some presentiment of death", were published after the war, in a book entitled *To Those Who Survive*[29] His poems begin with the excitement of youth but change as he looks into the future in 1943, and he never finishes his poem "Spirit of Things Gone".

Spirit of things gone,
Bring memories of the past,
Of other days that lingered on another land,
To me now exiled here at war's demand;
Bring heat and sunshine, for my heart is cold;
Bring old brown paddocks, gumtrees sparsely green,
The grass is here too bright, an alien scene.
The daffodils are beautiful and daisies star the grass,
But golden memories are mine of wattle in the mass.
Bring recollections of the days on fair Corinda rise,
The Brisbane warmly winding where an unhazed city lies;
Though storms blow down the river, and we curse the heat at night;
There is laughter and the shouting of the lads who swim and sun
Make all the world a peaceful place where even work is fun.
And I'd like to hear the voices of the friends I knew so well,
And see lantana on the hill, and watch the in-tide swell.
And up along Cloncurry way I think of winter time,
And flocks of grey and pink galahs, oleanders, red-dust grime,
The small white-gums and rust-red hills, my lonely loved ones all,
Where bullen-bullens whistle and the white corellas call.
I see now up Cooranga way the long and tawny grass
That robes the round hills void of scrub; I see the cattle pass
As the cow-boy on the chestnut mare rides bareback through
    the wheat
To bring the cows at milking-time – I watch him through the heat.

The verse is very different from poems written in 1939, 1940 and 1941.
They spoke of all things beautiful, of a young man looking forward to
meeting the girl of his dreams, of excitement for the future. In 1943 now
serving in Bomber Command Europe he wrote:

  There's sadness on my soul,
  For now I fear, the future near,
  That death may be my goal.
  The lights of earth have lost their mirth,
  Dim for war's tragedy,

Whose spotlights rake the skies and make
Battlefields there for me.
The friendly moon is now no boon
New hail drops form the clouds
Hate-lightnings form in this new storm:
Our planes become our shrouds.
But melodies are memories;
You'll hear them should not I,
And peace again will come to men –
For this we stake to die.

The book was likely both comforting and disheartening for his mother Emma because the ever present question was just what could her gifted son have achieved. Emma Galligan had lost a son in infancy and two in a war. Remembered as "a very gentle person", Emma Galligan suffered poor health and died in 1957. On her Australian gravestone were engraved the names of her two sons who had fought and died in a war in Europe.

LEFT: *Flight Sergeant Patrick James Galligan.* MIDDLE: *Pat and Ted Galligan in England.* RIGHT: *Emma Galligan's gravestone.*

Germany's second largest city was Hamburg and for a ten day period in July/August 1943 Bomber Command mounted a massive bomber operation. While OBOE was not useful for such a range, H2s was. Four major attacks took place in a ten day period, each consisting of in excess of 740 aircraft, wreaking havoc on the German city. "A total of 3,091 sorties were flown and nearly 10,000 tons of bombs dropped."[30] For the first time "window" or "chaff", (small, thin pieces of aluminium, metallic glass fibre or metallised film) was dropped to interfere with enemy radar and it proved very effective. On 17/18 August, 596 bombers were sent to destroy the Baltic German research centre of the V2 rocket. Authorities called it a success but 40 aircraft and their crews were lost. Many of those lost had been in the last wave – when the German night fighters had arrived. The V2 rocket was an alcohol and liquid oxygen single-stage rocket. The first A-4 (later called the V2) had been launched from Peenemunde on 3 October 1942. In 1943 Hitler decided to use the A-4 as a "vengeance weapon" for the bombing of German cities and ordered that the rockets, carrying cargoes of explosives, be launched on England. The damage inflicted by Bomber Command in August was only temporary and on 8 September 1944, the world's first long-range combat-ballistic missile was launched against London. It would be the first of more than 3,000 launched against British, Dutch, French and Belgium cities, killing thousands. V2 rocket sites would be priority targets for the rest of the war, something aircrew endorsed. After witnessing the horror Halifax Wireless Operator/Air Gunner, Flight Sergeant Max Norris would write:

These V2 rockets are certainly terrible things, even worse than the original flying bomb and have caused untold misery. I don't think there is anything too bad to do to those Huns. The whole German people are responsible as people are always responsible for their government. All of us derive intense pleasure out of unloading cargoes of death on them and seeing their whole world turn upside down.[31]

Hugh Edward Gilmour studied the RAAF form in front of him, it was indeed a long list of questions. Could he speak Japanese and if so, "With how many characters (Kanji) are you familiar?" Japanese was not a language taught in any Queensland school this grazier had attended – who would have thought in the 1930s you would have need of any Asian language, let alone Japanese? The questionnaire asked if he had any experience in engineering; architectural; or building experience; and many more occupations he had scarcely heard of – he had left school at 15. By the time he had finished writing "No" to everything he could be forgiven for being a little demoralised. The 20 year old was enlisted as "Guard", rank Aircraftsman 1 – he was at least in the RAAF. Hugh Gilmour (22776) would go on to rival for the longest RAAF training of any recruit signing on the dotted line on 21 May 1940. He received his LAC propeller six months later. That lasted ten months before he was ordered to remove the propeller from his sleeve as he was demoted for a re-muster. The demotion and re-muster were amazing, Gilmour could hardly believe it, he was aircrew, and what was more, he was now a "pilot trainee".

Unfortunately that didn't last as long as he wished. Hugh Gilmour was graded only "Average" in most flying aptitude tests and then deemed; "Below Average", when it came to "Natural Aptitude". The instructor's written comment was; "Aerobatics and co-ordination poor". The numbers didn't add up – only 417 out of 700. Hugh looked like washing out as a pilot and being re-mustered yet again, as a Wireless Operator/ Air Gunner. But he persisted and they gave him another chance. This time the numbers added up differently; and RAAF administration was running out of space on his service card. Gilmour was understandably pleased when he finally embarked for overseas service in March 1943, a long time since he enlisted in January 1940. Arrival in the UK did not mean an end to training, just a different type of training and it would still be twelve months before he was posted to RAF 75 Squadron. Though a circuitous journey, finally on 22 March 1944 he was officially on operations, and then promoted to Warrant Officer in May 1944. Just two months later, on 21 July 1944 Hugh Gilmour, was killed during a raid on Hamburg.

Hugh Gilmour's Bomb Aimer, Flight Sergeant Samuel (Sammy) Mills (425036) 32, who wrote occupation as "Grocer – Bee Keeper", was, like his pilot, from the Brisbane suburb of Southport and was also killed. So too, Wireless Operator/Air Gunner, Flight Sergeant John Edward Osborne (417877) 23, from Yunta, South Australia. RAF Engineer Sergeant Reginald Ernest Buzza (2203174) 24, and RAF Rear

Gunner Sergeant John Leonard Stephenson (2202048) who was 18, also died. The crew Navigator was from South Australia, Pilot Officer Lindsay Arthur Woodward (417257) 22, a former clerk with the Myer Emporium. He, together with RAF Middle Upper Gunner Sergeant W J S Ballard, became POWs. Woodward heard Hugh Gilmour call "Shit!" as they were attacked. The Lancaster burst into flames and went into a sharp downward spiral. As Woodward tried to get to an escape hatch, he observed Osborne shot in the chest and Gilmour slumped in the cockpit. He had no further recollection until he awoke in the air.

The Battle of Hamburg, codenamed Operation Gomorrah, raged from 24 July to 3 August. It was the heaviest assault yet in aerial warfare and would later be referred to as the "Hiroshima of Germany". Bomber Command Chief, Air Chief Marshall Harris, was commonly referred to as Bomber Harris. Harris was directed by prime minister Winston Churchill to pursue a doctrine, which Harris expressed as: "The aim of the Combined Bomber Offensive...should be unambiguously stated [as] the destruction of German cities, the killing of German workers, and the disruption of civilised life throughout Germany.[32]" It was a doctrine condoned privately by those who made top level strategic decisions, but few had the courage to publicly support this same doctrine.

Hamburg was Germany's most important port and targets included the U-Boat pens and oil refineries. Subsequently during World War II Hamburg was attacked 98 times but it was the four major raids of Operation Gomorrah that were devastating, particularly the raid by 777 aircraft on 29 July, which caused a massive firestorm in which more than 40,000 people perished. The Reverend John Collins' exchange with Bomber Command Commander-in-Chief, newly nicknamed "Butcher Harris" became predictably heated:

Collins: "I realize this is not a popular thing I'm doing..."
Harris: "Say what you've got to say."
Collins: "We began the war in the defence of humanity, with God on our side!"
Harris: "Did He tell you that? He didn't tell me."
Collins: "I think it so!"

Harris: "You're privileged, Collins. I was just told to win the war with every means at my disposal, but not God."

Collins: "Was it necessary?"

Harris: "What? Killing people? Barbarism? Savagery? If you are going to win a war, Yes!"

Collins: "No! But there are moral limits, surely!"

Harris: "You want me to admit it was a terrible thing we did to Hamburg? Right. It was bloody terrible. It was ghastly! Feel better now? Unless you can offer me alternative targets that will win the war quicker, shut up! You return to your conscience, and let me get back to the war. Okay?"

The destruction of Hamburg although agreed to by the British War Cabinet and personally encouraged by Winston Churchill, was a turning point in popular support for the bombing campaign. Authorities began to distance themselves – privately pleased that Harris was all too willing to assume responsibility. For the remainder of the war these same men in power would continue to distance themselves further from Harris and Bomber Command, unwilling to have "the blood of innocents" on their consciences. Unfortunately for the aircrew ordered to conduct bombing attacks on cities, they would be similarly accused at war's end. Some aircrew were already facing moral dilemma but were not entirely sure where the delineation was between fear, exhaustion, or lack of ease with their duties. "The poor bastard is afraid to fly but he's more afraid of the consequences of not flying".[33]

For Maxwell Alton Norris every skerrick of fitness and strength was now being tested. If the seriousness of the situation had not completely resonated it did when told to nominate next of kin and make out a last will and testament. Max would have liked to have been mustered as a pilot but Britain was now telling the RAAF what they needed most and volunteers were not given a choice. Max joined when the RAF stipulated it needed Wireless Operators/Air Gunners. Their first flights were in Wackett trainers: "Planes that struggled into the sky like bedraggled sparrows, flown by pilots whose only joy was to create a private hell for any wireless operator trying to gain contact with base."[34]

Having survived elementary training Max was sent to 3 WAGS Maryborough, Queensland, on 13 November 1942, to begin his Wireless Operator course. What ensued tested intelligence, stamina and patience, in what was a gruelling 24 weeks. If you could not master the technology you were re-mustered as a straight gunner and this was generally seen as quite a demotion. Training continued for six days a week, often with classes in the evening as well, the only respite was sport, physical training, and parades. Max used his one short leave to race home to Brisbane to visit his parents Alton and Gladys, younger brother Stewart, and convince new wife Hilda to travel to Maryborough for a belated honeymoon. Stewart (James Stewart Norris) like so many younger brothers couldn't wait to follow Max into the RAAF. On 8 October 1943 just over a month after his 18th birthday he joined as RAAF 435877. Their Commonwealth Bank Manager father, Alton, decided that he could at least perform administration duties in support of his RAAF aircrew sons and also enlisted in the RAAF in 1943 as a 48 year old Aircraftsman – "All in" the catch cry of World War I was even more relevant in this war with war raging on both sides of the globe and the Japanese seemingly beating at the gates.

The first accomplishment a trainee Wireless Operator needed was to receive and transmit radio messages in Morse code. A particular ear, limberness, and level of concentration were needed to distinguish the dots and dashes denoting the alphabet and much practice to attain the required speed of 20 words per minute. The dots and dashes came in saturation levels during long, long days, around 20 words a minute meant trainees needed to strike the transmitter key 300 times in 60 seconds. It was arduous and despite their efforts some "lacked the co-ordination of mind and muscles to achieve it".[35] There was also instruction on radio receivers, frequencies, and transmitters, and the requirement to contend with fluctuating and weak signals, interference and static. Familiarity with wireless technology was essential in case equipment broke down. When a trainee was considered efficient enough on land he took to the air in a Tiger Moth, an aircraft very ill-suited for Wireless Operator training. "The pilot occupied the rear cockpit, the wireless operator the front, sitting on his parachute, jammed behind his transmitter and receiver, trying to juggle his orders, code book, message pad and pencil, to work the morse key and controls as the light plane bobbed and bumped and the slipstream rushed by."[36]

When Max Norris was allowed he would cycle from the Maryborough base to the hotel where Hilda was now staying. That precious time seemed all too brief before he was posted to No.1 Bombing and Gunnery School, Evans Head, south of Ballina on the New South Wales coast and 111 miles (180 km) south of Brisbane. Four intensive weeks were spent there, although this still only allowed for the rudiments of aerial gunnery theory and practice. Aircraft recognition and theory of ballistics, meant more time in the classroom. In the air it was practice firing against a drogue towed behind another aircraft – Instructors accentuated that it really was not clever to shoot off your own tail plane nor should they shoot down the aircraft towing the drogue. For some misfortunate trainees working in the air came with air sickness and much to their chagrin they were henceforth relegated from aircrew to land duty.

Max Norris graduated and with his Sergeant's stripes and the half wing with WAG insignia over his left pocket, he returned to Brisbane for pre-embarkation leave. The pending departure for overseas service came with mixed emotions – this was what he had enlisted for, trained so hard for, believed in his gut was the right thing to do, but he was leaving a new wife and a secure and loving environment. On 10 September 1943 Sergeant Max Norris (426900) embarked in Brisbane for North America. On the quay below Hilda and family members waved, trying to look brave, wishing they actually were. Max wrote that parting was

Hilda Norris (née Ludlow).

Flight Sergeant Max Norris.

"a sweet affair with each avoiding any mention of the fear that it might be forever".[37] It was more difficult for those left behind.

Life had to go on but Hilda was greatly saddened to hear her friend Pilot Officer Hubert (Tom) Thomas Freeman (404240) was missing. The gentle giant who had hoped their friendship would blossom into more, had enlisted in the RAAF on 19 July 1940. He hoped his height of a shade over 6ft (1.8m) would not stop him from flying fighters. Fortunately most of his No 3 Course at 2 ITS, were destined for the cockpit, but 14 of his course would be killed. Tom left Australia in April 1941 and his RAAF career was varied. Following further training in Britain he was stationed in Malta, then Egypt, flying Wirraways. There was the odd accident along the way but he was also "Mentioned in Despatches" for "Distinguished Service". By September he was with RAF 155 flying a Spitfire over India, China and Burma. He was one of the 1,000 or so RAAF aircrew flying in this vast air space, disrupting Japanese supply lines and supporting Allied soldiers in the long campaign to recapture Burma. It is believed around 250 of these RAAF aircrew died during this campaign, and Tom Freeman was one of these – he was 23 and he and his aircraft were never found.

The French grave of Flying Officer John MacKay.

Pilot Officer Hubert (Thomas (Tom) Freeman.

Hilda then heard that their friend, John MacKay, had been shot down and was believed dead. Flying Officer John Duncan MacKay (405864) had achieved his dream too, to be a Spitfire pilot. Unfortunately the dream was short-lived. He was attached to RAF 129 when his Spitfire,

(MH442), took off from RAF Station Hornchurch, Essex, on 6 September 1943, tasked to protect bombers. Several Focke-Wulf FW190s dived across his path and John and another Spitfire pursued them briefly, shooting down one German fighter. The Spitfires climbed up in a spiral turn to 15,000 feet (4570 metres) before levelling out. A brief glint of metal caused them to climb towards the sun and 18,000 feet (5490 metres). From seven o'clock six FW190s attacked. "We broke left and continued to climb" one pilot would relate. The German fighters broke upwards under the Spitfires and made another attack from the right. Outnumbered, the air battle had become desperate. John MacKay was being pursued and he broke abruptly right causing one FW190 to overshoot his Spitfire. This desperate manoeuvre caused the fighters to collide. The FW190 broke into pieces and John MacKay's Spitfire went into an inverted spin with the whole tail unit missing. It was the 6 September 1943 when 23-year-old John MacKay crashed into French countryside.

Hilda visited John's father Duncan. Duncan was still struggling with the death of his wife Kathleen in August the previous year, and now the presumed death of his only son. The medical report marked 9 November 1943, said Duncan MacKay died of natural causes; those who visited the Mackay family Toowong corner store agreed that Duncan had died of a broken heart. A letter addressed to Duncan MacKay from the RAAF arrived two weeks after Duncan's death. It reported that John was buried in St Pierre Cemetery, Amiens, France. He would not be alone, dozens of Australian soldiers were buried there in 1918, victims of that war that was supposed to end all wars. Other members of the RAAF fighting this next war would join him later.

NINE

"Where was the justice of it all, and where was God in this mad slaughter?"

Sergeant Maxwell Alton Norris

Sergeant Maxwell Alton Norris (426900) had finished his Wireless Operator/Air Gunner Australian training and sailed for the United States. First stop the beautiful city of San Francisco. RAAF aircrew stood on the deck of their troopship and marvelled at the New World. The graceful Golden Gate Bridge, as ever cloaked in mist. The train trip across the United States took days but offered a great appreciation of the diversified American landscape. The experiences of these men in RAAF blue were the stuff of dreams, whether they came from the Australian bush or cities that clung to the rugged coastline, they were amazed by what they saw and the welcome they received in cities such as New York. The USA, in reality, surmounted the vision created in Hollywood.

The sea journey to the British Isles was treacherous and they tried not to think of the German U-Boats which could be lurking below. Finally they arrived to what most regarded as, "the Motherland". They had grown up with their parents referring to this as "home" and were surprised when they did not feel the same exhilaration. This land was not familiar at all. The skies were commonly grey and subdued and this seemed reflected in life. What was more it was a shock to the senses because they had come from a country barely touched by war to a country where the vestiges of conflict were everywhere.

Max Norris found himself at the RAF station, West Freugh, Scotland, in the winter of 1943/1944. This was the land of his forefathers but in January it was the coldest for years, even holding the pen as he wrote to his wife Hilda was challenging. Max and his course of Australian Wireless Operators would "take another step in their ultimate goal and proceed to OTUs". What could he say that sounded positive? He could not worry Hilda with his doubts and concerns, but he wondered if he, "could be as brave as his family expected, as he expected". Max sealed the envelope and dropped the letter into the box marked in large red letters CENSOR and pushed outside into the snow in time to hear a course mate mutter: "What a bloody country...why the hell didn't I join the army and get myself posted to New Guinea, at least I'd feel more at home with a bit of heat?"[1]

Moreton-in-Marsh, the home of No.21 OTU was set between low rolling hills. Through it ran the main road to Oxford University "England's premier seat of learning" – unless you spoke to someone from Cambridge. In Australia these places had conjured up romantic images, but Max gazed "with mingled awe and disappointment at this English hamlet brought back from its centuries-old tranquillity by the necessities of war". Perhaps it was the drizzle of sleet and the greyness that made this less than envisaged? Still, he had feelings of great anticipation as he arrived at Operating Training Unit because this was a major milestone in his RAAF career and here he was to become one of a "tight band of brothers. Max wondered if his crew would like him, and with a vague sort of panic, what if nobody wanted him in their crew."[2]

Could he "prove to himself, his future crew and his country" that he could fulfil his duties as Wireless Operator/Air Gunner? The all too familiar Nissen huts "with their queer appearance of a water tank cut in half" would be the draughty accommodation for as long as it took the latest Australian air recruits to qualify and crew up. On the airfield stood the Wimpys, described by Max Norris as "squatting like great short-legged birds". But for now it was the ranks of aircrew who were assembled and then left to work it out for themselves that held the attention. The dark blue Australian uniforms mixed with the lighter blue of other nationalities. The ranks of pilots with their resplendent gold wings now moved amongst the ranks of other airmen with their half wings and different letters; "N" for Navigators; Bomb Aimers with their "B"; the "WAG" of Wireless Operator/Air Gunners; "E" for Flight Engineers; and the "AG" of Air Gunners. "For the most part they sat in rather embarrassed groups gazing at each other in speculation, appraisal or disdain".[3] The ranks began to thin and that doubt started to occupy the senses yet again only to evaporate when finally an RAAF pilot walked up and asked that all important question – it was such a relief. Everything seemed to click, as small bands of aircrew in forage caps moved off to the local pub to cement what was hoped would become a successful and surviving bomber crew.

For Wireless Operator/Air Gunner trainees every 24 hours had its strict routine; parade at 0600, lectures, Morse practice, weary hours in "horror boxes" – small soundproof cubicles fitted up to resemble wireless operator's bomber compartments, with "ears ringing to the dits and dahs of morse". Then to the air and cross-country flights practising take-off routine, switching receivers to different frequencies, tapping out messages, logging incoming signals, and "feverishly taking bearings, urged on constantly by the acid tongues of their masters". It seemed ears grew to "twice their normal size" and "wrists ached with the incessant slapping of the Morse keys". Lectures on radar were followed by practice in turret manipulation and gunnery. Somewhere in the day Max needed to fit in physical training, hasty meals and study. "Lights Out" would echo through accommodation blocks at 2200 but Max rarely heard it as he was already asleep, study notes collapsed over his face.

For other musterings OTU was no less demanding. Navigators had their equivalent of "horror boxes", plotting courses to imaginary targets, taking sun and star shots with their sextants, solving seemingly impossible problems with one eye on the specially regulated clock, which turned two or three times faster than normal time. That clock and their race against it even filled their dreams. Bomb Aimers studied bombs and bombsights, navigation and gunnery, and suffered scenario after scenario of bombing simulated targets. Max Norris referred to Air Gunners as "gnome-like creatures, perpetually surrounded by the Perspex and weapons of their gun turrets or the long snake-like coils of ammo belts". The Pilots lived under Link Trainer canopies or "similar torturing apparatus". As for Engineers they were a bit of a mystery, men "with grease on their noses and with faces beginning to resemble petrol and oil pressure gauges".[4]

The real business of flying seemed too infrequent as the crew desperately wished to be together working as a unit. As a crew they were subjected to the decompression chamber, which reminded Max Norris of the vault in the Commonwealth Bank where he worked a quiet nine-to-five existence prior to all this. This sealed chamber was as unsettling as it was to walk past medical staff on the way in. Instructions echoed in: "We are taking you up to 30,000 feet [9,000 metres] in atmospheric conditions and at 10,000 feet [3,000 metres] I want all, except one of you, to clip up your oxygen masks and plug into the main oxygen supply line. The spare man will remain without oxygen until I give you the word and I want the rest of you to observe how this will affect him."[5]

For a moment they looked at each other, who would be the poor bugger, perhaps it should be the Flight Engineer – no one understood what he did anyway? Fortunately the decision was made with a pack of cards and whoever drew the lowest value was the victim. With flying helmets on they watched the altimeter needle climb, felt their ears pop and all but one donned their oxygen masks. All eyes were on the airman whose mask hung free, the altimeter showed 15,000 feet (4.600 metres) and the voice from outside asked this airman to solve some elementary arithmetic. They watched as his mental powers deteriorated rapidly, how the pencil started wandering hopelessly over the page shortly before he slumped down, when they rapidly applied his mask. It was a lesson they never forgot.

On the rare chance they got to fly in a Wimpy Max was amazed at the lack of space he had to squeeze into, a small black compartment behind his pilot. "The transmitting and receiving sets must have been fitted in with a shoe horn. The banks of batteries and other apparatus" left little room for the operator. Max was a slightly framed man and he wondered how larger men managed as he wedged himself into the small swivel chair. Having no window, no outside view was claustrophobic, and for a moment he wished he had been mustered differently.

Escape and Dinghy Drill caused much mirth. In theory each crew member had to follow final instructions before leaving the fuselage mock-up, collecting particular items as they made an orderly exit through particular hatches. The first attempt was a jumble of "collisions, mishaps and forgotten procedure". Two airmen collided, one got stuck in the top hatch one alighted triumphantly only to realize he had forgotten his delegated job of pulling the toggle to release the dinghy and his crew consequently "drowned". The routine was repeated until they became efficient but with little chance of beating the record of 23 seconds. The unanswered question was, would the forced exit from a damaged bomber allow for such a practised deliberate routine? At least it allowed Max to write with humour to Hilda that night but as he put pen to paper he "felt a hollow loneliness" for his new wife and home.

"Circuits and bumps" was an apt description of their first few flights – fortunately there was an experienced pilot in the cockpit with their less experienced pilot. Crew expectation was that this would be a "sightseeing tour". It was fine when the Instructor was at the controls, smooth as silk, not so when their own took over. The circuits were anything but smooth and the landing was very bumpy indeed. Hour after hour the same, aircrew and equipment jolted and tossed – and on the final landing after taxing to dispersal it seemed even the bomber "sighed gustily as the engines were cut". As the crew stretched and tested aching body parts they commented unmercifully to their pilot on his lack of ability -- they would never admit they actually believed the opposite. There were many more training flights and it was pleasing to see how they began to operate as an efficient and confident unit as the flights increased in length. On non-flying days they were sent on excursions, not all pleasant, such as floundering in a swimming pool in full flying gear, trying to clamber into a rubber dinghy. On that occasion they returned to base laughing only to find solemnity – an all Australian crew had crashed and been killed, including Brisbane Wireless Operator classmate, Flight Sergeant Edward Allen (Ted) Nayler (425885). It was 24 April 1944 and Max thought of the friend he had nicknamed "Lucky", how he would no more "see that cheery face" of the 20 year old. Words echoed through his brain "in a ghoulish merry-go-round". "Why did it have to be good natured Ted, who wouldn't intentionally hurt a fly. Why? Where was the justice of it all, and where was God in this mad slaughter."[6]

For Max Norris and his crew training was nearing an end and they were sent on their first and very memorable operation. As they passed over the French Coast Max vacated his Wireless Operator seat and moved to the pyrotechnics chute, where he proceeded to drop out "Windows", the bundles of strips of aluminium foil dropped to flood German radar. It was hard to believe that "these insignificant strips of silver paper should be able to disrupt the elaborate radar detection equipment of the enemy".[7] Ahead lay a carpet of anti-aircraft fire, "mushrooms of orange-coloured flame", which increased until the darkness "was split asunder with an inferno of bursting flame and shrieking shrapnel". The Bomber Stream bounced through the turbulent air like corks, occasionally the dancing long white fingers of searchlights would lock onto an aircraft – its pilot would weave quickly but occasionally there would be the flash of an explosion and the bomber was no more. Max retreated into his small black Wireless Operator compartment, perhaps this was not such a bad place to be after all. There was no missing the sound of Browning machine guns and intercom comment – Max could but hold his breath. When they landed there were a few metal souvenirs, nicks and tears. The gunners were on a high, chattering as fast as their guns had until the adrenalin wore off and they had to be manhandled into their beds.

Everything seemed to be going well with Max and his crew and he had just received a bundle of letters from Hilda including a couple of photos, which he immediately slipped into his wallet. They had been married a year now but had spent a mere few weeks together. Life was moving very quickly for both of them but in very different circles. Hilda, too, was now in uniform, the khaki uniform of the Red Cross, working as Secretary to Arthur Harcourt Perry the Director of the Field Force Section. The enemy propaganda machine was cranking out ridiculous information about how Australians should return home because Australian cities were filling up with American GIs who were "over paid, over sexed and over there". It did seem a little strange that he was over here in the UK fighting a war and "they" were "over there" fighting a war to save Australia from the Japanese.

His thoughts were interrupted when told to report to administration. Max was pretty certain he had passed all his Wireless Operator/Air Gunner qualifying so was perplexed. The officer proceeded to tell Max that not only had he qualified with excellent results but his promotion to Flight Sergeant had come through with back pay. Then totally unexpected bad news; "Your crew is going onto Tactical Air Force, flying Boston Medium Bombers". It was a slap in the face, Wireless Operator/Air Gunners were not needed on Boston Bombers so the crew was leaving without him. The officer's voice continued, there was another crew who needed a Wireless Operator/Air Gunner, would he think about it? The next trip to the sergeant's mess was awkward as his crew tried not to show their delight with the posting – for Max it was difficult to have come this far and not feel he was back at square one. His new crew seemed nice enough but it would take time to feel as comfortable in their company as his own crew already were in each other's. Max hoped this was not as bad an omen as it felt right now, a month at 1663 Conversion Unit, Rufforth, in windy Yorkshire, learning how to operate in four engine bombers, would sort them out one way or another, but he realised all too well he had to prove himself all over again.

LEFT: *back row left to right: Boon, Laird, Norris, Edmands; front row left to right: Hammond, Reason, MacKinnon.* RIGHT: *Hilda Norris (nee Ludlow).*

There was a saying that if you survived the conversion unit you "had a pretty fair chance on squadron" because the aircraft in the unit were generally believed to be "the duds, the lemons, the old clapped out ex-squadron survivors"[8]. Max observed his new crew operating and they him. Other than Aussie pilot Flight Sergeant Ronald Lindsay Reginald Laird (410500), all were RAF. Sergeant John Boon was the elder of the crew and Navigator; Flight Sergeant Ted Edmands was the largest bloke in the crew yet was the Rear Gunner; Sergeant Harry Hammond was the Bomb Aimer; Sergeant Ken MacKinnon was the Engineer, and the pint-sized Sergeant Bernard (Tich) Reason was the Middle Upper Gunner. Their coolness toward him gradually warmed and Max began to relax.

At 1663 Heavy Conversion Unit they were introduced to the Halifax four engine heavy bomber and if Max and crew had not been too enamoured with the "Hally", as the Halifax was known, in the beginning they soon became comfortable and fond of the bomber. The early model configuration of twin rudders had proved inadequate and plain dangerous as the aircraft wouldn't taxi straight on take-off and tended to overbalance and be unresponsive at low speeds. The latest model was earning a reputation for its ability to withstand heavy damage. One crew returned from an operation with 64 sq ft (6 sq m) of their Halifax starboard wing showing daylight as well as having their navigation equipment shot away. Yet another crew arrived back to their base relieved – their Halifax had only three working engines; the starboard elevator, aileron, flap, and wing had been smashed by flak; and the starboard rudder and fin were missing. Max decided after his first ops, "the Lancaster got all the hype but the Halifax would do me". Max found flying exhilarating

I am writing this 18 feet up. We are testing a plane and as I don't
have to do much on these test flights, thought I would drop
you a line. It is lovely up here. Down on the ground it is foggy
and overcast but we climb right through it all and now have
mountains and valleys of cloud down below us. No doubt about
this flying. If you don't like the weather down below you can
chase it up here. The only trouble is that we have to suck oxygen.[9]

Assigned to RAAF 466 Squadron the tempo and accompanying dangers increased dramatically as the second half of 1944 came and went. Occasionally words of concern would creep into Max's letters home. "The trip today was a little bit of hell but we came out unscathed. You know I don't think those Germans like us. I have quite a few more 'ops' to do, about 17. The total number has been increased so it looks as though I might see the finish to this war here."[10]

His crew survived many raids into the Happy Valley, operations against German cities like Hamburg, Bottrop, Cologne and Gelsenkirchen. It was during an attack on Gelsenkirchen that Max, his crew and their Hally came unstuck. The flak was a veil of lead and although they did their very best to avoid it German defence was mighty this night. Max Norris and crew were immediately reminded of those stories about Halifax bombers and their ability to withstand heavy damage and still return – as they assessed damage to the "kite" and human bodies they hoped their sortie would add to that reputation. "U/S (not operating) port outer engine; starboard feathered; no hydraulics; Skipper wounded through windscreen; Bomb Aimer with shrapnel in ribs and arm; Wireless Operator/Air Gunner peppered with shrapnel; Engineer out cold."

It seemed a long way back to base as they limped across the North Sea. Perhaps they would have an opportunity to test all those escape and dinghy drills, but the North Sea would be rather cold this time of year, and it was unlikely wounded crew would be able to remember the drill let alone carry it out. Max continued to send signals. And there it was – not exactly the white cliffs of Dover – but this part of the English coastline looked pretty dammed good, white or not. A question came over the airwaves into Max's earphones; "How shot up are you?".

After what seemed an eternity, they were instructed to divert to Kent's RAF Manston emergency aerodrome. Max could scarcely believe the next message, this time from Manston control. In "a frightfully English accent" the instruction was to land to a particular side of the airfield because repair work had just been completed after the last crash landing and it would be a shame to mess it up just yet. Surely this bloke was kidding, though there was no humour in his voice? Max would have liked to say plenty of things in reply; someone really needed to take this man on operations, but he stuck to procedure and replied they would attempt to comply with all instructions. The Hally wobbled a few times as the approach was made and the crew muttered prayers as the bomber touched down in an inelegant manner, groaned, and shuddered to a halt.

Vehicles and personnel quickly arrived and in stark contrast to the person in control were lavish in their caring attention. For this crew their war was over for now. Max continued to understate the situation in his letter to his mother Gladys.

We went on a trip to the Ruhr and wiped out a big oil refinery. Anyway we got rather shot up in the process but staggered back to an emergency landing field. ...Harry our Bombadier was rather seriously wounded but wouldn't let us fix him until we got back after helping to navigate us back. ...Mac, the engineer, got a scalp wound and I got peppered in the shoulder – all this by flak...these Hallys are great kites and take an amazing lot of punishment. It was altogether quite a hot time. Anyway please don't worry as that is probably the worst trip we will ever have.[11]

The Bombardier was awarded a DFM and there was hospital and convalescence for several. They had all suffered a big scare. Max Norris had some additional news, his first crew, posted to Boston Bombers without him had been killed. After recovering from their injuries they were back in the skies.

We have been rather busy. We have done trips to Cologne, Essen, two Dutch targets and a couple others in these last few days. Essen was a tough nut to crack and their gunners did their best to bring us down. However we made a terrific mess of the place and smoke was rising thousands of feet up in the air. Had a bit of engine trouble and just managed to hobble back to the drome where we crash-landed that other time.[12]

At least this time the Control personnel was more hospitable; "Hullo strangers glad to see you back again".

The winter of 1944 would be the "coldest since 1895. It started early and would endure well into 1945. The weather was, according to Max Norris, "the chief topic of conversation as it has caused the cancellation of a lot of our ops". Crews would "even get right up to getting dressed and going out to our kites and then it was 'scrubbed'". The strain was beginning to take its toll:

> It certainly looks like a very white Xmas this time again. I hope this is the last one I see over here. The only thing that keeps me going is the thought that someday I'll be going back to sunny Australia. If anybody ever mentions 'White Xmas' to me they will be murdered on the spot."[13]

Later he would write how he hoped he "might get back to Aussie before I'm too old to enjoy myself. I've got a personal grudge against this war. He was losing friends at an ever-increasing rate. "Another pal of mine was blown up with his crew, one day you are talking to them, next day an empty space". He was also concerned that his 19-year-old brother James (Stewart) Norris (435877), was approaching the end of his RAAF training. "I hope there is nothing left for him to do. It's funny you know, I don't mind the Jerries having a go at me but I hate the thought of them doing the same to my young brother."

Max's skipper and friend, Ron Laird, suffered a burst eardrum, and was grounded, the crew were suddenly "spare bods" each called on to fill in for aircrew out injured or ill. It was unsettling not to have those you most trusted beside you anymore, "we as a crew have ceased to exist and all our faces are far from cheery".

Max found himself on a month-long navigation course at York, preparing him for Mosquitos. It wasn't until January 1945 when life seemed almost whole again; he was recalled and reunited with his old crew. RNZAF Squadron Leader Lindsay Renolds (402899)[14] DFC, had been looking for a crew with whom he could complete his second tour of operations. He tested each airman and decided they would do just fine. They were posted to RAF 158 Squadron – more Halifaxes, but that suited them just fine as well. Over the next months Renolds chose his own operations. This meant fewer operations but not necessarily exclusion from the more dangerous and difficult, nothing less was expected from a pilot whose nickname was "Orbit Renolds", and there would be enough adrenalin laced scary operations ahead for RAAF Warrant Officer Max Norris (426900) later Flying Officer Norris.

Max Norris, his rejuvenated crew with new pilot Squadron Leader Lindsay Renolds, DFC, RNZAF.

On their first operation the Renold's-skippered Halifax returned with three large flak holes. Max was amused by his pilot's calmness and comment "that's beastly of them". A slower tempo of operations unfortunately meant it would be longer for other crew to complete their first tour, "it looks like it will be a good 18 months" before Max might return to Australia. He confided this in a letter to mother, Gladys, "but please don't tell Hilda that" he added. Max wanted the war over because he could not avoid the nagging doubt that he would not make it back, because he had just heard another of his mates was dead, "of 14 of my close air force friends only two remain".

For Max his English/Scottish ancestry ensured no immediate moral dilemma, it was natural that he would expect and be expected to fight for the British Empire. For Ray Dallwitz the situation was more complicated, the home of his forefathers was Kortnitz, Germany.

August Hermann and Maria Magdalene Dallwitz settled originally in South Australia's Barossa Valley but moved to Culcairn, NSW. Theirs was a big family with sons; Edwin John, Arthur Herman, Vernon, John Gerhard and, Raymond was the youngest. Daughters Erna and Marie meant the household would have some younger female input. One Christmas: "Ray was given a teddy bear, the bear growled when it was tipped over (something very special) but by the end of the day Ray had managed to remove the 'growl' with a knife or scissors, stuffing spilling out of the teddies gut!! He got into strife for doing this."[15]

Navigator Flight Sergeant
Ray Dallwitz.

Rear Gunner Flight Sergeant
Sydney Jackson.

Farming was just plain hard and the Dallwitz children were expected to do chores before and after school. There was little money for clothes and the boys went to school without shoes, tying hessian bags around their feet secured with string. The family moved to another farm in Eldorado, Victoria. Life became even more difficult when their home burnt down. They moved into a shed until another house could be built. The depression hit and Ray, Arthur, and John, drove an old car to Mackay, Queensland, to cut sugar cane by hand on a three-year contract. The Dallwitz boys lived in a tin hut for those three years, fed by the land owners, but received no pay until the three-year contract was finished. With their pay they returned to Victoria and purchased a wholesale merchants store in Wangaratta. As soon as they could afford they brought the rest of the family to be with them. Their hard work turned to profit and life was settled – then a German dictator emerged and European diplomacy and political solutions failed. German ancestry or not the Dallwitz children wanted to prove they were children of Australia. Arthur and Marie enlisted in the Australian Army and Ray joined the RAAF at 24 in October 1941.

Bomb Aimer Flight Sergeant
John Francis.

Middle Upper Gunner
Flight Sergeant Ron Wellington.

It was German guns on the Dutch Frisian Islands which sent a hail of flak into the night sky on 3/4 October 1943 striking RAAF 467 Lancaster JA906. Ray Dallwitz, endeavoured to navigate his crew to safer air and his pilot Pilot Officer Geoffrey Joseph Smith (414365) did his best to weave and evade the flak. As the Lancaster lost altitude German fighters attacked. It was an impossible situation and the Lancaster hit the North Sea. The 21-year-old Brisbane pilot struggled out of the sinking fuselage and was picked up by a German boat. After many months as a POW he would return to Australia and retire from the RAAF in 1954. The Australian Middle Upper Gunner, Flight Sergeant Ronald Gordon Wellington (421483) 30, formerly a cellarman with Penfolds Wines, would suffer badly from POW incarceration and spend time in a Medical Rehabilitation Unit on his return to Australia in 1945. The RAF Engineer Flight Sergeant Alexander McB Proudfoot (1551970) also scrambled out of the top of the fuselage to become a POW. For the men positioned in the bottom section of the Lancaster there was no hope as the aircraft sank quickly and they drowned. The Rear Gunner, 20-year-old Flight Sergeant Sydney Edward Jackson (416679), a lad educated in the difficult-to-pronounce South Australian school of Booboorowie, and had no hope of escaping his turret. His body would eventually be washed ashore. So, too, would the body of Flight Sergeant Raymond Ernest Dallwitz (409669). Both would be buried in Flushing, Holland. The 20-year-old Bomb Aimer, Flight Sergeant John Edmund Francis (409579), former student of Bendigo High, was never found. No remains of Brisbane's 23-year-old former apprentice joiner, Wireless Operator/ Air Gunner, Flight Sergeant Roy Edward Brook (414460) were found either. "Ray was the golden-hair son...a truly wonderful and much-loved brother...Ray's death affected the whole family dreadfully."[16] No one could question the national loyalty of the Dallwitz family. They had sacrificed too much, and their emotional pain was eased only slightly by the words of the Commanding Officer of RAAF 467: "His loss will be felt very much in the Squadron as he was a keen and capable member of a very fine crew and was well liked by all his colleagues."

Arthur Hoyle differed from many wishing to enlist in the RAAF – he had no wish to be a pilot and instead strived hard to be a navigator. With months of training behind him, aged 21, he and his crew were posted to RAAF 460 Squadron at Binbrook in 1943. The Battle of Berlin was underway and the rookie navigator together with his novice operational crew quickly realised that the Commander-in-Chief, Air Chief Marshall Harris, had a "fanatical determination to bomb Germany into total destruction with no apparent regard to the losses among his crews".[17] On 2 December 1943 they found themselves listed on the Order of Battle. Because navigators had the most preparatory work to do, they attended their own early briefing before the main briefing and consequently were the first to know the target. When Sergeant Arthur Robert Hoyle (420884) nervously looked at the map, "I saw the coloured string which set out the route, leading almost directly to Berlin. Momentarily, I felt my stomach tighten". His first thought was "This was not to be the easy first trip which was usually given to brand new crews".[18]

Hoyle would write; "Our first operation as a crew should, by rights have been our last." The Lancaster seemed to struggle under its massive load of fuel and bombs. Arthur Hoyle worked behind his blackout curtain fixing their position every six minutes. He stared at the chart in front of him, which was a grid of longitude and latitude lines and coastline of

Europe and the route outlined. Also on his desk was a box of 16 pencils which he had sharpened at both ends, erasers, a square protractor, a set of dividers and his little computer for working out course changes. On his side of the aircraft was the Repeater Compass, an airspeed indicator, an altimeter and the Gee box. Occasionally he would speak via intercom to his pilot for a course change – each time hoping like hell he got it right. As they crossed the Dutch coast all navigation lights were switched off. At 24,000 feet (7,300 metres) the temperature had fallen to -45 degrees Celsius, Arthur breathed heavily into the oxygen mask and was glad he had taken the advice of the more experienced crew and worn long underwear and a heavy pullover beneath his battle dress. Over the Zuiderzee, Gee became increasingly more difficult to use as the distance from the signal sources increased and German jamming became more effective. He thought about using astro navigation but its lit bubble bounced up and down with the movement of the bomber. "The only man whom I knew to navigate regularly by astro navigation strayed over Amsterdam and was killed".[19]

Arthur Hoyle was becoming increasingly anxious, he ordered his brain to slow down, but prior to take-off he had listened to aircrew discussing *schrage musik*, incongruously meaning "slanted music", the name given to the newly acquired upward-firing 20 or 30 mm (¾ or 1¼ in) cannons mounted in the rear canopy of German fighters. These allowed German fighters to now approach unobserved and fire underneath Allied bombers without endangering themselves. "Debriefing officers refused to believe stories of these German fighters being able to fire upwards" and it was not "until after the end of the war" that this was acknowledged. Hoyle tried to tell himself he had confidence in his gunners and knew that they realised "the price of life was constant vigilance".

On this first operational flight it was not lack of gunner vigilance which nearly cost Hoyle's crew their lives – it was Hoyle. His navigation was out and they found themselves over Leipzig and not Berlin. Perhaps a more experienced crew would have dropped bombs and returned to base but Hoyle's rookie crew altered course and pressed on. When they reached Berlin Hoyle moved into the cockpit and looked below to see "the first city that I had witnessed burning to death".[20] Yellow and red fires raged punctuated by the occasional explosion and fireball – clouds of thick smoke drifted higher and higher. The crew looked around and realized they were alone. Bombs were released into the sea of fire and feeling incredibly vulnerable they turned for home. RAAF 460 Binbrook was a very welcome sight but Hoyle paid for his mistake "no one in the crew spoke with me...they ignored me...my confidence was at a low level". Only when it was learnt that five of the 25 bombers dispatched had not returned did the crew silence dissipate. Arthur Hoyle's first operation had destroyed the romantic notions of his teenage years.

It was a midnight take-off and Arthur Hoyle "soon found that I hated these departures for a rendezvous with death in the middle of the night". He knew he wasn't the only one who "felt low spirited and quite without desire to destroy Nazis", as they silently pulled themselves into the crew bus, encumbered with bulky clothes and heavy gear, always wondering if his knowledge and courage would find a way through the moonlight. Operations slid past in almost a daze and he found himself retreating further within himself, preferring not to join the others in the pub. The prospect of early death made men react in several ways Hoyle noticed. "Some got drunk...some gambled when the weather was too bad for flying", married men, it seemed "wrote long letters to their wives", a few "became religious" and others like Hoyle "retired into themselves". All became superstitious and Arthur was no exception.

Flight Sergeant Reginald William Rowley (409747) was from

LEFT: *Flying Officer Arthur Hoyle, DFC.* RIGHT: *A navigator at work.*

Bethanga, Victoria. The 29 year old was a former Albury Grammar School student whose father was a Grazier. For Reg Rowley it was his art that sustained him and during overseas war service Rowley painted a mural on the wall surrounding his section of five beds. Shortly after its completion the Victorian was shot out of the sky. Over the ensuing months unwitting airmen arrived and moved into the beds only to die a few days later. Arthur Hoyle firmly believed, "Nothing would have made us sleep in those beds". Hoyle himself refused to give up the stained sleeveless sheepskin vest he wore over his battle dress; "I would not fly without it", and no one else would dare suggest he should.

As new crews arrived, Hoyle could see his past self reflected in their naive enthusiasm. These new crews, known as "sprogs", were supposed to receive additional training flights to gain confidence before being launched into operations, but there were too many operations and too many crews dying in the last quarter of 1943 for this to be possible. The attack against Berlin on the night of 16/17 December 1943 was disastrous. German radar plotted the bomber stream with great accuracy and German fighters attacked as soon as it reached the Dutch coast – 25 Lancasters, 5.2 per cent of the force, many flown by "sprog" crews were lost. Hoyle recalled the operation as "taxing", but worse was to follow.

As weary crews and bombers approached England, they were met by low cloud and fog-covered airfields, and a "scene of terror and destruction ensued". Another 29 bombers crashed, with Group 1 suffering the heaviest losses.[21] RAF 97, Group 8, lost eight Lancasters. In total, "148 men were killed in the crashes, 39 were injured and 6 presumed lost in the sea".[22] Forty Australians were killed. From the 18/19 November to the last day of December 1943, with the emphasis on the destruction of Berlin, it was estimated 1,260 airmen were killed, 242 taken POW, seven interred in neutral countries and eight evaded capture.[23] In total, 155 Australians were killed.

Australians attached to Bomber Command were definitely not "Dreaming of a White Christmas" but if they were in the mood to think of Christmas 1943, it was the hot Christmas of home, even if their family traditionally sat down to a British Christmas dinner of roast chicken or lamb with all the trimmings, followed by Christmas pudding and hot custard – of course the pudding had to be "magic", with threepence and sixpence coins to be found. The temperature may have commonly hovered around 100°F (37°C) but Australians thought it no more unusual to have that customary hot Christmas lunch, than the standard practice of sending friends and relatives Christmas cards with snowy scenes. But here in the country which had handed on these customs it was hard to celebrate Christmas, they were too far away from those they valued most. It was also difficult to believe that by next Christmas they would be home; it was better not to think too far ahead and tempt fate, and instead to simply focus on the next operation.

For Australians at home, Christmas 1943, was also no time to be jolly. Their nation was in a titanic struggle to resist Japanese forces and there seemed no end in sight for the war in Europe. While not as bad as in England, foodstuffs were rationed so the Christmas table would be sparse. More importantly, in the majority of Australian homes there would be empty places at the table.

For Flying Officer Francis William Rush (30245) it was a little easier to think of that hot Christmas lunch his mother Myrtle would prepare. Rush was from Hobart, Tasmania, and on the odd occasion it was possible to get a short-lived white Christmas there. Rush had worked as a Machinist with that most Australian of chocolates, Cadbury's. Now 23, he was skipper of an RAF 7 Squadron crew who took off eight days before Christmas to bomb Berlin. His Engineer, Navigator, Wireless Operator/Air Gunner, and Rear Gunner were RAF[24]. The Bomb Aimer was Flying Officer William Verdun Scott (413277) 27, from the Sydney outer suburb of West Houxton, and the Middle Upper Gunner was Flying Officer Clive Luther (424546). Luther was 29 and had the unusual middle name of Prosdocimi, which was invariably spelt incorrectly by the RAAF. A Grazier on the family property near the New South Wales Central West township of Gingkin via Oberon, he was married to Elaine with a 17-month-old son called David Clive.

The RAF Engineer, Sergeant J S Ogg had baled out. He was taken in by a Dutch family, disguised, and worked on their farm as a labourer until he could return to England. Only then would Australian families learn that Ogg was the only survivor. The RAF Engineer had watched the aircraft crash and burst into flames. Virginia Luther would write, "I cannot believe my boy is dead, he was all in life to me". Tom and Laura Scott received a carton containing their son's effects. Among the items of clothing were 97 photographs. They were pleased their son had been a keen photographer because the images offered a precious insight into the life they had been unable to share. After the war they would be informed their son was buried in a grave near Stompetoren Parish Church in The Netherlands.

Flying Officer Clive Luther.

Flying Officer William Scott.

It was difficult not to dwell on who had been lost. Survival stories were invariably tinged with sadness. An RAAF 467 crew was captained by 31-year-old Flying Officer Colin Irwin Reynolds (426572) from Perth. But for the RAF Engineer Sergeant W King (1568124) the crew were all Australian. The Navigator was Flight Sergeant Eric Albert Joyce (410496) an Accountant with the Myer Emporium in Melbourne, who had studied for a Bachelor of Economics at Melbourne University. Flight Sergeant Henry Morton Vellenoweth (410494), from Melbourne, had worked as a Rigger and then as a Carpenter before training as a Wireless Operator/Air Gunner. Flight Sergeant Kenneth Nigel Bishop Davies (411293) was born in Auckland, New Zealand, though educated in Sydney's Randwick High before becoming an Insurance Clerk. In 1941, aged 20, Davies enlisted with hopes of becoming a Pilot. He washed out with the RAAF stamping his file "unlikely to become an efficient aircrew". The enthusiasm remained and he wrote to the RAAF:

I wish to tabulate the details of my Service Flying Training School, Wagga, and ask that consideration be given to my appeal for an opportunity to continue my training as a Service pilot. I completed my Elementary Flying Training School course and passed out as an average pupil. At Wagga I had 25 hours flying to my credit, and as I was within a fortnight of my "wings" I suggest that a little perseverance would have been warranted. In view of the present international situation, I think that my use to the country would be much greater if I were given the opportunity of completing this course rather than starting me on a course which will take another six months to complete...I ask that the opportunity be afforded me to prove that which I feel so confident of, my ability to become an efficient service pilot.

The RAAF agreed on condition Davies re-enter as a Bomb Aimer. He was now 21, it was March 1942. In October 1943 Ken Davies was finally posted to RAAF 467.

His crew had two young air gunners, Flight Sergeant Cecil Roland Frizzell (426572) and Flight Sergeant Robert Henry Keating (429461). Frizzell, 20, was from the tiny Queensland town of Pittsworth, near Toowoomba and educated at Toowoomba Grammar. Keating enlisted at 18 in October 1942 and was fully operational with RAAF 467 as a Rear Gunner within a year. Keating had turned his hand to boat building when he left school in Brisbane. The two young Queenslander gunners quickly formed a close bond. Shortly after midnight on the 4 December the crew taxied down the runway for an attack on Leipzig. As the Lancaster lifted off both port engines cut and the bomber swung violently tail first into another Lancaster. Frizzell being the "Tail End Charlie" was badly injured. The 20-year-old Frizzell unfortunately died of his injuries, as did Sergeant Laurence Maurice Parker (9359) RAAF, another Queenslander, from the Bundaberg district. Parker was a member of the ground crew and was simply in the wrong place at the wrong time. They were buried in Cambridge City Cemetery. Reynolds and his crew struggled with the freakish nature of their Rear Gunners' deaths and their Christmas was much less bright without him. Another 20-year-old Rear Gunner, RAF Yorkshireman, Sergeant James William Neeve (1673669), joined the crew but it wasn't the same. On 3 January 1944 the crew celebrated Bob Keating's 20th birthday and two days later they were shot down on their 11th operation, an attack on Stettin.

Flight Sergeant Kenneth Davies.

Flight Sergeant Henry Vellenoweth.

Flight Sergeant Cecil Frizzell.

Flight Sergeant Eric Joyce.

News filtered through that RAF Engineer King was the only survivor and was now a POW. He reported Keating and Vellenoweth had been killed instantly. Florence Reynolds had found out some details from an English friend and wanted to know why the RAAF seemed poorly informed because she believed Australian families like her own should be told "our son did a good job" because "we are justly proud of him... it is the least we can do is to see that his remains are in consecrated ground". RAF red tape meant the crew could not be declared "dead" until confirmation. Richard Keating had lost his son and lashed out:

"I can't for the life of me see how you can still treat him as being missing, in view of the fact that six of the boys lost their lives and the only one that escaped was an RAF member. However, have it your own way, it can't make any difference to the issue."

Wilfred Davies, too, was angry, directing his grief at the death of his 23-year-old son Ken at the only agency he could, the RAAF. He had learnt that Ken was terribly injured and that King had pulled Ken's parachute ripcord and pushed him out of the bomber. King followed Davies out and survived, Ken Davies was found dead on the ground, the remainder of the crew did not survive the ensuing explosion. His son lay somewhere in Europe and no one could tell Wilfred where, even when hostilities ceased: "I consider such lack of consideration deplorable and grossly unfair. Surely it is understood how anxiously I await details, after all these years of sorrow and suspense." The RAAF was but a conduit and the RAF replied that investigations had been delayed due to "an extremely severe winter in Europe".

Air Marshall Harris's 1944 New Year resolution was no secret – it was the same as that of 1943, "Reduce Berlin to rubble". There may have been more important military or industrial targets but none carried the prestige of Berlin as far as Harris was concerned. As rostered crews entered the briefing room, the murmuring would begin, "The Big City?" and there would be many less polite retorts. For English aircrew there was perhaps the attraction of wishing to inflict on the German capital what they had witnessed during the London blitz. For all aircrew it meant a cold long ride and "nine hours of hell".

January and February 1944 saw too many bombers and their crews on operations against Berlin not return, with too many airmen killed. There was no easy approach to Berlin and it tested the extreme range of fuel and aircraft avionics; for crew it was physically and mentally punishing. Harris's estimate of 400–500 Bomber Command aircraft would prove vastly wrong. His "Battle for Berlin" cost 1,047 aircraft. Hunkered down in a bunker Harris believed that destroying Berlin would devastate the German spirit and will to fight, but this assault was personal to a people protecting their own, and German defences of Berlin would be understandably extreme and unforgiving. Even those largely unperturbed by human statistics, admitted later; "The enemy had ample time in which to make ready to defend his capital city. Surprise was virtually impossible".[25]

Any technical advantage bomber crews attained for self-preservation seemed to be rapidly overcome by counter measures. German defences managed to jam Gee and Oboe. German fighters were quickly equipped with honing devices which detected H2S transmissions. Naxos as it was called, was operational by the time of The Battle for Berlin. Radar stations sprinkled along coastlines of occupied territory alerted German defences as soon as bombers left English air space. Casualty figures of 10 per cent were mentioned in the office of the Commander-in-Chief, who considered this figure to be sustainable for the shortest of periods.[26] The deeper the attack into Germany the heavier the casualties were; leading to replacement crews, which were easier targets – it took just a split second to determine survival, and experienced crews reacted quicker.

Even on 1 January aircrews needed to be clear headed as 421 Lancasters were ordered to bomb The Big City. Night fighters directed by radar had no trouble finding the bomber stream. Twenty eight Lancasters, 6.7 per cent of the force were shot down; 20 Australians were killed and three were taken POW, and this officially was classed as a "minor attack". Another "minor attack" of 383 aircraft was put on route to Berlin the following night and 27 Lancasters, or 7 per cent, did not return from "another ineffective raid" on Berlin.[27] On these two raids nine RAF 156 Lancasters were shot out of the sky. The loss of so many Pathfinder crews, the most experienced airmen, would have lingering effects, and the danger facing all Bomber Command aircrew increased exponentially.

Pilot Officer Jack Weatherill's crew took off at 2313 to bomb Berlin on the second night of the New Year, having only joined RAAF 463 Squadron the previous week. This was their first operation and they were in the air less than two hours before being shot down by German fighters. Flight Sergeant William Donald Toohey (426401) was the Wireless Operator/Air Gunner. Wing Commander Rollo Kingsford-Smith, DSO, DFC, the Commanding Officer of 463, wrote to Brisbane's John and Gertrude Toohey telling them their 22-year-old son was "most popular and highly esteemed by his comrades", and how, "young men of his type are indeed a credit to their family and to the Service". The words were undoubtedly well intended to be comforting but Toohey and his crew had been sent to Berlin on their first operation. Pilot Officer Peter Louis Symonds (408054) was the 22-year-old Middle Upper Gunner educated at Scotch College, Launceston, whose wrote his occupation as "sheep farmer". Flight Sergeant Colin Hemingway (417839), 25, from Adelaide was the Rear Gunner. The Navigator was RAF Flying Officer John Watson Gage (151085) 24, from Northamptonshire, and the Engineer also RAF, Sergeant Albert Edward Cowell (1860362). Flight Sergeant Francis Noel Looney (423290) was the son of John Francis and Viola Doris Looney, of Maroubra, NSW. He seemed too young to have the responsibility of Bomb Aimer, but he was the same age as his pilot and this was a war that sacrificed the youngest and best. Among the belongings returned to his parents were prayer books and a "piety kit" indicating his faith, and John and Viola took solace in this and the belief their 20-year-old son was now in a better place and with his God.

The pilot, Pilot Officer Jack Weatherill (410021) from Melbourne was a fortnight off his 21st birthday. A year after his death his sister would write: "Twelve months ago today, my only brother...who was a pilot of a Lancaster Bomber was reported 'missing believed killed'". She needed more information "to ease my state of mind if you could inform me of the true position", because "the uncertainty of things as they are, is very upsetting". Her mother Annie was struggling with the shock and had written in May 1944 also pleading for information "to enlighten me as to the fate of my Boy". Annie's anxiety had been heightened by an article in her Melbourne *Herald* newspaper.

Since reading of the awful atrocities of the shooting of our gallant airmen in Germany. I feel half crazy with fear and grief that my own son may have shared this dreadful fate. Will you please send me all particulars regarding the finding of any other bodies...I have not troubled you before in this matter because I have just kept on hoping for the best but this article in tonight's

Herald has made me feel that I must know all. ...Do please help
me if you can, as I am sick with worry and suspense.

The press report may have been accurate, or may have been propaganda,
but little consideration was given the families of the many "missing"
Australian airmen. The Weatherill Lancaster had crashed into a Polder,
a small dyke, to the northeast of Vollenhove, through 2–6 feet (0.6–
1.8 metres) of earth and soft waterlogged sand, and sank 147 feet (45
metres) into water. It was deemed too difficult to retrieve the bodies
of Gage, Toohey and Symonds, and a plaque would be placed in the
Vollenhove Cemetery where the other members of the crew were
buried. Wing Commander Rollo Kingsford-Smith finished his letters to
the families with: "By their sacrifice and devotion to duty, he and his
comrades have added much to the glorious tradition of the Service and
have done grand work for our cause."

The Lancaster's bombload capacity could be varied. From the last
months of 1942 the most common bombload for a Ruhr Valley attack
was one 4,000 lb bomb, popularly referred to as "cookie", together with
12 small bombs loaded with 94 lb (42 kg) incendiaries. 8,000 lb (3.6
tons) cookies were also increasingly utilised. Depending on the target
the 12,000 lb (5.4 tons) "Tallboy" bomb could be carried by modified
aircraft and complemented Bomber Command's striking capacity,
which by the first quarter of 1944 was immense. This potential had
convinced Harris that he could end the war in the space of a few months
but also caused him to underestimate German defensive. Every month
212 Lancasters were being produced and of these Harris and his staff
projected that 171 Lancasters would be lost per month over the following
months.[28] The expected human cost within the Lancaster force alone
was 1,197 airmen in each month of 1944.

For a fleeting few days January winter weather caused Berlin to
be taken off the operational list and no aircrew complained. They did
complain, however, when they were asked to help clear the airfields
of snow so that attacks on other targets could proceed. On the night
of 14/15 January, 496 Lancasters and two Halifax crews were ordered
to attack Braunschweig. German radar picked up the bombers just 40

miles (65 kilometres) from the coast of England and 38 bombers, or 7.2 per cent, were shot down, eleven of which were Pathfinders. The attack was deemed "not a success".[29]

By the night of 20/21 January Berlin was back on the briefing chart. In total, 769 aircraft lifted off seemingly from the length and breadth of England leaving groups of ground crew standing in the bone-chilling cold, waving, cheering, watching as aircraft disappeared and wondering which aircraft, which crew, would return. As usual Berlin was cloud-covered and British Intelligence could never report on the success or otherwise of this attack. The report simply stated, "35 aircraft (4.1 per cent) lost".[30]

On the following night British Intelligence was again surprised when an attack on Magdeburg was "the worst night of the war, so far, for Bomber Command".[31] Some 648 aircraft took off on the first major raid against the city. German controllers again followed the bomber stream across the North Sea and although a little slow to identify the true target, the men who flew Lancasters, Halifaxes and Mosquitos, were soon at the mercy of the highly organized and efficient Luftwaffe. 8.8 per cent fell from the sky, three quarters of these to night fighters. Questions as to the vulnerability of the Halifax were again being asked after 15.6 per cent of the 224 Halifaxes sent were destroyed.

On the Magdeburg attack some very effective German decoy markings confused some crews. Pilot Officer Geoffrey Malcolm Drysdale Breaden (408323), a former Compositor from Hobart, Tasmania, joined the RAAF in November 1941 as an Observer. Magdeburg was his 12th operation as a Navigator with RAF 83 Pathfinder Squadron. The skipper was Flying Officer Wallace Kenneth Hutton (408296) 23, also a Tasmanian, and a Bank Clerk with the Bank of New South Wales branch in Devonport when he enlisted. Victorian Flying Officer Alan Fithie McInnes (410702) was unusual for aircrew, the Bomb Aimer had been selected in January two years prior when he was 32. He was married to Cathleen. Flying Officer Ronald Edward Walker (408430) the Middle Upper Gunner, was another Tasmanian, from Launceston, and was 19 when he was selected the same year. There were three RAF in their crew; Engineer Sergeant J O Lightfoot (1634342); Wireless

Operator/Air Gunner Flying Officer F W Houston (51221) and the Rear Gunner Sergeant R H Easton (1455823). When their Lancaster was attacked by fighters, Hutton dived in an attempt to evade, but the fighter sent streams of tracer and cannon fire down the centre of the fuselage, which narrowly missed Houston and Breaden and slightly wounded McInnes. Their own guns had ceased firing, when both their gunners were mortally wounded. On the third attack the fuselage burst into flames and Hutton ordered his crew to abandon the aircraft. Lightfoot jettisoned the forward escape hatch and jumped, followed by McInnes, Breaden and Houston, while Hutton attempted to keep the bomber steady – it then exploded and fell in three pieces. Breaden delayed opening his parachute and landed in the country and was captured by German troops two days later. The rest of the crew landed in Magdeburg, the town they had been bombing. Breaden would report later that crew members and other British airmen who parachuted into Magdeburg "were bashed and shot by enraged civilians".[32] His own Pilot, Hutton, had been uninjured when he was believed to have baled out "but we never saw him again". The raid was determined as "ineffective...industrial damage was insignificant".[33] The anger Breaden felt continued and on his release he would write: "Having been a POW in German hands and living on the very scanty and poor rations we were supplied with, I take this opportunity of saying that enemy POWs in this Country are treated in far too lax manner, and their scale of food rationing is in my opinion too good for them."

It is likely Warrant Officer Lyle Doust (420161) may have agreed with Breaden but he was reluctant to talk about his time as a POW and was grateful that at least he had been a POW, unlike most of his crew. It would take another generation to piece together their story and to forge a connection. Lyle Doust and his two younger brothers, Kevin and Rodney, were country boys raised with an affinity with animals and a hard work ethic. During World War I their father Bert served with the Light Horse Regiment in Egypt and then on the Western Front, he watched the developing rage in Europe knowing full well its consequences, and how another war would embroil his boys. Lyle proved good with his hands and it was decided he should move from the family home in Yass in country NSW, to live in Sydney with an aunt and begin a carpentry apprenticeship – and then Germany invaded Poland. It was difficult for men who had seen and suffered a bloody war to watch their sons show identical enthusiasm, naivety, and loyalty to King and country. Lyle opted for the RAAF and was accepted in October 1941, two months shy of his 21st birthday. Kevin joined the Light Horse (Armoured Corps), in September 1941 when he was 19 years of age; Rodney enlisted in the RAAF in July 1942 at just 18. Three sons, all overseas fighting, meant anxious times for Bert and Annie Doust.

By November 1942 Lyle Doust was in a white, wintery, Scotland, undergoing Observer Advanced Training. On New Year's Day 1943 Lyle took off in an Anson, on a cross-country course, in company with another Anson full of trainee aircrew, the weather was bad, "freshening winds and rain/snow showers". Lyle's Anson crashed into trees on the Cumbrian Mountains. Lyle and another injured airman used a parachute to drape over part of the aircraft in an effort to provide shelter for what would be a very cold night. It snowed heavily and New Zealander Sergeant William Alfred Leslie Babbington (NZ39816) died early the next day. Sergeant Lyle Doust (420161) was "seriously injured" and suffered "concussion, shock, lacerated limbs and forehead" and was admitted to Carlisle City General Hospital.

This was not enough to stop Lyle Doust and he returned to training with 15 OTU and joined the crew of Australian Flight Sergeant Conrad (Con) George Johnston (412066). Conrad's ancestors were pioneers in Wherrol Flat, near Wingham, in the mid North Coast in the 1840s. The family left the district in the 1920s to follow farming pursuits in the Northern Rivers of New South Wales. Conrad (Con) attended Taree High School to Intermediate level before becoming a Dairy Farmer at Nana Glen in the Coff's Harbour district. Dairy farming was hard work but Con still found the energy to take his sister Ada ballroom dancing on Friday and Saturday nights at the Nana Glen Hall.[34] He left Australia in November 1941 and disembarked in Rhodesia (now Zimbabwe) for additional pilot training. In November 1942 he was in the UK and choosing a crew. With Lyle Doust as his Navigator, he next chose New Zealander Johnny Dobson, an Auckland customs officer, as his Bomb

Aimer. Londoner, Sergeant Leonard William Wykes (1386942), a book binder, became the Wireless Operator/Air Gunner in this Wellington crew of five.[35] At 1663 Heavy Conversion Unit another Australian, Sergeant John Kevin Thompson (422757) joined as Rear Gunner. Thompson came from Sydney and his technical credentials were impressive, having studied at Swinbourne Technical High, Hurstville Central Tech, and Sydney Tech High, finishing the latter with first class honours in drawing, metalwork and woodwork. As a 19 year old in a hurry he opted to train as an Air Gunner on entry in May 1942. Sergeant John Fisher Morgan (1417169) 29, was from Swansea, and married to Violet. He became the Middle Upper Gunner. The RAF Engineer who was also in his late 20s, came from Bolton and was Sergeant Sydney Hennan (1028076).

The crew's operational life commenced on 1 September 1943 when

No. 466 (Halifax) Squadron RAAF crew No.85, and Johnston's No.87. Left to right: RCAF Flight Sergeant J A Dixon; RAF Sergeant S Hennan; RAAF Sergeant C G Johnston; RAAF Sergeant J F Thompson; RAF Flying Officer R Hodgson; RAAF Flight Sergeant L Doust; RAF Sergeant J F Morgan; RAF Sergeant S E Rayner; RNZAF Flight Sergeant J E Dobson; RAF Sergeant L W Wykes. By the end of the war only three of these men were alive.

they arrived at RAF Leconfield to join RAAF 466, "life was more ordered, noisier due to the constant flying at all hours, and with heightening tension".[36] Life was not dull for the next months and they were even made poster boys, following 466's Heavy Bombing debut against Frankfurt on the night of 20/21 December 1943. Forty aircraft and crews were lost on this raid, noted officially as "achieved little", but the press and government photographers were there to photograph those who returned. Conrad wrote home unimpressed saying: "I was tired and only concerned with getting to my bacon and egg and bed...I couldn't even eat it in peace however for ambitious camera men."[37]

On the 17 January 1944, Conrad (Mick) Johnston wrote home, he was showing the signs of stress: "Feeling a bit 'cheesed' or 'browned off' as they say over here meaning blue...bags of duff weather...I'll begin to grow some gills."

Three nights later on 20/21 January 1944, Flight Sergeant Conrad Johnson's crew took off in Halifax "K King" (HX312) to attack Magdeburg, Germany. The crew were relieved; they had successfully dropped the bomb load and were heading home. Oberleutenant Hans-Heinz Augenstein of the 7th Night Fighter Wing 1 was in the air in his Messerschmitt 110. His fighter was fitted with Lichtenstein SN-2 radar, and he was able to locate enemy bombers up to 4 miles (6.5 kilometres) away. Close to midnight the radar found Halifax 312 and Augenstein approached quickly. Just 35 minutes into the new day he fired his ¾ in (20 mm) cannons upwards into the wing of the Halifax.

Lyle Doust had just given Johnston a change of course to avoid flak. His pilot was weaving when the wing took a direct hit from below. Lyle Doust "remembered flying shrapnel and sparks and at least two loud bangs".[38] The skipper asked Syd Hennan to feather the propeller but the Engineer was unable to do so − Conrad ordered his crew to bale out. The front floor escape hatch was directly under Lyle's chair. Bending down he pulled at the hatch − it blew inwards knocking him unconscious. Bomb Aimer Johnny Dobson threw Lyle out of the aircraft and followed. Lyle Doust regained consciousness dangling from a tree, Dobson also landed in a tree. The Halifax was a fireball that hurtled into the ground at Losser in The Netherlands. German soldiers arrived to find four of the crew near the wreckage with chutes open; they were too close to the ground when they had baled out. The 20-year-old Rear Gunner Flight Sergeant John Thompson was still in his turret, he had been severely wounded by the straffing attack – Augenstein recorded his 23rd Allied aircraft "kill".[39]

Ada Johnston would continue to speak of her brother Conrad as being "gentle and sensitive...he was very musical and used to whistle a lot", and remember with a mixture of happiness and sadness the Friday and Saturday nights Conrad took his sister ballroom dancing at the Nana Glen Hall. His photograph would take pride of place in their widowed mother's home until she died, but a friendship between Ada Louise, and Fred and Sien Leus of Losser, who voluntarily tended Conrad's grave, led to a 45-year friendship, only ending with their deaths. One year the Dutch couple sent a gift of tulip bulbs, unfortunately they struggled in the climate of the mid-north coast of New South Wales.

Lyle Doust was treated in hospital for a five-inch (13-cm) long bone-deep gash above his right eye to his ear, and severe concussion. He and Dobson were now German POWs. Lyle Doust would survive time in Stalag VIIIB, and the ensuing "Death March". At the beginning of 1945, with the Soviet army advancing, the Germans would march POWs westward in groups of between 200 to 300. During the so-called "Death March" many POWs died due to exhaustion and the bitter cold – those unable to continue were shot or simply left to die. Lyle Doust would again be fortunate. Returning to Australia he would marry Marjory in April 1946 and have daughters Bronwyn and Merryn. Lyle would be a foreman carpenter on many major Canberra government buildings and retire in 1986. That year he and Marjory travelled overseas and one stopover was to visit the graves of his crew. In 1995 the citizens of Losser dedicated a memorial to the crew, they also subscribed money so that Lyle Doust could come to the dedication but he was not well enough to travel. Lyle Doust died in 2005.

The feeling of urgency and to a lesser or more extent, sense of doom, rarely left those who flew in bombers. Except for their six days' leave every six weeks they were seldom far from the base. With little respite crews would file into operational briefings wondering what target those who sat behind desks had chosen. Experienced airmen would notice aircraft were being fitted with overload fuel tanks, a clear sign that it was going to be another long night. Settling into briefing room seats they could observe the presence of many new youthful faces, replacements for those they had become accustomed to seeing. New aircrew wore masks which were a combination of nervousness, excitement, and fear, something that once reflected their own, until their own expression turned to one of indifference. The target map was unveiled and eyes followed the thin red line across the North Sea and its route which snaked across the map of Europe. The Squadron Commanding Officer would give a brief welcome, agree to the assembled men smoking and hand over to the specialist officers, navigation, signals, gunnery, meteorology, intelligence, and aircrew would concentrate as much as they could to mute that small voice that asked the question; "will this be the one I don't come back from". The same salient points would come from the official briefing, the tactic ever the same, the business was to attack, to push on and drop bombs on target regardless of what German defence came at your aircraft.

The intensity was beginning to show on the hearts and minds, but authorities unfamiliar with this sort of war and even less with the stresses placed on those they ordered to fly, made no allowances. The entire RAAF station was called to parade, with no exception made for aircrew who landed at dawn. A Sergeant had refused to fly an operation over Germany and was therefore guilty of Lacking Moral Fibre (LMF). He stood in front of every member of the Squadron with an expression unsettling to aircrew, most of whom would have preferred to have been anywhere else. In a dramatic gesture his half wing was torn from his uniform by his senior officer. His Sergeant stripes were then torn from his sleeve. In a matter of a minute he had been reduced to an Aircraftsman Second Class and a forlorn figure intended to discourage all others. In the Sergeant's mess opinions were mixed, some believed he deserved such treatment, some were sympathetic, others kept their thoughts to themselves as they attempted to use his dejected image to steel their own resolve.

On 15 February 1944, British Bomber Command was back with a

massive force of 891 aircraft dropping 2,642 tons of bombs.[40] RAF 35 Squadron Halifax LV861 that took off at 1736 had Australians at the extreme ends of the bomber. From Sydney 28-year-old Pilot Officer Colin Frazer Blundell (411116) was the pilot/skipper. Blundell was a Sydney accountant with AMP who enlisted at 21 in April 1941. He was one of the few Australians who received his training in Rhodesia and South Africa. African conditions resulted in his being admitted to hospital with dysentery. Flight Sergeant Jeffrey Eugene Pogonowski (418011) 22, from Melbourne, was the Rear Gunner, who enlisted in April 1942 at 20. Other than Pogonowski, Blundell's crew were RAF.[41]

Pilot Officer Colin Frazer Blundell.   *Flight Sergeant Jeffrey Pogonowski.*

The bomber was hit by flak while returning from the target and set on fire. Blundell gave the order to abandon aircraft before the Lancaster exploded in mid-air scattering wreckage near the Dutch city of Deventer. Three RAF crew evaded capture, the Australians at each end were not as fortunate, being killed along with RAF Sergeants Leslie Hazell (918657) and Ray Daniels (962612). Important war industries were severely damaged in this attack and Bomber Command lost only 43 aircraft and crew – 4.8 per cent, pleasing Bomber Commander-in-Chief.

Those who assembled for their orders for a raid on the night of 19/20 February, breathed easier when they realised the target was not Berlin. A summary of the attack that took place on Leipzig read; "This was an unhappy raid...the bomber stream was under attack all the way to the target". The winds were forecast to be calm but they were the opposite. The main bomber stream circled the target while awaiting

Pathfinders. Four bombers collided and 20 were shot down by flak.[42] The loss of men and aircraft was catastrophic, 9.5 per cent made up of 78 bombers and crews. Halifax losses were terrible at 13.3 percent. Their vulnerability at the extreme end of their range meant Halifax Vs and IIs would no longer participate in deep operations into Germany. Twenty seven more names were added to RAAF killed in action lists and more to those of POW.

Amiens, Augsburg, Frankfurt, le Mans, Schweinfurt and Stuttgart were targets added to log books. Aircrew were thankful when their excursions into foreign lands ended with their return to England and they fervently wished that few of their peers would be left behind. In February/March 1944 their prayers were answered: losses were lighter than usual, at around 4 per cent. On the night of 24 March the next destination was Berlin again. Crews sat quietly as if they had some dreadful premonition. Australians seemed intent on hastily writing letters home – Berlin had that effect. How many more of these excursions to the German capital would they be ordered to undertake?

Aircrew awoke to observe changing weather. Met officers would make the decision, if weather was deemed difficult the force would fly to Brunswick; if they believed it good enough it would be Berlin. The weather worsened and crews were surprised when they were told Berlin was still the target. It was daylight when they took off and climbed to set course for the Frisian Islands and soon the grey North Sea was beneath them. Over the intercom came the words "Enemy coast ahead", the aircraft's course changed south. The light began to fail and then there was complete darkness – flying at 18,000 ft (5,500 m) and with no moon. With no cockpit light the luminous instruments reflected brightly on the windscreen, and from the exhaust ports of the four Merlin engines came red streams of flame. The first light flak and tracer shells climbed skywards towards them. Pathfinders and the initial bomber stream commenced pushing bundles of windows foil strips through the chute into enemy territory. Wireless Operators spun radio receivers over the short-wave band seeking German fighter controller voices. They could send a burst of noise in the hope that it might blot out transmission to the fighter. On maximum alert, the gunners swivelled in their turrets scanning the sky for any unusual glint and their adrenal glands worked overtime.

Those responsible for the wind forecast had got it badly wrong. Some navigators figured it out and called upon their pilots to correct speed and course. Others decided to abide with the official weather prediction, and as a result the bomber stream began to break up and these aircraft strayed badly off course and at scarily slow speeds. The bomber stream quickly scattered adding to their vulnerability. Suddenly orange-red incandescence and a Lancaster burst into flames with fire quickly engulfing the fuselage from nose to tail. For aircrew nearby it was a terrible sight. Every detail lit up so clearly, and they held their breath and muttered aloud as they waited for parachutes to billow out from the bomber's belly – none came as the aircraft sank just before the bright red explosion tore metal and men apart. Who would be the next target? From above fighter flares lit up the bombers to assist the Messerschmitts and Focke-Wulfs in their attack.

Bomber crews knew they were over Berlin because of the massive flak blanket. It didn't matter how many times they had seen it, there was always the same tightness in the muscles and fear rose from deep down no matter how hard they tried to suppress it. A few religious words, and a few not normally used in mixed company, were muttered over the intercom – welcome to hell. Some crews had been pushed well past the aiming point by the strong tail-winds and found it impossible to turn around for a second run over the target. Below bombs burst and fire-lit smoke was everywhere. Pilots struggled to hold aircraft steady as their bomber swam through the slipstreams of other bombers, and was buffeted by ack-ack bursts. The bomb aimer's voice came over the intercom, and he could see the pathfinder flares and adjusted his sights. His sequence always seemed so agonisingly slow: "Steady...steady... right a little...steady...left...hold it skip...bombs gone". Bodies rose as the lightened bomber leapt upwards and the sense of relief was huge. "Bomb doors closed" called the captain as he turned onto the course home, weaving to avoid the cones of searchlights which would result in a heavy concentration of flak.

The coast was close when the excited voices of the gunners came over the intercom. They had sighted ghostly white aircraft. It was quickly evident that they were neutral fighters from Sweden, making a non-hostile token gesture of neutrality defence. It was almost surreal. Here was a European nation not wishing to be involved as thousands and thousands of fellow Europeans were killed and a bunch of Aussies were risking their lives to set Europe free.

As if protected by some supernatural force, Berlin was again the graveyard of many British airmen. ...The lighter Mosquito Pathfinders were pushed off course leaving them open to heavy radar-laid flak batteries. In total, 50 British aircraft were shot down by flak and 22 by night fighters – 8.9 per cent lost. Bomber Command's report on this attack on Berlin would read it was another "night of the strong winds. ... No industrial concerns were classed as destroyed but several important ones were damaged".[43]

Ordinary men were doing extraordinary things. Pilot Officer Harold Callaway Wills (412787) 24, was the pilot of a RAAF 466 Halifax ordered to attack Stuttgart on the night of 15 March 1944. He was a Linotype Operator before enlistment and was married to Raynor and had a daughter called Suzanne Elizabeth. Flying at 20,000 feet (6,000 metres), the bomber was intercepted by a night fighter. Gunfire caused a fire in the compartment which housed oxygen supply bottles. The fuel tank burst into flames. Despite the imminent explosion, Wills told his crew to bale while he held the aircraft steady. By the time Wills left the cockpit flames had severely burnt his face and hands and he was admitted to a German hospital. Flying Officer Harold Wills survived his POW internment and returned to Australia in 1945. Saving the lives of subordinates during a land incursion with the enemy would have received military recognition, but not so for Wills and other bomber captains who risked their own lives for their crews – bravery it seemed had mostly been defined as "returning fire".

RAF 158 Halifax LW718, was manned by seven personnel, with five RAF aircrew sandwiched between two Australians. In the cockpit sat 25-year-old Pilot Officer Keith Simpson (414166) who had been born in Texas, Queensland, but whose family now lived in Mackay, Queensland. By coincidence the Rear Gunner was 21-year-old Flight

Sergeant Malcolm John McKay (425042) – with a different spelling of the surname but good enough to confuse the English crew. They took off from RAF Lissett, Bridlington, at 1855 on 24 March to attack Berlin. Within four hours a radio message was sent from the bomber indicating major engine problems had caused them to abandon the operation. Somehow they kept the bomber flying and must have felt relief with the sight of the craggy English coast. Simpson was confident they could survive a crash landing onto sand dunes near the Norfolk town of Winterton-on-Sea, but was unaware that this part of the coast was mined. As the Halifax touched down a mine exploded and the crew died instantly. Civil defence workers removed the crew's bodies and then dealt with their unexploded bomb. Five of the crew were buried in a collective grave in Cambridge Cemetery.

TEN

"Rest peacefully, youngster, rest peacefully."

Lenie Baars

Sir Arthur Harris clung to his anathema regarding targets like Berlin and Leipzig because of his unshakeable view that nothing but the systematic destruction of the Third Reich from the inside out, would convince the German High Command to finish the war. Between the 1 January and 24 March 1944 eight major raids were launched against Berlin at terrible cost. In total, 351 aircraft, (112 Halifax, 234 Lancasters and five Mosquito) were lost; 1,787 airmen killed, 506 had become POWs and 25 had evaded capture. Combined Battle of Berlin first and second phase figures revealed that during the 16 major Berlin attacks, 606 aircraft were lost and more importantly, 3,047 airmen were killed, 748 became POWs, 33 evaded capture while seven were interned.[1] During The Battle for Berlin 20,224 sorties had been flown, critics said the battle had failed, others disagreed. Aircrew merely followed orders. The British War Cabinet and Allied Command, with eyes on the bigger picture, were increasingly concerned.

If Berlin was a failure Nuremberg was catastrophic. During the afternoon of 30 March 1944 crews noticed the wind was increasing and clouds were gathering on the horizon giving them confidence that the raid would be scrubbed. The regular routine continued as experienced airmen shook their heads and new crews looked increasingly nervous. The set course also raised dissension as it was standard practice that diversionary course changes were incorporated and on this operation they were to fly direct leg of some 270 miles (435 kilometres) between Charleroi and Fulda. Into the mission the realisation that the weather forecast was indeed, as their gut had told them, wrong with high winds beginning to scatter the main stream. Still a long way from the target massed German fighters launched an air battle and quickly the route was strewn with burning bombers in their death throes. Nuremburg was covered in dense cloud.

It was an RAAF 467 crew had taken off at 2148 from Waddington. The skipper was another Australian with a name synonymous with the ANZAC legend, Simpson.[2] Flight Lieutenant Arthur Bruce Simpson (408881) was born in Euroa, Victoria, and had been managing his family hotel in Numurkah when he enlisted in June 1941 at age 25. By September 1943, he was with RAAF 467 and become engaged to Joyce. Arthur Simpson and his crew had already had their fair share of excitement when on an attack on Hanover on the night of 8/9 October 1943, they collided with an FW190 night fighter in the skies over Germany. The Lancaster's front turret was torn off and an icy gale blew in. Simpson gave the order to bale. Flight Sergeant John William O'Connor (420990) born in the town of Coonabarabran, NSW, a town nestled in the foothills of the blue peaks of the Warrumbungle National Park, was the 20-year-old Wireless Operator/Air Gunner. On hearing the instruction he baled immediately and became a POW. His Skipper, Arthur Simpson, re-assessed the situation and decided he would attempt to fly back to England. It was a truly hairy trip back. When the aircraft was finally on the ground Simpson and his Navigator the Launceston, Tasmania-born Flying Officer Raymond Carson Watts (401842) were taken to hospital suffering frostbite. They were awarded DFCs.

It was back into the fray quickly for Simpson and crew with seven trips to Berlin, one to each of Brunswick, Schweinfurt and Essen, two raids on Frankfurt, and three to Stuttgart, between that eventful October trip to Hanover and this 30/31 March 1944. He was confident as he released the brakes and the Merlin engines roared into the sky.

Simpson had 190 flying hours; this was their 23rd sortie, and at least they weren't off to Berlin. He checked with his crew; Pilot Officer Geoffrey Johnson (414801) was a 21-year-old former Grazier from Roma, Queensland, and now the Wireless Operator/Air Gunner. In the Middle Upper Gunner turret, from Brisbane and still only 19, was Flight Sergeant Colin Argyle Campbell (426306). Flight Sergeant Kenneth Walter Manson (408375) the 20-year-old Bomb Aimer was Tasmanian, and hoping the front turret would not be ripped off this time. The RAF Engineer Sergeant C P Curl likely hoped the same. Londoner Pilot Officer R Weedon was sitting tight and alert in the Rear Gunner turret.

Clearing Belgium on the outward flight Lancaster LM376 was picked up by a German ME110 night fighter piloted by Major Martin Drewes. Simpson's gunners made a quick visual and shouted at their pilot to weave. Cannon fire raked the side of the British bomber. The rear gun was quickly out of action, the rudders and hydraulics were shot away as well as the instrument panel. The Lancaster was on fire and efforts to extinguish the flames were useless. Simpson ordered them to bale out; he was the last to leave at 12,000 ft (3,700 m). Simpson's Lancaster was Drewes 53rd kill and his 33rd Lancaster. The German ace did, however, follow the burning bomber down and in not firing allowed the crew to bale out.

Colin Campbell lost consciousness on the way down but it at least meant his body was relaxed when he struck the ground. His brain was fuzzy but he freed himself from the harness and hid his parachute. Soon after he came across Simpson and the two spent three weeks in Belgium before they could be gradually smuggled out through Switzerland by the Underground. Mary Campbell was overjoyed that her son was in "neutral territory", she had sent five parcels to him care of his squadron believing deep down that he was alive. She knew that he would be able to enjoy the birthday cake she had posted, Colin was to turn 20 on 26 April – the cake would stay fresh enough. It was September when Simpson, Campbell, Johnson, and the two Londoners, Weedon and Curl, met at 'Coger's', a hotel in London, just as they swore they would. A few pints were consumed, and there were several toasts to missing mates, Manson and Watts. They had learnt via the Red Cross that the two Tasmanians, Navigator Watts and Bomb Aimer Manson managed to evade capture for a month before becoming POWs.

The Nuremberg operation was referred to by some as a "fiasco" and others; "In a nutshell, it is a tale of almost unmitigated disaster."[3] Out of a force of 795 aircraft 105 were shot down, 71 damaged – 11.9 per cent of the force. An estimated 537 airmen were killed and 157 taken prisoner.[4] Forty five Australians were killed on this raid and eleven became POWs. Yet again meteorological intelligence was wrong and for British crews it was like being in a German shooting gallery. One crew caught up in the mêlée was very experienced and from RAAF 460. Lancaster ND361 was still outbound when shot down by a night fighter. Most of the crew were mature, had been decorated, and were on their second tours. The pilot, RAAF Squadron Leader Eric Arthur Utz (403438) 30, from Armidale, New South Wales, wore a DFC and bar. RAAF Pilot Officer Arthur George Jackson Chadwick-Bates (412480) 33, from Cammeray, New South Wales, had been awarded a DFC. RAAF Pilot Officer Jack Hamilton Thomson (412774) 28, from Forest Lodge, New South Wales, had DFM after his name. RAF Flying Officer John Howarth (50972) gained his DFM for gunnery skill while on a sortie to Hamburg in July 1942, nearly two years previous. The death of so many aircrew particularly such decorated and seasoned veterans like Utz, Chadwick-Bates, Thomson and Howarth, caused a large drop in morale as less experienced airmen wondered how they would survive when these heroes had been killed.[5]

Bomber Command Europe aircrew had faced withering duty and hardship in the first months of 1944. Seeing personal effects placed into boxes, sometimes by members of the Women's Auxiliary Air Force (WAAF), failing to hide their sadness and tears, had become too frequent. It appeared that the attacks of 1944 bordered on insanity, with so many lives lost for seemingly so little effect. Unbeknown to those harnessed with the responsibility of flying bombers, Nuremberg was the end of a large chapter in the history of Bomber Command. From April 1944 Bomber Command came under the auspices of the Allied Supreme Commander, American General, Dwight D Eisenhower, for what would be known as "The Transportation Plan"; and as a consequence those who flew with Bomber Command Europe found their chances of survival rose exponentially. A list had been prepared in March 1944 of 79 railway targets, repair and servicing centres, and the majority of these were in France and Belgium. The French railway network came in for special attention – the plan being to paralyse northwest Europe, to isolate the coast and delay enemy reinforcements. The inherent dangers of flying over occupied territory remained but it felt more inspiring to bomb aircraft factories, railways, mining, supply dumps coastal defences, military camps and radar installations, than cities.

Arthur Harold Probert, born in Dorrigo, New South Wales, was a 23-year-old clerk living a settled, predictable life with his wife Irene in Sydney in 1939. On 11 April 1944 he was the pilot/skipper of a Lancaster bomber on a raid on railway yards at the French town of

Flight Sergeant
William George Hogg.

Flying Officer Arthur
Harold Probert.

Flying Officer
Robert Bruce McDougall.

Flight Sergeant
Austin Hardcastle Palfreyman.

Aulnoye-Aymeries, and life was anything but settled and predictable. Flying Officer Probert (420054) had a sprinkling of French blood in his ancestry and his thoughts likely considered this as he flew over occupied France.

Close by his 20-year-old RAF Engineer Sergeant Basil George Wiseman (1603151) monitored the control panel festooned with switches and gauges to record engine performance. The Wireless Operator/Air Gunner was also with the RAF, Sergeant Dennis Robbins (1338956) 22. The Navigator was Flying Officer Robert Bruce McDougall (410609) 24, an arts degree student at Melbourne University. Also from the Victorian capital was 20-year-old Middle Upper Gunner Flying Officer Keith Francis Ryan (418695), a former engineering labourer who enlisted at 18. There was a degree of interstate rivalry because Flight Sergeant William George Hogg (429322) and Flight Sergeant Austin Hardcastle Palfreyman (425207) were both Queenslanders, from the same region. The Bomb Aimer, 22-year-old Palfreyman had attended the esteemed schools, Toowoomba Grammar and Brisbane Boys' College, but he never fancied the indoor life and chose to work as a jackaroo. His family lived in Miles, Queensland. The 19-year old known as "Young Will" was of a large Hogg Clan that were well known in Queensland's Darling Downs. Not long after his 18th birthday Young Will was mustered Air Gunner. They joined RAAF 460 as a crew on 25 January 1944.

Immediately following the end of World War II air force casualty reports would convey the grisly process of exhumation and identification of aircrew lost in Europe. When bombers exploded there was little left; the remains of a crew of seven could fit into one coffin. Positive identification of Probert and his crew was delayed, not only by the condition of the remains, but by "evil doers". According to the report, "three young men", locals, had stripped the bodies of "watch", "money", identity discs", a "signet ring" and "pocket book". In time, authorities would visit homes in the French village of Neuf-Mesnil and recover possessions that enabled them to place crosses with names over graves. As the sad news filtered through to the families, the sister of Flying Officer McDougall requested no further information be sent directly to her widowed mother Christina because "she is under medical attention and confined to bed". Louise Probert would request a photo of the grave – "he was my only son". The RAAF complied and she expressed her gratitude: "It is a great comfort to me to see where he is laid to rest, were I a younger woman I would go England and France to visit the place where he fought and died for his Country."

The night of 3/4 May 1944 was a terrible night for Bomber Command when 360 aircraft attacked the German military camp near the French village Mailly-le-Camp. Communication problems delayed the main force, providing German fighters with adequate time to arrive. Significant damage was caused, but 42 Lancasters, 11.6 per cent of the attacking force, were shot down, and 300 aircrew died. RAAF 460 lost five Lancasters; one RAAF 463 and one RAAF 467 crew were also shot down – 23 Australians were killed on this operation. A week later three RAAF 463 crews and three RAAF 467 crews sent to bomb rail installations at Lille, crashed, the highest 463/467 loss of the war. RAAF 463 aircrew ranged 19–39 years of age with 23 and a half being the average. RAAF 467 ranged 17–41, the average being 24.[6]

There was little left for identification of the crew in which Flying Officer Geoffrey Philip Pinn (424212) 22, was the Navigator. Pinn was from Sydney and held a Bachelor of Economics degree and a Diploma of Education. The Bomb Aimer was Flight Sergeant Harold John Smith (410515). His education level wasn't as good as that of others in his Observer course. In civilian life he was a Transport Driver in Mepunga, Victoria. Smith enjoyed the work because it got him out on the open road, and the Shipwreck Coast and Great Ocean Roads were two of the most beautiful in the land. Flight Sergeant William Gertzel (427460) 20, came from Perth and was a Shoe Salesman before entering the exciting world of wireless and gunnery at 18. Flight Sergeant William Andrew Gillard (429849) was the Middle Upper Gunner. The 25 year old came from Houghton in South Australian wine country. His background was humble compared to some and he doubted this would get him into aircrew. His father Richard was a Labourer. William was employed as a Carpenter's Labourer so after hesitating over what position he would apply for he opted for Airman, Rigger Trainee. The first recruiter comments were fairly damning: "No trade experience whatsoever, next to nothing on engines". The next took a closer look at the man; "Fairly tall and well built, neat and clean in appearance, no obvious faults, suitable type", and stamped "Aircrew" on Bill's file.

Flying Officer Lavington Edmund John Frederick Chinnery (429924), another South Australian, dabbled in wine-making and was a Clerk. Being 32, married to Ruva and with a seven-year-old son called John and a five-year-old daughter known as Jacey, he was a most unusual Rear Gunner. The RAF preferred Engineers to come from the United Kingdom because it was easier to ensure they were properly trained on aircraft built there – so it was not unusual that the Engineer was RAF, Sergeant Alexander Mitchell Berry (1861471) who was only 19. Flying Officer Leonard Victor Barnett (418332) was pilot/skipper of their RAAF 466 Squadron Halifax. Barnett from Melbourne put his occupation as vegetable grower and was also 19 when he enlisted in May 1942. Barnett was 21 when the Halifax LV919 was shot down by a

Flying Officer Geoffrey Philip Pinn.   *Flying Officer Leonard Victor Barnett.*

Lavington Chinnery.   *William Gertzel.*   *William Gillard.*

The crew backlit in front of their Lancaster.

night fighter near Antwerp half an hour into 13 May 1944 – he and his crew had not even joined a squadron, they were still training.

A year later Clarice Gertzel confessed to RAAF authorities that she had finally admitted to herself "it is hopeless", to expect to see son Bill again. Annie Smith wrote thanking authorities for confirmation because; "The 17 months of suspense have been awful" and "although the blow is hard it is much better to have some definite news". On his RAAF application form under "Religion" Gertzel wrote: Salvation Army; Pinn and Chinnery C of E; Smith and Barnett "Pres" and Gillard "RC". They came from different Australia stratum; different educational levels; different states, they did not share a common religion; but in death they would share a communal grave and in 1944 a single cross bearing their names.

The fickleness of fate remained unfathomable. RAAF 467 Lancaster LM475 despatched to bomb rail installations at Lille, was skippered by RAAF Squadron Leader Donald Phillip Smeed Smith (400495). Smith was an industrial chemist living in Mosman when he enlisted in September 1940. He would be discharged in December 1945 and as well as being "Mentioned in Despatches" would be awarded a DFC. The 10 May 1944 operation was the last operation of his second tour and his 51st op.

Jack Royston William Purcell.

His crew were three RAF and three RAAF. Warrant Officer Royston (Jack) William Purcell (412686) 22, from Sydney was a Navigator and had done well in the RAAF. A pupil at St Joseph's, Burwood, he was a shop boy in the NSW Railways Chullora workshops, before being accepted. Flight Sergeant Alastair Dale Johnston (425413) a 24-year-old Wireless Operator/Air Gunner from Queensland's Kingaroy, was a motor mechanic who wrote on his RAAF enlistment application that he would "go where best suited". Flight Sergeant Gilbert Firth Pate (423311) 27, studied at Sydney's Kogarah High – and married Edith a week before he reported for RAAF training. Tonight he climbed into the rear turret of a Lancaster.[7] When the aircraft was hit it burst into flames and the explosion shortly after ejected the pilot. Smith landed uninjured, evaded German forces, and returned to England – his crew were killed.

There was a routine involved when attacking by night but the operation itself whilst having procedure could rarely be called "routine". Aircrew learnt by morning if they were due to fly that night when battle orders were pinned to noticeboards. Crew would verify with ground personnel that their nominated aircraft was fully functional. Aircrew were dependant on ground crew for survival. Members of the WAAF checked CO_2 bottles on life vests, better known as "Mae Wests", for signs of corrosion and leakage, and parachutes for damp which might prevent the chute unfurling properly and leave the unfortunate airman "roman candling", spinning round and round as he hurtled to the ground. They would also pack escape kits with silk maps of the hostile area over which crews would be flying this op, as well as rations and other items like a compass.

Briefing would begin mid-afternoon, detailed instructions for each speciality followed by general briefing. "Tea" followed commonly involving the ever-precious rationed eggs, and then the wait – the worst time because the mind was difficult to silence. If they were fortunate they would get hold of the *Daily Mirror*, the airman's bible, and assure disbelievers it wasn't just to see how many clothes the comic strip character "Jane" had removed. "Jane" after all adorned the nose of one of their very own Lancs.[8]

Just Jane.

Just Jane.

There was a disconcerting rumour circulating in the mess that French ops, day or night, would only count for a third of an operation and grumbling about it helped to pass the time. Then there was mirth when a Bomb Aimer admitted he really did lie on a steel helmet during the run-in over target, to protect his testicles – uncomfortable but better than the alternative. Cigarettes would be stubbed out as they boarded crew transport, which drove them to the dark silhouettes of bombers waiting in dispersal. Last thing before climbing into the aircraft was to form a line and see who could pee the farthest. Urinating during a flight was rather difficult so best to relieve oneself at the last opportunity and the competition became a bit of a ritual and last frivolity before the deadly serious duty began.

Wearing their flying kit and carrying parachutes, each member of the crew crouched and scrambled up into their space breathing the familiar smell of oil and metal. The worst obstruction inside the Lancaster was the huge main spar which attached the wings to the fuselage. It was difficult to climb over when dressed in full flying suit and carrying gear, negotiating the main spar in the dark when the Lancaster was damaged, awash with hydraulic fluid, diving, and on fire, incredibly so. With flying helmets on each crew member acknowledged their skipper over the intercom. The bomber's engines were run up to specified revolutions, controls checked, gauges and dials read. Then they joined the queue and taxied to the runway. Takeoff forced bodies against seats and it was here airmen held their breath, willing their chariot through the first danger point and up into a steep climb and turn. Only after this first danger point when the Navigator gave his pilot the initial compass course could they breathe freely again.

At operational height oxygen masks were applied. The wireless operator sat separated from the navigator by the radio equipment framework, a clutter of knobs, gauges and dials linked by a maze of wiring. The Gee receiver box stood on the left-hand side and the Morse key was on the right, separated by a narrow space for him to jot down on the log sheet. Under his seat were other appliances including the winch for winding in a trailing aerial and batteries. It was strict radio silence en route to avoid being detected but he would listen on pre-arranged frequencies for weather reports. Above the wireless operator was the astrodome and the navigator would stand beside him to take a sextant reading of the stars. In the clear front dome the bomb aimer began to take into account the height, course and speed for the estimated direction and speed of the wind and the ballistic performance of the particular bomb carried deep in the belly below. A narrow passage from the front of the bomber led to the middle upper gunner and rear gunner turrets – they would clear guns, arrange ammunition belts and increase their vigilance as they approached the European coast. Commonly it was -45°C/-49°F and there was no insulation in the aircraft. After nine hours or so crew were frozen stiff and their bones hurt.

The summer of 1944 brought a much needed morale boost, Bomber Command aircrew could almost see the light at the end of the tunnel – this long war was finally moving in the right direction. For so long they felt that they were the only ones taking the fight to the heart of the enemy and in this summer of hope they no longer felt alone. The operation rate continued to rise but this brought with it most welcome benefits. The closer and less risky targets improved their chances of survival and whereas they needed previously to complete around nine months of operations for a tour, the frequency of ops meant they now commonly needed only six. In May it had become apparent that something big was about to happen, military personnel were everywhere – it was a wonder England did not sink beneath the weight of equipment and military personnel. While troops waited, aircrew continued their relentless operations on German installations. During the first days of June bombing operations began on the region of Pas-de-Calais. These were diversionary, not that crews realized this until later. The Normandy landings occurred on 6 June. It was impossible not to be caught up in the excitement of the invasion of occupied Europe. In total, 1,211 aircraft, each resplendent with additional broad black-and-white bands painted across each wing and round the fuselage, attacked coastal fortifications, dropping a record 5,000 tons of bombs.[9] Returning crews regaled in the amazing sight of the largest invasion force ever assembled sweeping across the English Channel and onto the beaches of Normandy. Four Australian bomber aircrew died this night, for Allied soldiers making French landfall this dawn, casualties would be much greater – around 10,000 would die on the opening onslaught of "Operational Overlord".

Bomber Command C-in-C Harris made no secret of the fact that he was unhappy with this diversion of his force from the strategic destruction of Germany which he steadfastly continued to believe would win the war. Nonetheless, when the Allies landed at Normandy his crews were pivotal to the land invasion[10] and during June 1944 Bomber Command would despatch 15,963 sorties, whereas in June the previous year the number had been just 5,816. Harris became annoyed that public recognition was lacking for these aircrew and in a 1 July letter to the Chief of Air Staff he complained of the:

> lack of adequate or even reasonable credit to the RAF in particular and the air forces as a whole, for their efforts in the invasion. ...I for one cannot forbear a most emphatic protest against the grave injustice which is being done to my crews. There are over 10,500 aircrew in my operational squadrons. In three months we have lost over half that number. They have a right that their story should be adequately told.[11]

In the first weeks following D-Day aircrew casualties were higher than those suffered by the British Second Army at Normandy. General Eisenhower remarked on the value of "pre-D-Day bombing" which had delayed the "completion of the defence works, and the unfinished state of the gun emplacements (which) rendered them considerably less formidable than anticipated".[12]

Exposed to danger in the skies over Europe the men of Bomber Command could have been forgiven for believing that with this last invasion their worst hours were over, but the following months of 1944 brought with it a level of operational activity far beyond expectations. "Tactical Support" resulted in weary aircrew wondering "where in Europe have I not been?" In almost a blurr the names rushed past; Boulogne, Thorigné-Fouillard, Sterkrade, Watten, Wesseling, Hömberg, Wizernes, Villers-Bocage, St-Leu, d'Esserent, Vaires-sur-Marne, Nucourt, Kiel, Stuttgart, St Cyr, Givors. The geography and language lessons were different to any they could have imagined or wished to imagine. In mid 1944 the names mattered little, the scenery was the same; the fiery green and red trails of target indicators; a pyrotechnic display of bombs igniting, of a blazing target area, of ack-ack shells exploding all around; and the knowledge that waiting above were German fighters, their pilots watching as bombers were silhouetted by dropped flares.

Much has been written about the affinity between pilots and their navigators but air gunners shared a similar bond. Their duties were the most warlike; theirs had the most direct engagement with the enemy and there was an adrenalin rush when firing machine guns fast and accurately. Gunner positions were the most exposed and commonly targeted first by night fighters. Flight Sergeant Patrick Edward Thomas Tiernan (426711) was the Middle Upper Gunner on RAF 77 Squadron Halifax MZ715. His mustering was a little unusual given that Pat was a graduate of Brisbane's esteemed Nudgee College, and was studying Law when he joined up in July 1942 at 28. He came from Murgon, Queensland, a speck of a town 139 miles (223 km) from the state capital. Pat's great mate, Rear Gunner, Flight Sergeant Alfred John Burns (424711) 21, a clerk from Sydney, was like a younger brother. Burns, a former Sydney Clerk, applied a few times before being admitted to the RAAF.

Their pilot was Pilot Officer Alan Irvine Crain (415308) in whom they had faith not only because they considered him a good pilot but also because he was Australian. Alan Crain enlisted at 18. Some would describe Alan as a "larrikin", though the RAAF probably did not use this endearing term. He was fortunate to keep his rank and position after several run-ins with authority. The former Assistant Cost Clerk with Commonwealth Oil Refineries came from Hollywood, Western Australia. His misdemeanours included "while on Active Service [he] was not carrying a respirator in Geraldton" for which he received three days extra duty; then the "whilst on Active Service at Georgina doing Guard duty was insufficiently alert" for which he got 14 days extra duty. He was severely reprimanded for "not being in possession of a valid pass in London"; also for "without authority, wearing the uniform of a Sergeant Pilot of the Royal New Zealand Air Force" – alcohol and a dare was responsible for that. But, there was a war on and his differences with the hierarchy did not affect his skill as a pilot. Crew Engineer was

RAF, 19-year-old Sergeant Vic Gledhill (1592716). The Navigator, Flying Officer Trevor Rhy Davies (146291), was another member of the RAF, as was the Wireless Operator/Air Gunner A J Owen. The Bomb Aimer was an Aussie, Warrant Officer Alexander Albert Braid (408562) 26, from Mitcham, Victoria; a former Melbourne Technical College merit student who became an architectural draughtsman. With RAF 77 Squadron less than two months, the crew was ordered to attack a synthetic oil plant at Sterkrade on 16 June despite a poor weather forecast.

The target was shrouded by thick cloud, Pathfinder markers disappeared quickly and the operation was unsuccessful. More disastrous was that the specified course took the bomber stream close to the German night fighter beacon at Bocholt. In total, 21 British aircraft were shot down by fighters and another ten succumbed to anti-aircraft

Patrick Edward Thomas Tiernan.

Alfred John Burns.

ABOVE: *The graves of two Australian gunners, Flight Sergeants Pat Tiernan and Alf Burns.*

fire; seven were from RAF 77 including MZ715. Shell entered the belly of the fully laden Halifax and the violent explosion spread metal and men over a wide area. Owen amazingly was blown clear. Although injured he made it to the ground and became a POW. Crain, Braid, Gledhill and Davies were buried in Uden. Gunner Pat Tiernan was a Roman Catholic and his personal effects contained prayer books and the New Testament. Alf Burns was not religious and possessed no such books – it made no difference. By strange coincidence the remains of both gunners were placed in a single grave, two Aussie mates tucked away in a corner, the only foreigners in the Dodewaard Cemetery, The Netherlands.

The news shook Emily Burns badly; "It is unnecessary for me to stress the fact of my anxiety, for as you know I am a widow and he is my only child". It was a simple sentence that carried a world of pain. Her husband was a casualty of World War I and now her only son was a casualty of this war. The letter from the Commanding Officer of RAF 77 did little to assuage her grief: "We all honour the gallant sacrifice your son has made, so far from home, in the cause of freedom and in the service of the British Commonwealth of Nations."

Grief takes many forms mostly weighed down heavily by cultural mores. For British men in the 1940s tears were deemed a weakness, an embarrassment. John Tiernan helped run the Tiernan's Australian Hotel in Murgon, an establishment proud of its "First Class Cuisine", "All Conveniences" and "Moderate Tariff", but losing a brother was difficult for John to accept and anger was all that was allowed him. He justifiably took exception to the news of Pat's death coming via sources other than the RAAF. He would receive a letter from his brother's RAF Commanding Officer. It was identical to that received by Emily Burns, just a different name. This gave John Tiernan no more comfort than it offered Emily Burns. He wrote complaining how some of Pat's personal effects had not been returned – all the precious items. John also wanted to know where the many gifts sent from home to celebrate Pat's 30th birthday were, because his brother died six days before he could turn 30.

It was always easier being with other Australians but Flight Sergeant Alan Milne Duggleby (418928) 22, from the Australian-Football-League-crazy Melbourne suburb of Essendon, and had joined an English crew and RAF 102 Squadron. He had been raised in a household that emphasized tolerance and compassion yet had a proud tradition of military service. Alan's father was the Reverend John (Jack) Taylor Duggleby. Jack, was from a family of English grocers and came to Australia to join the Home Mission Department of the Methodist Church in Victoria. He was appointed Home Missionary at the curiously named El Dorado Methodist Church in the Wangaratta Circuit. The stipend was £100/-/- per year and transport was a bicycle. Jack moved from church to church until a war broke out.

In December 1915 Jack Duggleby enlisted in the Australian Medical Corps of the 1st Australian Imperial Force. Motivation came in part from courting Helen (Memie) Eliza Milne, because Helen joined the Royal Australian Army Nursing Service and sailed from Melbourne in November 1915 for service in Egypt, England, France and later Germany, with the Occupational forces. Jack sailed for France in 1916 and while with the 5th Field Ambulance, was awarded the Military Medal for bravery in the field during operations east of Amiens, France.

Jack and Memie had continued to correspond and became engaged when both were on leave in France. Upon his return to Australia, Jack was ordained a Minister of the Methodist Church and appointed to Wodonga, Victoria. He and Memie were married in December 1919, Alan Milne Duggleby, was born in January 1922. By 1932 Jack was Superintendent of the South Melbourne Methodist Mission. It was a difficult eight years in which he witnessed the Great Depression; and outbreaks of scarlet fever, typhoid, diphtheria and polio, which caused the most vulnerable, particularly children, to die or be permanently weakened.

Between 1940 and 1942, Jack and Memie's son Alan demonstrated the family nurturing, caring trait as a student teacher.[13] His father was known to have great ability in "giving encouragement and hope" and Jack and Memie, having witnessed some of the worst of World War I, were likely in need of both when their only son asked permission to enlist. At least there seemed hope in the fact that Alan joined the RAAF, a service portrayed by the media as privileged, clean, and largely protected. Flight Sergeant Alan Milne Duggleby (418928) was killed

Alan Milne Duggleby.   *Flight Sergeant Alan Milne Duggleby.*

when his Halifax was shot down by a night fighter during the bombing attack on Sterkade on the night of 16/17 June 1944, and was buried in Steenderen Cemetery, Holland – he was 22.

England came under increasing attack from German V-1 flying bombs (buzzbombs) and V-2 missiles during the summer of 1944 so Bomber Command had an important new responsibility. Over the ensuing months V-1 flying bomb manufacture sites and the large, elaborate, and heavily protected V-2 missile installations at Watten, Mimoyecques, Siracourt and Wizerns in France were targeted. Whereas names like Essen had struck fear into the bellies of new aircrew now other destinations like St-Leu did the same. District caves in St-Leu formed one of three major underground V-1 flying bomb storage depots. There were also blockhouses, bunkers, a railway link, and flak emplacements. On the night of the 4/5 July tallboy bombs were used unsuccessfully to collapse the caves limestone walls and roofs. Twelve aircraft were lost including two from RAAF 463, 14 Australians died. On the night of 7/8 July another attack this time successful – 32 aircraft failed to return, including two RAAF 467 Lancasters;15 Australians died.

Bomber Command casualties per operation became lighter as Allied armies advanced. However, the number of Bomber Command operations increased and the lists of missing and dead continued to clatter through teleprinters in the offices of the RAAF Casualty section in Melbourne. Personnel continued their grim work of pulling service records and informing relatives. It was difficult to remain detached, so many files, so many youthful faces, so many distressing details. They were supposed to remain objective but phone calls and letters from grieving families made it impossible to remain immune to the sad legacy of the bombing campaign and the toll exacted on those left behind.

Members of the WAAAF attached to Casualty Section, who were responsible for checking details tried to believe it was easier if an airman came from a large family – an only son, or an only child, seemed more heartbreaking. They found it difficult to get the names of the dead men and the heartbroken pleas of their parents out of their minds. Some cases would remain in the mind such as that of the service file marked: "FO Thomas Edward William Davis (420173)". The 21-year-old pilot was homebound from an attack on Revigny-sur-Ornain railway junction on 18/19 July 1944 – his 30th operation. The Lancaster crew was attacked by a night fighter whose first gunfire killed 20-year-old Brisbane Rear Gunner, Flight Sergeant Colin Frederick Allen (434218).[14] RCAF Middle Upper Gunner, Pilot Officer E F Haddlesey left the bomber only to collide with the tailplane, which nearly severed his right leg above the knee. He would become POW from where he was sent to hospital and had his leg amputated. His pilot was not as fortunate. Tom Davis baled out with his helmet still on and was strangled by the attached intercom lead.

The shocking sacrifices of Australians in World War I were still fresh in the minds of many Australians. Women had lost fathers and husbands, and children had grown up never knowing their fathers except for a faint grainy photograph in a black-bordered frame. History could never prepare families such as Tasmania's Brock family for the sacrifices they would make. The Brocks had much to celebrate as sons and daughter grew into teenagers. Henry James was born on 23 January 1922 and Harold Eric on 9 August 1923. They were champion athletes and gifted scholars at Launceston Grammar. Harold (Harry) went on to study first-year engineering. Life for the Brock boys was good and their future was clear. Upon leaving school Henry, known as Jim, would assume charge of the family's 120,000-acre property "Lawrenny". The property also presented a working option for Harry. First, however they would travel about as far away from Tasmania as one could, to fight a war in Europe. The 18-year-old Harry beat his elder brother into the RAAF, joining in April 1942. He was mustered Navigator and departed for overseas at the beginning of 1943. The navigator course did not work out and he returned to Australia to be re-mustered for Wireless Operator/Air Gunner. When he finally left Australia in November 1943 wearing Sergeant stripes and the half wing embossed with "AG", some of the naive enthusiasm had already waned as he was pushed prematurely into manhood. Jim entered service at the beginning of December 1942 and mustered as Pilot, possibly to his younger brother's chagrin.

By 1944 they were both in the UK and grieved together upon hearing of the death of their father Harold. They appreciated that this would put additional strain on their mother Jean, sister Judy, and uncle Eric, who were trying to keep the property running – best they get on and help finish this war so they could return to Tasmania.

Henry (Jim) James Brock. Harold (Harry) Brock. Sgt Harold (Harry) Brock.

Neither of the Brock boys returned to Tasmania. It was their sister Judy who opened the door to accept the telegram in August 1944, which started with those dreaded words; "We regret to inform you..." her 21-year-old brother Warrant Officer Harry Brock (408396) had been killed and buried in Germany. In February 1945 the next telegram arrived to advise that 23-year-old Jim (428102) had crashed into the North Sea, somewhere off Scotland. His body washed ashore and was buried in Jutland. Following the war the family property Lawrenny was sold for a small price as a soldier settlement project.

Bomber Command continued to attack in support of Allied ground forces. France was liberated and the honour of entering Paris on the 25 August was given to the French army. Two bombing raids were sent against Stettin, a target known as "flak city". Bomber Command's strength continued to increase and entered a stage referred to as "Operational Climax". From 15 September Air Chief Marshal Harris was again in charge and intent on destroying German industry and Germany. Almost half the total tonnage of bombs dropped by Bomber Command during World War II would be dropped in the last nine months of the war.[15]

On 14 October 1944 "Operation Hurricane" was launched to "demonstrate to the enemy in Germany generally the overwhelming superiority of the Allied Air Forces". British Bomber Command launched a day raid of 957 aircraft dropping 820 tons of incendiaries and 3,547 tons of high explosives on Duisburg. During the day the USAAF attacked Cologne, Gremberg, Gereon and Euskirchen. With aircrew ordered to fly eleven hours in 24, Bomber Command aircrew revisited Duisburg the night of 14/15 October and dropping a further 4,540 tons of bombs and incendiaries in two waves -- the largest total bombload on any single day in World War II.

A quieter but still exciting operation was conducted by an RAAF 460 crew – to ferry Lancaster "G George" back to Australia. "George" had completed 90 operations and was Bomber Command's "most operational bomber".[16] The pilot was Flight Lieutenant Edward (Eddie) Arthur Hudson (404506) from Rockhampton, Queensland, who had completed two tours and been awarded a DFC and bar. Prior to their departure the Duke of Gloucester, Governor-General Designate to Australia, sent the following message: "I wish you and your crew a safe and speedy journey to Australia. I hope that when your veteran Lancaster arrives in Australia, it will soon be joined by many Australian-built Lancasters which will help to bring the war against Japan to a rapid and successful conclusion."[17] "G George" would eventually take pride of place in the Australian War Memorial.

On 2 November 992 aircraft attacked Dusseldorf, and on 4 November 749 attacked Bochum. Two days later 738 aircraft were sent to bomb Gelsenkirchen. Since 1943 the Luftwaffe had employed the night-fighter intercept tactic called Zahme Sau (Tame Boar). At the first indication of a raid, fighters were scrambled. They would orbit one of several German radio beacons to be directed en masse by wireless communication into the bomber stream. Once attacking, the fighters would make radar contact with individual British bombers. This tactic was rendered less effective when Bomber Command conducted short duration attacks. As 1944 progressed and the German war effort crumbled, the Luftwaffe became so starved of fuel it ceased to endanger those who flew British bombers. The increased presence of American Mustang fighter escorts also allowed British bombers to conduct more daylight attacks. November and December were months of intense activity for the men of Bomber Command and in support of their army brethren they performed their duties with courage and skill. A 12 November diversion from normal ops came when specially modified Lancasters sank the German warship Tirpitz with 12,000 lb (5.4 tons) tallboy bombs.

Mosquito HP934 from RAAF 464 flew on the night of 27/28 November 1944, tasked with carrying out night-intruder operations to bomb and strafe road and rail junctions at the towns of Unna and Cloppenburg, Germany. The pilot was Flying Officer Lionel James Colgan (413075) and his Navigator was Flight Sergeant Ross Arthur Stoner (417901) 22, who hailed from an address more fitting to the land he was attacking than the land he was from – Black Forest was an inner southern suburb of Adelaide, South Australia. Stoner was a clerk when he enlisted at 19 in July 1942. The 26-year-old Colgan was a shipping clerk in Sydney prior to the war. His RAF instructor referred to him as "A quiet, conscientious type...should do well. ...Is keen on operational flying...cool and determined character".

Flight Sergeant Ross Stoner.   *Flying Officer Lionel Colgan.*

As the Mosquito crossed the Dutch coast and approached the Arnhem region of The Netherlands at low altitude, they came under ¾ in (20 mm) gunfire. Colgan weaved and focused on the instruments in front of him –there was no visible damage, yet he could have sworn that they had been hit. Six minutes later the aircraft was rocked by two explosions. The aft of the aircraft was on fire and Colgan lost control of the Mosquito. The emergency hatch was jammed and Stoner kicked at it until it gave. The Mosquito was very low and Colgan regained some control and fought to get it up to 1400 feet (4426 m) for Stoner to bale out. The navigator had a head injury and this combined with the jerk of his parachute knocked the wind out of him. He saw a flash as the aircraft crashed. The next he knew was being in a patch of young trees. Before he could remove his parachute harness four young Dutchmen approached him – one spoke English and instructed Stoner to follow quickly because German soldiers were close. He was hidden in a barn where 26 evacuees were living and a doctor arrived to tend the deep gash on his head. The following day Germans arrived to search farm buildings but the Dutch declared the inhabitants had diphtheria and the

Stoner and Colgan (courtesy Wolter Noordam).

soldiers left in a hurry. Stoner was collected by the Dutch Underground on 8 December 1944 and was sent back to England. It was only then that he discovered that Colgan had been killed, possibly because he was intent on getting the Mosquito higher so that Stoner could bale out. Colgan was buried in the woods of Amersfoort. Stoner would return to Adelaide in June 1945, a very different man from the one who left the city of churches.

Most Australians who served with Bomber Command Europe would return physically and emotionally very different, yet most would think of themselves as "lucky" because they actually returned. Flight Sergeants Robert (Bob) Isaiah Hunter (426882) and Stanley David Jolly (426606) considered themselves "lucky" to survive an operation in May of 1944. Bob Hunter, 21, a former Clerk from Ipswich, Queensland was the Wireless Operator/Air Gunner. Stan Jolly, 22, from Brisbane, a former Salesman, was the Bomb Aimer of the RAAF 467 crew. Their Lancaster, JA901, was part of a force of 362 Lancasters sent to attack the German 21st Panzer Group base at Mailly-le-Camp on the night of 3/4 May 1944. In total, 42 airmen, or 12 per cent did not return. Their pilot was Flying Officer Colin (Dick) Dickson (422038) 23, from Kempsey, New South Wales. The Navigator was Flight Sergeant Oscar Skelton Furniss (423700) 22, from Sydney, who was a graduate of Hawkesbury Agricultural College. Flight Sergeant Hilton Hardcastle Forden (424403) 20, from Adelaide was the Rear Gunner. The Engineer was RAF Flight Sergeant Philip Weaver (1836169), a 33 year old from Wales; while the Middle Upper Gunner, also RAF was Flight Sergeant Horace Skellorn (2209827) from Manchester. He was just 19.

Bob Hunter was excited by the operation, he wrote: "Feels as though we are really in the war now; pranging the German military camp...from low altitude of 5,000 ft. I wonder if we will be able to see the buggers run?"[18] Their attack turned sour when they were instructed to orbit rather than bomb – there was a problem with the Bombing Leader's radio. After what seemed an eternity they moved over the target and heard the sound of "bullets hitting metal" and "the kite shook all over, like a tree in a windstorm". The Lancaster burst into flames and Bob Hunter emerged from the Wireless Operator/Air Gunner compartment and moved to the navigator's compartment and the front hatch. Whatever he saw stopped him in his tracks – his pilot, engineer, and navigator would never leave the aircraft. Turner turned, hurdled the main spar, and ran towards the blazing tail section. "The aluminium fuselage, the oil from the burst hydraulic lines to the turret, everything was burning". The Lancaster was in its death throes and shielding his eyes with his right hand, hunched over to protect his parachute, he moved into the fire. Ammunition from the rear turret was exploding and he was hit by a red hot shell case which burnt deeply into his right leg. Hunter grabbed hold of the rear hatch but it wouldn't budge. The floor gave way and the lower half of his body fell through, he was "suspended by my parachute on my back, completely surrounded by flames." Driven by survival instincts and with the flesh on his exposed face and hands afire he pushed as hard as he could. The slipstream caught him and swung him around in the opposite direction. "I was completely exhausted and fast giving up all hope because my parachute would not go through the hole".[19] By this time Hunter "was badly burned on my hands and face and different parts of my body." The thought of his family gave him strength for one last push and he fell back into what was left of his bomber. On his hands and knees he crawled to the rear hatch and this time the door gave and he fell into open sky, at least "I was free of the flames and turning over and over". His badly injured hands wouldn't work as he attempted to pull his ripcord, "perhaps a dozen times". Somehow on the 13th attempt he managed and it barely seemed to open before he crashed into a plantation of fir trees which broke his fall.

Barely conscious, Hunter looked at his hands, "the skin had peeled off the palm of my right hand and was hanging down". The lower part of his body was naked, his clothes having burnt off. The pain was horrific and he staggered on driven by the desperate need to find assistance, it did not matter which side, he needed help. Most people were too frightened and turned him away, but one brave woman took him in. "The pain was intense and I just paced the floor for several hours, until some members of the French Resistance came".[20] The French placed themselves in great danger by carrying him on a stretcher for a considerable distance to a safe house. Hunter was still in immense pain and dizzy. "By this time my hands were a tremendous size" and his father's wedding ring was cut from his finger.

Hunter would learn later that his host family were "shot by the Germans two days later". The French doctor was pessimistic and said he needed a hospital straight away because his hands, with practically no blood circulating, had begun to turn gangrenous and needed to be amputated. Hunter was dropped off at a hospital and placed in the charge of Roman Catholic nuns and the Germans informed of his presence.

Bob Hunter drifted into a drug-induced sleep realising his immediate future was grim, he had been asked "three times for permission to amputate my hands, but I was so close to being dead I did not answer". He remained unconscious for nearly two weeks and woke to the best news – his hands had been saved. The doctor was about to cut off his hands when the doctor's wife intervened, pointing out that because Hunter was so young "I would be better dead than without my hands". A second doctor concurred so they proceeded to make incisions to allow the swelling to subside. "After I had regained consciousness the Gestapo tried to take me away, but the doctor did not grant permission". The Gestapo persisted in their attempts to interrogate him but Hunter kept gesturing to his burnt and badly swollen lips pretending he was unable to speak. The Allied armies were getting closer and on 22 August the Germans began evacuating the hospital, including captured Allies. A French doctor gave Hunter an injection to raise his temperature, and sent him to an isolation hospital as a scarlet fever case – the Germans left without him.

Hunter could well be forgiven for believing he had already had more than his share of excitement and trauma but now he had to survive opposing armies. The Germans blew up the bridge near the hospital and then the Allied assault commenced with artillery shells screaming overhead. About 100 German soldiers "bearing rifles and light machine guns" passed along the road. The US Third Army arrived and the battle was on in earnest. Hunter crept to the door of the hospital for a better look and immediately a piece of shrapnel from a shell passed through his trouser leg and embedded itself in the wall. He decided it was better to stay well away from doors and windows but kept the shrapnel as a souvenir. It would be five days before the last of the German snipers were killed or withdrew. The French Resistance then began rounding up suspected collaborators and beat them, but it was the treatment of the women "I shall never forget". They were stripped, "their whole bodies were shaved, a swastika was painted on both the front and back" and the women "were then marched naked down the street to the gaol".[21] The French were "drunk with freedom" and alcohol. For days they continued to drink heavily and shoot at mythical snipers and at each other and some "died from these accidental wounds". Hunter believed that in this part of France "more of the Resistance died from accidents than from combat with the enemy".

The Australian tried to keep his head down until "their ammunition was finished", but just when he thought it safe to come out an American tank unit arrived and "opened up with 2 and 3 in (50 and 75 mm) guns. Tracer was flying our way" and a tree branch above where Hunter was standing was shot through and came tumbling down. On 13 September 1944 Hunter was flown back to England in a Dakota and met up with his Bomb Aimer Stan Jolly, who had his own story to tell and neither could decide who had been the luckier.

Stan Jolly had been in the front dome of the Lancaster. He knew he was falling to earth beneath the canopy of his parachute watching the ball of fire which had once been a Lancaster crash, and his spirits sunk further when he saw only one other parachute. Jolly owed his initial freedom to Madame Berque, who took him in and dissuaded Jolly from following the RAF recommended route to Spain because there were too many German troops. As dangerous as it was, she made it her responsibility to get him on to a train for Paris. Jolly shared a carriage with German soldiers and quietly chastised himself for not discarding some aircrew clothing he wore beneath borrowed civvies – he was scrutinized but not challenged. At the Paris railway station he was met by Bernard Mannin on the next part of his journey to freedom. It would take a couple of months and several safe houses but Jolly was in Paris when the city was liberated. After reporting to the Americans he was transported to England, and so, "ended 16 weeks on the run...

thanks to the courage and kindness of a number of French people".[22] Jolly and Hunter returned to Queensland and met regularly for the rest of their lives, and with others of the Royal Air Forces Escaping Society, Brisbane Branch. Sometimes after a few beers the stories would become a little embellished but this could never detract from the amazing truth.

Some remarkable people were involved with Allied escape lines and were responsible for saving many an Australian aircrew. If caught by the Germans their treatment was merciless. One of the most colourful and well known was the strong-willed English born Comtesse de Milleville. She was born Mary Lindell and during World War I served as a member of the Voluntary Aid Detachment (VAD) and then the Secours aux Blesses, a division of the French Red Cross. Her meritorious service would result in her being awarded the Croix de Guerre and the Russian Order of St Anne. Her marriage to the Comte de Milleville failed but the mother of three continued to live in Paris and her striking beauty and spirited personality ensured she remained a favourite in the city's high society. With the fall of France she again donned her Red Cross uniform, continued to be admired, and at a Paris cocktail party she convinced the German commander in Paris, General von Stulpnagel, that she needed a permit to cross into Vichy France to continue her humanitarian work. Her beguiling manner saw the German commander agree, agree also to her "mechanic" travelling with her, and supplied them with petrol to collect a sick child. Her mechanic was, in fact, an officer of the Welsh Guards who had been wounded and hidden from the enemy. On route to Limoges the Comtesse even insisted on giving a lift to a Luftwaffe pilot who subsequently entertained her in his officers' mess. Meanwhile her mechanic was on his way back to England where he would brief authorities about the remarkable woman who saved him. Mary would assume the alias "Marie Claire" and continue to drive evaders to safety. In January 1941 the Gestapo arrested and interrogated her. For nine months she was kept in solitary confinement in the infamous Fresnes prison. Upon release Marie Claire crossed the Spanish border and appeared at the door of the British Consul. She wanted to continue her underground work regardless of the consequences. Mary Lindell was the first woman trained by the British government to establish an escape route. She returned to France despite the danger and ensured the "Marie Claire Line" passed many Allies into Spain and freedom.

By Christmas 1941 German suspicions were again raised and an attempt was made to kill her. Mary was seriously injured but she discharged herself from hospital before the Gestapo could interrogate her. As soon as she recovered Mary again supervised the Marie Claire Line, with her son Maurice now undertaking the more physical demands. In May 1943, Maurice de Milleville was arrested and tortured by a Gestapo anxious to expose those involved with Allied escape routes. He was released and Mary's next son Oky was arrested and tortured. Oky was transported to a concentration camp and never heard of again. As the war progressed the "Maire-Claire Line" was flooded with more and more British airmen. They were commonly given false identities and introduced to a young woman who would instruct them not to speak, and would accompany them by train to the south of France. The train trip was always nerve wracking as they rubbed shoulders with German troops. Disembarking at Ruffec, they were taken to the Hotel de France where they were greeted by a loud English voice – Marie Claire. It was here that Australian pilot Allan McSweyn ended up.

On 30 June 1941 Pilot Officer Allan McSweyn (402005) and his crew took off in his RAF 115 Wellington to attack Bremen. The bomber was hit by flak and then shot down by an enemy fighter. McSweyn followed his crew out. Having survived, been taken prisoner and believing he stood a better chance of escape as a soldier, McSweyn exchanged identities with Private John McDiarmid of the Seaforth Highlanders. Next he teamed up with army driver, New Zealander, Geoff Williamson, who not only spoke fluent German but was acquainted with the German railway system. Clever POWs who manufactured something out of seemingly nothing had provided both men with civilian outfits and a small case, as well as money and chocolate. McSweyn would travel as a Frenchman unfit for further work in Germany and forged a medical certificate which declared he had "TB of the larynx". "I was wearing a pair of brown slacks, brown double breasted coat and carried a small attaché case, while Williamson had a pair of plusfours, a black coat and also a small case. We each had 400 reichmarks and chocolate for the journey.[23]"

Williamson and McSweyn "entered the tunnel on 19 September, a Sunday, at 1300". A camp football match was organized to coincide with the escape and of course the game deteriorated into a free for all which kept the guards busy. They had emerged from the tunnel and were walking away when there was a shout from a sentry. The men froze and Allan McSweyn may have wondered "not again".

The sentry was angry that two "civilians" were in a restricted area and told them to hurry away – they were very happy to obey his directive. When they arrived at Lamsdorf station they had to walk through the guards' living area, and still they were not stopped. On the Berlin express train they were subjected to "Gestapo checks, but we got through". With increasing confidence on arrival in Berlin the two escaped POWs booked into a hotel for the night. McSweyn observed bomb damage with pleasure but hoped his mates in Bomber Command would not revisit the region until he was clear. Leaving before the routine check of the hotel register they boarded a train for Mannheim and then another to Saarbrucken close to the French border. When they arrived in Saarbrucken they met the Frenchman who would guide them over the border. The crossing meant negotiating barbed wire fences with sentry boxes and twitchy guards so they stayed hidden and waited until the nearest sentry turned away to cross one at a time. The Frenchman led the way and an unseen German soldier immediately challenged and walked towards the Frenchman with raised gun. McSweyn acted on instinct: "I sneaked up behind him and hit him with a rabbit punch on the neck, and then grabbed him around the throat until he passed out."[24]

After what seemed an eternity they were finally in safer territory and had joined the "Maire-Claire Line", and travelled to Ruffec, the headquarters of the indomitable "Comtesse de Milleville" – "Marie Claire" – Mary Lindell.

Altogether McSweyn spent around six weeks in Ruffec at the Hotel de France while arrangements were made to get across the Pyrenees. More Allies arrived and they were split up into two groups – Geoff Williamson was moved to the second group and would follow McSweyn's a couple of days later. It was the Comtesse herself who ventured out with the Australian pilot's group of South African and Canadian airmen. They were to travel by truck to Limoges and then take a train. Their truck broke an axle and although Marie convinced a farmer to lend them his truck by the time they arrived the train had departed. The group spent the night at a hotel and Marie insisted on speaking English loudly at dinner even though there were German officers dining. The Australian pilot was impressed, "she had no regard at all for the Germans and thought they were idiots".[25] They caught the train the following day and at the foot of the Pyrenees met another contact, two Basque guides, and said their farewells to Marie Claire.

The mountain crossing was supposed to take six hours but the weather turned the escape into an ordeal. Within a couple of hours it started to snow and became bitterly cold. Their clothes were unsuitable for the conditions and a Canadian airman complained of chest pains, and begged to be able to rest. An uncomfortable night was spent in a cowshed, with a roof but no sides. The following day they trudged on through deep snow and a blizzard and spent another night in a mountain hut. They continued on into the third day since there was no safety. Conditions deteriorated and at one stage they had to "crawl, across a small gap of about 18 in (45 cm) with a drop of about 300 ft (98 m) on either side".

Mike Cooper was a Canadian who had been flying Spitfires with the RAF. He became ill as did one of the guides. They urged the frozen men on but the guide collapsed. Attempts to revive him proved hopeless so the party continued on to the next hut. Being able to start a fire, dry their clothing, and warm up, proved the difference between life and death. Come morning the desperately tired men dragged themselves down the mountain side. Arriving at a Spanish sentry post they surrendered, "We were so weak we had no option other than to surrender".[26] The hot drink and bread was heaven but then the local police "stuck us in a filthy cell". Locals were bribed to send for the British Consul and when he arrived six days later he bailed out the evaders and drove them to Madrid. McSweyn was sent to Gibraltar, and it was here he learnt that the second group had also run into the blizzard in the Pyrenees and Geoff Williamson had died. Flight Lieutenant Allan McSweyn returned to England on 21 December 1943, undertook flying refresher courses, but was no longer posted to Bomber Command. He was awarded the Military Cross and the Air Force Cross and returned to Australia. Marie Claire was severely wounded, captured, and deported to Ravensbruck concentration camp at the end of 1943. She survived and was liberated in 1945. In her absence her organisation continued to smuggle Allies out of occupied territory. Mary Claire (Lindell) died in 1986 at the age of 86.

Bomber Command Europe lost 3,298 aircraft on operations during 1944.[27] Since the war began 10,141 had been lost on operations. By the end of 1944 another 11,267 were lost in non-operations and on the ground.[28] The horrific human casualties could not be calculated until the war was over and too many Australians, like Tom Lennie, would be among the dead.

Flying Officer Thomas John Lennie (425684) 31, was a school teacher from Maryborough, Queensland. He joined RAF 98 as the Navigator to Victorian Flight Sergeant Bruce Llewellyn Williams (428538), a former furniture salesman, who was ten years his junior. The Battle of Arnhem was drawing to a close at the cost of around 1,700 Allied servicemen. On 25 September 1944, Williams and his Mitchell bomber FW194 crew were on a supporting raid to Schaarsbergen. Having dropped their bombs accurately they were turning for home when attacked by a Focke-Wulf Fw190.[29]

Flying Officer
Thomas John Lennie.

Flight Sergeant
Bruce Llewellyn Williams.

Frits Baars was a local resident and by strange coincidence his wife's name was Lenie. It was early evening and the Dutch couple watched as an airman drifted down in his parachute. "Suddenly we heard shots, fired by a German soldier. He shot at the pilot who was sailing to the ground, a pure war crime". The couple were forced to take shelter in their home as the battle raged. The following day the Battle of Arnhem, an attempt to liberate The Netherlands, was lost and the Allies were in retreat. Frits and Lenie were saddened to see the airman's body still lying where he had come to earth. It was "so lacking in respect and so sad", and they ventured out to bury him in a field – his uniform had "Australia" on the sleeve and on his identity disc the name Williams, Bruce. The body would later be re-interred to Arnhem military cemetery at Oosterbeek, as would that of Australian Navigator Flight Officer Tom Lennie. The Baars visited the grave occasionally and latterly in September 2009. Frits is 85 and Lenie 89. They describe what they saw as if it were yesterday and not 65 years in the past. "They shot him dead in the air, so vulnerable hanging on his parachute, not standing a chance. Atrocious." Frits says; "This is so very emotional". His wife strokes the gravestone bearing Bruce Williams' name and whispers "Rest peacefully, youngster, rest peacefully".[30]

ELEVEN

"Five aircraft were a heavier loss we were reminded, than the five crews."

Flight Lieutenant Don Charlwood

New Year 1945 could be welcomed with so much more positiveness than the previous four – which seemed like an eternity. The Allies were pushing through Europe from various fronts, victory was now a probability and just a matter of time. Australians in Bomber Command Europe split into two categories. There were those who wanted to return to Australia as soon as possible; they were weary of war; had lost too many mates; and had survived thus far with no desire to further test their luck. The second group were new arrivals who had no real inkling of what war was; they might never openly admit it but they just hoped the war did not finish before they had the opportunity to test themselves, and win some glory – had they not been taught it was the blood of Anzacs that determined their national ethos?

Don Charlwood was trying to keep track of those who had embarked with him for overseas service in September 1941, and were part of No.35 Observers Course, at No.2 Air Observer and No.16 Elementary Flying Training School, Edmonton, Canada. Those who sewed the half wing with a large "O" above their left pocket, he named the Twenty Men.[1] Within months of their arrival in England Twenty Men a name applied with such enthusiasm had begun to sound like a macabre version of the song "Ten Green Bottles".

Sergeant Joseph Albert Turnbull (411555) was a survey foreman with the New South Wales Forestry Commission in Grafton and was married to Lynette. He struggled to pass his RAAF fitness test and was referred to by Charlwood as the "most vociferous and rubicund" in the class. Turnbull was the first killed, never making it out of 27 Operating Training Unit. His crew-in-training were detailed to attack Bremen on 13 September 1942 but got no further than the airfield precincts when their Wellington stalled, spun, crashed and burst into flames. Eerily Joe had told Don Charlwood that he believed he "would be dead within the week" and he was.[2]

Sergeant Joseph Albert Turnbull.

Another two of the Twenty Men died in separate RAF 12 Lancasters. They were Flight Sergeant Colin McDowell Miller (401848) and Pilot Officer Wilfred Gordon Burrows (411739). Colin Miller was 29, educated at Melbourne High and entered the Melbourne Teachers' College in 1935. He taught at the Higher Elementary School, Coleraine. Gordon Burrows, 25, was a former Clerk with The Australian Gas Light Co., on his eleventh operation. Their crew attacked Berlin in the night of the 17/18 January 1943 but were lost over the North Sea, and the only sign that they had ever lived would be their names engraved on the Runnymede Memorial in Surrey, UK and a war memorial in Melbourne. They were just two of 20,327 airmen with no known graves.

Flight Sergeant Ian Victor Heatley (405310), was also with RAF

12 Squadron, and the next to die. Heatley, whose father was a grazier, had attended All Soul's School, Charters Towers, Queensland, before becoming a Bank Clerk/Ledger Keeper. Heatley and his crew took off on the night of 3/4 March 1943 to bomb Hamburg and did not return – he was 22.[3]

With each death of a classmate, the sense of doom within Don Charlwood rose. On the 21 January 1943, Don Charlwood sat down for an RAF 103 briefing, he was surprised to see that a couple of rows in front was his good friend and Twenty Men classmate Flight Sergeant Keith Robert Webber (411452). Charlwood was surprised to see him because Webber and crew were supposed to be on that well-deserved six days off. Keith, from Sydney, was a thinker like himself, and there had been many in-depth discussions between them. Like himself, Keith was older, 31. Keith's skipper was Western Australian Flight Sergeant Edward Vivian Laing (406693) 22. Their Bomb Aimer was Flight Sergeant Douglas George Williams (411566) also 22, an ex-student of Sydney Grammar and Audit Clerk with a firm of chartered accountants. The Wireless Operator/Air Gunner was Flight Sergeant Frank Lawrence Boyd (412101) another 22 year old, born in Fremantle, but now living in Wellington, New South Wales, and an invoice clerk in his former life. Frank was so enthusiastic about wireless that he attended the Marconi School of Wireless on his own initiative.[3]

> Ted Laing, plump and happy-looking, his complexion always glowing, as though he had emerged from a shower: Keith stooped, serious and intent; Tony Willis, rosy-cheeked and black-haired. Again and again my eyes were drawn to them, to Keith's greying temples and to Ted Laing's fresh complexion. Ted in particular looked so vibrant that my forebodings were hideous by contrast.

Bomber Command was short of numbers for this attack on Essen and leave had been cancelled. Charlwood's and Webber's crews had travelled the same training route and enjoyed RAF 103 squadron camaraderie, but that which bound them most was their nationality. This was just another operation, but also another night over Germany. They shared transport to dispersal and Webber, Laing and crew alighted first, "We exchanged the usual words with them, then they were gone". Don Charlwood never saw Keith Webber or his crew again.

Flying Officer Thomas (Tom) Hector McNeill (405381) 32, born in Gympie, Queensland, was another of the Twenty Men. On his RAAF application he had written his occupation as; "warehouse assistant, United Felt Hats Pty Ltd., Brisbane". He operated with RAAF 460 from February to March 1943, when on his eighth op, another Berlin attack, he was shot down by a night fighter.[4] On the night of 14/15 April 1943, another of Charlwood's classmates died. Flying Officer Ronald (Ron) Wheatley (412053) and his RAF 35 Halifax crew were shot down by a night fighter during an attack on Stuttgart.[5] Ron had been born in Lemington-on-Tyne, England. His family migrated to Sydney to give Ron the opportunity for a better life, only to see him return to England, lose his life in a war, and be buried in Germany – he was 21.

Nine of the remaining 13 of the Twenty Men of No 35 "O" course, who graduated in Canada on 10 October 1941, met at a London Hotel. Don Charlwood wondered why he saw no anger in the men left, instead there were masks of indifference. He realised he too wore the same mask. The only accepted ritual following the loss of good friends was to get drunk. As he regarded these Australian men, Charlwood wondered how they could "go on like this...someone must stop the whole insane business".[6]

Next of the Twenty Men to fall was Flight Sergeant William (Bill) Roy Kenneth Charlton (411121) 25, a former Sydney clerk, who had been posted to RAAF 460. On an attack against St-Nazaire on 22/23 March 1943, his Lancaster was badly shot up by a night fighter. The Aussie pilot Sergeant David Edward White (408896) with some brilliant flying kept W4879 in the air and crash landed the Lancaster in England without injury to his crew. The RAAF obviously had observed raw talent in White because they streamed the Victorian former Bank Clerk as a pilot when he was 18. The RAF agreed after the St-Nazaire operation: "Nothing but the highest praise goes to the pilot who, with a fully laden and practically uncontrollable machine, remained cool". White was still only 20 and awarded a DFC. His Bomb Aimer Flight Sergeant Francis Henry Ward (411207), who was married to Mary and had a ten-month-old daughter, Mary Elizabeth, received a DFM, for helping to dislodge a hung up bomb and assisting White with the Lancaster's controls on the return leg. Another in the crew was Sergeant Bruce Knilands (9431) 22, one of an unusual breed; the Victorian Fitter and Turner was a Flight Engineer. Flight Sergeant Robert Henry Baker (401730) 28, from rural Wereneth, via Ballarat, was a former employee of Victorian Railways, and was married to Aileen, with a six-year-old daughter, Leah. He was one of the Air Gunners; and the Wireless Operator/Air Gunner was Flight Sergeant Alfred Kenneth Parker (412265). Parker, 30, came from a pretty spot on the New South Wales Central coast, called Carrington, and was married to Mary. The report on their March 1943 crash landing referred to those who flew with Bill Charlton as a "well disciplined crew".

Charlton and Don Charlwood had met one morning in Wales, Don recognized Bill from a distance – his "tall, angular figure, pacing intently about the lawns, his hands clasped behind his back". Don believed life in the air war had changed Bill "less than any of us. In repose his face was still serious, almost ascetic", and conversation showed "he still gave the impression of being about to share some tremendous joke." The two men were delighted – it had been six months since they had last seen each other. Don had flown 20 ops and Bill Charlton deduced an unease in Charlwood. Ignoring the misty rain they walked up into the Welsh hills and for a brief time the war was forgotten. Less than a month later on the night of 16/17 April 1943, Bill Charlton and his brave crew took off to attack Germany. Flight Sergeant James Scott Stewart (409331) 22, an Engineering Draughtsman with his family's Melbourne firm, was onboard for experience, as second pilot. Charlwood and Charlton's classmate, Flying Officer Robert Maxwell Bryant, wrote in his diary: "This morning I heard the worst news the war has brought me. Bill Charlton is missing on Stettin".

Sergeant Geoffrey (Harry) Harold Theodore Waddell (413815) of the Sydney suburb of Burwood was an accountant. In the UK, on completion of training, Waddell was posted to RAF 106, then RAF 44 on 15 Jan 1943. A friend from Burwood Sydney, and fellow accountant was George Bruce Loder (412160). Loder, was 22 when he enlisted in June 1941. Both men were mustered as Observers, and classmates of Don Charlwood. Charlwood had nicknamed Harry as the "cheerful pessimist", and George, the "imperturbable".

Don Charlwood, Waddell, and Loder took some recreational time and as the friends climbed to the summit of Scotland's Ben Nevis, Harry Waddell declared to his companions that their chances of survival were negligible – and then laughed uproariously. Waddell was killed, when his RAF 44 Squadron Lancaster was shot down on an attack on Lorient, France, on 7/8 February 1943 and crashed into the sea. He was 33. He and his crew have no known grave.[8] Waddell had been employed in the Probate Branch of the Public Trust Office and they would now settle the affairs of their own.

Harry Waddell.

George Loder.

George Loder was delighted to hear he and his wife Betty were now the parents of a baby daughter. He kept "thinking of it, over and over again" as he tried "to see you and baby. ...Darling I was thrilled...and to know that you were well". George Loder had no difficulty in expressing the strong emotions he felt: "It will be a lovely baby and if it grows into as sweet and wonderful a woman as you my own darling, its father will be as happy as can be. Oh darling I adore you more than I would ever have thought possible and I am full of tenderness for you and our little baby. I long so much now to be home." [9]

In May George Loder was selected as a Pathfinder and was presented with his badge, "a gold eagle on the left eagle on my left pocket". At this stage Harry Wright had "done the most of the lads in our course – 36 [operations]". Wright had even been introduced to the King and Queen during their visit to the district. Loder mentioned that Don Charlwood had taken a short break after completing his first tour, Loder and most of the remaining class had completed 20. His letters were by necessity a mixture of the worst and best of his life and he knew where he wished to be and what was important to him: "I could never now be happy without you life would lose its meaning you and our dear little baby are far and away the most precious things in life to me."

Loder was attempting to sound unaffected by this war but struggled with the loss of his closest mates. On 13 June 1943 his letter to Betty revealed the death of another Twenty Men classmate; "spent some very pleasant evenings with Max Bryant but I won't be spending anymore with him. ...What a shock". A clearly dispirited George Loder now: "Had the unhappy job of writing to tell Don (Charlwood). Don will take it very hard I know. Max said to me not long ago 'He [Don] was badly shaken when Bill Charlton went. If I go it will be the last straw'. "

Flying Officer Robert Maxwell Bryant (411748), Don Charlwood's best friend, was killed when his RAF 156 Squadron Lancaster crashed just off the Dutch coast on the night of 11/12 June 1943 during an attack on Munster, Germany.[10] His body was recovered from the sea by Dutchman Urk Dike, of Friesland, who would also die at the hands of the enemy, a year later in a concentration camp. Four of Max Bryant's crew were buried in Dutch cemeteries – their average age was 23. Max had been 20 when caught up by the war recruiting drive. He found the world outside Cowra, NSW, utterly exciting – from the food on the troopship across the Pacific to the amazing sights and sounds of New York. War had been an adventure and he died at 21. George Loder's letter chilled Don Charlwood to the bone: "Believe me, I know what a blow this is to you. I feel it perhaps just a little less myself, for although I wasn't associated with him as close as you, I was tremendously fond of him – one couldn't help liking and admiring him."[11]

Don Charlwood wrote "few of my friends remained", of the eighteen of the Twenty Men who had gone to Bomber Command, "ten were missing or dead. Among the remaining seven I have two close friends, George Loder and Johnnie Gordon".[12] It was a very upset Don Charlwood who would write to John and Mary Bryant.

> I had hoped that it would never be my lot to write you this letter; indeed, even now it seems impossible to me that Max is not still safe in England. I assure you, I can write of him as of one of my own brothers I would be tremendously proud of. It is not yet a month since he failed to return, so I am still very hopeful that he has managed to bale out and even hope that he will turn up unexpectedly some day in the way that I found typical of him. ...A few days later Syd Cool flew over here bringing Max's personal belongings – his two cameras, his snaps and his diaries, things as familiar to me as my own belongings. I shall take every care of them and shall see that, when I am in any danger, that they are in safe keeping. I expect that you will know as much of me from Max as my people know of Max from me. Most of our overseas experiences we have shared together. We left Somers together, sat at the same table aboard ship and did all our training together. Max worked hard and was naturally clever and he left me floundering in his wake. His efforts led him to Ferry Command and we parted very miserably in Moncton, not expecting our ways to cross again. But in about three months we were together here at Lichfield and eventually we finished up at the same squadron. It was primarily Max's outstanding ability as a navigator that resulted in his crew being posted to a Pathfinder squadron and it was from this squadron that he was eventually lost. I know that, whatever the outcome, he would not have had things differently. With unbounded enthusiasm he tackled his new job as he tackled everything else. I can confidently say that their loss would certainly have nothing to do with navigation. Max just didn't make mistakes in the air, and many was the occasion on which his watchful eye detected a slip in my work as we flew in Canada. I could quote letters from others and pieces from my own diary that would reveal to you just how high Max stood in the opinion of

those who knew him. I loved him for being so intensely human and so generous-hearted and he was always absolutely natural, never varying whether in humble or exalted company. The war broadened him a great deal...I am very glad that we shared our last leave. Max no doubt wrote to you of our days in Exeter and Somerset...15 months ago he gave me your address and I gave him my home address, "just in case" remember if we do not see him again that he was very happy that he did his job well. He did it more than well, he did it splendidly.

Flight Lieutenant George Loder, second from right, and his crew (courtesy Elizabeth Webby).

George Loder's RAF 156 Lancaster took off on yet another operation, the night of 20/21 December 1943 to attack Frankfurt. The pilot was New Zealander, Flight Lieutenant Michael Acton Sullivan (414697) DFC, RNZAF, 23, from Auckland. With the exception of the Flight Sergeant George Edward Mason (1007560), DFM, the RAF Middle Upper Gunner, his crew was Australian. The Wireless Operator/Air Gunner was Pilot Officer Eric Whitby Ritchie (412189) DFC, 30, a former clerk with the Adelaide Steamship Co; Warrant Officer William (Bill) Liness Charles Hickling (400433), DFC, 21, a former student of Melbourne's Wesley College was the Rear Gunner. While Bill Hickling was a clerk he had completed a three-year course in turning and fitting. Warrant Officer Cyril William Knox (22170) DFC, a 25-year-old former Mechanic from Murgon, Queensland, was one of a rare breed, an Australian Engineer. Flight Lieutenant Rex Henry Wedd (408200) 29, DFC, from Lenah Valley, Tasmania, was a school teacher before he became a patrol officer in New Guinea. It seemed unusual to find him as a Bomb Aimer on a bomber over Europe, or perhaps first-hand knowledge of the New Guinea highlands had resulted in his never wishing to fight there.

Flight Lieutenant George Bruce Loder (412160) and his crew died when their Lancaster was shot down by night fighters over Laubach, Germany. He and his decorated crew were on their 45th and last operation.[13] Their regular Bomb Aimer Flight Lieutenant Vincent Joseph Givney (20205) from Tamworth, New South Wales, had fallen from a vehicle and broken an arm. Hospitalised, he was unable to accompany them on this "operation". Superstition about breaking up of a crew of long standing was again validated – Givney survived the war.

Flying Officer John (Johnnie) Irvine Gordon (412218) DFC, was from Cessnock, New South Wales, and saw himself as an elder within the Twenty Men – he was about to celebrate his 32nd birthday. Gordon had a BA and Dip Ed and Don Charlwood was impressed with his intellect as much as he was with Gordon's self-confidence. "He wore his cap in a manner that ridiculed his uniform, and he marched in a manner that ridiculed drill."[14] Gordon had been shot up on a couple of ops and when knocked down riding a motorbike during black-out his regular crew finished the tour without him. It was disturbing to have to finish the tour with a different crew but his letter to Charlwood was vintage Gordon: "I don't know a soul on the squadron now, as the place has been entirely taken over by a whole horde of cheeky new crews. I am aloof and unknown, but I've got a whole bottle of Algerian wine that I had been saving to drink at interrogation on our last trip. Since our tour ended in chaos and I'm left alone and cold, I'll drink the bloody lot myself."[15]

But Gordon wasn't as carefree as this letter suggested because "Sometimes my conscience troubles me about blind mass murdering". He believed "Bomber Command's policy is fixed too relentlessly on mere victory by annihilation. That is impossible". Clearly he had pondered long and hard on the dilemma he faced and confided in Charlwood: "Britain at present seems to lack men who can look beyond the victory. Bomber Command's policy, though it makes the victory more certain and earlier, may make a real peace impossible."[16]

Johnnie Gordon survived the rest of his tour of operations with "a cheeky new crew", and then volunteered for RAF 617, better known as The Dam Busters. RAF 617 attacked only military targets. He did not like the idea of instructing after his tour was completed because he hated the thought of sending young men on bombing operations. His young brother Flight Sergeant George Wallace Gordon (413852) had just been killed, at the age of 23. He was also now engaged to an English girl, Mary. Don Charlwood was the best man at Johnnie and Mary's wedding; "the bride slim and fair; the bridegroom, newly commissioned and wearing the ribbon of his recently awarded DFC".[17] As Don said farewell to the couple, Johnnie asked if he would personally deliver a letter to his mother Mildred Gordon when Charlwood returned to Australia, "telling her all I could find out about my brother's death, I don't suppose it would get past the censor". Johnnie Gordon spoke with urgency, "If we get through this mess, we must never let the others down".[18] On 13 February 1944 Gordon's crew's attack on the Antheor

Betty Loder and three-year-old daughter Elizabeth receive George Loder's DFC from the Duchess of Gloucester.

Viaduct was aborted. The pilot was Canadian Squadron Leader William Reid Suggitt (J/15131) DFC, RCAF, "A" Flight Commanding Officer. On their return to base bad weather over Sussex caused Suggitt to drop the Lancaster to low altitude – the Lancaster was too low and hit a tree. A farmer hurried to the wreckage and found all but Suggitt dead. The pilot was still strapped in his seat shouting: "Turn the engines off". Suggitt lapsed into unconsciousness and died two days later. Johnnie Gordon had been married six weeks.

Don Charlwood was weary. He lay on his bed willing sleep to take him from his thoughts of the enthusiastic, naive men who left Australian shores in 1941. Just seven of the Twenty Men remained alive, only five of those attached to RAF Bomber Command.[19] The number five brought to mind an RAF official reminding crews of the importance of bringing their "kites" back to the UK; "Five aircraft were a heavier loss, we were reminded, than five crews".[20] It had been said in such a matter of fact manner that it chilled Charlwood. Having completed 30 ops, Don Charlwood spent some time as an instructor before returning to Australia via Canada so he could revisit primary school teacher Nell East, the daughter of a host family. He and Nell married and settled in Australia. He worked 30 years in Civil Air Traffic Control. The love of writing remained and he would be accredited with several of the most thought-provoking, emotive books about service in Bomber Command. *No Moon Tonight* and *Journeys into Night* would reflect how fortunate he believed he was to survive. The latter title was launched by Professor Elizabeth Webby of Sydney University. She is the daughter of George Loder one of the Twenty Men. Elizabeth was a small girl in a large bonnet she travelled with her mother to Government House, Sydney, to receive her late father's DFC from the Duchess of Gloucester – a father she never knew.

The sense of sadness and total cynicism that hung heavily over Don Charlwood was not unusual. Don Charlwood joined the RAAF in 1941, Warrant Officer William (Bill) Elliott Kelly (425325) joined RAF Bomber Command much later but he, too, was introspective, and moved rapidly "from exuberance to despair, from ethos to pathos" his convictions altering as dramatically as his definition of war which to him altered from being synonymous with adventure and duty to "Tragedy or Disillusionment".[21] Kelly would quickly take exception to the term Blue Orchids because members of the other military services used it in a derisive manner, suggesting that war service for aircrew was easy – that they were "pampered, privileged, and having every comfort, in fact, as hot house flowers". Kelly could laugh it off in the early stages of his RAAF service and could explain that because bomber crews spent so much time at 20,000 ft (6,000 m) "in unheated and un-pressurised aircraft, parts of the body can turn blue with intense cold". He would continue, depending on the company and explain how "orchids are identified by the two tubers at the base of each plant likened to testicles", so although detractors had not figured this out, the term "Blue Orchids", was probably quite accurate in that sense.[22]

Bill Kelly was a country boy, born in Winton, in Queensland's west, a town purported to have been where Banjo Patterson wrote the words for "Waltzing Matilda". His family moved frequently wherever shearing contracts took them until settling at Blackall on the Barcoo River so Bill could start school. "I was a true bush kid and in this town of a dozen pubs I was able to run flat-out, sometimes in bare feet."

He became an avid reader and anxious to explore the wider world. Perhaps it was this which made him so open to the recruiting hype. Young men he believed were "supremely confident about their invincibility" and he was not immune to that or the enticement of being taken into the wide world. He also felt alienated by the broadcast Nazi hyperbole with regards to being the "master race". Before he knew it he was one of the 7,000 volunteers applying to join the RAAF in May and June 1941, except he really wasn't quite eligible, he altered his birth certificate from 1923 to 1922. He had not allowed for the fact that the RAAF could not train 7,000 right away and by the time he was accepted he was 18½, really. He did manage a further piece of subterfuge, using someone else's urine for the medical so they would not discover his asthma. The first part was giddy, "the jam-packed cheering crowds waved, yelled and showered us with paper".[23] It would be a photo he would ponder later – "how few of these proud men came back to Australian shores?".

William (Bill) Elliott Kelly (left) and right Kelly and his Queensland RAAF
intake marched proudly down Brisbane's streets. (courtesy Lyn Kelly).

The chest beating was wonderful, so too the bus ride to Sandgate and Initial Training School – he knew no one but there was "much camaraderie and singing of blue ditties on the hour-long ride".[24] Once the regimented life of the RAAF began the mood was very different as he became a number and everyone seemed to metamorphose into one. In June 1942 all the rookie pilots-to-be descended on RAAF Amberley west of Brisbane and then Narromine, NSW. Gradually one by one they failed pilot training, including Bill Kelly, he "bent the bloody aircraft!" when attempting to land – a never to be forgiven crime. The RAAF reacted rapidly and he was remustered "I was absolutely devastated".[25] He and the other scrubbed trainees commiserated by drowning their sorrows in the nearest pub. The new direction of his training was about to begin and he wasn't impressed but at least he was sent via Sydney and – what an enormous city it was – he was a long way from Western Queensland. Kelly was now a Wireless Operator/Air Gunner trainee and the going was tough until he attained the Morse speed of 22 words a minute without mistakes.

If Sydney had appeared foreign, the British Isles certainly was. He was challenged when sent to an RAF squadron and found himself the only Australian in an RAF crew. He was very impressed with his skipper, a very experienced pilot "his manner and confidence were the epitome of all things the skipper of a bombing aircraft should be."[26] But

Kelly was used to "socially homogenous Aussie servicemen" and this was not the case in this squadron or even his crew, officers were treated very differently, and expected to be so by Non-commissioned Officers. He also struggled with certain standards of morals embraced by several of his crew, which was exacerbated by his shyness with women and his reluctance to join the wild nights on the town, whatever town, they were in at the time. Bill Kelly retreated more and more within himself.

His first impression of his pilot was quickly justified and it extended to the fact that they never received "clapped out" aircraft. And then just as the rookie crew qualified to go to war, their experienced pilot ceased to operate on "medical grounds". It was a great disappointment but Kelly was willing to give him the benefit of the doubt. Other crew members were not so gracious and Bill Kelly wondered how they could call this man a coward. They were given an RAF rookie pilot, which meant they again marked time while he tried to qualify. Kelly had major misgivings concerning the new pilot's ability and also his sloppy, casual manner. Three months on and the crew were in conversion training on Stirlings and then on Lancasters. Kelly was surprised that they were rushed through training regardless of the "alarmingly hard landings". He was finally "cheesed off" and made a disparaging remark when they had to abandon the aircraft due to "bad teamwork". In the heat of the moment Kelly "criticised the Pommies and to stir the pot, very unfairly, their country" – he was not surprised when the crew decided to stay with the pilot and opt for another wireless operator/air gunner, "preferably from the RAF". It was a lonely feeling – he was the only Australian and the English crew had closed ranks against him. Clearly he was not popular for having the temerity to question squadron administrators on their judgement. Bill Kelly was given one last opportunity to prove himself in the squadron and was posted to a crew with a New Zealander as the skipper. Clearly matching one colonial to another was deemed the best fit, and it was. Less than two months later the crew that had abandoned him was killed – the news came as an "unbelievable shock".[27]

In July 1944, Bill Kelly could truly sympathise with Londoners as they faced the onslaught of flying bombs (V1s), referred to as Doodlebugs. They were the stuff of nightmares, as they could be heard overhead and then the motor cut and they would descend rapidly to the earth and explode. In just two weeks approximately 1,600 Londoners were killed and nearly 5,000 injured. With his squadron close to London the occasional stray V1 exploded in their airfield. Bill Kelly would happily volunteer to bomb German flying-bomb sites. By the time his crew began operations it was the last months of 1944 and casualties were on the rise again, "the chance of survival was the same as playing Russian roulette...only now with the odds of three bullets instead of one".[28] With little notice the crew was posted to the Middle East. Kelly found the place fascinating, and then they were back outside London. He met up with an Aussie classmate and was stunned to see how this "outgoing, likeable...rugged Australian" was showing signs of war stress and how readily he admitted that his feelings when over targets were "scared, in fact, bloody SHIT scared".[29] Worst news was to come when he discovered another friend had been sent back to Australia with a nervous breakdown.

The weather was fair so the order came to proceed with the operation. It was March 1945 and because double daylight saving time had commenced it would mean they would not take-off in total darkness. At operating height the electrically-heated flying suits were not really warm enough. When the need arose to remove gloves and touch equipment it invariably resulted in mild frostbite, and without the oxygen/intercom face mask in place, icicles formed in the throat from breath, preventing clear speech. Arriving over target the firestorm on the ground was enormous and the flak peppered the underside of the Lancaster, Warrant Officer Kelly wrote in his log "scared". The outward-bound leg seemed so very quick, yet the return leg seemed to take forever, and finally they were down with their Lancaster sporting multiple shrapnel dints. First the fear of the operation and then the elation as they returned home safe and then the weary aircrew stumbled into debriefing –"The excitement was electric".[30] Kelly found he wasn't the only fearful airman this night, it seemed a common consensus, and they all received half a glass of rum. His crew seemed to carry an awful lot of talismen after that, "our whole crew had become overly superstitious" and each began carrying some personal item they would never fly without. Bill Kelly ensured his Australian penny (with the kangaroo emblem) was in his pocket when they took off on their next trip in April – but why were they ordered to attack on Friday the 13th?

They survived the op, but with a minimum of sleep before they were again on an operation to bomb Berlin. Over the target they were "coned". The silhouette of their Lancaster stood out above the firestorm below. Their skipper dived and twisted and two of the engines cut out. The sharp popping/thudding noises of flak meant they were still locked in the searchlights. Another Lancaster lifted quickly and just in time to clear their air space. Then the intercom went dead as they plunged towards the earth. Teamwork laced with a frantic self-preservation instinct meant that they got power restored and their aircraft lifted again. Kelly went into well-practiced mode and struggled down the narrow corridor to open the rear hatch in preparation for the crew to bale out. Below was a raging inferno and into this they were supposed to parachute? His pulse thumping, Kelly was aware of the "fleeting hiatus between life and possible oblivion".[31] And then it was over, the bombload was expelled, the Lancaster began to hum again, they turned for home, and Bill Kelly surprised himself by writing in his log "not so scared this time", but he wondered in amazement, "How on earth did others who had completed their tours of duty ever sustain"[32]. Bill Kelly was becoming increasingly "concerned when non-combatant civilians were destroyed during bombing raids".[33] He knew he was not alone in this dilemma, but it was something that could not be discussed.

The first months of 1945 were bitterly cold. Operating at heights meant the atmosphere was chronically cold for aircrew. Ice was a problem for aircraft not only on the airfield, but as the bomber penetrated cloud, when thick frost would coat windscreens. As the frost broke away, large chunks of ice flew off whirling airscrews, and crackled through the turret ventilators in handfuls. Ice could break off props and cause a total loss of power. On 4/5 January nonetheless, it was decided to launch a raid on German fortifications defending the Gironde Estuary, at the mouth of which lay the French port of Royan. With only seven aircraft shot down the raid on Royan barely rated a mention in Bomber Command records, but Australians were on six of the seven aircraft destroyed and 15 Australians died. In what clearly would be the last months of World War II, Bomber Command was caught up in the crescendo.

On 14/15 January 1945, 21-year-old skipper Flying Officer Kenneth Alan Cook (418227) drew the short straw and was given NN722, an RAF 9 Squadron Lancaster with a bad history. NN722 had been damaged the previous month on an attack against Munchen. A repair party spent 597 hours working on the bomber, but under pressure to release the aircraft declared NN722 sound for service. Ken Cook had been an Audit Clerk and enlisted at 18. The Bomb Aimer was Flight Sergeant Bruce Cowper MacKnight (428879) 20, a clerk from Sydney's Neutral Bay; Wireless Operator/Air Gunner, Flight Sergeant Maurice James McNamara (429719) 22, was a school teacher from Melbourne. One Air Gunner was Flight Sergeant John Erskine Brown MacLean

Flying Officer Kenneth Cook.   *Flight Sergeant Maurice McNamara.*

Flight Sergeant   *Flight Sergeant*   *Flight Sergeant*
Bruce MacKnight.   *Michael John Kerrigan.*   *John MacLean.*

(434641) 21, from Toowoomba, Queensland, a former student of the Christian Brothers school, Toowoomba, and latterly studying at Gatton Agricultural College to become a stock agent. The second gunner was Flight Sergeant Michael John Kerrigan (434528) 27, a former Kogarah High student and "electric clock worker".[34] The Lancaster and its crew never made it back to England. Whether the bomber failed or was shot down was not clear. Kerrigan survived but died two months later in a POW hospital.

The letter to the Cook family in Ballarat from the RAF Commanding Officer of RAF 9 showed how war had taken its toll. The stiff upper lip of years gone by had dropped – clearly he had wearied of writing letters of loss:

> I realise what a terribly anxious time this will be for you, and you have all the sympathy of myself, the officers and airmen of the Squadron. Your son had only recently joined this Squadron but in the short time he was with us showed himself to be a first class operational captain of aircraft, and his loss is a great blow to us all. I wish I could tell you how much we, in this country, appreciate the way Australia is helping us in this war, and how bitterly we regret the loss of her sons.

Ken Cook's father, Edgar, needed to release emotion, and RAAF red tape provided him with that outlet. To a second letter requesting acknowledgement of receipt of Ken's personal effects, the grieving father took exception, "I beg to differ. I personally sent a registered letter stating that we received the trunk and bag". His wife, Ivy, was grief stricken and her husband wrote "when Mrs Cook is well enough to open the same" the last piece of paperwork, which required the next of kin to tick each itemised personal item within, would be signed and the RAAF could close the file on his son's life – but in the meantime; "doctor's orders are to leave it intact".

For the Kerrigan family the news was more painful. They received a cable from their son; "Shot down over Germany. Prisoner in Hospital. Don't worry. I shall soon be better". Inez Kerrigan was overjoyed and wrote to the RAAF, "'Prisoner of War' is not so very nice to hear but it is a great relief to know he is alive". There was no further communication, which they reasoned was due to the chaos of the last months of the war. But it became more perplexing when Michael senior and Inez opened their *Sydney Morning Herald* to be confronted by the announcement by the Australian Minister of Air that; "only three prisoners of war had not yet reported as returned safe". Inez wrote immediately asking "does that include my son?" because his camp, Stalag IV-A, "had become a part of Russian occupation?" A cable arrived via an agency in England and made shocking reading: "Flight Sergeant Michael John Kerrigan died on 22nd March 1945". Michel Senior demanded to know why news came directly from overseas and not via RAAF Casualty. Why had authorities in Australia, who had encouraged young men like his son to join the RAAF and fight a war in Europe, been so "poorly informed?" Only then was he informed that his son had been admitted to a POW hospital in January suffering: "Injuries to his left leg, which necessitated the amputation at the knee. Following the operation septicaemia developed causing his death at 0730 on the 22nd March 1945."

The officious tone continued; "Your son's remains were buried in Berlin" and "any further questions should not be sent to the Department of Air, but to the Imperial War Graves Commission". In a far more gracious manner Inez Kerrigan would write; "Although we lost our dear son at least we are fortunate enough to know where he is laid to rest". For them this was better because so many others "do not know where their loved one is buried". It did, nonetheless, seem cruel that Michael John Kerrigan was buried in Berlin, and far away from his crew and farther away from his own country. The Kerrigans requested a photo of Michael's grave and when it had not arrived by 1955 they asked yet again only to be told that "due to difficulties in Berlin there has been a delay". It had already been a decade since their son had been killed. Allies had turned to foe and in 1961 a wall would be built to divide Berlin into "East" and "West", indicative of how quickly the political landscape would continue to change.[35]

The media was heralding victory after victory and how the end of the war was nigh, but "Killed in Action" names continued to be transmitted to RAAF Casualty Section, Melbourne. During the first week of February, the file marked "432755. CHEATLE, Raey Hilton", was one of those which caused personnel to inhale suddenly. Noel and Mabel Cheatle, of Sydney's Bankstown, were just regular Australians, the type who worked hard to survive in the city and make a comfortable home for their twin boys. Noel was a Carpenter but he was pleased Allen and Raey were better educated and managed to obtain positions as Clerks. They both wanted to enlist in the RAAF but had to mark time until they were 18. Allen was accepted in December 1942 and Raey, who referred to himself as "the younger twin", in January 1943. Both became Wireless Operator/Air Gunners.

Flight Sergeant Allen Leonard Cheattle (432305) never made it out of training. He and his crew were practising night circuits when the starboard inner engine failed and his inexperienced pilot was unable to stop the dive into English countryside. Allen died of injuries two days later, on 25 July 1944, a fortnight after his 20th birthday and was buried in England's Stonefall Cemetery, Harrogate.

Warrant Officer Raey Hilton Cheatle (432755) was killed on 8 February 1945. He was a Wireless Operator/Air Gunner on an RAF 97 (Straits Settlements) Squadron Lancaster; one of 177 Lancasters and 11 Mosquitos ordered to attack the Dormund-Ems Kanal near Ladbergen, with delayed-action bombs. Something went horribly wrong and Cheatle's Lancaster collided with an RAF 83 Squadron Lancaster and crashed. Raey was only 20, and now one of the many Australian aircrew with a grave in Eindhoven, The Netherlands. He was known in his crew and squadron as a bloke with a mischievous grin and sense of humour, and a ladies' man writing to four young women at home and one in New Zealand. Within Bomber Command he was just another airman from the Dominions. Noel and Mabel Cheatle had lost both their twin sons, and the future they had worked so hard for, was now severely diminished.

In February 1945 "Operation Thunderclap" was sanctioned. With Allied forces pressing on two fronts Bomber Command was sent to attack Berlin, Dresden, Leipzig and Chemnitz. In four raids between 13 and 15 February 1945, a combined British and US force of 1,300

Flight Sergeant Allen Cheatle.

Warrant Officer Raey Cheatle.

heavy bombers dropped more than 3,900 tons of incendiaries and high explosive bombs on Dresden. The result was catastrophic with the resulting firestorm devastating the city and killing an estimated 25,000. It would be the bombing of Dresden which would result in much post-war moral debate and condemnation of Bomber Command and ostracism for Harris. Although the British prime minister, Winston Churchill, would later attempt to distance himself from the attack on Dresden "he took a direct hand in the final planning".[36]

Though a generation had grown up with the adventures of pilot, adventurer, and hero, James Bigglesworth, their exploits in World War II were proving more thrilling than anything *Biggles* attempted. There was the story of the bomber pilot who held his burning aircraft level to aid his crew in baling out. As he rose and moved toward the hatch the aircraft blew up and he found himself in inky darkness falling without a parachute. His thoughts were erratic and when he bumped into something, he instinctively grabbed at whatever it was. His rapid descent was stopped and he floated safely to earth hanging onto the legs of one of his crew.

Flight Lieutenant Roberts Christian Dunstan (419018) was very much of the *Biggles* genre. Dunstan enlisted in the Australian Army in June 1940, writing on enlistment papers that he was born in Bendigo, Victoria, on 4 November 1919. The army was satisfied it had found a fit and enthusiastic 21 year old for 2nd Battalion 8th Field Artillery Company, and after training Dunstan sailed for the Middle East. His war was short. He was hit by a shell splinter in January 1941 and as a result his right leg was amputated. He then admitted to being born in November 1922. "I had lost my leg...lied to get into the army...I had put up my age so that I could be here so that I could take my place among men. Now I was 18 with one leg."[37]

He was discharged from the AIF in early February 1942. A "stirring RAAF poster that shouted 'It's a man's job!'" inspired him to apply for aircrew.[38] Though the initial interviewer was sceptical, Dunstan continued to pester the RAAF, insisting he was perfectly capable of fulfilling duties that did not require two legs. He wore them down and was accepted in June 1942, two years after he enlisted in the AIF and he was still only 19 – really.

Attached to RAAF 460 Dunstan used crutches to get to his aircraft and then crawled through the fuselage to reach the rear turret. He was not deterred by the unlikelihood of his escaping a crashing bomber, and completed a full tour of 30 operations, the day before his 21st birthday. The citation for his DSO included the words "unique determination". He was discharged from the RAAF on 2 October 1945. In 1956 Dunstan was elected to the Victorian Parliament as the Liberal Party member for Mornington. He served in two ministerial positions before leaving Parliament in 1982. He died on 11 October 1989.

Flight Lieutenant Robin Ordell (422251), DFC, was a natural to play *Biggles* in any post-war movie. Not only did he have the dashing

Flight Lieutenant Roberts C Dunstan.

good looks of a matinee hero, but he had the presence and confidence of someone who had already appeared on the silver screen in a starring role; as well as coming from Australian entertainment royalty. His father Talon (Tal) Ordell worked extensively on Australian stage and screen. Tal Ordell's work largely featured the bush ethos, playing characters like Dad Rudd twice on film; starring in movies like *On Our Selection*, *The Hayseeds' Come to Sydney*; *The Gentleman Bushranger*, *While the Billy Boils*, *The Sentimental Bloke*. He turned to writing and directing and wrote, acted, produced and directed, *The Kid Stakes* in 1927. Based on the popular comic strip, *Fatty Finn*, the film starred his six-year-old son Robin as the leader of a gang of irrepressible, scruffy, Woolloomooloo kids. Tal Ordell continued to be heavily involved in film, vaudeville, and stage productions, but recognizing the demise of the theatrical business he became a radio storyteller.

LEFT: *Flight Lieutenant Robin Ordell.* RIGHT: *Robin Ordell as Fatty Finn.*

After education at Sydney Grammar School Robin established himself as a radio announcer and looked to continue his own career under the bright lights of theatre and cinema. Due to his father's reluctance to sign the enlistment form Robin needed to wait until he was 21 before joining the RAAF. His confidence impressed recruiters and few Australians were not familiar with his father's starring roles if not his own in Australia's last silent movie, and he was streamed "Pilot". Training proved easy and by April 1944 Robin was in England with 27 Operating Training Unit choosing his crew. Perhaps it was due to his sense of fun that Robin chose Ian Ronald Osborne (422251), later Pilot

Officer, as his Navigator. Ian enlisted at 18 in September 1942. He was a former student of North Sydney's Church of England Grammar School (SCEGS, known also as Shore). There were plenty of jibes between the two about whose school was superior, and then the Wireless Operator/ Air Gunner, 21-year-old Flight Sergeant Keith Kevin Reynolds (424306), would cut in and say they both had it wrong because he attended the King's School. Reynolds was still a student when he enlisted at 19 in August 1942. He had represented King's in tennis, and had been one of the 1st XI and XV. It was certainly unusual to have members of three of Sydney's most prestigious private protestant schools represented in the same crew.

Pilot Officer John Killen.

Flight Sergeant Keith Reynolds.

Pilot Officer
Ian Osborne.

Flight Sergeant
James Harper.

Flight Sergeant
Ray McKaskill.

The Bomb Aimer, Pilot Officer John Gordon Treatt Killen (421913) 24, had his own pedigree, and was working with his father, John, on the family property at Goobragandra via Tumut, New South Wales. Melbourne was the hometown of both gunners, 19-year-old Middle Upper Gunner Flight Sergeant Ray McKaskill (431183), and 20-year-old Rear Gunner Flight Sergeant James Harper (117739). McKaskill couldn't claim to have attended a top school – he spent his education at Boolarra State, and no one had the slightest idea where that was. When he enlisted at 18 in June 1943 he had been working as a Grocer's Assistant. Harper, too, did not come from the comfortable lifestyle enjoyed by his skipper. He was 18 when he applied for RAAF entry. His education was modest at Belmont State School, Victoria, and then he left for gainful employment. He was studying at Geelong Tech at night and was an Apprentice Cabinet Maker by day. A referee recommended Jim because he was "honest and reputable" with "a clean interest in life". The RAAF originally thought Jim Harper should be placed in a trade but tests were mixed and he was delighted when they decided to send him to aircrew training as a trainee pilot. He tested well on "Persistence" and "Endurance" but did not so well on "Leadership". He excelled at gunnery and aircraft recognition so became an Air Gunner, and was pleased to be selected by Robin Ordell as Rear Gunner.

The crew was complete when RAF Sergeant Charles Scurr (1077176) 24, from Durham, was appointed Engineer. They joined RAF 100 and in June 1944 Robin Ordell was commissioned Pilot Officer, then Flying Officer, and by November the confident, good looking pilot was Flight Lieutenant. He was awarded a DFC on 2 February 1945 with the citation: "Ordell has completed and was captain of the aircraft for numerous operations against the enemy, in the course of which he has shown the utmost fortitude, courage and devotion."

Tal Ordell was pleased as punch and everyone heard of Robin's starring role in the RAAF. Ordell, Killen, and Osborne were all commissioned and looked forward to a time when the rest of the crew would also be commissioned. That extra rank and slightly more dapper uniform certainly was worth having. The Australians were popular and having a "movie star" as a skipper certainly helped socially. Even if his father's Australian films were unheard of in the finer English establishments, let alone his own Fatty Finn character, his crew were sure to let everyone know and they were happy to be guilty by association.

Lancaster PB569 shook to the full roar of the Merlin engines, Robin Ordell released the brakes and the bomber gained momentum until it lifted skywards with the slipstream flattening the grass. It was 1605 on 3 February 1945 and the destination was the Benzol works at Bottrop, Germany. The dwindling view of the English coastline would be the last view of it for all bar one crew member. Even this late in the war German anti-aircraft defences were lethal. For the last five months this crew, like others, had danced with searchlights. Robin saw the searchlights and knew they would be relentless in their pursuit of bomber targets. As they moved towards his Lancaster Robin followed the standard drill of turning towards and through the light. In the excitement of the moment inexperienced pilots did not heed the advice of seasoned veterans and attempted to outrun the searchlight and be found by the master beam, a great wide blue thing that enabled anti-aircraft guns to fire on a target, which was lit up as brightly as any day. Once coned by the light a pilot could weave, or even climb, but not dive, which seemed more the natural tendency. The searchlights came and went and the Lancaster was buffeted by light flak, but then it all went horribly wrong and they were hit. The bomber burst into flames, which engulfed the fuselage with incredible speed. Jim Harper heard no voices acknowledge what he believed was Robin's faint order to abandon the aircraft. He had begun to turn "the rear turret by hand in order to get out", the bomber was diving fast from an altitude of around 12,000 ft (3,600 m). Next he knew he was "seeing the stars and cloud" as he regained consciousness at about 3,000 ft (914 m) and pulled his ripcord. Harper was unaware he was the only survivor of his crew. The Lancaster crashed into a minefield and disintegrated. Advancing British troops found the wreckage and carefully recovered the shattered remains of five airmen from what was left of the bomber – Ian Osborne's body lay a distance away.

Harper landed in a field and with the sound of battle all around he hid in a deserted house. The following morning he was startled by German soldiers and was lucky not to be shot. They were excitable, menacing and in retreat. He was marched off with them and soon there were more POWs and more German soldiers. It was raining, they had no food, and it was clear that if they couldn't keep up they were liable to be shot and left. As the column of forlorn POWs approached a small town, American P51s screamed down on an attack killing POWs along with their guards. Those who survived arrived at Moosburg a prison barrack, which was "filthy and crawling with lice and bed bugs". Harper would spend two months as a POW before being freed by American soldiers. James Harper was flown back to England and discovered his luminous crew had perished. Asked if he required immediate evacuation to Australia – Harper's response was an emphatic "YES". James Harper returned to Australia, still only 21, his adventure had been "memorable" but he had no answer for the question which humbled him, "Why me?"

Tal Ordell received the dreaded telegram in March followed quickly by a letter written by Robin prior to his last flight. Tal's health weakened and several months later he apologised to the RAAF for his lack of communication. He then asked if they could tell him more about how a son he believed could have achieved so much, had died; "I would be glad to have any further news you have received re the loss of my son". In May 1946 Tal Ordell found the strength to write again asking why he had not received "my boy's effects" as he was led to believe they were supposed to be sent the year before. The RAAF apologised and advised they would be dispatched as soon as possible. The body of his son along with those of Ian Osborne, John Killen, Keith Reynolds, and Ray McKaskill were exhumed and buried in Mierlo War Cemetery in The Netherlands. RAF Engineer Charles Scurr had been buried in Venray, but George and Sarah Scurr, in concert with the other families, decided their boys would have liked to be buried next to each other – because in life they had so enjoyed each other's company. When asked what inscription they would like on the headstones, Tal Ordell and Ron and Mabel Osborne decided to continue the fun and competitive spirit between Robin and Ian, so below Robin's name was inscribed "Sydney Grammar" and below Ian's, "SCEGS". Tal Ordell had been described as, "A versatile actor, proudly Australian, and above all a comedian", but the pride and laughter had gone from his life with the death of son Robin, and Tal Ordell succumbed to coronary vascular disease on 8 June 1948.

By March 1945 the Bomber Command operation was at its peak and a massive 67,637 tons of bombs were dropped, more than any other month in the war, and as much as the combined tonnage of the first 34 months of World War II. Mannheim, Cologne, Kamen and the Dortmund-Ems Canal, Chemnitz, Dessau, Hemmingstedt, Harburg, Essen, Kassel, and Hamburg all felt the massive striking power. Wessel, in the German Rhineland encapsulated the fury. The city was "97 per cent destroyed" after being bombed on 16, 17, 18 and 19 February, and again on the 23 March; tactical support of the British 21st Army Group push over the Rhine on 24 March. Commander of the British Army Group, Field Marshal Bernard Law Montgomery, affectionately known as "Monty", sent the message: "My grateful appreciation for the quite magnificent co-operation you have given us in the Battle of the Rhine. The bombing of Wessel was a masterpiece and was a decisive factor in our entry into the town before midnight.[39]

Although the campaign in the Ruhr continued it became a race to Berlin, but the battles on the ground resulted in a tenuous future for downed airmen. The German military was stretched and in life and death struggles on many fronts, there was not always the opportunity, or the inclination, to take prisoners. The situation was in flux as societies crumbled and militaries were in desperate attack mode. Aircrew who floated to the ground from burning aircraft into Germany increasingly faced the wrath of civilians. There was little safety anywhere in the maelstrom – lucky aircrew would evade the enemy and not be shot by friendly fire. On the 22 and 24 March 1945 two crews would be caught up in a horrific sequence of events, both skippers were Australian, the first was Flying Officer John Edwin Paradise (426148) and the second was Flying Officer Philip Henry Morris (423161).

John Paradise was a 22-year-old former Clerk from the Brisbane suburb of Indooroopilly. He eased RAF 51 Halifax MZ348 into the air and banked onto a course to attack the Dortmund Ems Canal on 21 March 1945. The Canal had claimed the lives of many aircrew so the operation wasn't expected to be easy. Onboard were fellow Australians, Navigator Pilot Officer Bruce Frederick Greenwood (424584) 22, a former draughtsman from the Sydney suburb of Bexley. Flying Officer Keith William Berick (424950) 24, a Farm Hand from Wyalong, New South Wales, and now Wireless Operator/Air Gunner. The Engineer was from Sussex, 19-year-old RAF Sergeant Richard (Dick) Francis Gunn (1721922); the Bomb Aimer was RAF Flight Sergeant Alexander Armstrong (1567638) a 22-year-old Yorkshireman; and both Air Gunners Sergeant W Hood and Flight Sergeant L Hart, were RAF.

Flying Officer John Paradise.

Flying Officer Keith Berick.

Armstrong, lying in his Bomb Aimer position in the front Perspex dome, had just called "Bombs Gone, well done Skip" when there was a warning shout from the Middle Upper Gunner. It was too late – their Halifax was clipped from above by the bombs of another. A bomb went through the port wing knocking off the fin – the rudder controls were useless and Paradise lost no time in calling "fit parachutes and jump". With the Halifax losing height rapidly one by one the crew threw themselves out of the aircraft, Paradise was watching closely, "How many?" seven parachutes – such a relief. On the ground he met up with Bruce Greenwood, Keith Berick, Dick Gunn and Alex Armstrong, but this was Germany and they were immediately rounded up by some very unhappy men who propelled them to the police station. They were questioned and searched, then they were pushed, shoved and hit during a trip to military headquarters. On arrival they were "stripped, searched, and given third-degree interrogation". Refusing to say anything, they were locked in a room without food or water.

Just before sundown on the 22 March the three Australians plus Armstrong and Gunn, were taken outside and ordered to march down the road to the railway station from where they would be transferred to a POW camp. Behind them walked a number of armed Germans. The group walked about a mile when in the failing light the soldiers opened fire. Paradise, Greenwood, Armstrong and Gunn fell forward, Berick flinched as two bullets struck his body. Instinct took over and Berick was running for his life. Although concentrated fire came in his direction he stumbled into brush, tripped and fell – the trip saved his life. Momentarily the gunfire stopped before starting again "from the scene of the murders, presumably completing the execution". Well into the night the Germans searched with dogs for Berick, but he evaded and remained at large until taken POW on 1 April – 28 days later he was liberated by the Americans and discovered that both his gunners were also safe. After medical treatment in England Berick returned with authorities to look for his crew, and grimly confirmed that half buried decomposing remains, shot in the back and head, were the men he had flown with. Berick stayed until he identified the soldiers who murdered his mates.

Keith Berick returned to Australia in November 1945, his war experience a nightmare rather than the great adventure he had anticipated. The following year he was expected to give testimony at the War Crimes Trial but the Australian government believed it was the British government's responsibility to cover Berick's travel costs back to Europe – the British government disagreed and officials continued to quibble. Fred Greenwood was angry and demanded to know if Berick's statement was sufficient for a guilty verdict, appalled that two governments should dispute "such paltry expenses" given his son and so many sons had lost their lives – he would "gladly pay the expenses out of my late son's account". Fred Greenwood suffered in the knowledge of how his son Bruce had died and was pleased: "That a further seven

Germans in addition to Karl Amberger have been condemned to death for the atrocity concerning the murder of my son...I am pleased to learn that the Intelligence Dept and the War Crimes Commission have been successful in tracing these brutes and I hope at a later date to be notified of their paying the full penalty of death."

In due course he was advised that the perpetrators had been hanged. He continued to struggle particularly with "the Authorities attitude of re-interring their bodies into a cemetery in Germany". If this must be done he hoped at least his son's crew "were not separated from him when they were re-interred".

Two days after the murder of four members of RAF 51 Halifax MZ348, RAF 150 Lancaster, PB853, took off to bomb Dortmund. Like those who flew the Halifax, these baby-faced men had barely lived. Flying Officer Philip Morris (423161) 23, from Sydney was the pilot. The Engineer, predictably, was RAF Flight Sergeant John Clement

Flight Sergeant James Gillies.   *Flight Sergeant James Noel Griffin.*

Flight Sergeant Kevin Anthony Kee.   *Flight Sergeant Harvey Bawden.*

Davis (1814561). Flight Sergeant Kevin Anthony Kee (430174) was the Navigator, Flight Sergeant James Henry Gillies (433557) was the Bomb Aimer; Flight Sergeant Robert Lockyer Masters (432681) the Wireless Operator/Air Gunner; Flight Sergeant Harvey Hayward Bawden (419835) Middle Upper Gunner and Flight Sergeant James Noel Griffin (435186) the Rear Gunner. Masters was a School Teacher from Tumut, New South Wales. Griffin attended Christian Brothers College, Warwick, before studying Accountancy. He was 16 when he entered the Air Training Corps and impatiently waited until he finally made it to 18 to enlist in the main game in March 1943. Griffin hoped to be a pilot and made it through the first training regime before being rejected and re-mustered Air Gunner.

Harvey Hayward Bawden (419835) didn't look old enough to leave the family home, but had enlisted at 18, in a hurry lest the war finish before he qualified. He had attended Bendigo Technical before becoming a sheep farmer on the family property Mulvra. Kevin Kee was an 18-year-old student when he first applied to the RAAF. His interviewer wrote; "Clean and smart. Good appearance but shows signs of Chinese extraction". Australia was an Anglo Saxon nation: Chinese workers who had been present since the early 1800s had few opportunities to be accepted as true Australians. Kevin's Chinese father was deceased and his next of kin was his Australian-born Chinese mother Ethel. The next RAAF interviewer looked further than skin colour and Kevin Kee's qualifications were impeccable, first class passes in all subjects in Intermediate and Leaving Certificates at Melbourne's Scotch College; he was now a second year Civil Engineering Diploma student at Melbourne Technical College; he had spent five years in the Scotch College Cadet Corps and four months in the Air Force Training Corps. The RAAF recruiter wrote: "Quiet, reserved type. Keen and intelligent. Quite suitable for aircrew. Recommended".

The Navigator, Flight Sergeant James (Jim) Henry Gillies was born in Maryborough, Queensland, before the family moved to Sydney. He was just 19. He did not go without, and life was privileged. Educated at the exalted King's School, sporting involvement included "golf, tennis and billiards". Employment as a Junior Clerk while studying

Accountancy at night school, proved unfulfilling unlike the RAAF where he trained in different parts of Australia's eastern seaboard before embarking for overseas training in August 1943. Like so many before him, Jim Gillies could not foresee how his future war experience would be so vastly different to that which the recruiting brochures and newsreels would have him believe.

With crew training completed in October 1944, and after a month with RAF 153, the "sprog" crew found themselves attached to RAF 150 at the end of November 1944. On 24 March 1945 their operation was to attack the synthetic oil plant at Harpenerweg, Germany. As they approached the target they felt the light flak. Jim Gillies was lying down in position speaking to his skipper on the bombing run when the Lancaster bucked and the starboard inner engine caught fire. With the rudder shot away or jammed the aircraft began to dive to starboard and Masters shouted at his crew to abandon the aircraft. Jim Gillies remembered looking at the inferno below and was relieved when he glided into an open field. Gathering the silk canopy he was "bailed up by an elderly man with a pitchfork". For an instant he wondered how he would explain this to the others, "an elderly man with a pitchfork!" so much for imagined bravado, but then four other men arrived. He was stripped of his possessions and shoved in the direction of a town. Dozens more gathered along the route and Jim Gillies was "struck with numerous blows with sticks, fists and boots". He attempted to shield himself but by the time he arrived at the makeshift police station, he had suffered a "deeply cut scalp...severe general swelling of my face and head and bruising of my body". He was taken to gaol and thrown into a 9 x 6 ft (2.75 x 1.8 m) cell with five others. There was no bedding, and they were given a loaf of bread to eat. The latrines were "in shocking condition".

Gillies heard Harvey Bawden in another cell. Harvey had thrown himself out of the rear hatch but unfortunately hit the tail plane. He heard a crack and felt searing pain – his left femur was broken. Harvey Bawden was thrown into gaol for three days without medical treatment. Bawden and Gillies were finally moved to a hospital where they stayed for 15 days with little care. The hospital had few medical staff and limited medical supplies and even less food, but plenty of patients – the situation was chaotic. The two Australian aircrew wondered what had happened to the rest of the crew because they were confident that they had all baled out. It was a relief when the US army arrived and they were flown to England. Warrant Officer Harvey Bawden had just turned 21, and was classified "A class invalid" and a priority case to return home.

It took a post-war enquiry to find the remaining members of RAF 150 PB853. Jim Griffin was caught up in the burning Lancaster and was found close to the wreckage. German witnesses said that six bodies were found near the wrecked bomber, but when military enquiry members found a flying jacket and boots in the possession of a citizen of Herbede, ten miles (16 kilometres) south west of Dortmond, the shocking truth was pieced together. One of the crew landed by a farm and was struck down by a German soldier. A crowd gathered and he was "beaten to death by blows to the head with a hammer". Another was captured on landing by two German soldiers and taken to a camp. Soon after, the local Ortsgruppenleiter, the local NAZI party leader, and a crowd, succeeded in forcing the soldiers to hand him over. The young Australian was beaten up and then shot by the Ortsgruppenleiter. Later the same day the remaining two crew members were brought to the same camp by members of the local anti-aircraft unit. Again the Ortsgruppenleiter enforced his authority and they too were beaten and then shot.

It was September 1948, before the hopes of families of the missing aircrew were dashed and speculation and anxiety replaced by unfathomable sadness. There was no way to lessen the impact of the terrible news that their sons had landed safely, but "later that day they lost their lives at the hands of the Germans". Officials hoped that though "greatly distressing" the truth would avoid further distress by dispelling "inaccurate accounts", and that those responsible had been "convicted and their sentences ranged from 5 to 20 years imprisonment to death by hanging". Jim Gillies who had left a fortnight after his 19th birthday, returned just after his 21st a very different man. He would return to study and become a Sydney Dental Surgeon, a thoroughly less exciting career than he experienced between 1943 and 1945, but that was reassuring.

The last Bomber Command attack on Berlin took place on the night of 21/22 April as Soviet forces prepared to enter the city centre. Small tactical support raids continued over ensuing days, but the destruction of the oil refinery at Vallo, Tonsberg, Norway, by 107 Lancasters on the night of 25/26 April was Bomber Command's last major strategic raid. On 7 May 1945, General Dwight D Eisenhower, accompanied by British, French and Russian authorities accepted the unconditional surrender of German forces from 0001 on 9 May 1945.

TWELVE

"No one has asked me before how much I have missed my brother all these years"

Lionel Rattle

Wild flowers cover the red earth across the flat endless horizon. This year the yellows and white blossoms and clusters of sturt pea triumph over salt bush and scrub. Water fills previously hard-cracked water courses, flows over banks and submerges the bases of eucalyptus. Menindee Lakes had been a virtual dry plain mere months ago – now it is Menindee Ocean – small waves picked up by the fresh westerly wind lap bitumen, which had never seen water before. In western New South Wales the people rejoice – it is the 100-year flood bringing so much new life – after the 100-year drought. This is how it is in the harsh Australian outback – a land of extremes where only the most resilient survive. It was to this region of extremes that the Chigwidden family came, from Wales, UK. The shared experience of these regions was mining, but in every other way the region of birth and the land to which they came were truly a world apart. Jim Chigwidden is a sprightly 84. Having lived in Broken Hill all his life he knows the harshness of Australia and also its beauty – the strong colours that inspired artist Pro Hart to escape the gloom of the mines. Jim speaks of escaping the mines and of how his brother John (Jack) couldn't wait to escape the pit – Jack joined the RAAF and went to war.

Their father Peter Chigwidden was one of the devout Catholic Welsh pioneers who journeyed so far at the end of the previous century. He was one of 12 children and he and wife Kathleen (Kit) added seven to the Chigwidden clan, with Jack being the eldest and Jim the youngest. Seen through the eyes of a young boy life was simple. In hindsight Jim realises how poor they were growing up. The family regularly went without and often the only meat they had was the rabbit Jack and his brothers caught. It was taken for granted that they would descend into the mine as soon as they were old enough. "Jack hated the mine" Jim recalls. It was black, dirty, stifling, claustrophobic, exhausting and dangerous. The stark Broken Hill Miners' Memorial attests to the dangers. Boys as young as 12 and men as old as 65 were killed, and the reason for their deaths: "Fell down shaft, Explosion, Rock Fall, Crushed by Ore Truck, Lead Poisoning, Struck by Loco". Jack Chigwidden trained as a carpenter but there was little other work in Broken Hill not directly involved with the mines. For him the advent of World War II was a blessed relief, although this could never be suggested out loud.

On the other side of the world in a different century, a tall lanky Dutchman studies a tablet in a neat local cemetery in the town of Tilburg, The Netherlands. One gravestone is engraved:

28155 Flight Sergeant J J Chigwidden
Royal Australian Air Force
21st July 1944 Age 33

His Duty Nobly Done Always Remembered

Jack Chigwidden never returned to Broken Hill. Tilburg City Archivist, Gerrit Kobes, was touched by the grave of the airman from so far away and determined that the town records should contain more information about the man. The more he investigated the more Australians he found; each left behind a grieving family; each airman was their own story. Another Jack, Flight Officer Jack Stewart Nott, had perhaps the most remarkable and tragic story of all the Australians who flew British bombers and who are now part of Tilburg history. Gerrit's quest is

Gerrit Kobes and Commonweath Graves Tilbury.
The grave of Jack Chigwidden.

typical, of a strong bond that formed between individuals of different nationalities brought together by the vestiges of war.

Jack Chigwidden (28155) lost no time in enlisting. Yes there was the desire to protect the world from Nazi rampage, but it was also an escape from the pit, and the opportunity to travel to Wales, the home of his forefathers, which Jack could never envisage affording. He was fit and 29 and very willing to undertake anything the RAAF asked of him. There was no space left on his "Application for Air Crew" forms, Jack wrote everything he could think of. He had passed his Intermediate exam but hoped they wouldn't notice he failed maths A and B, English and chemistry. He worked in his father's butcher shop until he attended technical college and studied Carpentry, Drawing and Maths. He wrote Timberman as his occupation when he enlisted at the mobile RAAF recruiting centre in June 1940. The RAAF initially considered him for a trade but Jack failed the Carpenter's test. The recruiting officer, however, wrote that Jack was of a "Clean and tidy appearance. Pleasant sort of chap. Appears to have cheerful disposition and good manners", and suitable as "Airman Guard".

Jack Chigwidden stuck to his desire to be aircrew and convinced the RAAF that they should test him – he was deemed "exceptional".

Considered observer material his instructor wrote; "Was so keen on the subject matter...he undertook a preliminary course on navigation", and that Jack was, "keen, diligent and with good service spirit". Jack was delighted because he realised, at 31, he was approaching an age too old for aircrew. He had at this stage been in the RAAF for 15 months and was a Sergeant. Never had anyone been so happy to be demoted to Aircraftsman – Jack had made it, he was aircrew. In March 1943 Jack bade farewell to Beatrice, his wife of two months, as well as the large Chigwidden clan, particularly little brother Jim, and left the strong hues of the New South Wales far west.

LEFT: *Flight Sergeant Jack Chigwidden front left with the Queen and Princess Elizabeth.* RIGHT: *Jim Chigwidden with Jack.*

It was May 1944 when he and his crew joined their first operational Squadron, RAF 622. In July 1944, King George VI, the Queen, and Princess Elizabeth, visited RAF Station Mildenhall, Jack was introduced and had his photograph taken with Queen Elizabeth and the Princess. To him, it was amazing that a "timberman" from Broken Hill had gone to England and met the Queen. How far was he from the Broken Hill coal pit? Sixteen days later Jack and his crew were shot down over Holland.

There was a valued connection with Holland that continued for the Chigwidden family of Broken Hill. Dutchwoman Annemarie Vossen and her husband Jan were members of the Dutch underground and had aided Allied flyers with shelter, food, clothing and money, and helped return them to England. After the war they were concerned by the 77 Allied war graves in the Tilburg cemetery, graves of young men from countries distant, "who gave their lives for our freedom in the war". They maintained the graves and contacted many families, some of whom visited. Jan died in 1959 and authorities agreed he could be buried "with his Allied friends". Annemarie continued to care for the graves and families and the lively 80 year old travelled to Australia to visit the Chigwidden family in 1979. She marvelled at how vastly different the terrain and colours were when comparing the countries from where Jack came and where he had lain since July 1944.[1]

Annemarie Vossen tending the Allied war graves in the 1950s and visiting Broken Hill in 1979.

When responsibility for war graves was taken over by the Commonwealth War Graves Commission the involvement of Dutch volunteer carers did not cease. Individuals continued to lay flowers and observe anniversaries and birthdays of the men who lay in their village cemeteries and importantly they maintained communication with their families. Men like Tilburg archivist Gerrit Kobes ensure the link between then and now continues. He can speak knowledgeably about Flight Sergeant Peter (Stuart) Wade (426719) and Flight Sergeant Malcolm Henry Graydon (419443), two young Australians who should not be forgotten, because they are buried in his town of Goirle.

Stuart Wade laboured with his brothers on their father's property known as Glengyle, Brookstead, via Toowoomba, Queensland. He wouldn't take umbrage with being called a "bushie", but unlike his brother Bob, who was a natural with horses, and who would join the Light Horse regiment, "Stuart hated the sight of horses and would rather ride a bike".[2] Stuart had faster, modern mounts in mind and desperately wanted to join the RAAF as a pilot. He knew there were spaces in his 1941 application form, particularly with regards to education. He attended Cecil Plains State School and the Toowoomba's Bullocks' College where he sat for his Junior Certificate, but he had to write "No" to the question of "Was certificate obtained?" and "Unknown" to the questions as to what subjects he had passed and which he did not. Stuart had second thoughts about the nationality of his parents William and Violet, and crossed out "British" and in its place wrote "Aust". Something caught the recruiter's eye and Stuart was enlisted six months later when he was still 21. His wings resplendent on his uniform, Stuart Wade departed for overseas on 25 May 1943, and was killed exactly a year later on 25 May 1944.

Posted to RAF 76 Stuart's crew was English with exception of Malcolm Graydon his Wireless Operator/Air Gunner.[3] The two Australians felt comfortable in each other's company, were the same age and Graydon had also been born in a rural township, Korumburra, nestled in the scenic foothills of the Strzelecki Ranges in Victoria's South Gippsland. Having travelled around the globe together they died together, shot down by night-fighter pilot, German ace, Hauptmann Heinz Struning, who claimed their Halifax as his 47th kill.[4] According to their Commanding Officer, Stuart Wade had impressed. He "could be relied on in an emergency" and because of "his cheerfulness he had made many friends". They had been attacking Aachen, Germany. Only the Rear Gunner, RAF Sergeant R J Head survived to become a POW – the average age of the six killed was just 21. All Stuart's parents could do was "pray he will be reported safe and well". When his death was confirmed Violet Wade wrote to her friend Mary Hogg; "We do feel so sad. Stuart was such a good boy and a favourite with everyone".[5] In this letter she also mourned a member of Mary's family, Young Will Hogg.

Mary's RAAF husband, Thomas (Tom) Ballantine Hogg (8765) had been sent to the UK as ground crew, and led to believe he could qualify as a Flight Engineer. The RAF did not agree, but would not allow Tom to return to Australia. At least in England he could keep an eye on his nephew, Young Will. Tom Hogg was the youngest of six sons and had lost a brother, Jim, in World War I at the 1917 Battle of Messines. Jim had been struggling to keep the family's Darling Downs farm on track with two of his brothers already serving on battlefields overseas. One day he received a white feather from some misguided and ill-informed district ladies, so he enlisted and never returned. Brother William Hogg, father of Young Will, was a Light Horseman in Egypt, Gallipoli and France, and lost an eye, but returned to the family's Queensland rural interests. Brother Richard (Dick) also served with the Light Horses in Egypt, at Gallipoli with his brother William, and in Palestine before returning home. Their brother George got as far as Egypt before World War I ended. But this was another world war and the two youngest brothers enlisted. Joe, a Doctor, was deployed to New Guinea, and Tom, was stuck in England as airforce ground crew.

William Hogg had lost a brother in a European war in 1917, and been wounded himself; now in another European war, he lost his son. Flight Sergeant William George Hogg (429322) was dead at 19; his RAAF 460 Lancaster was shot down in the skies above France where William himself had fought in World War I. Young Will's remains were buried in Maubeuge-Centre Cemetery, close to the border with Belgium, 81 miles (130 km) from where his uncle was killed. RAAF Corporal Tom Hogg, stuck in England, was bereft now that his young nephew was dead. Violet Wade, speaking of her son Stuart, and Young Will: "We really had great hopes...it was an awful suspense waiting. We were so sad. ...We must be brave as these boys certainly were. They have made the supreme sacrifice that we may live in peace."

The parents of Flight Sergeant Malcolm Graydon were also struggling to make sense of it all. Malcolm Graydon senior, like the father of his son's pilot, had survived World War I. Private Graydon (No.869) had been a member of the 4th Reinforcement 4th Light Horse, having enlisted in November 1914. He was then moved to the Australian Army Ordnance Corps and in April 1918 suffered a "gunshot wound". He continued to serve in France, with the "Cyclist Corps", then as a Lance Corporal with Corps Armourers. He survived the European carnage of 1914–18 when so many of his mates had not, but the horrors of the battlefield remained. By the late 1930s he was enjoying working with his son, selling groceries and hardware in Melbourne. Malcolm Graydon believed his son of the same name would be safer in the skies than in the trenches. Warfare had changed though and the words "cannon fodder" were applied differently now.

Flight Sergeant Malcolm Henry Graydon

Flight Sergeant Peter Stuart Wade (courtesy Bob Wade).

In a quiet part of Tilburg, just one Dutch city to which Australian families are tied, there is a memorial, an imposing rock on which there are the names of three airmen. They came from three nations, England, Canada and Australia, three airmen who were killed close-by, not in an aircraft crash, but who were murdered and have no known graves – the Australian was Sergeant Jack Stewart Nott (421543). Jack Nott like Jack Chigwidden was a man who worked with his hands, a blue collar worker, a bricklayer, whose life would be honest and hardworking but with limited opportunities. His world was turned upside down and for a couple of years his life was the stuff of fiction, wilder and more dangerous than he could ever have imagined. Jack Nott's family came from Armidale, NSW. He enlisted on the 1 February 1942 at 23 and was mustered Navigator. He needed to apply himself to exacting courses but passed and arrived in the UK with others as keen as himself to fight against the Nazi regime. After additional Bombardier training he joined RAF 77 Squadron in November 1943 as a Bomb Aimer, his first flight was the same day. In keeping with the axiom, his first five flights were hazardous and fortunate. Against Leipzig mechanical trouble caused an early return. Against Berlin another early return when the port outer engine stopped. The next flights were no less eventful but at least nothing ceased working, just the odd flak souvenir. In February, attacks against Leipzig and Berlin, and three mine-laying operations. March there were raids against Meulan, Trappes, and Le Mans, and April brought more mine laying.

Flying Officer Jack Stewart Nott (courtesy Tony Nott).

Letters home were not easy to write; there was so much to say but so little that would escape the censor's block-out pen. Jack had married Airlie and his son Anthony was born on 30 June 1941 before he departed from Australia. He could write that he had been commissioned, but like others he was unable to include anything of his real feelings, of how the strain may have been beginning to take a toll; how leaving Australia in July 1942 meant he had missed precious months of his son's life. Sometimes, being the only Australian in an all RAF crew attached to an RAF squadron was lonely. As much as his crew endeavoured to include him, they could return home on leave to their wives and growing families.

Flying Officer Jack Nott (421543) and his RAF crew took off in their Halifax on the night of 16/17 June 1944 to bomb Sterkrade. The bomber was shot down over Holland and only three survived the crash.[6] Jack was one of them and set out on his own managing to evade German patrols. Crew members Navigator Flight Sergeant J M Bulmer (1474195) and Wireless Operator/Air Gunner Flight Sergeant J W Needham (1459553) were not as fortunate and became POWs. Nott's luck held out and Jack connected with the Dutch Underground. At the Van Kampens home in Neunen he met up with 21-year-old RAF pilot Flight Lieutenant Ronald Arthur Walker (149550). Walker had been the sole survivor when his RAF 83 Lancaster blew up and he found himself on the ground, stunned, but alive. The two were handed along the line from one safe house to another. On 29 June dressed in civilian clothes, the airmen set off with Dutch underground members on bicycles to ride to the village of Waalre, about 6 miles (10 km) from Eindhoven. When the German police stopped the first in the party and examined the Dutchman's papers the others quickly took evasive routes. They linked up again and Jack and Ron Walker were hidden in a linen factory owned by Frans van Dijk. Next they were taken to the home of the four van Moorsel sisters. The risk these Dutch citizens were taking was not lost on the airmen. There was now a third member of their party, 23-year-old Canadian Flight Officer Roy Edward Carter (J/28855). Together they stayed in the Tilburg home of Jacoba (Coba) Pulskens. False papers had been received and it was hoped that shortly a car would arrive to take them to a point from which they could be smuggled back to England.

Their spirits were buoyant and they felt relieved enough to be able to consider their future freedom, but this boy's own adventure story would not have the standard happy ending. Having tortured a member of the Underground the Gestapo was alerted to the imminent transfer of Allied aircrew. Cars arrived and members of the German Security Police burst into the Pulskens home on Sunday 9 July 1944 – the three unarmed British airmen were still at the breakfast table. Ordered outside into the yard they were shot by machine gun by Michael Rotschoff. Karl Cremer came over the wall into the yard and shot the prostrate bodies of the

British officers to ensure they were dead. Coba Pulskens was ordered to fetch a sheet to cover the bodies. The 60-year-old Dutch woman went into the house and returned with a large Dutch flag which she had been keeping until The Netherlands was liberated from German occupation. The possession of Dutch flags was forbidden and this last brave act sealed her fate. Coba spent seven months in solitary confinement before being deported to Ravensbruck Concentration Camp. In February 1945 she took the place of a woman with small children in an attempt to save their lives and died in the gas chamber.

In an attempt to hide their crime the Germans took the bodies of the murdered airmen to the Vught Concentration Camp for cremation and the ashes were scattered. For some time, all the Nott family was told was that Jack was "missing". After the war the nephew of Coba Pulskens came forward. Nico lived opposite his aunt and witnessed some of what took place. Other neighbours came forward to speak of the bravery of Coba and the defencelessness of the Allied flyers. In a July 1945 War Criminal Trial four Germans were found guilty of the murders and hanged.[7] In 1947 the city of Tilburg erected a plaque in memory of Coba and the three airmen. On 27 October 1994, a large granite memorial stone was unveiled in the green area opposite the Pulskens home, as part of the 50th anniversary of Dutch liberation. Relatives of the English and Canadian airmen were present as was Tony Nott, the son who never knew his father.

LEFT: *The memorial to Coba Pulskens.*
RIGHT: *Tony Nott and the memorial to his father Jack.*

Australians could be forgiven for not knowing where Wagin is. It is a very small town in another of Australia's harsher, but more colourful, landscapes. Wagin, Western Australia is a pale reflection of a more prosperous past. Families followed the jobs and the jobs moved with the mining revolution north of Perth. In a quiet street there is a beautifully restored home, a bed and breakfast owned by Beverley and Brian Anderson. Beverley called it Buckinghams because it was Buckingham Mill, Western Australia where her father was born. "I am not an emotional person but whenever I think of my father I get teary". She would have liked to have known her father, Pilot Officer Edward (Eddie) Oliver Deveson (415625), husband of Eileen, of East Fremantle, but she was only three when he was killed. Edward Deveson was a foreman at Westralian Soaps before he enlisted in the RAAF at 26. "Dad was only 5 ft 4 in [1.62 m] but apparently he made up for it in his physique. He was gymnast and very strong". By early 1944 Air Gunner Eddie Deveson found himself attached to RAF Pathfinders Squadron 635. He excelled and was appointed Squadron Gunnery Leader.

LEFT: *Eileen, Beverley and Eddie Deveson*
RIGHT: *Pilot Officer Edward Oliver Deveson.*

Family clearly meant a great deal to Eddie Deveson because among his personal effects were 53 telegrams, 73 letters, and 72 airgraphs – they were his connection to the family he had not seen since early 1942. It would not be from RAF or Australian authorities that Beverley learnt more of her father's crew, last operation and death, but from the people of the Dutch town of Hoogeveen. Albert Metselaar grew up with stories of brave British aircrew who crashed and were buried in his village cemetery. It was very early on the morning of Friday 24 March 1944 when villagers saw "a big bomber flying above Hoogeveen like a burning torch". Deveson's crew were returning from bombing Berlin when they were hit by flak. The aircraft was very low and flying toward the town, but suddenly banked and altered direction. A Dutch fire warden observed the Lancaster flying over the German anti-aircraft station: "The German soldiers could see the left engine was on fire. Over the radio they called on the pilot to land. Then the Germans said 'Go to Hell'."

Those on the ground watched while a German fighter "gave the death-blow to the burning machine with a few volleys of gun-fire". When the bomber exploded in the air, wreckage and bodies disintegrated. One body was retrieved from a house roof. The Dutch asked German soldiers if they could douse the smouldering fuselage and remove the remaining two. As far as the villagers were concerned the sudden final change of course was to avoid crashing into the middle of the town. It was also believed that with wounded crew onboard unable to bale out, Eddie Deveson stayed. They looked upon the pilot and his crew as heroes and were displeased when the Germans would not accord the men a military funeral, and gave the Hitler salute, because they referred to the crew as "terror flyers". Under the menacing guns of German soldiers the Dutch clergyman insisted on speaking English as well as German during the ceremony and six villagers placed themselves in further danger by walking to the graves and reverently throwing handfuls of dirt onto the coffins below.

The connection between Beverley and those who tended her father's grave was tangible and important and encouraged her and Brian to make a pilgrimage to the gravesite. Unbeknown to the couple, Albert Metselaar organised a special ceremony for the occasion and townsfolk attended in support. They were accorded great care and prominence by the people of Hoogeveen. On 4 May each year, the Dutch people honour all Allied foreign military who died in World War II and are buried in Dutch soil. For this ceremony attended by villagers Albert organises

ABOVE: *Albert Metselaar and* (BELOW) *the graves of Pilot Officer Edward Deveson and crew.*

Dutch defence personnel, a band, a bugler and school children to attend the graves.

The home of Ada de Lange-Timmerman is distinctively Dutch, the beautifully cared for old stone building is mere steps from the canal along which barges have plied the region's trade. Ada knows a great deal about Australia and keeps the long-standing correspondence she has had with two West Australian women in a large folder. In a neat home in Perth another woman is also pleased to share her correspondence and photographs received from her Dutch friend Ada. Most of all Marjorie speaks of her brother John Parr Ion.

Flight Sergeant John Parr Ion (427833) came from the Perth suburb of Wembley. He was the middle child and only son of Thomas and Olive Ion of Wembley. Flicking through the black and white family photos Marjorie wondered where the time had gone, from when John stood with her and their sister Norma, the little boy slightly knock kneed but with his characteristic happy expression. He was a reasonable student at South Perth State School, Perth Boys' School and City Commercial College. John was one of those blokes with an easy cheerful grin.

LEFT: *Flight Sergeant John Parr Ion.*
RIGHT: *John Marjorie and Norma Ion (courtesy Marjorie Manley).*

The simple innocence of their middle class family was lost when a war intruded. Now John at 18 was in the RAAF, and the family really did not know what to expect. He seemed excited and happy even though: "They didn't make me a pilot like I wanted to be but made me a Wireless Air Gunner". John had been "working the hardest I have ever done. When I left Perth I did not know what I was in for". After months of hard "swatting" he passed his course at No.1 WAGS Ballarat, in December 1942. His only excitement since leaving Perth was the four days leave he took in Adelaide after gunnery training at Victor Harbour; "the people of Adelaide were grand to us especially the girls, boy and I can tell you there are some beauties". With characteristic youthful, naive optimism, he wrote, "I'll soon be a Squadron Leader", because he had already passed "from the rank of ACII to Leading Aircraftsman". If he passed "all my courses, I will be a Sergeant in another seven months".[8]

On 27 August 1944 John wrote to his sister Marjorie, giving her some typical John banter about her impending marriage. He added "for goodness sake don't smash the (family) car. ...I will want the car to drive down to City Beach at Christmas time" because after a couple of years in England "I can get some of my good Australian suntan back again". Clearly John was counting his hours and operations and confident he would be home for Christmas 1944. He didn't think that he would be free of war but that he "would be out there bombing the Japs in our Lancasters". He promised to write in a week.

Flight Sergeant John Parr Ion (427833) was the Wireless Operator/ Air Gunner of RAAF 460 Lancaster PB176, which took off at 1303 on 31 August 1944 to attack the V2 storage site at Raimbert, France. The skipper was Australian Pilot Officer Linley Joseph Grey (418394) 22, from Melbourne. The Navigator was Flight Sergeant William Edward Hathaway (432167) 31, from Long Jetty. Sergeant Rex Coates (417699) 21, from Adelaide was the Bomb Aimer, and the Engineer was RAF Sergeant Ronald Tomkinson (1750255) 21, from Lancashire. The guns were manned by Warrant Officer Robert Le Gay Brereton (412546) 22, from The Rock, New South Wales and 23-year-old RAF Sergeant Ronald Robert Curphey Morris (1494879). Nothing further was heard from the crew of PB176. The body of John Parr Ion was washed ashore at Colijnsplaat on 3rd October 1944.

To Joseph and Viola Grey the RAAF 460 Commanding Officer would write: "The loss of your son has deprived the Squadron of a Pilot of outstanding skill, and his devotion to duty and high standard of courage in face of dangers inspired us all." To Tom and Olive Ion the RAAF 460 Commanding Officer would write: "The loss of your son has deprived the Squadron of a Wireless Operator of outstanding skill, and his devotion to duty and high standard of courage in face of dangers inspired us all." To Herbert and Nellie Coates the RAAF 460 Commanding Officer would write: "The loss of your son has deprived the Squadron of a Bomb Aimer of outstanding skill...". And so the letters went to each Australian family.

There were only eleven months between John and his younger sister Norma and she would recall with great affection how close they were as young children particularly in mischievous undertakings. It was a bond that endured as they became teenagers: "I still recall watching him walking up our street, rucksack on his back, as he turned around for a final wave before boarding the trolley bus for Perth and eventual departure. ...more and more families received telegrams advising them that their loved ones had been killed or were missing in action, but somehow we bathed in the belief this wouldn't happen to us – but it DID." It was important for Norma to save her money so that one day she could visit "where John was buried". It took 40 years but she got there and on John's grave "I placed a rose for Mum and brought her back a small stone to keep".

The connection with The Netherlands, and with the succession of women who cared for the grave of John and the unknown: "Soldier of the war 1939–45" buried in the other grave became increasingly important. For many years Ada de Lange-Timmerman had travelled with a friend to place flowers on John's grave on his birthday. In August 2004 she wrote to John's sisters Marjorie and Norma:

> This special month my mind is particularly on your late brother John. On the 31st of August it is 60 years ago that he died and found his last place in the grave in Colijnsplaat. ...I will go to the cemetery...and bring flowers, on behalf of you. ...We all, you in Australia and we here in Colijnsplaat shall have communication in our minds and our hearts. Together we shall think of John and so many young boys of that time and saying prayers for them. ...Sorry for my poor English. ADA

By coincidence, the sisters of Pilot Officer Allan Robert Hart (412434), the only son of Norman and Ruby of Murrumbarrah, New South Wales were also named Norma and Marjorie. Allan was destined for the family farm known as Tiverton, so after his Intermediate Certificate at Murrumburrah Intermediate High, he ventured onto Yanco Agricultural College. Allan was working on the farm, when at 20, he was caught up in the nationalistic furore, which accompanied the RAAF recruiting team through Harden in mid-1941. So many country lads working on farms with limited opportunities joined the AIF in the previous war, excited by the glamour, mystique and travel opportunities that now attracted country boys to Australia's newest defence force.

The following months were one big adrenalin rush. Nine days shy of his 22nd birthday Allan was with 14 Operating Training Unit. There he teamed up with a Navigator, 20-year-old Flight Sergeant Harold James Boal (409497). Harold was born in Echuca, Victoria, where he attended Barmah East State before gaining first class honours at Nathalia High. When Harry enlisted in September 1941 he was only 18 and was working as a Clerk in the accounts branch of the PMG Department, Melbourne. The children of Charles and Lily Boal were close, Val Duncan clearly remembers Harry as a "sensitive, gentle, loving boy" who surprised the family by enlisting – it seemed out of character, perhaps it was because his elder brother was deemed medically unfit for military service.

Allan Hart (courtesy Jo Jordan).   *Harold Boal (courtesy Val Duncan).*

The crew with the baby-faced pilot and navigator were a mixed bunch. RAF Sergeant Leslie Clifton (1146496) 24, was from Nottingham. Warrant Officer Gordon Ivan Williams (R/119950) 21, the Bomb Aimer was from Manitoba, Canada. The Wireless Operator/Air Gunner was RAF Sergeant William Joseph Jones (1131932) 21, from Liverpool, while RAF Londoner, Sergeant Douglas Frederick Hicks (1397995) was the Middle Upper Gunner. Flight Sergeant Charles Melville Price (R182206) from Toronto, Ontario, was positively old at 30, as well as being the only married man in the crew. Their first operational Squadron was RAF 97, which was strange given this was a Pathfinder Squadron. The crew was killed 22 days later, another inexperienced crew sacrificed on the altar of Berlin. It seems Allan Hart realized this would be their future because on the day of this operation he wrote to his mother "its curtains for me tonight".[9]

Lancaster JB659 was attacked by a night fighter on 31 January 1944 and the cockpit, blasted with cannon fire, separated from the fuselage and plummeted to earth with Hart and Williams inside. The rest of the aircraft, with two of its four engines still running, crashed into a farmhouse and burst into flames. Six members of the Van der Bijl family, who were asleep in their home, were killed. Older children sleeping in a separate barn survived. The bodies of Allan Hart and Gordon Williams were recovered but such was the force of the crash that the Lancaster had penetrated 26 ft (8 m) into soft earth taking the rest of the crew with it. The RAF investigation team would list 2,210 pieces of wreckage from the crash, which was strewn over a wide area. The holes in the ground made by the engines were clearly visible after the war, and in fact, the large crater caused by the Lancaster was later turned into a lake. Authorities deemed it too "impracticable" to retrieve the fuselage with five airmen within: "It is proposed that the spot where the aircraft is buried should be accepted as the grave of the crew who must be presumed to have been in the aircraft when it crashed and whose bodies have not been recovered, and a suitable memorial erected on the spot."

The families and Dutch citizens campaigned to have the bomber raised so that the men within could be given a Christian funeral. Fifty seven years later, excavation for expanded port facilities at Amsterdam eventuated in the Lancaster being raised. It was with very mixed emotions that relatives attended a ceremony on 29 November 2001, in Zwanenburg, Netherlands. Crates of parts of the Lancaster had been retrieved and returned to RAF Wickenby with plans to rebuild JB659. Forensic investigation determined the remains of five crew members, but all that remained could be buried in a single coffin beside Allan Hart and Gordon Williams. Jo Jordan, niece of Allan Hart, and Val Duncan, sister to Harold Boal, were present. They were invited to the UK to observe the initial rebuilding of JB659. Val Duncan declined. In time the Port of Amsterdam Authority created a memorial, which featured a twisted propeller from the Lancaster and a plaque describing how seven airmen from three nations and a family of six had died in war, for which Val was grateful. Trees were planted for the crew, two eucalyptus trees for the Australians, two maples for the Canadians and three oaks for the Britons.

Jo Jordan would recall: "My grandparents never got over Allan's death. They remained very sad". Before they died James and Ruby Hart paid for a stained glass window in St Paul's Anglican Church, Murrumburrah, New South Wales, in their only son's memory. Val Duncan grew up in a family deeply saddened by the loss of a son and brother. "My elder brother regularly attended Sunday church but after Harold's death he would no longer go and said 'There is no God'". It has been nearly 70 years but tears trickle down Val Duncan's cheeks for a lost brother, but also for the part of her lost on that terrible day in January 1944.

The Perth suburb of Subiaco catered for those attracted by the discovery of gold in the Yilgarn district in the 1880s. Separated from the wealthy suburb of West Perth by a railway track Subiaco became known as a "working class suburb", a description which never fazed those living there. For most, Aussies Rules was a religion they pursued with the strongest conviction, and as long as they could watch Subiaco play footie, life was good. Bob and Phil Emrose were typical district kids, who felt utterly free riding their bikes to district jetties to fish for gardies and yellowtail, or leaping into the cool waters to escape Perth's scorching summer heat. The Emrose boys realised they were more fortunate than many of their neighbours because their father, Stanley, was a commercial traveller for W D & H O Wills Tobacconists, and their family could afford their home and the basics of life. Although their father's presence was missed during the week, the weekends were wonderful. Stan had a car at a time when this was less common. He would take his sons and their friends further afield to swim at Cottesloe, and one year he took them to the Australian Grand Prix held at Applecross – life was innocent and good. Trevor Preston was a close friend of the Emrose boys: "Australia was at war, but life in Perth did not change much – except for the presence of slit trenches in backyards and streets, blackout provisions at night, petrol rationing, and an occasional air-raid alert as the year wore on.[10]" But then life changed forever.

Bob Emrose was a good student and finished his formal education at Wesley College, before assuming a clerical position as a shipping clerk while studying Accountancy at night. Bob, predictably called Ginger due to his auburn hair, convinced their father Stanley to sign the RAAF enlistment papers when Bob was still only 18. It was 4 August 1942 when his war began and Bob, now RAAF 427592, was mustered Wireless Operator/Air Gunner. Soon he was in the UK and feeling great to be chosen by an RAAF pilot in a crew that included five Aussies. Together the crew were posted to RAAF 467. Better still was the fact that they were all from Western Australia so the Australian Football League was much discussed. Eventually they hoped to convince the two Englishmen in the crew that this was "the only football code worth following".

Flight Sergeant Robert Keith Emrose.   *Mick and Phil Emrose.*   *Phil, Ina and Bob Emrose.*

The pilot was 22-year old Flying Officer Alexander (Alec) Carlisle Findlay (415937), born in Northam, Western Australia. RAF Sergeant Harry Hemingway (1492963) was 21 and the Navigator. The other RAF member was the Engineer Sergeant David Henry Francis Burton (1593192). The Middle Upper Gunner Flying Officer William (Bill) John Woods (415002) 27, was born in Katanning, Western Australia. He was the son of George and Kathleen Woods. The family moved to the Perth suburb where Bill worked as a clerk before he enlisted in June 1941.

Flight Sergeant Carl Francis Larkin (427387) 29, was the Bomb Aimer, born in Beaconsfield, close to Fremantle, and was a school teacher. Flight Sergeant Neil Willington (436767), though born in Broken Hill, New South Wales, moved to Western Australia, and was a dairy farm worker before enlisting three weeks after he turned 18 in April 1943. His place was in the rear gun turret. Their operational life lasted less than a week.

On the night of 19/20 September 1944 their target was Rheydt, near the German city of Mönchengladbach. The Bomb Aimer Carl Larkin remembers the relaxed attitude just prior to the operation. The crew "sat in the grass...smoking and talking". The bomb doors of the Lancaster were open so Larkin went to inspect the bomb load. Several crew members wandered over and chalked "remarks" on the bombs, none that Larkin believed he could repeat. Very soon the recurring mixture of "tension and restlessness" took over and they were pleased to get onboard and into the familiar routine. They were quickly over target and Larkin lined up the bombsight as they commenced the run in. With bombs gone they had begun to pull away when Neil Willington shouted there was a fighter approaching. Larkin said "my inside seemed to compress together" red flecks of tracer shot up from below. The Lancaster was thrown violently as if hit by a great force and someone shouted "We are on fire". Larkin went to remove the front escape hatch cover but the wind caught and jammed it across the opening. The bomber went into a steep dive and Larkin shot forward into the nose. He remembered thinking "If I don't get out of this I'll be killed".[11] After a great deal of pushing and shoving and good luck, Carl Larkin found himself "swinging gently in the darkness" beneath a canopy of silk but watching with horror at the Lancaster "hurtling towards the ground...lit by the fire trailing from beneath".

Pilot Alec Findlay evaded capture, Larkin and Willington, became POWs but Dennis Burton, Jack Woods, Harry Hemingway, and the boy from Subiaco, Bob Emrose were all killed. For a short period Stan and Ina Emrose had a flicker of hope as the RAAF notified them that their boy's crew were POW. Then on Bob's RAAF record a clerk wrote: "Previously incorrectly reported as 'believed prisoner of war' remains 'missing air operations'". Such misinformation was cruel on families awaiting word. Shortly afterwards the large red letters spelling "Deceased" were stamped on Robert Emrose's service record. He was 21.

Phil Emrose, his brother, enlisted in the RAN rather than the RAAF, and served on corvettes. He survived the war and lived a full life, which included raising seven children. It would be his son Michael who visited Bob's grave in Bergen-op-Zoom, Holland, on behalf of a father who lost his only brother in 1944.[12]

Jeffrey Laing and Phil Emrose never met, which is a shame, because they had a great deal in common. Both mourned a brother lost in their 21st and 22nd years, respectively. The Laing family owned farms that surrounded much of Denmark, a pretty town close enough to the Great Australian Bight to feel winds loaded with salt spray. Ted was good at school and trained to be a school teacher. His brother Jeffrey remembers Ted as being "a great worker, reliable and friendly". It is likely that this was why Ted sped through his pilot training and was in England by July 1942. At Operating Training Unit he teamed up with Twenty Men Navigator, Keith Webber. On a night cross-country training flight their Wellington had a near miss. The bomber lost its starboard airscrew, but Ted was able to make an emergency landing. This impressed instructors and the crew were posted to RAF 103.

On 1 January 1943 Ted wrote a letter to a fellow Lancaster pilot about

LEFT: *The graves of Flight Sergeants Edward Vivian Laing and Keith Robert Webber.* RIGHT: *Jeffrey Laing with a photograph of Ted.*

the fun in the sergeant's mess over Christmas and how he mourned the operational death of a mutual mate – "tough luck" Ted called it. Twenty days later Ted, Keith Webber and their crew were ordered to attack Germany. As they taxied to take-off a mechanical fault became evident. The fault was fixed and authorities insisted they continue with the raid even though it was well known that a single bomber was an easy target. In Holland on the night of the raid 13-year-old Ada Jongedijk, who lived in the Dutch village of Enschede, heard a loud noise and ventured outside. "The plane was on fire, I saw the pilots strapped in their seats. Their heads were forward so they were unconscious or already dead. ... Terrible was the fate of those airmen."

Some 60 years later the Lancaster pilot to whom Ted wrote on 1 January 1943, finally found Ted's brother, Jeff, and gave him the letter.

The colours are softer in Griffith than further west in New South Wales. The town that would become a city was established in 1916 as part of the Murrumbidgee Irrigation Area (MIA). Griffith and neighbouring Leeton were fortunate in many ways, not least of all being designed by Walter Burley Griffin, the architect of the nation's capital, Canberra. The Riverina towns would soon boast abundant fruit, vegetables and wine. The Gibbs family were pioneers of an earlier period and their farming interests were more the traditional grazing. William (Lionel) Gibbs was a remarkable bloke by any stretch of the imagination.

He wrote Farmer Grazier on his RAAF application, but flying was in his blood. Lionel spent time on horses and was a member of the local Light Horse militia, but was fascinated by being in the vast spaces above. The son of William and Isabella built a glider in 1935 with the assistance of his brother Oswald. Younger brother Harold (Digger) held the lantern. They worked at night, hand crafting pieces over three years. The glider project caused some mutterings among the old timers who were more at ease with things as they were than with "new fangled things", and who firmly believed "man was not meant to fly". Lionel was determined he and the glider would fly and it was hauled into the air by a 500ft- (152m)-long rope attached to a new 1936 Chevrolet Ute on the Gibbs Willow Bend property. It took a few attempts but the glider became airborne for approximately 13 minutes before plummeting to earth.

Lionel Gibbs flew briefly before his glider returned to earth.

It surprised none in the Gibbs family that when war came Lionel applied for RAAF aircrew. He married Dorothy on 9 December 1940 and sailed overseas three days after Christmas. Following wireless operator/air gunner training in Canada and the UK Lionel found himself at 25 Operating Training Unit a year later. He had written to his brother Digger in September, not long after his arrival in the UK, to say "The English people do not seem to be nearly so hospitable as our former hosts, the Canadians". He had "not seen, nor heard, hide or hair, of a fritz or his machines". That changed quickly when his crew was posted to RAF 49 in April 1942, and within six months they were sent to Pathfinders RAF 83. Pilot Officer Lionel Gibbs (402922) and his crew took off in Lancaster W4955 from RAF Wyton in the first half hour of 13 May 1943 to bomb Duisburg, Germany. The Lancaster was hit by anti-aircraft fire and then attacked by a night fighter. The only other Australian onboard, Flight Lieutenant Horace D'Arcy Meadows Ransome (404486), an audit clerk/accountant living in the Brisbane suburb of Corinda, survived, and was taken POW. Pilot Officer Lionel Gibbs and RAF members of his crew were buried in the woods at Amersfoort, Holland.

After the war a parcel from a Dutch farmer arrived at the Gibbs' family home. Lionel's body had fallen onto his land. The farmer removed Lionel's flying helmet and buried it in a tin before the German soldiers arrived. He thought it might be something Lionel's family would like, and it was. In 1986 the Griffith Shire Council received a letter from the Historical Society of Eemnes, a small town in the middle of Holland, seeking information about Pilot Officer Lionel Gibbs of

Willow Bend to be included on a plaque. The following year Lionel's wife Dorothy and brother Digger travelled to The Netherlands for the unveiling of a memorial to Allied aircrew who lay in district cemeteries. Horace Ransome also made the journey, and with much ceremony the memorial was unveiled by Dutch royalty. The sculpture was of five dancing children to symbolize a brighter future than the past.

In Griffith's Pioneer Park 40 historic buildings set in 45 acres (18 hectares) capture that past. From the ceiling of one hangs a dusty, slightly bent, red timber glider in which a young bloke called Lionel Gibbs defied the sceptics and flew.

On 12/13 June 1944 an attack was ordered against the Nordstern synthetic-oil plant in the German north Rhine city of Gelsenkirchen. It was declared a success and would cause a loss to Germany of some 1,000 tons of aviation fuel a day for weeks.[13] Like all operations this came at a human cost and 17 Lancasters or 6.1 per cent of the bomber force did not return. Many of these Lancasters carried Australian aircrew.[14] This was just one Bomber Command Europe operation yet it demonstrated how the effects of the loss of life of Australian aircrew

The war memorial at Eemnes.

rippled across Australia. The legacy would endure long after the death of grieving parents, many decades later as eyes moisten with tears the same comment would be made; "No one has ever asked me before how much I have missed my brother all these years".

One RAAF 460 Lancaster participating in the 12/13 June Gelsenkirchen raid was piloted by 26-year-old Pilot Officer Austin Frederick Roche (5136). Roche grew up with sister Betty in a sprawling comfortable home in Balwyn, north east of the centre of Melbourne. Austin was quiet and reserved and studied at Trinity Grammar intending to become a doctor like his father Cedric, or a veterinarian. His grades did not reach University entry level for those degrees and he worked in several unsatisfying positions until a war gave him both status and a challenging role. His crew was made up of the Navigator, who was Flying Officer James Rollo Fry (422165) 33. Fry was the youngest of six and after attending North Sydney High School he studied Accountancy. This was not his first trip to Europe, since back in 1933 he had travelled to Hungary to attend the 4th World Jamboree as a Scout. Wife Jean gave birth to daughter Glenn while Rollo was in Canada.

Flight Sergeant Robert (Bob) Trevor Hill (20076) 24, was the Bomb Aimer. Born in the New South Wales mid-north-coast town of Bellingen, Bob was one of eight children, although twin sisters died during their first year and his eldest sister Nellie died at 12. The family moved first to Dorrigo where Bob was schooled and then to Bowraville. Bob applied to the RAAF eight times before his persistence wore them down. The training route was a little bumpy and lengthy and it was nearly three years before he was part of this crew. Flight Sergeant Mervyn Thomas Whittenbury (417920), the Rear Gunner, was one of six children, and studied at South Australia's Naracoorte Primary and High Schools. He was another 19 year old eager to leave his junior clerk position and accountancy studies to begin RAAF air gunner training. At 27 Operating Training Unit he was chosen by Aussie pilot Roche. He thought it was great that fellow Air Gunner, RAF Sergeant Gerald Gordon Barker (1894666) was also 19. RAF Flight Sergeant Thomas (Teddy) Edwin Sage (1543242) was the Wireless Operator/Air Gunner, and the Engineer was RAF Sergeant Joseph Beaddie Ross (1673067).

*Flying Officer
James Rollo Fry.*

*Flight Sergeant
Mervyn Thomas Whittenbury.*

The outward flight was incident free, but this only heightened nervousness. The bomb load was gone when the operation came to an abrupt end for Lancaster ME785, Roche and his crew. The Kloosterboer family were woken and saw the bomber on fire and only about 1,000 ft (305 m) off the ground before it exploded. The wreckage landed on or near their farmhouse and barn. They found the bodies of the seven aviators close together, a few with open parachutes, but the rest unopened, indicating that there had been too little time. Hill's wristwatch had stopped at 0130. The crew were buried in the Dutch Olst (Duur) General Cemetery. In a letter posted to his family just before he climbed into the Lancaster, Flying Officer Rollo Fry wrote, "only 8 missions to go".[15] Keith Whittenbury served with the Australian Army and survived the war – his 21-year-old brother did not. Keith continued to speak of his brother, 21-year-old Mervyn, and the effect his death had on his family.

Against Gelsenkirchen on the night of 12/13 June, the skipper of RAF 199 Lancaster ME777 was RAF Flying Officer William George Grant (152306) a 23 year old from Hampshire, who had been awarded the British Empire Medal (BEM). The other Englishman onboard was the Engineer RAF Sergeant Joseph Eric Bawtree (1893164). The rest of the bomber crew were Australians. In the Rear Gunner's turret sat Flying Officer Keith James Moses (432231) who had turned 20 the day before. His parents Frank and Florence lived in the village of Long Flat, on the southern banks of the Hastings River, 18 miles (30 kilometres) from Wauchope. Keith was a typical country lad who enlisted at 18 desperate to find something more exciting than his clerical job. The 22-year-old Wireless Operator/Air Gunner was Flight Sergeant Leslie Thomas Hunt (423242) from Sydney, who was the son of a Newtown butcher. He wrote his occupation as "Photogravure, Associated Newspapers". The longest name in the crew belonged to the Middle Upper Gunner Flying Officer Harry Arthur Bulgar Brown (432525). Harry was 27 and from Blenheim, New Zealand, before relocating to Australia to be a farmer. The Navigator was Flying Officer John Henry Stopp (419738) 28, an accountant with Steamships Trading, Port Moresby, and who was married to Alisa. Though born in Australia's far north town of Cairns, his name would be included on the roll of honour plaque in Mitcham, South Australia. The Bomb Aimer, Flying Officer Herbert William Davies (422143) 34, from Cootamundra, had a Bachelor of Arts and was working as a law clerk. He was married to Sadie. For several of the crew this was their ninth operation, for others it was their seventh.

With no information for more than a year Sadie Davies and Alisa Stopp became increasingly anxious. Sadie wrote how it had been "such a terrific strain all these months, waiting for news", and Alisa said that she still had hope, but "the suspense is terrific". Authorities in Melbourne were awaiting more positive information because they felt they could not partake the only knowledge they had, it would be too upsetting for both widows to know there was a single grave bearing the names "Stopp/Davies" containing "a torso and little else" and further investigation was pending. Amy and Tom Hunt were also struggling with the lack of information of:

Our missing airman, our only child...we both were very upset about the sad news, I had such hopes of him being still alive and that he may have been a nerve case or loss of memory after all the time of waiting for news of him. We both would have been very happy to hear of him being still alive and we would have done all we could for him. I still can't make myself believe he is taken and hope for better news than we got. I am sure you can quite understand how we feel about him. And we miss him terribly our dear boy.

Amy Hunt enclosed two recent photos of her 22-year-old son, who was better known as Mike, just in case he was found suffering from "loss of memory" and added that she was "very worried about his father also". Tom Hunt also wrote begging authorities to "please help find our dear boy". The slightest hope was extinguished when confirmation came that Flight Sergeant Leslie (Mike) Thomas Hunt was buried in the Dutch Zelham Cemetery.

Flying Officer
Harry Brown.

Flying Officer
John Stopp.

Flying Officer
Herbert Davies.

Flight Sergeant Leslie (Mike) Hunt.

Flying Officer Keith Moses.

In a modest home in Queensland, four generations of the Delacour family sit at a table sorting through a collection of documents, photographs, medals, and memorabilia. This is all that is left of Bertie Delacour. It is his nephew Shane Delacour who, with his father Allan, ensures that Bertie, who was shot down on the night of 12/13 June 1944 on an operation against Gelsenkirchen, is not forgotten. The words "Aussie Battlers" fit easily with the name Delacour. These hard-working Australians have a strong sense of family. There were ten children to John and Mary Delacour so they had their hands full, but John was delighted to be surrounded by so much new life and childhood exuberance. John had served on the Western Front in World War I where the lives of so many young men had been extinguished.

Herbert (Bertie) Samuel Delacour was the eldest son in the Delacour tribe and although he grew up in Charters Towers, Queensland, a district better known for hardy, physical men, Bertie was a sensitive bloke who loved to write. His short stories were published in the *Townsville Bulletin* and *The Northern Mine*. Bertie wrote journalist on his RAAF application. Bertie's life, to date was one intent on delighting a reading public with an entertaining yarn. In his new life Bertie was mustered Pilot and left for overseas looking forward to new adventures and hoping that his crew would never hear that he was terrified of frogs. It could be embarrassing to admit that if he got into a fight with his sister Edna, she would chase him with a frog until she prevailed.

On the night of the 12/13 June 1944 Pilot Officer Bertie Delacour (425136) found himself pilot/skipper of an RAF 514 Lancaster full of English and Canadian servicemen. Bertie had chosen an Englishman for his Navigator and he and RAF Flying Officer Roy Picton (151087) worked very well together. RAF Flight Sergeant George Palamountain (1433141) was the Bomb Aimer. RAF Sergeant Albert G Bonham (1580616) was the Wireless Operator/Air Gunner. The Engineer was RAF Sergeant Gerald Martin (1625906). The Middle Upper Gunner was Pilot Officer Spurgeon F Williams (J87116) and Canadian Flight Sergeant George (Don) Savage was the Rear Gunner. Whenever the crew were briefed that the target was Gelsenkirchen, there was a tug at the stomach and lower quadrant of the torso. At this stage of the war only the knowledge that Berlin was the target had a worse effect on the crew. Bertie and his crew couldn't help but be nervous because the night operation would be their last of their tour. Their war would be over, well perhaps, because the crew had been asked to undertake another tour with the elite Pathfinders. It would tempt fate to make any decision just yet, they needed to complete their first tour this night. The crew hoped the operation would be a "milk run", a short, easy operation – but it wasn't, the target on 12/13 June was Gelsenkirchen. In keeping with procedure for a last operation there was a second pilot in the seat next to the 20-year-old pilot. Canadian Flying Officer Samuel A Phillips (J16550) would assume command of control Lancaster LL678 "Lily Mars", after this operation.

At a German fighter airfield in Leeuwarden, young crew men like Bertie Delacour were relaxing in the summer sun. Their uniforms were different, as was their native tongue, but they were alike in many ways. They had similar dreams for the future; they loved to fly; they believed in their cause; and they followed orders from older men. The German pilots discussed the Allied advance. They had been more confident when Allied forces were on the other side of the English channel – now it seemed German forces were in retreat. British bombers had been wreaking havoc on German cities for years now and they believed they needed desperately to safeguard their homeland and citizens. They looked to the skies and knew that it would likely be bombers that would come again tonight and they would again go into battle.

LEFT: *Bertie (courtesy Delacour family).* RIGHT: Lily Mars *and crew, Pilot Officer Herbert (Bertie) Samuel Delacour (third from left) (courtesy Delacour family).*

The bomb load of LL678 Lily Mars had been released and Bertie Delacour and his crew were relieved to be on their way home. It was too early to relax just yet – only when they were off the Dutch coast could they really begin to relax and break out the coffee and sandwiches. Unbeknown to the British crew they were being carefully observed. The youthful, good-looking Oblt Dieter Schmidt, shadowed the Delacour Lancaster. He was careful to position his Bf 110G just at the right height and distance to avoid detection by the bomber's Rear Gunner. The soft spot of the Lancaster was between the engines and when it came into his gun sight, he pressed the trigger. For the British crew the attack came unseen and incredibly quickly and the blast of 30 mm rounds penetrated the wing and fuselage. Fire and explosions follow and Bertie struggled to control his Lancaster while ordering his men to bale out. The second pilot grabbed his parachute but while pulling on the harness, he pulled the ripcord and his canopy emptied. Only the Bomb Aimer Flight Sergeant George Palamountain, Sergeant Gerald Martin, the Engineer, and the Middle Upper Gunner Pilot Officer Williams survived. It will never be known why Bertie didn't bale out. It could have been that observing the second pilot's hopeless situation he stayed onboard with the thought of attempting a crash landing. The fire spread rapidly and the Lancaster crashed with its Pilots, Wireless Operator/Air Gunner, Navigator and Rear Gunner still onboard – they would be buried in the small Dutch town of Bathmen.

RAF Bomber Command Europe flew 364,514 sorties in World War II, the raid on Gelsenkirchen, Germany, on the night 12/13 June 1944 was just one – yet it deeply affected many families throughout Australia. It is with great sadness that Lionel Rattle looks at a photograph of himself as a young boy. He is in his late eighties and his sadness is for lost youth, not his own, but that of the handsome man who stands behind with an arm draped around small shoulders. William (Bill) Frederick Harvey Rattle was Lionel's hero. Given the age difference Bill displayed an abundance of patience for a little brother who, in hindsight Lionel realises, must have been a bit of a pest sometimes. Bill fitted the hero role well. He was handsome, clever and very athletic. "He let me do all the things that I wanted to do that Dad didn't, by that I mean Dad was quiet and not very active...Bill did all sorts of things with me, we used to sail model yachts in a big pond in Centennial Park."

Bill sailed for real, "in an 18-footer. They were massive things.

They'd carry about a dozen fellows, all big fellows to keep it down", these were sea-going boats and "you'd look up at the sail area. Gosh, these modern 18-footers, long slim things, are different altogether today." Bill loved it and occasionally would stow his little brother onboard. Bill loved speed, sailing, and flying, "joy rides and all sorts of things". There was nothing Bill Rattle could not do. He was good at baseball and was a "very good golfer". When war broke out Bill Rattle "did not want to have anything to do with the war", but "he knew darn well that he would be conscripted into the army and he wasn't going to have any part of that... he was going to fly".

Lionel looks back to the days when he was 16 and his hero was 29. "He was a keen photographer and wanted to be a journalist", but while he waited for an opening Bill was apprenticed to the *Sydney Sun* as a newspaper rotogravure operative. Bill was delighted when the RAAF deemed him pilot material and went on to train at Narranderra and Uranquinty. "He held his own against the bright young men in his course. He was very determined to succeed." Returning resplendent in his uniform adorned with gold wings helped cultivate the hero status. Through Operating Training Unit and conversion training Bill Rattle gathered three Aussies and three Englishmen and once finished the qualifying circuits and bumps they were posted to RAF 622.

LEFT: *Lionel and Bill Rattle.* RIGHT: *Flying Officer William (Bill) Frederick Harvey Rattle (courtesy Lionel Rattle).*

As crews went, Bill's was fairly exotic. The Bomb Aimer was Flying Officer Walter Richard Tanner (424230) a 27-year-old former clerk with the Australian Gas Light Company in Sydney. He was married to Lillian with a three-year-old son and one-year-old daughter. He embarked for overseas when his daughter was just two days old. The Wireless Operator/Air Gunner was Flight Sergeant Richard Paul Percival Holden (429323). Though born in Sydney and educated at Paddington Public and Edgecliffe College, his parents moved to Dubbo, New South Wales. Richard had already tried several occupations, message boy, grocer's assistant, and then a junior machinist, but was so enthusiastic about the RAAF that he joined the Air Training Corps until he could enlist at 18 in September 1942. The Air Gunners were both RAF Sergeants. The one with the thick Irish accent was Martin Dea (1798041) 24, from Ballacolla, County Laois, Ireland, and the other was Reginald Bramley (2220988) 26, from Wollaton, Nottinghamshire. Sergeant Francis Michael Leaney (623992) 27, had RAF after his name, yet his parents Reg and Louisa lived in Sydney. The Navigator, Flight Sergeant Richard John William Moore (423433) 24, was born in Trivandrum, South India. He was the son of a tea plantation owner. Richard studied at Hurlstone Agricultural High School, Hawkesbury Agricultural College, and Sydney Technical College, to prepare him to become manager of a large landholding. Tall and well set, he was an excellent sportsman and was working as a jackaroo on a sheep station when he went off to war.

When the news came that Bill and his crew were "missing" on the operation against Gelsenkirchen on the night of 12/13 June 1944, his quiet "very shy" father surprised Lionel. "He heard that someone a couple of streets away also had a son missing on the same raid. He went up to the house knocked on the door and when this fellow's mother came to the door, he introduced himself and they just hugged each other. So out of character for my father but they shared the same terrible news."

Official confirmation was slow in coming. For five months the families waited and again news of death and burial came from sources other than the RAAF. Muriel Moore wrote "Surely it is bad enough to lose one's only son without being caused needless sorrow and pain". Bill Rattle's story eventually emerged and he proved to be a hero to the last. Shot up before reaching the target he made the split second decision not to jettison either the cookie onboard, or crash land Lancaster LL812 into the town of Eindhoven. They were low and there was no time to bale out so he aimed at a forest, "cut the tops of the trees clean off...Bill was a beaut exceptional bloke...outstanding waste".

Lionel still has his brother's prized Perfex 22 camera – it has been a long time since the camera took a photo but that doesn't matter. He returns to the present and pauses, shaking his head and says in an unsteady voice: "Bill had so much to live for, a lovely wife...a terrible time the war, nothing good came of it. It was dreadful. Our mother never got over it. Neither did Dad, and do you know no one has asked me before how much I have missed my brother all these years?"

Lionel Rattle with brother Bill's prized Perfex 22 camera.

THIRTEEN

"You know our mother never recovered from losing Michael. Michael was the very best of us."

John Skarratt

Grief is a difficult beast, impossible to define and something that affects everyone differently. No one can understand the depth of someone's grief – they may have travelled a similar road but never the same so consequently it is a road that must be travelled alone. On another level each family needed to find a safe release and to find closure, but for the families of RAAF aircrew attached to Bomber Command, there was seldom closure because they lived on the other side of the world and their father, son, brother, cousin, uncle, was buried in a grave too far away.

Life has been a struggle for the diesel-engine driver, Jim Noel Eastcott, and it might have been just that much easier and more enjoyable had his brother Flight Sergeant Thomas (Tom) Frederick Eastcott (427076) not been killed. Tom was the Rear Gunner, part of an RAAF 466 crew lost on 15 February 1944. The crew, bar the RAF Engineer Sergeant John Thomas Darwood (1164922) were Australian. Flight Sergeant Francis Kevin Williams (412869) was the 25-year-old Navigator. Flight Sergeant Colin Sheldon (426168) was 22 and the Bomb Aimer. Another 22-year-old, Flight Sergeant Hubert Cecil

Lloyd Thomas (410191) was the Wireless Operator/Air Gunner. The Middle Upper Gunner turret was occupied by Flight Sergeant Rex John Newell (423003), aged 21. Their Halifax HX293, took off from RAF Leconfield at 1711 on 15 February 1944 to bomb Berlin. It was shot down by a night fighter piloted by Lieutenant Kurt Matzak and the crew were buried in Grootegast (Opende) Protestant Churchyard, Holland. Flight Sergeant Jack Dudley Wormald (420326) was the 21-year-old skipper. On Jack's file a bureaucrat wrote, "Clothing returned to stores. Balance of flying clothing lost". Frank Eastcott, can only wonder what his 19-year-old brother might have achieved, and how good their relationship may have been – in his memory he named his own son Thomas.

Thomas Frederick Eastcott.

Jim Eastcott, with his wife Beryl, wonders how enriched life would have been.

For Philip Charley, World War II took his cousin John (Jock) Ross Charley, who had been more like a brother: "We were great friends... my earliest memories are of us, aged seven and eight, going to our grandfather's magnificent residence "Belmont Park"...for Sunday lunch...Jock and I would play games in the vast cellars beneath the house or on the beautiful lawns where the whole family would relax after lunch...we grew up together." The boys attended Shore School, joined the school cadets, and worked in a family laundry during school holidays. Civilian employment separated the men. Philip travelled extensively in the world of radio broadcasting. The cousin who was schooled at Tudor House, Moss Vale, and Shore, North Sydney, went off to be a jackaroo, and then enlisted in the RAAF at 18 in October 1942. Jock was mustered Wireless Operator/Air Gunner. As he approached his second year in the RAAF he wrote to Philip and his letter concerned his cousin a great deal. "This is my 21st sortie and my luck has held so far, but I have a feeling it may not last much longer."

The next news that Philip heard was that his cousin and friend was dead, the 20-year-old son of Herbert and Eileen Charley, of Summer Hill, New South Wales, was killed three days before that second anniversary of his RAAF enlistment. Jock's RAF 78 Squadron Halifax and his RAF crew took off from RAF Breighton at 1430 on 6 October 1944 to bomb Gelsenkirchen. Halifax MZ310 collided in the air with another RAF 78 Halifax. Both aircraft fell on, or near, the Dutch Reform Church at Oude-Tonge (South Holland) on the island of Overflakkee. No one survived the explosions. In May 1946 the Charley family were advised that Jock's watch had been recovered from German authorities and sadly that was all that was left of him.

Sergeant Angus Milne of SA (courtesy Robert Milne). *Flight Sergeant John (Jock) Charley of NSW (courtesy Philip Charley).*

For Robert Angus Lace Milne, it was the uncle whose name he bore, in keeping with the saying "I am not forgotten if someone mentions my name"; and there was the responsibility for the memory of another

Milne uncle also. The Milne family property was in the rich lands surrounding the town of Wirrabara, South Australia, 146 miles (235 km) from Adelaide. Angus Milne was very fond of White Park where he was born along with elder sister Marcia, and younger siblings Ian, Donald and Janet. The family's isolation nonetheless necessitated a move to the coastal area of Victor Harbour, south of Adelaide, so that the children could attend school. Angus moved back to White Park as soon as his formal schooling was over, with the intention of remaining on the land. Ian joined him and the brothers farmed and played cricket and tennis locally. They watched as the shadows of war lengthened over Europe and decided that if they were to get caught up in this feud, then they would fly. Both joined the local air school in Port Pirie. Ian proved a natural aviator, but Angus did not.

Ian Arthur Lace Milne (407078), later Flight Lieutenant, enlisted in May 1940 and perfected his pilot's skills at Narromine, New South Wales, and Ottawa, Canada. Ian Milne was delighted to be streamed into fighters and was embroiled in the latter stages of The Battle of Britain. The two brothers spent leave together in England. Both wore RAAF blue; Ian with pilot's wings and Angus wearing the half wing of a Wireless Operator/Air Gunner. On 20 April 1941, after amassing 404 flying hours, Ian crashed. The engine of his spitfire was shot up over the French coast and he hoped desperately it would cough, splutter and glide far enough to get him back close to England to be picked up by Sea Air Rescue. The spitfire died over the English Channel. Fellow pilots failed to see Ian emerge and presumed he was dead. No rescue boats came and Ian drifted for three days and two cold uncomfortable nights until a French fisherman sighted and reported him to the Germans. It was another six weeks before the Red Cross confirmed he was a POW, and it would be another three and a half years before he eventually returned to White Park – unfortunately, he would farm there without his brothers Angus and Donald.

The first operational raid for Sergeant Angus Milne (407091) was on Berlin on the night of 18/19 August 1941. It was on the return flight that RAF 51 Whitley Z6811 collided with an enemy fighter. A survivor, by chance, met up with Ian Milne in a POW camp some months later.

He told Ian that their pilot was injured but ordered the crew to abandon the bomber while he kept the Whitley steady. Angus was last seen, feet out of the hatch, ready to bale, yelling at the pilot to leave the controls. It is believed that Angus may have gone back to assist his injured skipper – neither managed to escape. Angus Milne was buried in a cemetery in the Dutch city of Uden. His name would be added to the Wirrabara war memorial with that of his brother Donald.

Flight Sergeant Donald Harold Milne (416596) followed his brothers into the RAAF, enlisting in July 1941 at 20, mere months after his brother Ian became a POW and less than a month before Angus was killed. Donald, too, became a pilot and was attached to RAF 35 Squadron. His operational career was brief. On his first raid as skipper he successfully landed his damaged bomber in the North Sea and he and his crew were rescued. On his second operation he was again the only Australian on Halifax HR673, tasked to attack Cologne. Donald was killed when his bomber was shot down and he was buried in Heverlee, Belgium. Eve Milne: "Like thousands of mothers, battled five years of torment, afraid to answer the telephone or the front door. Within a month two telegrams, Angus gone, Ian presumed dead, and Donald gone 19 months later."[16]

In 1988 Ian Milne and his wife travelled to Europe to visit his brother's grave in Holland and another brother's grave in Belgium. They carried with them two vials and on reaching each "immaculately cared for grave" they sprinkled White Park soil, liberally "watered in with tears". Ian Milne remained on White Park until he died in 1992.

They were a bunch of young Australians, good mates, and they should have been standing around in someone's backyard on the day before Christmas drinking a cold beer and burning sausages on the barbecue. Their ages were 22, 20, 20, 25, 21, 21, and their conversation should have been about the cricket and the Boxing Day test – it would surely be great to beat the "Pommies" and retain the ashes. Granted there were a few Victorians and a South Australian, but this was the Australian summer when there were no arguments about which football code was the best; cricket was universal. Instead this group of young Australians with bright futures were in the land of snow and ice listening to an operation briefing to bomb rail yards at the German city of Cologne.

Michael Carleton Skarratt had been born in London but the extended family came to Australia to oversee business investments and his grandfather, Charles Carleton Skarratt would become director of the Mount Morgan Gold Mining Co. Michael's family was wealthy and Michael enjoyed the lifestyle this afforded. He could have been called a "larrikin" but that was not the vernacular used in well-to-do homes on Sydney's north shore. Nonetheless he managed to get himself into a fair amount of trouble. Normally Michael could charm himself out of the repercussions – but not always. Brother John remembers the mischief and the charm and: "when I had to collect him after a night of solid drinking. I was annoyed but when I arrived and found him on a park bench looking decidedly dishevelled, he fixed me with that grin of his and my anger disappeared."

Michael was having trouble deciding upon a career. He worked as an accountant but found it incredibly boring so went off to the country to be a jackaroo. World War II promised a new direction and what Michael believed would be a great adventure. He badly wanted to be a pilot and was delighted when the RAAF, impressed by his schooling and lineage, agreed. The 19 year old entered in November 1941, applied himself enthusiastically and became a Sergeant Airman Pilot in November the following year. John remembers how excited and determined Michael was when he returned for his brief "pre-embarkation" leave before sailing out of Melbourne in January 1943.

So this was England, the motherland. Bournemouth was pleasant and full of men in RAAF uniform, but Michael was there way too long, two months, "why?" he was trained and itching to fly. Over the radio waves came the voice of William Joyce, nicknamed Lord Haw Haw. Joyce was the prominent English-language broadcaster used by the Reich Ministry of Public Enlightenment and Propaganda in an attempt to demoralise Allied military personnel and the British population. "We know you Australians and Canadians have just arrived in Bournemouth. We'll pay you a visit before long. In any event, most of you will kill yourselves in training".[2]

Patience was not one of Michael Skarratt's virtues and the RAF messed him around – he had arrived in Bournemouth on 17 March 1943 and didn't leave until 20 July when they finally sent him to the Advanced Flying Unit at Snitterfield, near Stratford. He had not flown an aircraft since November 1942, "eight months and there was supposed to be a war on". Nor was he flying continuously after that. Within two months he was back at yet another Personnel Despatch Centre. Michael was posted to Italy and RAF 69, but couldn't understand why given that the Italians were all but destroyed, and he was sure he would be better put to use attached to an English-based squadron. Instead, he was messed about for more months, not getting the flying he needed. Sure enough he wasn't needed in Italy and was sent back to England. It was now June 1944 and he was with 27 Operating Training Unit in Lichfield, England. The period from this date to the end of the war would be the busiest of the war for Bomber Command.

The time came for Michael to choose a crew. Although he was born an Englishman and raised in a cultured English household transplanted to the dominions, he chose Australians. His charm, warm grins and strong presence made it easy to find a crew. Flight Sergeant Robert (Bob) John Dickie (430773) wrote on his RAAF application that he was 5 ft 5 in (1.65 m), the RAAF medical wrote that he was 5 ft 4¼ in (1.63 m). He was short in any man's language. At 20 years of age he was Michael's choice of Navigator. Bob Dickie came from Dunkeld, Victoria, a tiny town nestled at the bottom of the spectacular Grampian National Park. He was a Grocer's Assistant when he enlisted in March 1943, a month away from turning 19, and did not arrive in the UK until April 1944.

Flight Sergeant Cyril Keith Deed (30953) at 25 would be the old man of the crew. He hailed from Maryborough, Victoria, and was the fifth child of Edward and Esther, and a carpenter/painter by trade. He originally was entered into the RAAF as an aircraft hand in March 1941, then as a carpenter general. Two years after his enlistment, he was re-mustered as aircrew, and demoted from Corporal to Aircraftsman II. At ITS under close scrutiny he received mixed comments that could possibly have been influenced by being severely reprimanded because he, "behaved towards his superior officer in a manner unbecoming an NCO". Cyril Deed was mustered as an Air Gunner.

Flight Sergeant Graham Fowler Day (433717) was another 20 year old and the Rear Gunner. His father Donald was a commonwealth public servant in Canberra before his premature death. Graham struggled with his father's death and dropped out of Queanbeyan High at 14. He tinkered with motorbikes before knuckling down and studying for the Public Service Clerical examination at Canberra High. He was a slight 5 ft 6 in (1.67 m) who had his heart set on joining the RAAF, preferably as a Flight Engineer. While he waited, he was appointed a messenger to the Commonwealth Prices Branch and joined the ATC. Graham was delighted when his RAAF posting arrived. It was May 1943 and he was still only 18. He was told it was very unlikely that the RAF would train and allow him to serve as an engineer in the UK, Graham immediately elected for the faster route to war, and became an Air Gunner. Graham Day arrived in the UK in April 1944.

Flight Sergeant Russell Ian Stewart (434335) had an excellent education at University High, Parkville, Melbourne, to leaving level, achieving first class honours in most subjects. Now in the UK having recently turned 21, he was hoping quietly but desperately, that as hundreds milled around over tea and sticky buns, someone at Operating Training Unit would select him for a crew. Stewart was delighted when the charming Michael Skarratt approached him and asked if he would be his Wireless Operator/Air Gunner. Flying Officer John Michael Ward (437237) another 21 year old, a former law clerk in Adelaide, quickly joined them – his job would be to master the intricacies of Bomb Aimer. The crew were delighted to join RAAF 460 on 3 November 1944 and welcomed the remaining crew member, RAF Engineer Sergeant Thomas Charles Newman (923554).

It was Christmas Eve 1944 when the Lancaster Michael Skarratt was piloting was struck by anti-aircraft fire and exploded. With a full bomb load, death came instantly and there was very little left of the young Englishman and the Australians who showed so much promise. Their remains were buried in the small village of Oostelbeers Roman Catholic Churchyard, Holland. Ellen Deed wrote several times pleading for more information, "I'm very worried and long for news of my dear one. Sincerely a sad mother", then; "I am most anxious to find out all I can about my dear son". Anne Day also struggled with the lack of information, "he is my only son, and as I am a widow, I will be grateful for any information", she felt it necessary to add "at the same time I apologize for intruding on your busy hours". The most hideous details were not disclosed by the RAAF to the mothers. The crew was eventually identified by the RAAF watch issued to Stewart. A letter from a member of the Royal Netherlands Legation to Annie Day was not so pleasant and she was told the crew "were mutilated beyond recognition and scattered over a wide area...therefore it was impossible to bury them separately".

Realizing his personal effects would soon arrive she asked if they could be sent to her place of employment – the Australian War Memorial. A small carton containing Graham's modest belonging was so delivered. Anne was surprised to find a pair of ice skates, clearly an activity he had enjoyed in a distant part of the world. She would treasure his stamp album, a hobby he had pursued since a small boy, and took counsel in the prayer book which she would often hold. Michael Skarratt graciously left a letter for those who would be required to dispose of his personal effects, a group rather oddly named The Standing Committee of Adjustment, with the message: "Hoping sincerely that I have caused you as little inconvenience as possible". He enclosed, "a meagre gift for doing a job that receives no thanks".

The white gravestones are stark in the small Roman Catholic churchyard,

Flying Officer Michael Carleton Skarratt (courtesy John Skarratt).

John Skarratt.

but there is plenty of colour in the flowers, foliage, and small trinkets that adorn the freshly raked soil. Across the front a sign fashioned from wood and foil spells "Bedankt", which is Dutch for "in gratitude". This is the work of the grade seven class of St Joseph School, Oostelbeers. Joke van Ham is the teacher who ensures each year her students learn "everything that has happened" to these young Australians and Englishman "during their last flight". She would write to John Skarratt:

> Each year on May the 4th people remember the victims
> the Second World War. ...The children of my class hold
> their own commemoration of the dead...the children of my
> class remember your brother and his crew. It was a serious
> remembrance. The children read self-made poems in which you
> can hear much thankfulness for our liberty and a call for peace
> all over the world...(they) make flowers for the graves. ...we keep
> two minutes of silence. ...We also went to the crashsite in the
> woods.

Later John would receive a letter from a student to say that although Joke van Ham was no longer his teacher he promised: "I also keep visiting the graves, my grandmother's grave is nearby, the grave of your brother Michael...My grandfather has seeing the airplane from your brother that in World War II was crashed."

Michael Skarratt would have thought there was a strong possibility he would die while with Bomber Command, but he would never have envisaged that every year since his death in 1944 residents of Oostelbeers, particularly the children, would care for his grave and those of his crew. His brother John has been greatly consoled by the reverence but he still needs people to know, "You know our mother never recovered from losing Michael. Michael was the very best of us".

The effect of the European air war on Australian families was profound. The experience of the Holmes family was unfortunately not unusual. The Holmes were a close knit family with five sons. The family Draper Shop was one of the first stores in the town of Theodore, Queensland, and the boys, when not at school, would help out or work in their father William's Picture Theatre. Flying Officer Kenneth (Glad) Gladstone Holmes (405017) son of William and Annie, was a teacher before he enlisted in January 1941. He was killed whilst attached to RAF 100 Squadron on 21 May 1943 – he was 23. His brother Flight Sergeant Ross Primrose Holmes (4144351) enlisted in September 1941 and was killed whilst attached to RAAF 467 Squadron, just two months later, on 28 July 1943 – he was 21. Allan Holmes would name his children in honour of his brothers – there seemed so little else he could do.

Eileen Sheean proudly wore a mother's badge with stars representing two sons in the RAAF. Brian Leo had been a star pupil at both, St Patrick's College, Ballarat, and Warrnambool High. At the latter he was house captain, athletics captain, and captain of the 1st XI. He was a student teacher when he enlisted at 19 and returned to Ballarat to train at 1 Wireless Air Gunner School. By 17 February 1944 he was with RAAF 466.

Flight Sergeant Lorin James Sheean.   *Flight Sergeant Brian Leo Sheean.*

His elder brother entered the RAAF in November 1941, the month after Brian. Flight Sergeant Lorin James Sheean (410014) was a dairy farmer who mustered as an Air Gunner. On the night of 20/21 December 1943, during an attack on Frankfurt, Lorin's RAF 76 squadron Halifax, was shot down by a night fighter and disappeared into the North Sea. His Commanding Officer wrote Lorin Sheean displayed a: "Fine fighting spirit under a calm, quiet, manner". Struggling with the death of their 24- year-old son, Edward and Eileen Sheean were told their son Flight Sergeant Brian Leo Sheean (409855) had been killed, his RAAF

466 Halifax shot down by night fighter on the night of 11 April 1944, crashing into the same expanse of water. Brian was a fortnight shy of his 21 birthday. His body was eventually washed ashore and buried in a French cemetery – Lorin's body was never found.

Another Victorian couple, William and Eleanor Osborne, from the farming community of Goorambat, near Benalla, could identify with this depth of sorrow. Like most brothers theirs were good mates and also competitive. Flight Sergeant Edgar Thomas Leslie Osborne (409272) was a farmer, someone who lived life as if there were no tomorrow and wrote on his RAAF application form that although he was only "21 and 9 months" he had been in "various occupations". Ed even thought his three first names took too long to write. Ed was married to Heather, was studying electrical engineering by correspondence, and by October 1941 was the father of Glenda Janice. Edgar Osborne was a man in a hurry for action and was delighted when mustered pilot. By November 1942 he was in England, by 28 May 1943 he was flying a "Tiffy", an RAF 198 Typhoon fighter, and by 2 September 1943 he was dead at 24, killed whilst attacking German warships in a Dutch harbour.

Ronald Henderson Osborne enlisted on 23 May 1942 at 19. His elder brother had beaten him into the RAAF and whilst he may have wished to emulate Ed's accomplishments he was a very different person. Ron was less physical and more studious. Ed found school boring whereas Ron loved books, enjoyed attaining knowledge, and graduated from Benalla High School with excellent Leaving Certificate results. He studied further, taught French for half a year, before his Accountancy qualifications gained him the position of audit clerk, in the Commonwealth Public Service. The RAAF believed he was better qualified to be a Navigator regardless of what Ron hoped. His training was longer so Ron did not reach England until April 1943 and was still training when news came of his brother's death. Eight months later to the day, 21-year-old Flight Sergeant Ron Osborne (418560) was killed. His crew was attacking French railway yards and stores depots when their RAF 218 Stirling crashed on 2 May 1944. The crew had time to bale but Ron's parachute failed to open and he died in an area where too many youthful Australians had died in the previous war, the Somme. By

1977 it was a very different world, enemies of old had prospered, all it seemed had been forgiven, but Edith Campbell could not forget or even forgive. Her deceased parents, struggling with their grief, had disposed of the heartbreaking RAAF telegrams and letters which changed their lives, causing Edith to write: "I hope to go to Europe...my two brothers, Edgar Thomas Leslie and Ronald Henderson Osborne...were killed in action...I would like to visit their graves...could you please advise me as to where I would find their crosses? And the number of the cross? Or any other relative information which would help me to find and visit them? ...I do realise that I am giving short notice, however the opportunity to visit these parts has only just occurred." The RAAF sent a hasty reply, Ed was buried in Bergen-op-Zoom, Canadian Military Cemetery, Holland; Ron was buried in a churchyard in Pois-de-la-Somme, near Amiens.

With the war over Australian aircrew gradually returned home, to a nation quite different to the one they had left. Even though they realised they were the lucky ones, the transition from uniform to civilian life was challenging, none more so than for those who had endured years as POW. The 8,000 Australians captured by Germany and Italy were generally treated in accordance with the Geneva Convention, but this was nonetheless war. The majority of the 8,000 were taken during the fighting in Greece and Crete in 1941, but the next largest single group were the 1,400 aircrew shot down over Europe. After months and years there was the exhilaration of freedom savoured by men like Albert (Stoppy) Adrian Stobart of Melbourne and Cyril Borsht from Brisbane – but it was a freedom that came with responsibility.

Brisbane lad Cyril Borsht was a junior draughtsman before he enlisted and left for overseas service as an RAAF pilot. When it came time to choose a crew his first question was, "I am a Jew – do you mind?" The extent of Nazi crimes against humanity were not yet fully comprehended but the world understood that under Hitler's regime people of the Jewish faith were suffering unprecedented persecution. It was added motivation for Cyril to fight but he also appreciated that if he and his crew were captured his religion would likely place others in added peril. Few had reservations and his crew quickly filled. The Navigator slot was taken by Flight Sergeant Brian (Snow) O'Connell from Sydney, a Clerk with the Department of Agriculture also studying economics at Sydney University. The Wireless Operator/Air Gunner was Flight Sergeant Maxwell Ray Staunton-Smith (428029), a natural sportsman, and still a student when he enlisted in 1942, at 19, from Hobart. The Middle Upper Gunner turret was taken by Flight Sergeant Thomas Patrick Lonergan (432828), and Pilot Officer Ronald Glyn Sheers Cooper (434622) from Rockhampton, slotted quickly into the Rear Gunner turret. The Engineer was RAF Flight Sergeant Eric Leigh (2204264) and another Englishman, RAF Flight Sergeant Tom Laing (1561720), took on the Bomb Aimer duties. The crew quickly became good friends, to the point where they combined their savings to purchase a Vauxhall car even though only Cyril and Max knew how to drive. Their first op was on D Day, a decoy run over the English Channel. 25 operations later their RAAF 463 Lancaster was hit by flak on the bombing run on German coastal gun emplacements at Flushing, The Netherlands.

The bomb bay doors were open and Engineer Eric Leigh was badly wounded in the stomach. Fire spread quickly from the bomb bay into the interior of the fuselage and the 22-year-old pilot lost no time in giving the order to abandon the Lancaster. The bombs were still onboard regardless of the efforts of the Bomb Aimer to jettison the load. Both the bomb aimer and navigator baled out, Borsht left his seat and pushed his wounded engineer out of the forward hatch and followed. Dutch citizens watched as the bomber descended gradually and then burning badly dived into the sea. Pilot Officer Cyril Borsht landed almost on the German gun emplacements he had attempted to bomb. At the sight of German soldiers he began to run but with their urgent screams the Jewish bloke from Brisbane stopped and raised his hands wondering what would be his fate. The navigator evaded capture and Borsht was told his engineer did not survive; the rest of his crew became POWs.

Borsht's critique of his POW camp included: "Three tier beds, poor lighting, one store, 18 to a room, a sixth of a loaf of bread, potatoes, noodles – poor quality (rations), one stove per hut." The next camp was worse. There were 200 to a hut; the loaf ration was reduced to around a tenth of a loaf, and this and the soup and potatoes were of a very poor quality made worse by the fact there were "no cooking facilities". Liberation was wonderful.

Flying Officer Cyril Borsht (courtesy of the Borsht family).

Flight Sergeant Stobart (408934) became a POW when his RAAF 460 crew were shot down by a night fighter during their 11th operation, an attack on Berlin on 3 September 1943. The 22-year-old Rear Gunner assisted the RAF Middle Upper Gunner, RAF Sergeant J B Hilton, and they baled out together. They were the only survivors. Their Australian skipper, Flight Sergeant Robert Barr McPhan (413788) 30, from Kanwal, New South Wales, and Flight Sergeant John Andrew Spence (421135), the 31-year-old Bomb Aimer from Sydney, would remain in a Dutch cemetery. Albert Stobart would be sustained during his two-year internment not just by the company of other POWs but by the girl he left behind. In a book entitled *My Trip Aboard* Albert Stobart gathered paintings and poems from as many of his fellow POWs as he could, whatever their nationality, asking them to "just write or draw something". Stobart found an artist willing to paint a portrait with paints derived from all sorts of elements from a battered photo, one of the very few possessions the young Air Gunner had.

Camp internees, "Had built a wireless set which the Germans never found. We would listen to the news every night so knew exactly where the Allies were." Then one glorious day Russian Cossacks rode in, "rode the length of the camp, down to where the Russians POWs were held and then rode away". The Russians later put guards on the camp gate; the POWs were now being guarded from angry, disgruntled German military and civilians, rather than by them. But British and American POWs "were concerned that the Russians might take us to Moscow, so we just left the camp and eventually found the American lines". Albert Stobart carried the portrait back to Melbourne and married his girl, and they were still married in 2010.

LEFT: *Albert Adrian Stobart, later Warrant Officer, and Noel, the girl he left behind in 1941 (courtesy Albert Stobart).* RIGHT: *Together still, more than 60 years later, with the portrait painted by a POW.*

The question "Why me, why did I survive and not the others", would forever remain for aircrew, as did the "responsibility to dead mates to live a good life". The adjustment after months and years in overcrowded and cramped quarters would take time; as would plentiful food after poor rations. It also took time to adjust to the luxury of being able to shower as often as one wished; and to good sanitation, after watching and smelling seepage into the sleeping huts from the urinals. There were no barbed wire fences; no uniformed armed guards; just freedom to do what you wished when you wished – it would take time to adjust to all this and it was made all the more difficult by the political and public views of the aircrew's wartime duties.

Britain's Prime Minister Winston Churchill failed to acknowledge the contribution made by the men of Bomber Command in his victory speech. Bomber Command's activities had become increasingly controversial as the war progressed, not only among segments of the British government but also within the general public. Bomber Command had ceased being a political asset. Indeed, it was an embarrassment. Some believed its existence was "a tacit admission that Britain had seriously violated the war convention and that those in authority knew she had done so".[3] Of Harris one critic wrote: "He pursued the strategy of area bombing with an almost religious fervour and with a contemptuous disregard for even marginal quibbles about the pragmatic or moral correctness of such a strategy."[4]

Harris received little recognition from his masters and was shunned by the RAF. He received a baronetcy in 1953 but this was seen as a minor honour. There was no specific campaign medal for Bomber Command aircrew, young men who undertook their duties at the behest of others.

Whereas other warriors were invariably lionised, aircrew were demonised. Those who participated in land combat were "unreservedly lauded" while society offered only "faint praise" for those who flew in bombers. While memorials were raised to lesser men Bomber Command aircrew were left to deal with their own doubts and demons. Many Australian Bomber Command aircrew felt spurned by organizations such as the Returned Services League (RSL), and it would only be in their twilight years that some joined an organisation that was supposed to care for all returned servicemen. It would also be an indictment of Australian cultural awareness, and how their nation's military tradition was disseminated, that there would not be greater appreciation of their deeds and their deaths, as there was in small communities throughout Europe. Not until June 2012 would a Bomber Command memorial be unveiled by Queen Elizabeth II in London's Green Park. The 9 ft (2.74 m) tall bronze sculpture of a crew of seven would come too late for the vindication of the majority of Bomber Command veterans.

Bomber men had been of the utmost importance during the war. Their duties were of the adrenalin-charged life and death category, but after the war they were decidedly less in number and few cared. They were of vital importance to five, six, or seven brothers in arms. Their responsibility had been to themselves and each of their crew. Now they were responsible for a wife and children. People wished to move on, to forget the war, to look to the future, yet the better part of them seemed enslaved to that past.

Max Norris did not involve himself in the RSL until post-retirement and did not march on Anzac Day. He struggled upon his return home to build an interrupted life and adjust to the priorities of post-war existence. He had left a career with the Commonwealth Bank to become an RAAF Wireless Operator/Air Gunner on Halifax bombers. He saw service with RAAF 466 and RAF 158 squadrons, but returning to the duties of a bank clerk diminished who he had been. Today there is counselling for post-traumatic stress disorder (PTSD) but in the late 1940s and early 1950s there was only ignorance. During his first week at work Max Norris was unwisely placed on the front counter. A female customer approached and said in an aggravated tone, "My son is in the army with the occupied forces in Japan, why is a fit young man like you here?" Max left the bank that day and struggled to find meaningful work. It took time and loving commitment from his wife Hilda, before he settled into a nine to five job in the Commonwealth Public Service, and the responsibility for three children made this inevitable. Only in the latter stages of his life did he join RAAF aircrew organizations and find solace, companionship, and most of all, the unspoken understanding that only those who had flown in bombers shared.

When hostilities finished Arthur Hoyle had flown 50 operations and he was still only 22 years and 9 months. Arthur "had seen death frequently, I had known that chilling fear". He struggled to describe how he felt when late in November 1945 the cliffs of Sydney Harbour appeared out of the mist, "I was home and the greatest adventure of my life was over". In retrospect he was torn, resenting "that my youth disappeared so quickly", one day he, "was a lad and a few weeks later I was a man", but he missed, "the intense comradeship of a flying crew". "I learned to know myself. Fear and the frequent sight of death stripped away many of the illusions about myself which I might have retained in a peacetime world. ... survived...I had a good war but I never want to see another." [5]

Bill Kelly was only 17 when he applied for RAAF entry in 1941, he falsified his birth certificate and hoped authorities would not discover his subterfuge: "I went to war with oxymoronic wonder. In the end, the abandonment of ethics by the warmongers was, for me, the inevitable alienation."[6]

It was with delirious relief "overcome with happiness, emotion, memories and hope; a confused paradox" that Bill Kelly celebrated the end of the war. He danced the night away with "riotous celebration". He and others gathered around the mess piano singing at the time what seemed a "hilarious parody, to the waltz tune. "'After the Ball'". The first line went "After the war is over" and the last "up those who did fuck all", followed with great gusto by the two fingers "V" for victory sign inverted. Kelly had been encouraged to enlist by stories of the Anzacs, proud, noble, defiant, and Australian. His war had been none of these things and furthermore unlike those in land battles, he had been unable to comfort his mates when they died; instead his mates died in isolation, "strapped in aluminium compartments hurtling through the sky", their remains being scattered from the heavens over foreign lands. Coupled with these thoughts Bill Kelly had lingering visions of the plight of "unfortunate citizens" of cities he had been ordered to ravage.

Bill Kelly returned to Winton, Queensland. As he approached his home he saw his mother working in the sub-tropical garden, she stood up and:

> We hugged and kissed in the late afternoon sunshine. We both started crying and suddenly my tears could not be controlled. Overcome by happiness, pride, humility, and awe of being human, I continued to weep late into the night and all the next day. It seemed too much emotion for a grown man. But I was not alone, for all my mates who had been killed were here with me.[7]

It would largely be left to following generations to understand as best they could how their fathers, grandfathers, uncles, and great uncles, served in the air war, and they would become more and more determined that this service should not be subsumed by more popularised war service. On the first weekend of June Bomber Command aircrew are commemorated, and not more so than by the hundreds and hundreds who gather by the dramatic and stunning Bomber Command memorial on the lawn of the Australian War Memorial. Few remain who can speak first-hand of the air war, but the frail, bent bodies weighed down by campaign medals, and aided by walking sticks and walking frames, who stoically move forward to lay a wreath, are all who remain of the best of the best.

Around 125,000 aircrew served with RAF Bomber Command. Of these 9,838 became POWs and most importantly 55,573 were killed. Their average age was just 22.[8] For every 100 aircrew, 56 were killed in the air or died of wounds; 12 out of every 100 airmen became POW.[9] In the nine major cemeteries and half a dozen smaller Commonwealth War Graves Commission cemeteries, World War II air force "dead is more than double that of the army with a staggering 17,630 graves of known and unknown airmen", the vast majority of whom flew with Bomber Command. It is not known exactly how many Australian aircrew served with RAF Bomber Command, Europe. Numbers differ wildly from 10,000 to 20,000. It is known that 3,486 were killed in action and a further 500 died in training accidents. Against Germany 9,572 Australians were killed in action or as POWs – 5117 of these were RAAF. Although just over one per cent of Australian World War II defence personnel were enlisted in the nation's air force they made up 20 per cent of Australia's World War II dead.

But statistics are statistics and living in a world which celebrates statistics removes the human stories behind the figures. Ultimately the deaths of so many, is profoundly sad – not just because these young men never really lived, but because Australia would have been profoundly richer for their presence. There is also pride as younger Australians in increasing numbers, appreciate the commitment of this generation. We will always walk in the shadow of this generation of naive, gullible, but hardworking, proud and heroic Australians – may we never forget their service and sacrifice.

Pilot Officer Bertie Delacour was only 20 when he was shot down and buried in a Dutch cemetery, among his personal effects was the following letter...

Dear Mum and Dad,

I hope you never get this for if you do it means I did not return from the operation I am about to set out on.

I have no feeling of premonition – nothing at all, but the reason I'm writing this is an expression of gratitude to you, which I want you to know I feel very much.

I've often wondered how it was I was so lucky to be born to such parents as you and Dad. No other mother in the entire world could have been so good, kind or understanding, or, to sum it up in one word GRAND as you have been to all of us ... And the same to Dad. Together such parents in this whole, wide, wicked world of ours could never be found.

Do not grieve over me too much Dad and Mum. Oh I know you will grieve and the pain in your heart will burn badly for a while, but please Mum and Dad, remember I've died the way I've always wanted to die and died the way so countless numbers of other fellows are dying every day on this earth. I am just merely your contribution to a better, cleaner, freer world. May you obtain that world Mum. And again remember it is you who are left behind who are the real heroes not us who die. It is you who bear the sacrifice, so grin and bear it and remember that famous motto time heals all wounds. Yes time will erase that burn from your heart Mum and then, you and Dad and the family shall know that what you suffered was, after all, just a minor affair, an everyday happening in this world.

I can't express here how much I love you Mum and Dad for it is beyond all expression. I hope Edna, Alma, Myra, Stanley, Betty, John, Allan and Graham all grow up to have happy successful lives. I will not say goodbye Mum for it is not goodbye for one day we shall all be again united in a much better land than this.

So I'll only say
For the present
Lots of love to you all,
From your loving son,
Bert.[11]

ENDNOTES

Chapter 1

1 *Sydney Morning Herald*, 4 September 1939.

2 4,044 taken POW, 397 died while captive.

3 *Statistics of the Military Effort of the British Empire During the Great War, 1914–1920*, The War Office, (London 1922); AWM133 Nominal Roll of the AIF abroad; AWM144 Roll of Honour Cards, First World War.

4 *Age*, 2 September 1939.

5 McCarthy, J. *A Last Call of Empire: Australian Aircrew, Britain and the Empire Air Training Scheme*, Canberra, AWM, 1988, p 2.

6 After WWI the defence of Australia lay with the part-time soldiers of the Citizens Military Force (CMF), also known as the Militia. The Militia was organised to maintain the structure of the First AIF and kept the same numerical designations. Units were distributed as the original AIF units. In 1937 it was decided to raise a new infantry battalion in the Ipswich-Brisbane region. The local Scottish community wanted Queensland to have its own Scots regiment. They lobbied for the newly raised 61st Infantry Battalion to be linked with a Highland regiment. In 1939 the 61st was linked with the Queen's Own Cameron Highlanders and became the "Queensland Cameron Highlanders".

7 Spurling, K. *Cruel Conflict: the Triumph and Tragedy of HMAS Perth I*, New Holland, Sydney, 2008, p 43.

8 The first operational flights did not occur until 27 May 1915, when the Mesopotamian Half Flight was called upon to assist the Indian Army in protecting British oil interests in what is now Iraq.

9 Stephens, A. *The Royal Australian Air Force, The Australian Centenary History of Defence Vol II*, Oxford, 2001, p 5.

10 Ibid, p 25.

11 Ibid, p 57.

12 Parliamentary Debates, Commonwealth of Australia, Vol 162, p 1,699.

13 *Sydney Morning Herald*, 5 January 1940.

14 *Sydney Morning Herald*, 13 June 1940.

15 Hoyle, A. *Into the Darkness: A Personal Memoir*, self published, Canberra, 1989, p 2.

16 McKernan, M. *ALL IN!; Australia During the Second World War*, Nelson, Vic, 1983, p 17.

17 Hoyle, A. *Into the Darkness: A Personal Memoir*, self published, Canberra, 1989, p 2.

18 McKernan, M. *ALL IN!; Australia During the Second World War*, Nelson, Vic, 1983, p 19.

19 Ibid.

20 Cutlack, F.M. *Official History of Australia in the War of 1914–1918, Vol VIII, The Australian Flying Corps in the Western and Eastern Theatres of War, 1914–1918*, pp xxv–xxvi.

21 McCarthy, J. *A Last Call of Empire: Australian Aircrew, Britain and the Empire Air Training Scheme*, Canberra, AWM, 1988, p 13.

22 Ibid, p 14.

23 Ibid, p 20.

24 Robertson, J. *1939–1945 Australia Goes to War*, Doubleday, Sydney, 1981, p 62.

25 Waldon, R. Diary, Waldon Family Papers.

26 Stephens, Alan *The Royal Australian Air Force, The Australian Centenary History of Defence Vol II*, Oxford, Vic., 2001, p 78.

27 Stephens, A. *The Royal Australian Air Force, The Australian Centenary History of Defence Vol II*, Oxford, Vic., 2001, p 85.

28 Pilot Officer C C Bennett, Pilot Officer Francis Walter Cale and Flying Officer Richard Lindsay Glyde of Perth, Pilot Officer John Dallas Crossman, Flight Lieutenant F W Flood, Sergeant K C Holland, Flight Lieutenant P C Hughes, Flight Lieutenant J C Kennedy, Pilot Officer B M McDonough, Pilot Officer R F G Miller, Pilot Officer W H Millington, Flight Lieutenant R C Reynell, Flight Lieutenant S C Walch, Flight Lieutenant L C Withall,

were killed in the Battle of Britain, Flying Officer R W Bungey, Pilot Officer J R Cock, Pilot Officer A N Constantine (K), Pilot Officer A L Hamilton, Flight Lieutenant C G C Olive.

29 Hayes, M. *Angry Skies: Recollections of Australian Combat Fliers*, ABC, Sydney, 2003, p 23.

30 Middlebrook, M. And Everitt, C. *The Bomber Command War Diaries: An Operational Reference Book, 1939–1945*, Midland, UK, 1996, p 148, reports that no aircraft was lost on this operation. Chorley disagrees, p 46.

31 Hayes, M. *Angry Skies: Recollections of Australian Combat Fliers*, ABC, Sydney, 2003, p 20.

32 Ibid, p 21.

33 Bingley, A.N. *Australian Airmen: Lest We Forget Europe 1939–1945*, self published, WA, 2002, p 2.

34 Ibid, p 3.

35 Ibid, p 5.

36 Ibid, p 3.

37 Ibid, p 3.

38 Goldie, P. Diary published in full in Bingley, A.N. *Australian Airmen: Lest We Forget Europe 1939–1945*, self published, WA, 2002, pp 99-194.

39 Ibid.

40 Wilson, D. *The Brotherhood of Airmen: The Men and Women of the RAAF in Action 1914–Today*, Allen and Unwin, 2005, p 58.

41 A9300, 257540, National Archives, Canberra.

42 Chorley, W.R. *Bomber Command Losses Vo.2 Aircraft and Crew Losses 1941*, Redwood, England, 1993, p 98.

43 Sgt R E E Fotheringham (pilot), gunners were Sgts S A Dyer, P E Hare, and D M MacKinnon.

44 Chorley, W.R. *Bomber Command Losses Vo.2 Aircraft and Crew Losses 1941*, Redwood, England, 1993, p 129.

45 Ibid.

46 Ibid, p 19.

47 An additional 36 Blenheims were lost in "non-operational flights". Statistics compiled from Chorley, W.R. *Bomber Command Losses Vo.2 Aircraft and Crew Losses 1941*, Redwood, England, 1993, p 198.

48 Also in crew were RAF Sgts A G Harris and R V Griffiths.

49 Bingley, A.N. *Australian Airmen: Lest We Forget Europe 1939–1945*, self published, WA, 2002, p 90.

50 Letter, 6 February 1942, RAAF HQ WA., to Secretary, Air Board, Melbourne, in A705, 406450, National Archives.

Chapter 2

1 Hoyle, A. *Into the Darkness, self published*, Canberra, 1989, p 6.

2 Ibid, p 9.

3 Waldon, R. Diary, Waldon Family Papers.

4 Ibid.

5 Butterworth, D. "One Man's War", unpublished manuscript, Butterworth Family Papers.

6 Butterworth, D. "One Man's War", unpublished manuscript, Butterworth Family Papers.

7 Ibid.

8 Ibid.

9 Ibid.

10 Butterworth, D. "One Man's War", unpublished manuscript, Butterworth family papers.

11 Firkins, P. *Strike and Return*, Westward Ho, Perth, 1985, p 18.

12 Ibid, p 18.

13 Ibid.

14 Interview with Mary Cheese-Walker, 10 February 2010.

15 Ibid.

16 Letter in Cheese family papers, courtesy Mary Walker.

17 Ibid.

18 Hayes, M. *Angry Skies: Recollections of Australian Combat Fliers*, ABC Books, 2003, p 41.

19 Ibid, p 43.

20 Ibid, p 45.

21 Crashed at Tondern in the vicinity of Neumünster, where the crew were initially buried. They have been subsequently re-interred in the Hamburg Cemetery.

22 Chant, C. *Allied Bombers 1939–1945*, Amber, UK, 2008, p 32.

23 A705, 400080. Dansey, Arthur. National Archives.

24 Letter in Cheese family papers, courtesy Mary Walker.

25 A705, 400080, National Archives, Canberra.

26 Firkins, P. *Strike and Return*, Westward Ho, Perth, 1985, p 25.

27 Ibid.

28 His crew were taken POW. Pilot Officer I F Keys, Flying Officer H R Train, Sergeant J M Stephenson and Flying Officer R R Ferry were all veteran RAAF. The middle upper gunner was a New Zealander, Sergeant S H Sharp.

29 Butterworth, D. "One Man's War", unpublished manuscript, Butterworth family papers.

30 Berry (407281) joined another RAAF 460 crew and just months later, on 22 November 1942 his Lancaster (W4273) was shot down while on an operation to bomb Stuttgart. He survived the crash and was taken POW. Flight Lieutenant Berry returned to Australian and was discharged from the RAAF on 13 February 1946.

Chapter 3

1 Sergeant Archibald Cowen Honeyman (404549) son of Archibald and Lillian Honeyman died 10 June 1942 and his body was never found. He is commemorated on the Singapore memorial wall.

2 Squadron Leader Geoffrey Francis Jackson (400414) son of Francis and Mabel Jackson of East Malvern, Victoria, was shot down on 23 January 1943 and his remains were not recovered. He is commemorated on the Malta Memorial.

3 Goulding, A G. *Uncommon Valour: The story of RAF Bomber Command, 1939–45*, Cheshire, Goodall, 1996, p 11.

4 Chant, C. *Allied Bombers 1939–45*, Zenith, UK, 2008, p 32. The 1400 men were killed, missing or POW.

5 Ibid.

6 Crew: Sergeant A J Higgison RNZAF; RAF Sergeant K G H Davies, Pilot Officer J D W McCallum, Sergeant G H Mayor, Flight Sergeant C G White AFM, Sergeant A W D Frost.

7 HMSO, B*omber Command: The Air Ministry Account of Bomber Command's Offensive Against the Axis*, September, 1939–July 1941, London, 1941, inside back cover.

8 Goulding, A G. *Uncommon Valour: The story of RAF Bomber Command, 1939–45*, Goodall, UK, 1996, p 67.

9 Ibid.

10 Ibid.

11 Barker, R. *The RAF At War*, Time-Life Books, USA, 1981, p 131.

12 In McCarthy, J. *A Last Call of Empire: Australian Aircrew, Britain, and the Empire Air Training Scheme*, AWM, 1988, p 39.

13 A9301, 400524, Brodie, Hugh Rowell, National Archives, Canberra. The aircraft was piloted by Flight Sergeant Solomon Levitus, (402910) RAAF, 22, from Sydney. The other Australian in the 460 crew lost on the 2/3 June 1942 Essen operation was Rear Gunner James Albert Gaiter (405020) 26, from Cloncurry, Queensland.

14 Bean, C. *The AIF in France: 1917, The Official History of Australia in the War of 1914–1918, Vol 4*, Sydney, 1941, p 788.

15 B2455, Silk, Frederick John, 6358, National Archives, Canberra.

16 Education Department, Victoria. War Service Record 1939–1945, Melbourne, 1959.

17 Mawdesley Family Papers.

18 Ibid.

19 A705 401073, Mawdesley, National Archives, Canberra.

20 A705, 163/96/120, Christsen, Walter Irvine (Sergeant), National Archives, Canberra.

21 Born on 14 July 1918 in Salzburg, Austria, a member of the aristocratic Austrian House of Lippe. His father was Prinz Alfred zur Lippe-Weißenfeld. The family lived in an old castle in Upper Austria called Alt Wartenburg. He had piloted gliders from age 14. He joined the Austrian Bundesheer in 1936 at the age of 18, initially serving in the infantry. In the aftermaths of the 1938 Anschluss, the incorporation of Austria into Greater Germany by Nazi Germany, he transferred to the German Luftwaffe. He was transferred to the night-fighter wing Nachtjagdgeschwader 1 (NJG 1) on 4 August 1940, based at Gütersloh, and then Leeuwarden, The Netherlands. By October 1940, he had taken over command of an independent night-fighter commando at Schiphol and later at Bergen. On his first encounter with the Royal Air Force (RAF) bomber, the night of 16/ 17 November

1940, he claimed a Vickers Wellington bomber from No. 115 Squadron RAF. The night of 15 January 1941, he shot down an Armstrong Whitworth Whitley N1521 of No. 58 Squadron RAF over northern Holland. A year later he was awarded the German Cross in Gold (Deutsches Kreuz in Gold) and the Knight's Cross of the Iron Cross (Ritterkreuz des Eisernen Kreuzes) on 16 April 1942 after he shot down four RAF bombers on that night of 26/27 March 1942. He had now shot down 21 British aircraft; by July 1942 he was one of the leading German night-fighter aces with 37. By October 1942 he was promoted to Hauptmann and Gruppenkommandeur of the I. Gruppe (1st group) and had claimed three more. In May 1943 he took command of III. Gruppe (3rd group) of NJG. A month later his tally was 45 British aircraft and he was awarded the Knight's Cross of the Iron Cross with Oak Leaves (Ritterkreuz des Eisernen Kreuzes mit Eichenlaub). After a crash and hospital stay, Weißenfeld was promoted to Major and made Geschwaderkommodore of Nachtjagdgeschwader 5 (NJG 5) on 20 February 1944. He and his crew, Oberfeldwebel Josef Renette and Unteroffizier Kurt Röber, were killed in a flying accident on 22 March 1944. Prinz Egmont zur Lippe-Weißenfeld and

Prinz Heinrich zu Sayn-Wittgenstein are buried side by side at Ysselsteyn in The Netherlands.

22 A705, 420071, Snape, D. National Archives, Canberra.

23 Chorley, W R. *Bomber Command Losses of the Second World War, Vol 3*. 1942, UK Midlands, 1997, p 79.

24 His mother was Mary and his wife was Ruth Roberts of Malvern.

25 A705, 163/115/85, Gammie, Colin, National Archives, Canberra.

26 Gammie, Allen, Letters 12 June 2007 and 30 October 2009.

27 Middlebrook and Everitt, *The Bomber Command War Diaries*, p 238.

28 868 aircraft bombed the main target with 15 aircraft bombing other targets.

29 Firkins, P. *Strike and Return*, Westward Ho, Perth, 1985, p 27.

30 Broodbank, Eric. Correspondence.

31 A9300 McSweyn, A F (402005), National Archives, Canberra

32 Adams, M. (ed), *Against The Odds: Escapes And Evasions By Allied Airmen, World War II*, published by the Executive Committee of the Royal Air Force Escaping Society, Australia Branch, Queensland, 1995, p 19.

Chapter 4

1 Adams, M (ed) *Against the Odds: Escapes and Evasions by Allied Airmen, World War II*, The Royal Air Forces Escaping Society, Brisbane, 1995, p 20.

2 Ibid, p 20.

3 Ibid, p 21.

4 Major Arkwright and Captains Coombe-Tennant and Fuller connected with the "Comete Escape Line" and arrived back in England.

5 Adams, M (ed) *Against the Odds: Escapes and Evasions by Allied Airmen, World War II*, The Royal Air Forces Escaping Society, Brisbane, 1995, p 22.

6 A705, 163/63/156, Webb, Albert Ernest William, National Archives, Canberra.

7 McSweyn, A. in Adams, Murray (ed) *Against the Odds*, p 23.

8 Middlebrook and Everitt, *The Bomber Command War Diaries: An Operational Reference Book 1939–1945*, p 241.

9 Chorley, W R. *RAF Bomber Command Losses of the Second World War –1942, Vol 3*, Midland, 2001, p 101.

10 Chorley, *Bomber Command Losses 1942, Vol 3*, p 118.

11 Middlebrook and Everitt, *The Bomber Command War Diaries*, pp 274–279.

12 Eleven aircraft did not return.

13 Bomber Command, p 129.

14 Middlebrook and Everitt, p 280.

15 Middlebrook, M and Everitt, C. *The Bomber Command War Diaries: An Operational Reference Book 1939–1945*, Midland, 1996, pp 280-281.

16 Goulding, A G. *Uncommon Valour: The Story of RAF Bomber Command, 1939–45*, Cheshire, Goodall, p 65.

17 Charlwood, D. *No Moon Tonight*, Vic., 1987, Penguin, p 20.

18 Ibid., p 281.

19 Chant, C. *Allied Bombers 1939–45*, p 42.

20 Courtesy of Wayne Cumberland, 13th February 2011.

21 Spurling, K. Cruel *Conflict: The Triumph and Tragedy of HMAS Perth*, New Holland, 2008, p 127.

22 Kelly, W E (Bill) *Blue Orchids*, SA, 2005, Seaview, p 57.

23 Pilot Officer Douglas John Lovejoy (403752) was the pilot of a Hudson which crashed into the sea near Byron Bay, NSW, on 6 July 1942. No trace was found of crew or aircraft.

24 Middlebrook and Everitt, *The Bomber Command Diaries*, p 283.

25 Ibid.

26 Firkins, P. *Strike and Return*, p 33.

27 A705, 403409, Pilot Officer Charles Roland Lark, National Archives, Canberra.

28 A705, 163/180/15, Wyllie, Maxwell Joseph Andrew, National Archives, Canberra.

29 A9301, 40387, O'Brien, John Ormond, National Archives, Canberra.

30 Chorley, W R. *Bomber Command Losses 1942*, p 296.

31 Ibid, p 68.

Chapter 5

1 Turner, J F. *VCs of the Air*, Harrup, London, 1960, p 75.

2 Ibid.

3 Ibid.

4 A9300, 402745, Middleton, Rawdon Hume. National Archives, Canberra.

5 Chorley, W R. *Bomber Command Losses of the Second World War, Vol 3*, 1942, p 140.

6 Middlebrook and Everitt, *The Bomber Command War Diaries*, p 290.

7 Ibid.

8 Ibid, p 300.

9 Ibid.

10 Ibid.

11 Goulding, A.G. *Uncommon Valour: The Story of RAF Bomber Command, 1939–45*, p 81.

12 Chorley, *RAF Bomber Command Losses, Vol 3*, 1942, p 181.

13 Barker, R. *The RAF At War, Time-Life Books*, USA, 1981, p 105.

14 Ibid, p 9.

15 Ibid, p 12.

16 Ibid, p 15.

17 Ibid, p 17.

18 Martin Family Papers.

19 Son of John Bertmoore Shannon and Edith Muriel Shannon, born 8 September 1920, enlisted 19 July 1940, shot down on 30 November 1941 and is buried in a collective grave in Hamburg Cemetery, Germany.

Chapter 6

1 Chorley, W R. *Bomber Command Losses of the Second World War, Vol 3*, 1942, pp 175–176.

2 Garrett, S A. *Ethics and Airpower in World War II*, St Martin's Press, New York, 1993, p 41.

3 A705, 163/132/186, Keats Gilbert Carrington, 407794, National Archives, Canberra.

4 Ibid.

5 Middlebrook and Everitt, p 293.

6 He would be awarded a DFC with the citation "In various capacities this officer displayed great gall and determination in attacks against targets". He was described as having a "strong personality makes it easy for him to lead others". He would undertake a photography course at Farnborough and return to Australia on 15 June 1945.

7 Chorley, W R. *Bomber Command Losses of the Second World War, Vol 3*, 1942, p 141.

8 Middlebrook and Everitt, *The Bomber Command War Diaries*, p 308.

9 Hoyle, p 23.

10 Ibid.

11 Ibid, p 27.

12 Ibid.

13 Ibid, p 34.

14 Chorley, *Bomber Command Losses, Vol 3*, p 245.

15 Courtesy of Wayne Cumberland, 13th February 2011.

16 Also killed with O'Brien were RAAF Sergeants Terence Francis Breen McKenna (405162) 21, of Port Moresby and Keith Allen (401359) 31, of Elwood, Victoria and Harrington Warren Price (402539) of Sydney.

17 Gwenda Stanbridge, daughter of a first cousin of Jim Philpot.

18 A9300, 402745, Middleton, Rawdon Hume. National Archives, Canberra.

Chapter 7

1 Chorley, W R. *Bomber Command Losses 1942, Vol 3*, p 246.

2 Ibid, p 246.

3 Ibid, p 247.

4 Two British actors playing Dutch citizens would become well known to Australians. Googie Withers would marry Australian actor David McCallum and move to live in Australia following the war. Robert Helpmann would become iconic in the world of Australian ballet.

5 Bowman, M W. *Legend of the Lancasters: The Bomber War from England 1942–45*, 2009, Pen & Sword Books, Yorkshire, p 43.

6 Chorley, W R. *Bomber Command Losses of the Second World War*, 1943, Vol 4, 1996, p 7.

7 Bowman, p 28.

8 Ibid.

9 Chant, C. *Allied Bombers 1939–45*, Amber Books, UK, p 74.

10 Borrett family papers, courtesy Glenda Adams.

11 Winterbon family papers, courtesy Judith Knox.

12 Middlebrook and Everitt, *The Bomber Command War Diaries*, pp 400–401.

13 Chorley, Bomber Command Losses 1942, Vol 4, 1943, p 64.

14 A9301, 413469, Winterbon, Kenneth, and A705, 166/43/233, Winterbon, John; National Archives, Canberra. His crew were RAF Sergeant E A Duchene, Pilot Officer E G Grove; Sergeant W H Gordon; Sergeant J W Bembridge; Sergeant W P Smith and Flight Sergeant J S F V Crawley.

15 Warrant Officer R A Swan (404221), Flight Sergeant D G Hoffman (207799), Flight Sergeant D Reece (18984), Sergeant N D Woodhouse (18994), Sergeant K E Thompson (9167) and Flight Sergeant A M Belshaw (67878).

16 Charlwood, Don. *No Moon Tonight*, Penguin Vic., 1987, p 14.

17 Ibid, p 17.

18 The Land Army was an organisation of mainly women volunteers who became farm labourers, taking the place of men who had left for military service. Due to their service, the Land Army ensured badly needed agricultural supplies continued.

19 Bryant, M. PRO00275 Papers, Australian War Memorial, Canberra.

20 Charlwood, p 26. Burcher was from Neutral Bay, Sydney, and would be killed on 30 July 1943 when with RAAF 460 Squadron.

21 Bryant, Robert Maxwell, Flying Officer, PRO00275 Papers, Australian War Memorial.

22 Also killed was Sergeant James Gordon Milne (408774) 26, of Tatura, Victoria. It was 13 September 1942 and the target was Bremen.

23 Ibid, p 53

24 Charlwood, p 33.

25 Muirhead, Campbell. *Diary of a Bomb Aimer*, Spellmount, 1987, p 16.

26 Osborn, R B. "The last landing of 'C-Charlie', on Saturday 23rd January 1943: a review of the event written for Stewie Methven and Jack Conlon", unpublished manuscript, National Library, Cbr, p 9.

27 Osborn, p 18.

28 Ibid, p 9.

Chapter 8

1 Middlebrook and Everitt, p 362.

2 Tooze, A. *The Wages of Destruction: The Making and Breaking of the Nazi Economy*, 2002, pp 597–598.

3 Ibid, p 363.

4 Chorley, Vol 4, p 61.

5 www.awm.gov.au/events/ conference/2003/Nelson.Hank.

6   The Bomb Aimer was RAF Sergeant Ronald Cordingley.

7   Middlebrook and Everitt, p 379.

8   Firkins, P C. *Strike and Return*, Westward Ho, WA, 1985, p 81.

9   Ibid, p 79.

10 Chant, C. *Allied Bombers 1939–1945*, p 73.

11 Ibid.

12 Ibid.

13 Courtesy Jim Lundie. Doug Lundie would die in a drowning accident. David Lundie's crew would be buried in Ijsselmuiden General Cemetery, The Netherlands.

14 Fry, E. A*n Airman Far Away*, Kangaroo, NSW, 1993, p 143.

15 Ibid.

16 Ibid, p 100.

17 Ibid, p 19.

18 Ibid, p 124.

19 Ibid, p 126.

20 Ibid, p 134.

21 Ibid, p 139.

22 Ibid, p 139.

23 Ibid, p 154.

24 Ibid, p 162.

25 Ibid, p 163.

26 Courtesy of Robert Galligan.

27 The Engineer, Sergeant Dennis Mansell Lewis (1581747); Navigator, Sergeant Arthur Tooth (1438888); the Bomb Aimer, Sergeant Joshua Alan Sykes (657255); Wireless Operator/Air Gunner Sergeant Thomas Rees Jones (1379595); and Sergeant George Albert Denney (756167) the Mid-upper Gunner.

28 Engineer, Sergeant W Lowe, Navigator Pilot Officer E E Huxter, Bomb Aimer Sergeant A C Brooksbank, Wireless Operator Sergeant A J H Millin, Mid-upper Gunner Sergeant C W Sweeting.

29 Courtesy of Robert Galligan.

30 Middlebrook and Everitt, p 411.

31 Morris Family Papers.

32 Denson, J V. T*he Costs of War: America's Pyrrhic Victories*, Transaction Publishers, USA, 1999, p 352.

33 460 Squadron Veterans & Friends Group, July–September 2010, p 11.

34 Norris, M. "The Crowded Sky" unpublished manuscript, p 1.

35 Fry, E. *An Airman Far Away*, Kangaroo, NSW, 1993, p 52.

36 Ibid., p 54.

37 Norris, M. "The Crowded Sky" unpublished manuscript.

Chapter 9

1   Norris, M. "The Crowded Sky", unpublished manuscript, p 2.

2   Ibid, p 4.

3   Ibid, p 5.

4   Ibid, p 14.

5   Ibid.

6   Ibid, p 32.

7   Ibid, p 36

8   Norris Family Papers.

9   Ibid.

10 Ibid.

11 Ibid.

12 Ibid.

13 Ibid.

7   Norris, M. Discussion.

14 Renolds, Squadron Leader Lindsay Blair, DFC. Born Hawera, 2 Feb 1919; RNZAF 31 Aug 1940–17 Apr 1947; Pilot Citation Distinguished Flying Cross (9 Sept 1943): [466 Squadron RAAF (Wellington)] Although gravely injured in a crash, which occurred on return from an operational sortie, this officer resumed duty on recovery with determination and enthusiasm and has displayed a high degree of skill and gallantry in attacks on major targets. By his personal example and his work as deputy flight commander he has made a valuable contribution to the operational efficiency of his squadron. Crashed at 0500 on 30 Sept 1941 in a 102 Squadron RAF Whitley. While attached to the RAF, Squadron Leader Renolds also served with 1502 BAT Flt and Halifax Squadrons 640, 158 and 76 Squadron. Renolds was discharged from the RNZAF in the UK on 18 April 1947 (he had relinquished his acting rank of Squadron Leader with effect from 15 January 1947), and relinquished his temporary RNZAF commission with effect from same date. He had married in England in April 1945, and his last address was in Port Stewart, Northern Ireland.

15 Heather Maree Alexander (nee Dallwitz).

16 Ibid.

17 Hoyle, A, p 34.

18 Ibid, p 35.

19 Ibid, p 41.

20 Hoyle, A. Interview.

21 Hoyle, A. p 47.

22 Middlebrook and Everitt, p 459.

23 Chorley, Vol 4 1943, p 442.

24 Sergeants J S Ogg, K Wightman, H B Bushell and W R Buntain.

25 Searby, J. Air Commodore, RAF. *The Bomber Battle for Berlin*, Airlife, UK, p 10.

26 Ibid, p 60.

27 Middlebrook and Everitt, p 463.

28 Searby, J. p 77.

29 Middlebrook and Everitt, p 465.

30 Ibid, p 466.

31 Chorley, W R *Bomber Command Losses*, Midland, UK, 1997, Vol 5, 1944, p 51.

32 Johnson, S. and Winspear, B. (eds) *Tasmanians At War*, self published, Tas.,

2002, p 321. McInnes however became a POW.

33 Middlebrook and Everitt, p 463.

34 Courtesy of Jennifer Nielson and Don Coutts.

35 Waller, D. "Navigating the War", unpublished manuscript, 2010, p 15.

36 Ibid, p 19.

37 Courtesy of Don Coutts.

38 Ibid.

39 Augenstein was shot down and killed in December 1944 – he had shot down 46 Allied aircraft.

40 Middlebrook and Everitt, p 472.

41 The Engineer was Flight Sergeant Leslie Albert Hazell, (918657); Sergeant Raymond Valentine Montigue Daniels (962612) 24, was the Middle Upper Gunner.

42 Middlebrook and Everitt, p 473.

43 Ibid, p 485.

Chapter 10

1 Chorley, 1944, Vol 5, p 139.

2 Private John Simpson was in fact John Simpson Kirkpatrick, but while serving with his donkey on the Gallipoli beaches retrieving the injured he was known as "Simpson" and the donkey "Simpson's donkey". He was killed after three weeks of the most meritorious service.

3 Chorley, 1944, Vol 5, p 140.

4 Ibid, p 160. Another report states this as 94 bombers lost or crash landed.

5 RAF Sergeant Kenneth Edwin Green (1604776) Engineer, and Wireless Operator Flight Sergeant Tom Dawson (1372580) RAF also killed. Pilot Officer R J McCleary RAAF became POW.

6 www.467/463raafsquadrons.com.

7 The three RAF was Flight Engineer Sergeant Kenneth Harold Tabor (1850279); Air Bomber Flight Sergeant Jeremiah Parker (658844) and Sergeant Eric Reginald Hill (1352851) was the 22-year-old Middle Upper Gunner.

8 NX611, "Just Jane". Currently based at the Lincolnshire Aviation Heritage Centre at East Kirkby, UK, is expected to be flying again soon.

9 Middlebrook and Everitt, p 523, state it was 1,012 aircraft. Chorley gives the total as 1,211, p 256.

10 Chorley, W R. *Bomber Command Losses*, Midland, UK, 1997, Vol 5, 1944, p 163.

11 Goulding, A G. *Uncommon Valour*, Goodall, UK, 1996, p 151.

12 Firkins, p 146.

13 Courtesy Dr J C Duggleby, Victoria

14 Remainder of Australian crew Wireless Operator/Air Gunner Flight Sergeant Denis Vaughan Kelly (418751); Navigator Flying Officer Mark William Edgerley (417466); Bomb Aimer Flight Sergeant Lawrence William McGovern (424274). Engineer was RAF Sergeant V L Johnson

15 Middlebrook and Everitt, p 568.

16 Firkins, p 142.

17 Ibid.

18 Adams, M. *Against The Odds, Royal Air Forces Escaping Society*, Australia Branch, 1995, "Through Fire to Freedom", Flight Sergeant Robert Ian Hunter. (The official file has the name as Robert Isaiah.)

19 Ibid, p 125.

20 Ibid, p 126.

21 Ibid, p.128.

22 Adams, M. Ibid, "Mon Episode Francais", Flight Sergeant Stanley D Jolly, p 123.

23 Adams, M. Ibid, "Persistence Rewarded", Pilot Officer Allan F McSweyn, p 23.

24 Ibid, p 24.

25   Adams, M. Ibid, Pilot Officer Allan F
     McSweyn, p 25.
26   Ibid, p 26.
27   Middlebrook and Everitt, p 529.
28   Middlebrook and Everitt, p 530.

29   RAF 98 Mitchell FW211 was also shot
     down, onboard RAAF Pilot Officer Harold
     Morris Nottle (417104) 25, from Melbourne.
30   Sanders, C. "Execution over Arnhem", De
     Telegraaf, 19th September 2009.

Chapter 11

1   Colin Cherrill Cooper (405395), Wilfred
     Gordon Burrows (411739); Harold
     Theodore Waddell (412217), Joseph Albert
     Turnbull (411555), Thomas John James
     Cunliffe (411127) Robert Maxwell Bryant
     (411748), Colin McDowell Miller (401848),
     Donald Ernest Cameron Charlwood
     (408794), Edward Freeman (408678),
     Ronald Wheatley (412053), Ian Victor
     Heatley (405310), George Bruce Loder
     (412160), Ronald Bowen Anzac Pender
     (411517), Thomas Hector McNeill (405381),
     Harold John Alfred Wright (405611),
     Harold James Barker (405288), Keith
     Robert Webber (411562), John Irvine
     Gordon (412218), William Roy Kenneth
     Charlton (411121). Robert William Morgan
     (411585).

2   His pilot was Australian, Sergeant William
     (Bill) Fletcher (406476). Also in the crew
     was 26-year-old Sergeant James Gordon
     Milne (408774) from Melbourne.

3   Other Australians onboard the Lancaster:
     Navigator Flight Sergeant Donald Kerr
     (401646), National Bank Clerk, from
     Melbourne; Wireless Operator/Air
     Gunner Flight Sergeant Henry Herbert
     Brien (411281) 26, educated at Cowra
     Intermediate High and Wolari College,
     Orange, was a farmer/grazier on his father's
     property; Air Gunner Flight Sergeant
     Archibald John Marfell (400677), 21,
     who had been assisting his father in the
     family Victorian Grain Store. He married
     a Canadian and his wife and son lived in
     Kamloops. Their bomber was shot down
     near Rotenburg.

4   The Engineer was RAF Sergeant Anthony
     (Tony) Marshal Willis (925963) as were
     Air Gunners Sergeants Stanley C Brewer
     (1600029) and Ronald Taylor (648472).

5   Pilot Flight Sergeant David Harold Victor
     Charlick (416322); Bomb Aimer Flight
     Sergeant Eric Neil Cooper (403502);
     Flight Sergeant Gordon Vivian Hampton
     (408578) Middle Upper Gunner; Wireless
     Operator/Air Gunner Flying Officer F J
     Falkenmire (411445) survived. Also killed,

     RAF Sergeants P Perry (980250) was the
     Engineer and W P D Chapman (1361314),
     was the Tail Gunner.

6   His pilot was RAF Pilot Officer R E
     Wilkes (141103), Warrant Officer T G
     O'Shaughnessy (1262920) , Flight Sergeant
     F Hay (1002505), Warrant Officer F W
     Vincent (1174030), Flight Sergeant T
     L Brown (570690) , and the only other
     Australian Wireless Operator/Air Gunner
     Flight Sergeant Michael Albert Edward
     Bradford (411478) 27, former storeman
     who was studying accountancy with Sydney
     Tech and whose hobby was radio assembly.
     Wilkes, Wheatley, Bradford, and Hay, KIA.

7   Charlwood, p 48.

8   Other Australian was Sergeant A Knight
     (403519).

9   Family papers courtesy Professor Elizabeth
     Webby.

10   Lancaster ED935,156 Squadron RAF
     took off from RAF Warboys, Huntingdon,
     at 2338 on 11 June to bomb Munster,
     Germany. Nothing further heard. Crashed
     in the IJsselmeer. Their average age was
     23. Four bodies washed ashore in the
     Zuider Zee area RAF Flying Officer J A
     Cowley, DFM, (Second pilot) and Pilot
     Officer Bryant, buried in New Eastern. RAF
     Sergeant J R Drake (Middle Upper Gunner)
     and RAF Sergeant W J Drake (Wireless
     Operator) buried in Lemmer Cemetery.
     408724 RAAF Flight Sergeant K L LAY
     (Pilot- Capt) Son of Dr Leonard May and
     Kathleen Elizabeth May, of Chatswood,
     NSW, RAF Sergeants F E Ratcliffe
     (Engineer) and W Forster (Rear Gunner)
     not found. Lost on its first operation with
     No.156 Squadron; this aircraft had a total of
     21 hours.

11   Charlwood, p 169.

12   Ibid.

13   Flight Lieutenant Michael Acton
     Sullivan,(414697) DFC, RNZAF, 23, from
     Auckland; Warrant Officer Cyril William
     Knox (22170) DFC, RAAF, 25, from
     Kilkivan, Q; RAAF Flight Lieutenant Rex

Henry Wedd (408200) DFC, 29, of Lenah Valley, Tasmania; Pilot Officer Eric Whitby Ritchie (412189) DFC RAAF, 30, of Sydney; RAF Flight Sergeant George Edward Mason (1007560) DFM; Warrant Officer William Liness Charles Hickling (400433) DFC, RAAF, 21, from Melbourne.

14 Charlwood, p 170.

15 Ibid, p 171.

16 Ibid.

17 Ibid, p 178

18 Ibid, p 179

19 Survivors who returned to Australia were: Harold (Tib) Barker DFC and bar, who flew a total of 90 operations. Ted (Blue) Freeman DFC survived more than 50 operations. Harry Wright DFC and bar, DFM, flew 78 operations. Ron Pender became a POW on the night of 9/10 April 1943 when his 101 Squadron Lancaster was hit by flak while attacking Duisburg. Bob Morgan, DFM. Robert (Bob) William Morgan, DFM, flew with 112 Air Sea Rescue Flt at war's end. Tom Cuncliffe finished first in the course and elected to fly Transport Command.

20 Charlwood, p 27.

21 Kelly, W E. Blue Orchids, self published (Seaview Press), 2005. Interview with Lyn Kelly, April, 2010, p 1.

22 Ibid, p 2.

23 Ibid, p 19.

24 Ibid, p 19.

25 Ibid, p 28.

26 Ibid, p 54.

27 Ibid, p 64.

28 Ibid, p 69.

29 Ibid, p 83.

30 Ibid, p 87.

31 Ibid, p 90.

32 Ibid, p 92.

33 Ibid, p 96.

34 RAF Sergeant H Taylor (3011426) Flight Engineer; RAF Flight Sergeant R Watt (1579768), Navigator.

35 In 1989 the wall would be reduced to souvenir pieces of concrete.

36 Middlebrook, p 663.

37 Dunstan, R. and Graham, B. The Sand and the Sky, Robertson and Mullens, Melb, 1945, p 36.

38 Ibid, p 40.

39 Bowman, p 27.

Chapter 12

1 In 1984 Annemarie received a medal from the government of Tilburg – she died in 1986.

2 Interview with Bob Wade, July 2009.

3 RAF Sergeants R E D Robinson (25072) Flight Engineer; K H Allaker (1471670) Navigator; S Patterson (1553418)Air Bomber; and J Horrocks (2209732) Air Gunner.

4 On the night of 24/25 December 1944, Strüning was shot down by a RAF intruder. He baled out but struck his fighter's tail unit and fell to his death. Strüning was credited with 56 kills.

5 Courtesy Mary Sadler (nee Hogg).

6 Pilot Flight Lieutenant Sidney Edward Wodehouse (48319), Flight Engineer Sergeant Douglas Dean Roberts (1685090), Air Gunner Sergeant Robert Cottar (1348052) (also spelt Cotter), Air Gunner Sergeant John Henry Brown (2209145), Second Pilot Flying Officer Arthur Hanley Ford (139587) were killed.

7 Albert Roesener, Karl Klingbeil, Michael Rotschopf and Karl Cremer.

8 Courtesy of Marjorie Manley (nee Ion).

9 Lister, Jonathon. "World War II Bomber Pilot Allan Robert Hart and the JB659 Avro Lancaster Crew", school project.

10 Preston, T. "Growing up in Subiaco 1924–1942", 2006, Preston family papers.

11 Walley, B. (ed) Silk and Barbed Wire, Larkin, C. "An unwilling guest of the Third Reich", p 312.

12 Phil Emrose died in 2010.

13 Middlebrook and Everitt, p 527.

14 On an RAF 625 Lancaster: Australians Flight Sergeant Charles Stirling Dundas Tainsh (418583) and Flight Sergeant Jeffrey Gordon Lane (25514) were killed and Flight Sergeant John David Lindsay (419074) and Flight Sergeant Raymond Francis Ridge (417891) became POWs.

15 Courtesy Keith Whittenbury in Adelaide and Mike Kleinlugtebeld in Zwolle, Netherlands.

16 Courtesy of Robert Milne.

Chapter 13

1   Courtesy of Robert Milne.
2   Charlwood, p 54.
3   Garrett, p 37.
4   Ibid, p 38.
5   Hoyle, p 96.
6   Kelly, p 94.
7   Ibid, p 100.
8   Clint, p 69.
9   Chorley, Vol 6, p 182.
10 Courtesy Delacour family.

BIBLIOGRAPHY

Books

Adams, M. (ed), *Against The Odds – Escapes And Evasions By Allied Airmen, World War II*, Published by the Executive Committee of the Royal Air Force Escaping Society, Australia Branch, Queensland, 1995.

Barker, R. *The RAF At War*, Time-Life Books, USA, 1981.

Bean, C. *The Official History of Australia in the War of 1914–1918*, Vol 4, Sydney, 1941.

Bingley, A N. *Australian Airmen: Lest We Forget Europe 1939–1945*, self published, WA, 2002.

Bowman, Martin. W *Legend of the Lancasters: The Bomber War from England 1942–45*, Pen & Sword Books, 2009.

Chant, C. *Allied Bombers 1939–1945*, Amber, UK, 2008.

Charlwood, D. *No Moon Tonight*, Penguin Vic., 1987.

Chorley, W R. *RAF Bomber Command Losses of the Second World War, 1939–1940, Vol 1*, Midland, 1992.

Chorley, W R. *RAF Bomber Command Losses of the Second World War, 1941, Vol 2*, Midland, 1993.

Chorley, W R. *RAF Bomber Command Losses of the Second World War, 1942, Vol 3*, Midland, 1994.

Chorley, W R. *RAF Bomber Command Losses of the Second World War, 1943, Vol 4*, Midland, 1996.

Chorley, W R. *RAF Bomber Command Losses of the Second World War, 1944, Vol 5*, Midland, 1997.

Chorley, W R. *RAF Bomber Command Losses of the Second World War, 1945, Vol 6*, Midland, 1998.

Clutton-Brock, O. *RAAF Evaders: The Complete Story of Thousands of Escapers and Their Escape Lines Western Europe 1940–45*, Grub, London, 2009.

Cutlack, F M. *Official History of Australia in the War of 1914–1918*, Vol VIII.

Denson, J V. *The Costs of War: America's Pyrrhic Victories*, Transaction Publishers, USA, 1999.

Dunstan, Roberts and Graham, Burton. *The Sand and the Sky*, Robertson and Mullens, Melb, 1945.

Education Department, Victoria. *War Service Record 1939–1945*, Melbourne, 1959.

Firkins, P. *Strike and Return*, Westward Ho, Perth, 1985.

Fry, E. *An Airman Far Away*, Kangaroo, NSW, 1993.

Garrett, S A. *Ethics and Airpower in World War II*, St Martin's Press, New York, 1993.

Goldie, P. Diary published in full in Bingley, A N. *Australian Airmen: Lest We Forget Europe 1939–1945*, self published, WA, 2002.

Goulding, A G. *Uncommon Valour: The Story of RAF Bomber Command, 1939–1945*, Cheshire, Goodall, 1996.

Hayes, Mike. *Angry Skies: Recollections of Australian Combat Fliers*, ABC, Sydney, 2003.

HMSO, *Bomber Command: The Air Ministry Account of Bomber Command's Offensive Against the Axis, September, 1939–July 1941*, London, 1941.

Hoyle, A. *Into the Darkness: a Personal Memoir*, self published, Canberra, 1989.

Johnson, S and Winspear, B. (eds) *Tasmanians At War*, self published, Tas., 2002.

Longmate, N. *The Bombers: Royal Air Force Air Offensive Against Germany, 1939–45*, Hutchinson, London, 1983.

Kelly, W E (Bill). *Blue Orchids*, SA, 2005, Seaview.

McCarthy, J. *A Last Call of Empire: Australian Aircrew, Britain and the Empire Air Training Scheme*, Canberra, AWM, 1988.

McKernan, M. *ALL IN!: Australia During the Second World War*, Nelson, Vic, 1983.

Middlebrook, M. And Everitt, C. *The Bomber Command War Diaries: An Operational Reference Book, 1939–1945*, Midland, UK, 1996.

Muirhead, Campbell. *Diary of a Bomb Aimer*, Spellmount, 1987.

Parliamentary Debates, Commonwealth of Australia, Vol 162.

Robertson, J. *1939–1945 Australia Goes to War*, Doubleday, Sydney, 1981.

Spurling, K. *Cruel Conflict: The Triumph and Tragedy of HMAS Perth I*, New Holland, Sydney, 2008.

Statistics of the Military Effort of the British Empire During the Great War, 1914–1920, The War Office, London, 1922.

Stephens, Alan. *The Royal Australian Air Force, The Australian Centenary History of Defence Vol II*, Oxford, 2001.

Tooze, A. *The Wages of Destruction: The Making and Breaking of the Nazi Economy*, 2002.

Turner, John Frayn. *VC's of the Air*, Harrup, London, 1960.

Walley, B (ed) *Silk and Barbed Wire, Royal Air Forces ex Prisoners of War Association* (WA Aust), Sage, 2000.

Wilson, D. *The Brotherhood of Airmen: the Men and Women of the RAAF in Action 1914–Today*, Allen and Unwin, 2005.

Unpublished Manuscripts

Butterworth, D. "One Man's War".

Norris, M. "The Crowded Sky".

Osborn, R B. "The last landing of 'C-Charlie', on Saturday 23rd January 1943: a review of the event written for Stewie Methven and Jack Conlon", National Library, Canberra.

Preston, T. "Growing up in Subiaco 1924–1942".

Waller, D."Navigating the War".

Newspapers/Journals/Newsletters

Age, 2 September 1939.

Sydney Morning Herald, 4 September 1939, 5 January 1940, 13 June 1940.

De Telegraaf, 19 September 2009.

460 Squadron Veterans & Friends Group, July–September 2010

National Archives

A9300 RAAF Personnel Files

A9301 RAAF Personnel Files

A705 RAAF Accident Reports

Private Family Papers

Borrett Family Papers.

Butterworth, D. "One Man's War", unpublished manuscript, Butterworth Family Papers.

Cheese Family Papers

Martin Family Papers.

Mawdesley Family Papers.

Norris Family Papers

Waldon Family Papers.

Winterbon Family Papers

Bryant, M. PRO00275 Papers, Australian War Memorial, Canberra.

Web

www.awm.gov.au/events/conference/2003/Nelson.Hank.

www.elsham.pwp.blueyonder.co.uk/raf_bc/20_men

www.467/463raafsquadrons.com

Other books by the author published by New Holland Publishers:

Abandoned and Sacrificed. The Tragedy of Montevideo Maru, 2017.

Cruel Conflict: The Triumph and Tragedy of HMAS Perth I, 2008.

HMAS Canberra: Casualty of Circumstance, 2008.